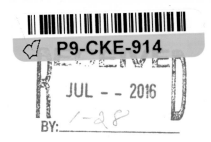

CITIZEN KANE

A

FILMMAKER'S
JOURNEY

ALSO BY HARLAN LEBO

Citizen Kane: The Fiftieth Anniversary Album
Casablanca: Behind the Scenes
The Godfather Legacy

CITIZEN KANE

A — FILMMAKER'S JOURNEY

HARLAN LEBO

THOMAS DUNNE BOOKS   ST. MARTIN'S PRESS   NEW YORK

THOMAS DUNNE BOOKS.
An imprint of St. Martin's Press.

CITIZEN KANE: A FILMMAKER'S JOURNEY. Copyright © 2016 Harlan Lebo. All rights reserved. Printed in the United States of America. For information, address St. Martin's Press, 175 Fifth Avenue, New York, N.Y. 10010.

www.thomasdunnebooks.com
www.stmartins.com

Excerpts from the 1973 lecture and Q&A with Bernard Herrmann provided by the George Eastman House.

Article from *Popular Photography* by Gregg Toland © Bonnier Corp. All Rights Reserved.

The words "Oscar" and "Academy Awards" are trademarks and service marks of the Academy of Motion Picture Arts and Sciences, copyright ©A.M.P.A.S.®

Designed by Steven Seighman

Library of Congress Cataloging-in-Publication Data

Names: Lebo, Harlan.
Title: Citizen Kane : a filmmaker's journey / Harlan Lebo.
Description: New York : Thomas Dunne Books, 2016.
Identifiers: LCCN 2015045237| ISBN 9781250077530 (hardcover) |
    ISBN 9781466889750 (e-book)
Subjects: LCSH: Citizen Kane (Motion picture) | BISAC: PERFORMING ARTS /
    Film & Video / History & Criticism.
Classification: LCC PN1997.C51173 L35 2016 | DDC 791.43/72—dc23
LC record available at http://lccn.loc.gov/2015045237

Our books may be purchased in bulk for promotional, educational, or business use. Please contact your local bookseller or the Macmillan Corporate and Premium Sales Department at 1-800-221-7945, extension 5442, or by e-mail at MacmillanSpecialMarkets@macmillan.com.

First Edition: April 2016

10 9 8 7 6 5 4 3 2 1

For Monica

CONTENTS

Acknowledgments ix

A Note on the Illustrations and the Text xi

Citizen Kane: A Recollection xv

PART ONE

1   Asking for the Impossible 3

2   The Beard and the Contract 15

3   The Script 35

4   The Consequences of His Actions 53

5   RKO Production #281 69

6   A Great Deal of Doing 81

7   No Visitors, Please 96

8   Giggling Like Schoolboys 123

9   Cryptic Notes and Bigger Hams 152

PART TWO

10   Conflict 175

11   Negotiating and Placating 190

12   Mr. Hearst 215

13   Release 233

14 Triumph 246
15 Walking on the Edge of a Cliff 249

Viewer's Guide to *Citizen Kane* 259
Cast and Production Credits 259
Gregg Toland: "I Broke the Rules in 'Citizen Kane'" 271
Bernard Herrmann: A Conversation at the George
    Eastman House 275
Citizen Kane: Scene-by-Scene Guide 279
The Budget 301
RKO Soundstages 305
Resources About Orson Welles and *Citizen Kane* 309
Notes 315
Bibliography 343
List of Illustrations 351
Index 353

ACKNOWLEDGMENTS

This book exists because the generosity of these people made it possible. With so many thanks:

William Alland, Kathryn Trosper Popper, Ruth Warrick, Richard Wilson, and Robert Wise, five participants in the making of *Citizen Kane,* for allowing me to explore their pasts and learn the answers to many questions that lingered about the production of this film. These patient people brought to life the creation of *Citizen Kane* in a way that no amount of digging through old files could ever accomplish.

Joseph Popper and Laura Popper, the son and daughter of Kathryn Trosper Popper, for everything they did to bring me the story of their mother's adventures working with Orson Welles on *Citizen Kane.*

Robert Carringer, who has written often and well about Orson Welles and *Citizen Kane,* for his invaluable guidance.

Ron Gottesman, for creating *Perspectives on* Citizen Kane, a collection of articles, essays, and related material about the film that was tremendously useful in writing this book.

Peter Bogdanovich, for graciously giving permission to reprint excerpts from his interviews with Orson Welles when I wrote my first book on *Citizen Kane.*

The librarians and researchers who guided me in this project—Julie Graham and Amy Wong at the UCLA Library; Ned Comstock from the Cinema-Television Library at the University of Southern California; Isabel Planton, Zach Downey, Rebecca Baumann, and Rebecca Cape from the Lilly Library at Indiana University, Bloomington; Philip Hallman at the University of Michigan

Special Collections Library; Dean Smith and Lee Ann Titangos from the Bancroft Library at the University of California, Berkeley; Rosemary Knopka at the Art Directors Guild, and the entire staff of the Margaret Herrick Library at the Academy of Motion Picture Arts and Sciences in Beverly Hills. These dedicated researchers and their colleagues provided assistance and insight that extended far beyond the normal call.

Juliet Demeter, who served as my guide through the Hearst Papers at the Bancroft Library.

Bob Sirchia, who long ago took time from his duties managing the facility that is the former home of RKO's studios in Culver City to show me the last remaining relics of Xanadu.

Joe Maddalena, Brian Chanes, and the staff at Profiles in History, the auction house that opened its doors to me to review a trove of treasures from *Citizen Kane*.

My agent, Felicia Eth, who supports my adventures in authorship with more patience than I deserve.

My editor, Peter Joseph—a great partner who made it all work so smoothly.

Neil Helgeson, David Bloome, and Joel Bellman, who put aside their natural sardonic tendencies to provide many helpful suggestions while I edited the first draft.

To my wife, Monica Dunahee, who makes it readable and coherent—a miracle worker.

And to my family and friends, who are patient, tolerant, and endlessly supportive of my writing adventures. For them, I am especially grateful.

A NOTE ON THE ILLUSTRATIONS AND THE TEXT

The Illustrations

This is the second book I have written about *Citizen Kane:* the first, for the fiftieth anniversary of the film, was a coffee table book with limited text that was created to showcase photographs of the production; it was published before the broad use of the Internet or easily searchable media such as DVDs and video downloads were widely available (as incredible as it may seem, there was such a time).

For this new book—which is meant to be read and not just perused—I chose a different approach for the illustrations. First, I have included images that show some of the background, people, and incidents that occurred before, during, and after the making of *Citizen Kane;* then, to complement your reading of the book and viewing of the film, you will find two guides:

- The Notes section, which will show you the exact time of every shot discussed in the text.
- To further assist your reading and viewing, I have also compiled a Scene-by-Scene Guide, which includes every shot in the film and the time each occurs.

Of course, there is no better source of illustrations than *Citizen Kane* itself. I encourage you to use a video of *Citizen Kane* as a companion to your reading—

especially the superb Blu-ray that was released in 2011. I hope the guides included here will amplify your exploration of the film.

The Text

This book was written using material drawn from interviews with participants in the making of *Citizen Kane;* reviews of more than four thousand pages of studio files, including production reports, business memos, script drafts, financial records; quotations from a score of books and unpublished research; details culled from articles and news accounts that appeared in film industry journals, daily newspapers, and magazines from 1938 to 1941; radio programs; information included in my first book; and, of course, notes gathered during dozens of full-length viewings of *Citizen Kane* and individual reviews of every shot.

Those participants in *Citizen Kane* who in conversations with me added their thoughts to the creation of this book—William Alland, Ruth Warrick, Richard Wilson, and Robert Wise—provided a dimension that would have been impossible otherwise. Sadly, these fine people, and most of the rest of the cast and crew who worked on the production of *Citizen Kane,* are now gone. Fortunately, our endless fascination with Hollywood offers readers a seemingly inexhaustible supply of biographies and historical accounts that chronicle the lives of key figures and events from the golden age of the motion picture industry.

However, in Hollywood legend blends easily with reality. The passage of time and the frailty of the human ego tend to blur the distinction between fact and invention, especially when events are recalled decades after they occurred.

These inaccuracies sometimes seep into other publications, both in print and—especially—online, where such "findings" are often accepted as fact without attribution. Orson Welles was a gifted storyteller, but with all due respect, he was also a font of erroneous information who would correctly recount the substance of an incident but often shape the characters and locations to suit his audience. "Seventy-five percent of what I say in interviews," he told Jean Clay in 1962, "is false." With hundreds of Web sites devoted to Welles and his films, "facts" as recounted by Welles and others about *Citizen Kane* tend to circulate and recirculate without citing an original source.

So whenever possible, I have relied on the original words of the people involved as found in their correspondence, memos, and confirmed quotes—and not the publications, online or otherwise, of others.

Finally: I am sure your enjoyment of this book will be enhanced by watching *Citizen Kane*. I believe that a fresh viewing will reinforce the most important point of this book: that *Citizen Kane* is a cinema experience unlike any other.

Happy reading—and viewing!

H. L.

Your comments about this book are welcome.
Please write to the author at
leboprojects@gmail.com

CITIZEN KANE: A RECOLLECTION

At the top of a private castle on a man-made mountain in Florida, newspaper publisher Charles Foster Kane lies dying. With his final breath, he whispers, "Rosebud." From Kane's hand slips a glass snow globe containing a tiny cabin, which shatters on the floor.

A newsreel company prepares a film obituary of Kane. But Rawlston, the head of the company, is not happy with the production; it captures the highlights of Kane's life, but not its meaning. The story needs an angle, so Rawlston dispatches Jerry Thompson, one of his reporters, to discover the significance of Kane's last word. "It'll probably turn out to be a very simple thing," Rawlston says.

From the recollections of five people, Thompson learns about the key events in Kane's life. In the memoirs of Walter Thatcher, Kane's deceased banker and guardian, Thompson reads the story of Kane's youth and how his mother became a millionaire overnight when a supposedly worthless gold mine given to Mrs. Kane by a defaulting boarder actually contains the "Colorado Lode." Kane's mother signs over management of the fortune as well as guardianship of the eight-year-old boy to Thatcher's bank.

Kane's wealth grows into the world's sixth-largest private fortune by the time Thatcher's guardianship ends on Kane's twenty-fifth birthday. But of all his vast holdings, Kane is interested only in the *Inquirer,* a failing newspaper. Kane takes over as publisher of the *Inquirer,* becomes a public crusader, and saves the newspaper, but not without resorting to grossly irresponsible journalism.

From Bernstein, Kane's general manager, Thompson learns about the early days of Kane's career—and his success in building a publishing empire. Kane writes a "Declaration of Principles" that promises readers he will provide the news honestly and without influence by special interests, and will serve as "a fighting and tireless champion of their rights as citizens and as human beings." Jed Leland, Kane's best friend and drama critic for the *Inquirer,* asks to keep the declaration, believing it will become an important document.

As a result of Kane's leadership—and scandal-filled stories—the *Inquirer* becomes the largest-circulating newspaper in New York. From Bernstein, Thompson also learns about Kane's passion for antiquities and his engagement to Emily Monroe Norton, niece of the president of the United States.

Thompson then meets Leland, long since estranged from Kane, who tells of the deterioration of Kane's first marriage, the rise of the publisher to political power, and his dramatic fall after meeting Susan Alexander, a sheet music clerk whom Kane befriends in an innocent relationship.

Kane becomes the leading candidate for governor of New York, but only days before the election, "Boss" Jim Gettys, a corrupt political leader, threatens to expose Kane's "love nest" with Susan unless Kane withdraws. Kane refuses, and the resulting scandal ends his marriage, his political ambitions, and his friendship with Leland, who transfers to the *Chicago Inquirer* after a quarrel with Kane about the publisher's motivations. Two years later, Kane's ex-wife and their son are killed in an automobile accident.

Kane marries Susan, and he engineers her career as an opera singer—a career he created for her because of Susan's offhand comment about how her mother hoped she would perform opera. But Susan, whose voice is weak, is incapable of singing grand opera. Nevertheless, Kane pushes her forward. Susan's debut at the Kane-built Chicago Opera House is a disaster; while Kane's paper is being filled with lavish puffery about her singing abilities, drama critic Leland drinks himself into a stupor after starting to write a bad notice about her acting. Kane finishes writing the unfavorable review for Leland just the way the critic started it. Kane then fires Leland and ends their professional association with a $25,000 severance check.

From Susan, who now runs a nightclub in Atlantic City, Thompson learns more about the horrors of her singing career. The morning after her debut, surrounded by newspapers filled with vicious reviews, Susan begs to give up performing. As she and Kane argue, a messenger arrives with Leland's $25,000 check ripped in pieces; with the check, Leland sends along Kane's original handwritten text of the "Declaration of Principles." Kane calls the declaration "an antique" and tears it up, then refuses to let Susan stop singing.

Eventually, the pressure on Susan overwhelms her and she attempts suicide, an act of desperation that finally convinces Kane to let her stop singing. Instead, Kane turns his attention to the construction of Xanadu, a private castle built on a man-made mountain on the Gulf coast of Florida. But Susan is bored and unhappy living in a palace. She longs for life in New York, but Kane refuses to leave. At an overnight picnic, Kane and Susan argue, and he strikes her; the next day, Susan leaves Kane.

Thompson then travels to Xanadu to interview Raymond, Kane's butler. Raymond tells him how after Susan's departure, Kane destroyed the contents of her bedroom in a burst of fury—but stopped his rampage when he discovered a snow globe containing a wintry rural scene. Raymond hears Kane say "Rosebud" without knowing what the old man means.

After Thompson's interview with Raymond, the search ends; he cannot discover Rosebud's identity. Thompson tells his colleagues, who have come to Xanadu to photograph Kane's relics, that to Kane, Rosebud may have been "something he couldn't get or something he lost." In Kane's life, Thompson says, "Rosebud is just a piece in a jigsaw puzzle—a missing piece."

The reporters depart, and the unwanted remnants of Kane's life are burned in a giant furnace. A workman throws a battered sled from Kane's youth onto the flames; across the front of the childhood toy is written "Rosebud."

CITIZEN KANE

A
FILMMAKER'S
JOURNEY

PART
ONE

1

ASKING FOR THE IMPOSSIBLE

There but for the grace of God goes God.
—Herman J. Mankiewicz, describing Orson Welles

The weather had been balmy in Southern California that August of 1940—a welcome contrast to the heat and humidity that had blistered most of the United States all summer. In Culver City, a town as much a part of "Hollywood" for moviemaking as the actual community of that name seven miles to the northeast, the sparkling blue skies and wispy clouds were ideal for filming outside.

But on August 15, two weeks into production of RKO Radio Pictures' most prominent and controversial motion picture of the year—or any year—the schedule called for work indoors on a soundstage down a long, narrow street shared with cozy California bungalows.

The full crew had not yet arrived when a reporter was ushered onto the soundstage to meet the young director, co-writer, producer, and star—all one person—who had been on the set since four A.M. preparing a scene for his first motion picture.

Escorted by an assistant, the reporter could ignore the chalkboard next to the stage entrance, on which was the polite but blunt message "No visitors, please." After they entered the soundstage, the thick soundproof door slid shut to close out the summer breeze and the bustling streets of the studio.

"On the set, all was cool and quiet," wrote the reporter. "Even the clatter of the hammers and saws seemed muffled."

The stage housed the set for a newspaper office, being meticulously designed and decorated in the style of 1890s New York. In the center of the newsroom clutter, a cinematographer viewed the set through lavender glass (a standard-issue tool for black-and-white filmmaking that transformed the world into monochrome) as he supervised his crew while they positioned lights on floor stands; the full ceilings on the set prevented the use of the overhead lights that were typical of the day. Seated at a table, the director, who despite his off-camera duties was in a full costume and test makeup that aged him by thirty years, consulted with his staff about script revisions.

The soundstage could have housed any motion picture production at the height of the Hollywood studio system. But Stage 11 at RKO in Culver City held a set for a film unlike any other: here was the office of the *New York Inquirer,* the newspaper at the core of a publisher's personal empire. The cinematographer supervising his crew was Gregg Toland, at thirty-six already renowned in Hollywood for his groundbreaking photography. And the young director-producer-co-writer-star was a recent arrival in Hollywood named Orson Welles, working on his first film, *Citizen Kane.*

The creation of *Citizen Kane* is a story of many contrasts: it is a celebration of artistic vision and a disturbing account of corporate conspiracy. It is a drama that played out in the make-believe world of soundstages in Hollywood as well as the real-life boardrooms of New York City and at a mountaintop palace high above the Pacific coast. It is the public story of a private witch hunt: how a media organization that claimed "genuine democracy" as its maxim sought to strangle the First Amendment, first by trying to suppress *Citizen Kane* and then by attempting to destroy it.

But most of all, the creation of *Citizen Kane* is a story that continues to amaze—and confound—those who explore how it unfolded: a twenty-five-year-old who had never worked in Hollywood created as his first production a motion picture often called the best ever made.

There is no formula for cinema excellence, but the journey to create it can be chronicled. This is the story of Orson Welles' journey.

In 1939—the greatest year for movies among many great years—it may have seemed inconceivable that Orson Welles, then only twenty-four years old and without experience in Hollywood filmmaking, would one year later make a motion picture that would be acclaimed as the finest in screen history. Welles' arrival in Hollywood that year became another step in a career that can only be described as meteoric: it began on Broadway, expanded onto the radio airwaves, and then—literally overnight—burst into the world spotlight.

"Were Welles' 23 years set forth in fiction form," *Time* magazine reported in

1938, "any self-respecting critic would damn the story as too implausible for serious consideration."

The often-told story of Welles' early years was indeed as improbable as one could imagine. Born in 1915 in Kenosha, Wisconsin, George Orson Welles was labeled a marvel from the moment he could speak—a youthful prodigy who has been described over the decades, with varying degrees of accuracy, as being able to read at two, discuss world affairs at three, and write plays before he was nine.

"The word 'genius' was whispered into my ear at an early age, the first thing I ever heard while I was still mewling in my crib," said Welles. "So it never occurred to me that I wasn't until middle age."

Welles' rapid progress was so impressive that it became an endless source of jokes, even among those closest to him. When in 1940, publicist Herbert Drake asked Dr. Maurice Bernstein, Welles' onetime guardian and surrogate father, for details about his former ward's childhood, Bernstein replied that little Orson "arrived in Kenosha on the 6th of May 1915. On the 7th of May 1915 he spoke his first words. . . . He said, 'I am a genius.' On May 15th he seduced his first woman."

Recognizing the many exceptional qualities in their son, Richard and Beatrice Welles provided him with a near bohemian upbringing filled with art, music, literature, travel, and theater. But his parents separated when Welles was four, and his father was an alcoholic. Young Orson's unconventional lifestyle—which became still more independent after Welles' mother died when he was nine years old, his father when he was fifteen—instilled in him an uncanny ability for creative expression early in his life.

As a teenager, Welles had the stage presence and free-spirited personality of an actor far beyond his years. While attending camp as a ten-year-old, Welles produced a stage adaptation of *Dr. Jekyll and Mr. Hyde*. Later, at the Todd School in Woodstock, Illinois (the one structured educational influence of Welles' life), he starred and directed in some thirty school plays—all before his sixteenth birthday.

His was not a perfect pathway to adulthood, however. With a lifestyle of his own choosing and without parents for guidance, young Orson was indulged by others without boundaries. He saw the unlimited possibilities in life but had no checks on his creative and personal appetites.

"In some ways," said Roger Hill, another father figure in Welles' life, "he was never really a young boy."

Still a teenager, Welles traveled to Ireland to paint, but when his money dwindled, he visited Dublin and tried to convince Hilton Edwards and Micheál MacLiammóir, cofounders of the renowned Gate Theatre, that he was not a young vagabond but actually an experienced Broadway actor. ("I don't know what possessed me to tell that whopper," Welles later admitted.) Neither Edwards nor MacLiammóir was duped, but they both recognized Welles' potential.

"I saw this brilliant creature of 16 telling us he was 19 and had lots of experience; it was obvious to us he had none at all," said MacLiammóir. "But he was more than brilliant, and we said, 'We simply must use that boy.'"

Welles was cast in Gate productions, in his first role (top billed at sixteen) as a nobleman in the stage version of Lion Feuchtwanger's *Jew Süss*. Welles then performed roles in *Hamlet, Death Takes a Holiday,* and more productions at the Gate and other theaters in Dublin before moving on to further adventures. (Two years later, Welles would himself direct Edwards and MacLiammóir in summer stock productions in Illinois.)

When Welles returned to the United States, he put his natural charm and commanding physical presence to good use. Welles advanced quickly: in July 1934, he was at the Todd School, producing local plays; five months later, he was appearing on Broadway. Still in his teens, Welles was becoming a sought-after theatrical performer.

But even in his early years, acting was not enough to satisfy Welles' unique creative yearnings, and he leveraged success as an actor into opportunities as a director. In 1934, he was noticed by producer John Houseman, who signed the nineteen-year-old to appear in his Phoenix Theatre production of *Panic*. The play survived only three performances, but the Houseman-Welles relationship continued in an alliance that was as professionally dynamic as it was emotionally explosive. On one day Houseman and Welles would be praising each other and exchanging effusive messages, while on the next they would be embroiled in explosive arguments—including, later, one very public display in Hollywood that involved flaming projectiles.

In spite of their frequent personality clashes, Welles-the-director and Houseman-the-producer mounted vivid theatrical productions. In 1936, for the Works Progress Administration's Federal Theatre Project (a New Deal–era program created to provide jobs for idle actors and production staff), Welles and Houseman staged, among other plays, a version of *Macbeth* with an all-black cast in a stunning Haitian voodoo setting. The production was so enthusiastically received that it broke all records for the presentation of the play in New York City by a single company of actors. Welles, not quite twenty-one, was a sensation.

In 1937, Welles and Houseman took the bold step of forming their own repertory company, calling it Mercury Theatre. It was a vibrant enterprise, with plans to mount innovative productions of classical drama. Mercury Theatre had its own "Declaration of Principles," a statement vowing that the company would cater to patrons "on a voyage of discovery in the theater" who wanted to see "classical plays excitingly produced."

On a scant budget, Mercury Theatre produced several of the most inventive productions ever seen on Broadway. Mercury's first production in the fall of 1937, a staging of *Julius Caesar* in modern dress and with a script shortened by Welles, was an artistic success and a visual triumph: Welles—only twenty-two—directed and appeared as Brutus, with the play performed on a stark platformed stage painted red, while the actors wore dark business suits or Fascist-style military uniforms dyed dark green.

"The Mercury Theatre which John Houseman and Orson Welles have founded with *Julius Caesar* has taken the town by the ears," said Brooks Atkinson, drama critic for *The New York Times*. "Of all the young enterprises that are stirring here and there, this is the most dynamic and the most likely to have an enduring influence on the theater."

Soon after *Julius Caesar* came *The Shoemaker's Holiday* and *The Cradle Will Rock*—two more hits that crowned Mercury's success. Each Mercury play, and Welles' other projects, found him running the show in a twenty-hour-a-day creative whirlwind of writing, editing, and directing—ever disorganized and demanding, and immensely creative.

"What amazed and awed me in Orson was his astounding and, apparently, innate dramatic instinct," said Houseman. "Listening to him, day after day, with rising fascination, I had the sense of hearing a man initiated, at birth, into the most secret rites of a mystery—of which he felt himself, at all times, the rightful and undisputed master."

By age twenty-three Welles had conquered New York theater, but it was his work in radio that brought him to the attention of most of the public. Welles had a rich compelling voice that critic Alexander Woollcott described as "effortless magnificence." While developing his stage projects, Welles also performed in hundreds of radio programs. He soon became a broadcasting star, using both his natural voice and dozens of accents and affectations for character performances (Welles recalled such a frantic performance schedule that he hired an ambulance to transport him from network to network). Of his radio roles, Welles is perhaps best remembered as Lamont Cranston, the mysterious crime fighter better known as "The Shadow." In a national poll conducted by the Scripps-Howard newspaper chain, Welles was chosen as the nation's favorite radio personality of 1938.

The media found Welles' combination of talent, stardom, and youth irresistible. By then he had already been featured on the cover of *Time* magazine: the photo on the front of the May 9, 1938, issue showed Welles, unrecognizable in old-age makeup for his role as the grizzled Captain Shotover in George Bernard Shaw's *Heartbreak House*. To *Time,* Welles was simply "Marvelous Boy."

With Welles established as a radio star, he and Houseman expanded Mercury Theatre into broadcasting. In the summer of 1938, Welles and Houseman created *Mercury Theatre on the Air* and produced a series of entertaining but low-rated weekly radio broadcasts.

It was the Mercury program that aired October 30, 1938—a seemingly routine adaptation of a science-fiction story—that elevated Welles to international celebrity status. Low rated though *Mercury Theatre on the Air* may have been, and despite commercial breaks and announcements that stated the program was fiction, the production of H. G. Wells' *The War of the Worlds* convinced millions of Americans that Martians had landed in Grover's Mill, New Jersey, and were massacring the human race.

"Radio wasn't just a noise in somebody's pocket—it was the voice of authority," Welles said. "Too much so—at least, I thought so. I figured it was time to take the mickey out of some of that authority."

What began as a routine radio broadcast soon stimulated a national panic. With the attention of a nervous world fixed on the escalating international tensions that would touch off World War II ten months later, it is not difficult to understand why so many people believed that the world was being destroyed.

But the real catalyst for the terror was the timing: millions of listeners tuned in to *The War of the Worlds* during commercials on other programs and did not hear the disclaimers. Instead, at that moment what they first heard was the quite realistic "news broadcast" of a reporter describing the opening of an alien spacecraft. Some studies estimated that thousands who changed stations to *Mercury Theatre on the Air* abandoned their homes in panic without listening long enough to hear the commercials and program announcements.

By the time Welles broke in late in the broadcast with his own urgent disclaimer ("This is Orson Welles, ladies and gentlemen, out of character to assure you that *The War of the Worlds* has no further significance than as the holiday offering it was intended to be"), it was too late. Welles—who sought only to air a Halloween stunt—was stunned by the real-life hysteria and the resulting international front-page news inspired by *The War of the Worlds*.

"The first inkling we had of all this while the broadcast was still on was when the control room started to fill up with policemen," Welles said. "The cops looked bewildered—they didn't know how you could arrest a radio program—so we just carried on."

Did Welles know in advance he would spark a nationwide scandal with his broadcast of *The War of the Worlds*? No one, not even an artist with an imagination as vivid as Welles', could have envisioned the combination of dramatic content and on-air timing that was needed to terrify millions. But once it was done, Welles certainly capitalized on the opportunity.

At a press conference the morning after the broadcast, Welles was as sincere as a choirboy, answering questions with a furrowed brow, the gentlest of tones, and shocked surprise at what had occurred the night before. Welles, a commentator said much later, "was masterful in his astonishment." Welles repeated over and over again how "deeply regretful" he was. However, he also carefully expressed his surprise that a radio drama could convince millions that the end of the world had come.

"It would seem to me unlikely that the idea of an invasion from Mars would find ready acceptance," Welles told reporters. "It was our thought that people might be bored or annoyed at hearing a tale so improbable."

(Three years later, Welles would send a less-than-subtle message in his first words during the newsreel in *Citizen Kane:* seen as an old man being interviewed on his return from Europe, Kane says, "Don't believe everything you hear on the radio.")

By the next day, Halloween 1938, the international spotlight shined on Welles.

"At the moment he was shocked and dismayed, but he was also aware that suddenly his name was on the front page of every newspaper all over the world," said daughter Chris Welles Feder sixty years later. "Overnight, he had become internationally famous as a result of this broadcast. I don't think he was sorry about *that*."

And famous he was. After *The War of the Worlds,* Welles was no longer solely a radio and Broadway star: the attention of the country was, for the moment, focused on this mildly amused twenty-three-year-old, whose Halloween prank had made him a sensation. Welles would continue to work in theater and radio, but Hollywood was already beckoning.

Film studio executives did not require a broadcast-inspired national panic to convince them that Orson Welles was a hot Hollywood prospect. A year before *The War of the Worlds,* when *Julius Caesar* made headlines, several film companies tried to entice Welles into motion pictures. Warner Bros. offered him three scripts, including a costarring role in *The Adventures of Robin Hood.* Welles must have seemed particularly appealing to Warner Bros., because the studio wanted him even though his 1937 screen test was, to be charitable, a quirky piece of film to showcase the young actor: Welles' first screen appearance shot by a major Hollywood studio recorded a wild-eyed, hammy performance of Welles reciting a brief scene from the play, *Twentieth Century,* followed by a 180-degree "inspection shot" of the decidedly baby-faced actor.

Independent producer David O. Selznick, already involved in planning *Gone with the Wind,* proposed that Welles serve in a management position in his organization—not acting or directing—with the authority to choose and develop projects. Perhaps surprising, given his growing inclination toward production rather than performance, Welles declined the position, saying it "did not represent a step toward my ultimate aim: my profession of actor-director."

After *The War of the Worlds,* Welles received more film offers. Before the end of 1938, the talk in Hollywood had Welles slated to appear in two major productions: *Napoleon* at Warner Bros. (at nearly six feet two, he would have been the tallest on-screen Napoleon ever) and *The Monster* at Paramount. Neither project was completed, with or without Welles.

Although all of the major studios sought Welles, the bait that finally hooked him was dangled not by one of Hollywood's biggest or most profitable studios such as Warners or Paramount, but by RKO, the least stable of the major motion picture companies.

From its creation in 1928, RKO (Radio-Keith-Orpheum) had a well-deserved reputation for lacking the machinelike consistency of the other major studios in Hollywood. Although created by financial dynamos Joseph Kennedy and RCA executive David Sarnoff, RKO was not as profitable as competitors such as MGM or 20th Century-Fox. The quality of RKO's productions drifted, and management changed frequently, as the studio's board of directors tried to find a leader who would manifest that elusive combination of business acumen and filmmaking ability.

Nevertheless, RKO produced some of Hollywood's most enduring hits, such as *King Kong, The Informer, Bringing Up Baby,* and the magical partnership of Ginger Rogers and Fred Astaire in delightful moneymaking musicals such as *Top Hat* and *Swing Time.* But the studio's success varied from year to year; for each Fred and Ginger spectacular, there were even more flops.

By the fall of 1938, RKO's tenuous financial condition forced the board to bring in another new president: George J. Schaefer, a film distribution executive who had worked in Hollywood since starting as a secretary in 1914. Schaefer sold the RKO board on a radical new direction for the company: "Quality Pictures at a Premium Price." Schaefer's plan emphasized creating more high-end (and higher-risk) films based on literature, original scripts, and top Broadway productions, many of which would be created by cultivating new writers, directors, and producers—some of whom had no experience in Hollywood filmmaking. It was a policy that would ignite opposition to Schaefer's rule as soon as he took over.

Among the notables Schaefer brought to RKO were Erich Pommer, the German producer of *The Blue Angel* and *The Cabinet of Dr. Caligari.* Soon to come to the lot was Alfred Hitchcock, on loan from Selznick International Pictures, who in 1940 and 1941 would direct *Mr. and Mrs. Smith* and *Suspicion* for RKO.

It was in this corporate climate that Schaefer began to court Welles in early 1939; he would soon create a deal that would satisfy even the reluctant young director.

RKO, like the other studios, had been intrigued by Welles since his early Mercury stage successes. In 1937, Lillie Messenger, RKO's East Coast story editor, urged then studio head Leo Spitz to take note of Welles' abilities as both actor and director. *Julius Caesar,* reported Messenger, was "brilliantly directed." Welles, she said, was "such a brilliant talent he cannot be ignored. There must be a place in a studio for this kind of talent." A year later, when Schaefer took over RKO and began his push for quality productions, Welles rose to the top of his list of prospects.

For RKO, Welles represented more than a potential producer-director who already had a high public profile. Welles radiated the physical presence of a movie star long before he arrived in Hollywood. With dark, transfixing eyes, a cerebral yet accessible persona, and a voice as well suited to motion pictures as it was to radio and theater, Welles was an ideal candidate to play film's most sought-after starring roles.

The vision of Welles, for example, as the tormented Rochester in the 1944 production of *Jane Eyre,* striding across the frozen moors, wind roaring, became one unforgettable star image among the many that Welles would bring to the screen. Although when not performing, Welles could sometimes appear rumpled and disorganized—actress Ruth Warrick, who knew Welles at CBS before she joined the *Citizen Kane* cast, remembered seeing him rushing down hallways with coattails flying and shirt untucked and described him as looking like "a bundle of laundry on the way to be done"—he was the model of perfection onstage, at the microphone, and (RKO hoped) in front of a camera.

So potent was Welles' aura that friends and colleagues would sometimes describe him in divine terms. When writer Dorothy Parker met Welles, she recalled the encounter as "like meeting God without dying." Micheál MacLiammóir from the Gate Theatre said Orson was "exactly the way he would have been if he had consulted God on the subject." Mercury publicist Herb Drake routinely described Welles in memos as "the Christ Child." And writer Herman J. Mankiewicz, who would soon have his own role to play in Welles' adventures, stated simply, "There but for the grace of God goes God."

Actress Geraldine Fitzgerald, who knew Welles in Dublin and later performed in the Mercury Theatre production of *Heartbreak House,* was more philosophical about him: "We used to say that Orson had a 'God's-eye view,' that he saw in you all the things that other people didn't see, all the wonderment and brains and beauty and wit you had," Fitzgerald said. "But what was disturbing about this beautiful light was that it was rather like a lighthouse. When the beam turned, somebody else was illuminated, and you were back in the darkness."

The one physical threat to Welles' potential as a screen idol was a gargantuan appetite that forced him, even at an early age, to constantly fight to control his weight. His routine consumption for lunch was an entire chicken and all the trimmings or a dinner of two steaks and a quart of ice cream. Another obstacle to his success as an actor was a different kind of artistic drive—his deep desire to write, produce, and direct as well as act on-screen.

The only other barrier to Welles' prospects for success as a filmmaker was the mountain of publicity he received before he arrived at RKO. The events that established him as a national figure and an artistic wonder boy also reinforced his role as a Hollywood outsider before his film career started. Otherwise, Welles was ideally suited to screen acting—but it was a job that he would find unfulfilling without the inducements that he sought behind the camera.

———

But there were practical reasons Welles may have turned to Hollywood for the next phases in his career: the "Marvelous Boy" may have had nowhere else to go.

Although Welles continued to resist film offers, his career needed a new direction. After *The War of the Worlds*, his theatrical work drifted; *Danton's Death*, Mercury's first play of the 1938 season, could not lure audiences and closed in less than three weeks. *Five Kings*, an ambitious compilation of five of Shakespeare's plays about the British monarchs, shut down before it reached Broadway. The Mercury's modest production of *The Green Goddess*, a short melodrama by William Archer that Welles had performed on radio, flopped when he converted the story into a vaudeville act. Welles was in debt from his Mercury projects— the beginnings of money problems that dogged him his entire life. Theater writer Sydney B. Whipple said of Welles, "Genius unchecked by practical considerations is its own worst enemy."

The critics were still enthusiastic about the prospects for Welles and his Mercury productions, but as critic Richard Watts wrote, "The honeymoon is over."

Welles could, of course, have continued to perform in radio or appear in plays staged by others, but he wanted to create and lead productions, not solely perform. He saw Hollywood as the financial means to return to Broadway.

Years later, Welles would recall the Hollywood offers as an inconvenience, almost as if they had been forced upon him.

"When you don't really want to go to Hollywood—when you didn't honestly want to go—then the deals got better and better," Welles said.

But if Welles had hopes of producing and directing, onstage or otherwise, he had to make a decision.

In the summer of 1939, the timing was ideal for Schaefer and Welles. RKO was looking for the big deal; in Welles, Schaefer saw a groundbreaking artist with a national reputation who could participate in his ambitious new plans for the studio.

Welles, with his artistic and financial troubles, was—even if he did not say so—ready to sign. But he continued to resist a contract, declining RKO's offers to appear in *The Hunchback of Notre Dame* and *Dr. Jekyll and Mr. Hyde*. However, after *The War of the Worlds* aired, Welles had the leverage he needed to negotiate his kind of deal with a studio willing to nurture new ideas about filmmaking.

"In my case I didn't want money, I wanted authority," Welles said. "So I asked for the impossible, hoping to be left alone, and at the end of a year of negotiations, I got what I wanted."

Schaefer engineered a deal that Welles would accept. Welles and Houseman traveled to California and, on July 22, 1939, signed an agreement with RKO on behalf of Mercury. And when the deal was announced, the uproar over its terms made the usual Hollywood infighting and political maneuvering seem tepid by comparison.

THE BEARD AND THE CONTRACT

A genius is a crackpot on a tightrope. Hollywood is watching Orson Welles, wondering if his foot will slip.
—VARIETY, AFTER ORSON WELLES SIGNED A CONTRACT
WITH RKO THAT GAVE HIM EXTRAORDINARY
CREATIVE CONTROL OVER HIS PRODUCTIONS

Although Welles clearly showed promise as an artist who could develop into a talented actor-director, no one outside of Schaefer's management team expected the contract to be anything but a journeyman's invitation into motion picture production. So when Welles and RKO reached an agreement that featured the most liberal creative terms ever granted to a director working within the confines of the traditional studio system—let alone to a newcomer—the news shattered Hollywood.

Despite the rumors about the concessions RKO would offer to sign Welles, insiders accustomed to the iron hand of studio rule refused to believe that George Schaefer would sign away its control of Welles' projects. But there it was—nestled within the usual legal verbiage about rights, money, and distribution—the phrase that stated it plainly: for Welles' productions, *"each picture shall be under the sole supervision and control of the producer."* Another clause reinforced the point: while RKO could confer with Welles on the cutting and editing, *"control of such cutting shall vest in the producer."*

The RKO insiders who opposed Schaefer's new "quality plan" were just as appalled by an annoyingly casual sentence that reinforced how much freedom Welles was granted: the contract stated that "the producer will, *from time to time,*" notify RKO about casting, staff, music, labor, material, and supplies needed for each production.

In short, Welles received full creative control of his work, including the precious right of final cut for the finished motion picture, and he was not required to explain to RKO what he was doing—concessions that enraged studio executives across Hollywood who had never granted to their most trusted directors a fraction of the creative control that Welles received before he ever set foot on a studio soundstage or shot a frame of film.

Welles soon found that many established directors supported him—perhaps seeing their new young colleague as a champion for artistic freedom that would benefit every filmmaker. But there were also those in Hollywood who opposed the contract because of their legitimate distress about granting a director the right to final cut. Without that control, the studios lost what they considered the best protection of their financial investment.

Eight years later, when Welles made *The Lady from Shanghai* for Columbia Pictures, studio boss Harry Cohn explained to Welles why he would never again hire him to produce, direct, and star simultaneously in a picture.

"Because," Cohn told Welles, "that puts the head of the studio in the position of being a janitor . . . of having no power, because you can't be fired."

But a Hollywood mogul with sensible concerns in 1947 was years away from the problem for Welles in 1939. It was an open secret in Hollywood that RKO had become sharply divided by Schaefer's leadership and his "Quality Pictures at a Premium Price" philosophy. Those disagreeing with Welles' contract included RKO executives who were intensely opposed to Schaefer's tenure as president and tried actively to push him out. Welles' contract galvanized opposition to Schaefer, which continued for as long as the new director was at RKO.

"In those days, studio politics, particularly at RKO and many of the big studios in Hollywood, were revolutions and counter-revolutions and every sort of palace intrigue," said Welles twenty years later. "There was a big effort to overthrow George Schaefer . . . and indeed a very definite effort to stop me by elements in the studio who were attempting to seize power. Stopping me or proving my incompetence would have won their case."

Welles' agreement with RKO—often assumed to be a single contract—actually began on July 22 as a general working commitment to confirm the deal, and was soon rewritten into a series of three detailed contracts that spelled out the relationships between Mercury Theatre, Welles, and RKO.

The first contract, between RKO and Mercury Theatre, committed Welles to serve as writer, director, and screenwriter of two films (an additional film was later added). For working on three jobs for each film, Welles would receive $70,000 for his initial project and $90,000 for the second.

As part of this arrangement, Welles could submit up to six story ideas for RKO to consider "in utmost good faith." If the studio found Welles' ideas unacceptable, RKO could counter with six subjects for Welles to consider. But regardless of the origin of the idea and the time it took to develop, Welles' first film would have to be completed by January 1, 1940—little more than five months after he signed his contract. (This deadline as well as other provisions of the agreements would later be revised when Welles' plans were delayed.)

The second contract was a guarantee for Welles' services under the production agreement. The third contract, an acting agreement, hired Welles to appear in two films: for the first, he would be paid $30,000 as an initial fee, plus 20 percent of the profits; for the second film, he would earn $35,000 plus 25 percent of the profits. Because of this profit participation, it was possible that if Welles created just a modest hit in either of his first two films, he would earn more for acting than for creating, producing, and directing his own film.

While Welles did receive what was billed as "total creative control" of his RKO films, his contract was not the license of absolute freedom that is often recalled in Hollywood history. RKO retained the right to approve the budget and the story if the cost of the picture rose above $500,000. The studio could approve the stories or reject ideas that Welles submitted, especially if the ideas were too political or controversial, and RKO wanted Welles to write his films (but would not push the issue). The studio could also edit footage, but only if required for censorship or for foreign-language requirements. Incredibly, RKO retained the right to participate in choosing titles for Welles' films, but not controlling the content of the motion pictures that the titles described.

Beyond those provisions, however, Welles' deal was unprecedented in the scope and control it granted him.

The real implication of the agreements could be boiled down to this: As long as he kept his budget under $500,000, Welles—only twenty-four when he signed his contract—could produce, direct, write, and star in his projects, or any combination of those jobs he chose, and he alone controlled the final cut of the film. Welles could shoot what he liked, spend studio money as he chose (again, up to $500,000 per picture), and with only minimal input from the studio, complete the finished film just as he wanted it.

But even if a film project exceeded the $500,000 threshold, Welles would be in charge. As amazing as it seems now, in 1939 the studios produced many of their top motion pictures with budgets under $500,000, and "B" pictures cost considerably less. For most of the Hollywood studios in the late 1930s, a production budget of more than $1 million was reserved for projects of special merit. At RKO, as Welles would soon discover, a request for a $1 million budget would trigger alarms.

Considering the business climate in the motion picture industry of the late 1930s, it is understandable why Welles' contract shocked Hollywood. In July 1939, the motion picture business was the eighth-largest industry in America and the world's premier producer of entertainment—success that was ensured by the tightly regimented system of production, distribution, and exhibition of film product that was controlled by the Hollywood studios.

To maintain this system, studio management, in particular production heads such as Darryl F. Zanuck at 20th Century-Fox, Jack Warner at Warner Bros., and Louis B. Mayer at MGM, and their corporate leadership in New York City, maintained autocratic control over every aspect of their filmmaking, including approval of scripts, casting, budgets, assignment of directors, and editing of the footage into a final print—a grip on the creative process that no one, not even the most bankable stars and directors, had the power to break.

RKO signed over almost all of this authority to Welles. While creative control was a central issue in the controversy over the contract, more remarkable was the list of responsibilities Welles would be permitted to assume as a neophyte filmmaker. Allowing an individual to write, produce, direct, and star in motion pictures was the rarest of Hollywood phenomena. Only Charlie Chaplin had regularly attempted so ambitious a challenge. But Chaplin created his pictures outside the traditional Hollywood system—he owned his studio not far from RKO and was the world's most popular film star by the time he assumed the three principal off-camera assignments as well as starring in his own projects.

Never did an individual serving in a major studio receive such control of the final product—at least not until Welles arrived. It was not long before the Hollywood vultures descended on him.

"RKO is going to rue its contract," cried an editorial in the *Hollywood Spectator*. Said *Variety* columnist George Phair, "I would be willing to bet something that Welles will not complete a picture. A genius is a crackpot on a tightrope. Hollywood is watching Orson Welles, wondering if his foot will slip." W. R. Wilkerson, publisher of *The Hollywood Reporter*, described the situation more concisely: "RKO President George Schaefer is just plain nuts."

Resentment and distrust compounded in July when Welles arrived in Holly-wood sporting a beard left over from his preparations for *Five Kings*.

"It was both the beard and the contract that did it," said Roy Fowler, who wrote the first biography of Welles in 1946 when the director was thirty-one. "Nobody liked the beard, everybody hated the contract. Like peeved little chil-dren, the population of Hollywood indulged in nose-thumbing at the errant genius newly arrived in their midst."

In September, after Schaefer announced pay cuts for studio employees, Wilkerson wrote, "If George Schaefer had come out with an announcement that the Orson Welles picture was too much of a gamble to take during these critical times and he had prevailed on Mr. Welles to step back his production effort for a while, the RKO president would have been a big guy in town yester-day. But Mr. Schaefer evidently does not think an investment of $750,000 or more with an untried producer, writer, director, and a rumored cast of players who, for the most part, have never seen a camera, is a necessary cut in these critical times."

Welles in general and the whiskers more specifically alienated some and amused others. Film industry press coverage of Welles and columns about him routinely referred to him by nickname, such as "Little Orson Annie" or "Kid Orson" or "Orson (Boogie Man) Welles." Guinn Williams, a character actor who played western roles and heavies, supposedly accosted Welles at the Brown Derby restaurant, slicing off his tie with a knife. (In another telling of the story, Welles remembered the encounter as being with actor Ward Bond at Chasen's restau-rant.) Errol Flynn, who was fast becoming a close friend to Welles, sent him the perfect Christmas gift for a whiskered actor: a ham with a beard attached to it.

However, as Welles began to move in Hollywood circles, many established directors—such as John Ford, William Wyler, and King Vidor—encouraged his work.

"King Vidor said to me a thing I never forgot," Welles recalled. "He said, 'A good director is a fellow who doesn't go on trying to get everything right, who knows when to walk away from something, and when to stay with something.' That's a wonderful definition, and I never forgot it."

Among the Hollywood pundits upset about Welles' arrival, opinion was divided between those merely resentful of any new arrival—especially one so young and with so much authority—and others with earnest concerns about the risks associated with granting artistic freedom to a beginner when so many proven filmmakers were shackled creatively. Given Welles' lavish contract and his newcomer status, it was hard to fault the critics; forty-five years later, Welles said, "I would have hated myself, too."

For some artists, Welles' contract served as a painful reminder of the good fortune of the haves and the misery of the have-nots in the Hollywood studio system. At a Christmas gathering in 1939, one of those who had snubbed Welles was director D. W. Griffith, a legendary pioneer in creating the motion picture industry.

By 1939, Griffith had fallen from the top ranks of directors and was almost forgotten in Hollywood. The man perhaps most responsible for developing the feature film as a medium for expression had not directed since 1931 and by the end of the decade could find employment in films only as the part-time producer of a caveman melodrama titled *One Million B.C.* As a reluctant witness to Welles' ascent, Griffith could only wonder why an inexperienced newcomer—four months old when Griffith's masterpiece, *The Birth of a Nation,* debuted—had been handed unheard-of control that other filmmakers could never hope to receive.

"We stared at each other across a hopeless abyss," Welles said of his meeting with Griffith. "There was no place for Griffith. He was an exile in his own town, a prophet without honor, a craftsman without tools, an artist without work. No wonder he hated me."

Welles' first film contract has become so ingrained in Hollywood lore as being a perilous corporate venture that, at the time, few acknowledged that the actual financial risk involved was relatively small. If Welles failed, his defeat would have created, at worst, only a comparatively minor loss among many losses for RKO. Given the relatively low cost of film production, ticket sales driven by the sheer publicity value of the young director's involvement in *any* project would have reduced the largest potential loss to thousands of dollars, not millions, certainly a risk worth taking in the always chancy business of running a studio.

Welles' contract may have granted him liberal control, but the money involved was modest, even by 1939 standards. In fact, Welles may have been a bargain. His $70,000 fee for writing, producing, and directing his first film—three jobs that would require months under the best circumstances—could not begin to compare with the $5,000-plus-per-week salaries earned by many of Hollywood's top directors, such as Michael Curtiz or George Cukor. And by signing Welles for all three of the most expensive off-camera jobs on a film for a single relatively low salary, the studio may have actually *saved* money on pictures by using Welles.

Welles' $30,000 acting fee was dwarfed by the salaries of James Cagney, Errol Flynn, Bette Davis, Clark Gable, and several dozen other stars who earned $2,000 to $7,000 per week in long-term contracts. Of course, as part of his salary to act, Welles was also granted a hefty percentage of any profits earned from his films—assuming profits were generated—but a bonus based on healthy earnings above expenses was a price RKO would gladly pay for a profitable performance.

Even the contract's much-maligned clause that granted Welles the final cut of his films could have been considered a giveaway with only modest risk. Knowing that Welles was coming to Hollywood with big ideas about highly visual, potentially expensive projects, RKO may have recognized that its new director would not hold his budget below $500,000 and thus would lose the right to his prized final cut. This is precisely what would have happened to Welles' first proposed project, *Heart of Darkness,* as well as *Citizen Kane,* if the studio had held firm on the $500,000 ceiling. Instead, the maximum amount Welles could spend and still retain control of the final cut was eventually raised to cover the costs of *Citizen Kane.*

However, if Welles succeeded under his RKO contract, the artistic and financial gains would have been more than worth the investment. By producing hits under his contract, Welles could have delivered major profits to RKO and set the tone for a filmmaking transformation at the studio, thus elevating George Schaefer to the status of executive mastermind among the movie moguls.

None of the potential benefits were relevant in the studio system of the 1930s. The real risk in Welles' deal was not the money involved, but rather the potential damage to RKO's credibility if the studio's ambitious venture with Welles failed.

In an industry so utterly dependent on image, each production chief recognized that maintaining his studio's standing in the industry was at least as important as profits, perhaps more so. For the RKO board of directors, losing money regularly was detrimental enough, but if Welles and Schaefer deliberately rocked the industry and then flopped—even with a minimal financial loss—their failure would further weaken the studio's shaky reputation with its stockholders and bankers.

Still worse, however, a failure by Welles would expose RKO to the most embarrassing public disgrace ever experienced in the film community, and many would savor the studio's anguish—for Schaefer, a consequence far more devastating than any financial loss. To Welles and Schaefer, their controversial business relationship had to be a triumph, or swiftly imposed consequences for all involved would be the penalty.

Welles came to RKO without experience as a Hollywood filmmaker, but he was not as unprepared for motion picture production as 1939 publicity and film history have suggested. Although he had been involved in professional theater and radio for less than five years, Welles was already lauded for the striking visual innovations he brought to his theatrical productions and the inventive use of sound he employed in his broadcasts. Those talents would shift seamlessly to his work as a filmmaker.

Welles had already gained some modest filmmaking experience: of little help was a project he co-created in 1934 as a student at the Todd School, an abstract film titled *The Hearts of Age*. (Years later, Welles was endlessly amused when film scholars sought to include this dalliance of a nineteen-year-old in his cinema "oeuvre.") But even *The Hearts of Age*, a grainy eight-minute film produced with fellow student William Vance, shows the beginnings of Welles' flair for visual, imaginative abstract images and (in heavy makeup and skullcap) hints of Welles' screen presence.

Much more telling is *Too Much Johnson*, which Welles created in 1938 as footage intended to be shown between the acts for his abortive revival of the 1894 farce by William Gillette. The film, thought lost until its 2008 rediscovery in an Italian warehouse, with restoration conducted in secret by the George Eastman House and a surprise release in 2013, offers more hints of a budding filmmaker.

Created in the style of silent slapstick comedies, *Too Much Johnson* featured Joseph Cotten in a romp through lower Manhattan, Yonkers, and New York City parks. Shot in crisp black and white, Welles used dramatic angles, intelligent camera placement, and deep focus. He also staged an overhead sequence showing a mass of boxes and baskets that on first glance is startling in its similarity to scenes he would film two years later for the end of *Citizen Kane:* the shots of hundreds of crates at Xanadu containing the mementos of Kane's life.

RKO executives, nervous about the creative control they were ready to bestow on Welles, hedged their bets by viewing the raw footage from *Too Much Johnson* and were enthusiastic about the results. (*The Hearts of Age* and *Too Much Johnson* can be viewed online; see "Orson Welles and Pre–*Citizen Kane* Films," page 312.)

Welles reveled in makeup, costumes, and lighting and thoroughly appreciated the importance of backstage crafts for a production. And unlike many theatrical directors, he viewed the stage not as a flat space with a single shallow plane for the action, but as a deep, three-dimensional platform, a perspective that would soon prove invaluable in his Hollywood projects.

All of these talents glowed in Welles' creations. For example, as anyone who saw Welles' productions of *Macbeth* or *Julius Caesar* could attest, his sense of the visual transcended the predictable in traditional theater. Welles' direction defied mainstream staging and featured imaginatively planned interplay of character movement, overlapping dialogue, unusual entrances and exits, distinctive lighting, and vivid designs—all the results of his self-taught education as a director and his deliberate rejection of the conventional.

"Going into the Maxine Elliott Theatre during rehearsals," wrote Hallie Flanagan, director of the Federal Theatre Project, about Welles' production of *Doctor Faustus,* "was like going into the pit of hell: total darkness punctuated by stabs of light, trap doors opening and closing, explosions, and properties disappearing in a clap of thunder."

More important was Welles' experience as a writer and editor, especially his success editing complex material down to its essence. In addition to the positive reviews he received for directing *Julius Caesar, Macbeth,* and Christopher Marlowe's *Doctor Faustus,* Welles was acknowledged by the critics for expertly editing the scripts of the classic plays—and without complaints from purists: *Julius Caesar,* for example, was reduced from its original five acts to a crisp one-act, ninety-minute production. Welles had also participated in writing and revising dozens of radio programs, routinely condensing classic books or plays into one-hour broadcasts under the unyielding pressure of broadcast deadlines, skills that would become vital when he moved into film production.

When Welles began shooting *Citizen Kane,* he would discover that his lack of knowledge about the practical day-to-day workings of Hollywood filmmaking would slow his progress—although only briefly. But regardless of his inexperience, by the time Welles arrived in Hollywood in 1939, he was thoroughly prepared as a visual artist and writer to begin his exploration into the possibilities for filmmaking.

However, the real key to Welles' potential was his steadfast conviction that cinema was yet another method of artistic communication to explore with the same energy and disregard for creative boundaries that had served him so well in New York. Welles was determined to confront the curious business of making movies and produce electrifying new methods of expression, just as he had in radio and the theater.

In July 1939, Welles arrived in Hollywood, settled in at the Chateau Marmont (the classic Hollywood hotel that today continues to be the home of choice for many a transient filmmaker), and signed his contract. He soon moved into a lush Brentwood estate on Rockingham Drive—a bachelor living in a forty-seven-hundred-square-foot, five-bedroom house, with staff and grounds—another example of his financial excesses. (Money problems would soon require him to move to a somewhat more practical home on Franklin Avenue in the Hollywood Hills.)

The week Welles signed his RKO contract, the studio trumpeted the deal. "And *what* a picture is planned for the first!" howled the studio's ads. But no picture was formally approved for production, though Welles' initial agreement with RKO called for him to prepare a screen version of *Heart of Darkness,* Joseph Conrad's novel about the adventures of Charles Marlow, an ivory trader on the Congo River in central Africa, and his obsession with Kurtz, a trading post commander. Unless Welles could create a budget under $500,000 for *Heart of Darkness,* RKO would have to approve the project before it would move into production.

As he started the planning for *Heart of Darkness,* Welles also began to indoctrinate himself in the ways of the studio system. He hired researcher Miriam Geiger as one of his first guides to the Hollywood "language" of film. To clarify the purpose of camera shots, Geiger asked the RKO editing department for frames of film for several different kinds of shots. She pasted them on a piece of paper and underneath each frame described the scene. For instance, Geiger wrote, "A long shot would show the country, the city, the place where you might wish your story to begin, preferably featuring a recognizable landmark. . . . The USA would be shown by the Statue of Liberty, the Eiffel Tower would indicate Paris."

Geiger meant well, but her documents had little effect. A year later, Welles would use exactly the opposite strategy with *Citizen Kane,* instead beginning his first film with a close-up—the "No Trespassing" sign on the fence at Xanadu—and then using each succeeding shot to tell a little more about Kane's crumbling estate. Geiger's notes may have served Welles by showing him the typical Hollywood way of doing things—for Welles, what *not* to do.

Of more value to Welles was prowling the RKO lot, meeting and greeting, learning what was where, and screening films. During these early days in Hollywood, Welles said he viewed John Ford's classic *Stagecoach* as a nightly ritual, accompanied at each screening by a different representative of an RKO department.

"I screened *Stagecoach* every night for a month with someone from the studio," Welles said, "and then asked questions."

Welles also began mapping out his plan for *Heart of Darkness* by analyzing every scene from Conrad's story.

"Welles started work on *Heart of Darkness* by pasting up the book in a large portfolio and going through it page by page, editing it and making suggestions to himself," Mercury publicist Herb Drake told a reporter. "After several weeks of this he began to dictate a breakdown on the story."

The product of this cut-and-paste analysis was a bound, 254-page volume that Welles used for planning sessions and meetings about set design and camera angles. "He went right through the whole story this way," Drake said.

And for the first time, Welles was experimenting with studio equipment that was the envy of filmmakers worldwide. He began to appreciate that motion pictures could, even more than theater, feed his need for creative expression.

"I had my first night with the movie cameras a few hours ago," Welles told Drake on October 18, "and I am wildly enthusiastic about the business."

George Schaefer recognized that *Heart of Darkness* was an ideal initial film vehicle for Welles to produce—if the price was right. Mercury Theatre had already performed *Heart of Darkness* on radio, and Welles created an ambitious adaptation of Conrad's novel for the screen that would have been a moody, lush journey employing inventive camera techniques (such as "first-person camera" to record the action from the lead actor's point of view), tropical sets, thousands of extras, and a host of featured players, including several colleagues from Mercury projects whom Welles imported from New York and signed, among them Ray Collins, George Coulouris, Everett Sloane, Erskine Sanford, and Gus Schilling—names that would pop up again when casting started for *Citizen Kane*.

But Welles had been planning for only a few weeks before a serious new issue far from Hollywood blocked his path: the simmering tensions in Europe exploded into full-scale war when Nazi Germany invaded Poland on September 1.

Almost immediately, the Hollywood studios felt the war's impact. Although the United States would not enter the conflict until Japan bombed Pearl Harbor more than two years later, within days of the Nazi attacks in Europe, the studios knew they were already losing markets, even in countries not under Nazi control.

In the United Kingdom and France—two of RKO's largest overseas markets—the movie business was hit hard. Central London implemented a six P.M. curfew, effectively killing the studios' business there, and only 40 to 50 percent of theaters across Britain were open. In France, which would not be overrun by the Nazis until June 1940, theaters remained open but with little business, and sending money out of the country was forbidden.

For the other major studios, the impact of losing overseas ticket sales was severe, but for ever shaky RKO, at the time the problem seemed like a disaster. Schaefer told colleagues that RKO would have lost money on *every* important film it produced in the previous five years without revenue from the United Kingdom, France, and Poland.

Schaefer wired his producers, "Never in my entire 25 years in [the] industry have we been so confronted with [the] need to use our ingenuity and eliminating all material not necessary for story value."

Two weeks after the war began, Schaefer told Welles about this grim analysis and sent him a desperate request about the budget for *Heart of Darkness*.

"All of this [is a] severe blow," Schaefer wired to Welles, "and puts us in [a] position where I must make [a] personal plea to you to eliminate every dollar and for that matter every nickel possible from *Heart of Darkness* script, and yet do everything [to] save the entertainment value."

At the time, Schaefer had no way of knowing that World War II would become the most lucrative period of the studio era. With travel restrictions in America and limited entertainment options, by 1944 more than eighty million people a week went to the movies. As a result, even RKO made money during the war years, and 1946 would be the studio's most profitable year ever. But in September 1939, with overseas revenue lost, the future of the movies looked bleak.

"We are watching very carefully hoping for the best," Schaefer said, "but certain we must be prepared for the worst."

Welles, of course, enthusiastically agreed to comply with Schaefer's request.

"Every cent will be counted twice in *Heart of Darkness*," Welles replied. "No single luxury will be indulged—only absolute essentials [for the] effectiveness and potency of our story.

"Thanks for your confidence expressed in times when confidence is expensive," he added. "I'm trying very hard to be worth it."

Welles had already cut two expensive sequences and continued to economize. At the same time, he was developing a spectacular script. When he sent the draft to John Houseman shortly after ordering a new home phone line and not giving the number to some of his closest friends, Houseman read the draft and wrote to Welles, "For again concealing your phone you are a booby. For writing a terrifically exciting script, you are a fine man.

"We shall have many arguments," said Houseman, "but the cumulative sweep and the final revelation of Kurtz before, at, and after death is just magnificent."

Welles worked closely with the studio to pare the costs, but it was not enough. On December 5, the studio's analysis of the project produced a budget of $1,057,761—far too large for a first production under any circumstances, but especially so given the uncertainty about wartime income. (Forty years later, *Heart of Darkness* would come to the screen—the setting shifted from Africa to Vietnam—as *Apocalypse Now,* created by a controversial director of a more recent generation, Francis Ford Coppola.)

In December, Welles and Schaefer met to review the problem and together decided that *Heart of Darkness* would be postponed until Welles finished a somewhat more traditional (and cheaper) motion picture. Welles' first project and his beard both disappeared as he moved on to his next idea.

As an alternative to *Heart of Darkness,* Welles proposed *The Smiler with a Knife,* an espionage thriller by Nicholas Blake that was packed with secret agents and international intrigue (Blake was the pen name for British poet—and later poet laureate of the United Kingdom—Cecil Day-Lewis, father of actor Daniel Day-Lewis). Originally, Herb Drake told Dr. Bernstein, *The Smiler with a Knife* was going to be produced while the sets for *Heart of Darkness* were being built, but when *Heart* fell through, *Smiler* continued. Welles, now under pressure to start any project, quickly revised Blake's original story, changed the setting from Europe to the United States, and asked the studio to assign Carole Lombard to star in the production. However, Lombard, one of Hollywood's leading ladies, declined the part.

Welles' next choice was Lucille Ball, at the time an RKO contract player who had limited box office success in starring roles (her true talents would shine twelve years later, when she became America's most popular TV star in her own hit series, *I Love Lucy*). But in 1939, Schaefer, unwilling to risk Welles' first film without a top actress in the lead, vetoed Ball for the role before he would grant approval to the story. Welles, always with an eye for the exotic, ignored other actresses already in America and decided that Dita Parlo, a German actress who was France's top film performer in the prewar years, should take the lead role, although she had appeared in only one modest American film.

But as the war intensified, Parlo was trapped overseas, and Welles and Schaefer realized that *Smiler*—even if identified as an in-between picture—would have been a major letdown after the huge buildup for Welles and his unprecedented contract. *The Smiler with a Knife* soon faded away.

The stress on Welles eased somewhat late in November, when Schaefer agreed to extend the deadline for his first picture until May 1, 1940. (Later, that deadline was extended to October 1, with the start of the second film scheduled for November 1.) Welles stayed busy; in December 1939, he "appeared" in his first Hollywood production, an uncredited performance as the narrator of Edward Ludwig's production of *Swiss Family Robinson*.

However, as the budget crunch continued and with no film project in sight, RKO forced Welles to take his Mercury players off the payroll. At an emergency strategy meeting at Chasen's restaurant for the Mercury team that included John Houseman, tempers flared, Houseman and Welles argued, and Welles threw a flaming chafing dish at Houseman, who stalked out. Their stormy creative relationship was over—for the moment, at least.

"We came to a parting," Houseman said. "I couldn't control him, and it simply wasn't fun."

But the budget problems at RKO did not stop Welles from his own lavish spending.

"Orson does not think of his income in concrete terms in relationship to his expenditures," said L. Arnold Weissberger, Welles' attorney and financial adviser, to Mercury assistant Richard Baer. "He does not ask how much he can spend in light of his income, but spends without regard to his income, and then has the payments arranged for as best can be done."

Without an approved film project, Welles was sinking financially. He was personally spending $800 a week, not including rent; his spending for two weeks would pay a studio secretary's salary for a year. Something had to change.

Meanwhile, the pressure intensified on George Schaefer to assign Welles to something less exotic than *Heart of Darkness*, in spite of the original reasons Schaefer hired him.

In May 1940, when *Citizen Kane* was already in preproduction, RKO commissioned Audience Research Institute, the national polling company operated by George Gallup, to survey Americans about the type of film they wanted Welles to produce. The top choice among viewers: *Invasion from Mars*, an adaptation of *The War of the Worlds*. Some interpreted Gallup's findings as simply representing the convenient choice of moviegoers who selected a subject they associated with Welles. However, for many at RKO, the results of the poll were another validation that audiences had no interest in seeing new approaches to filmmaking, not even from the "Marvelous Boy."

The survey results were presented to Schaefer, who continued to support his young protégé's interests in developing unusual projects, although support for Welles was weakening the studio chief's own position.

"The only way I was able to secure Orson originally was because of my sympathy with his viewpoint—that he did not want to go out and be tagged and catalogued as 'the horror man' by appearing in a picture such as the *Hunchback* [*of Notre Dame*] or immediately go into a picture such as *The Men From Mars*," Schaefer wrote to RKO executive Harry Edington on June 5. "He was anxious to do something first, before Hollywood typed him. This has been uppermost in his mind and I know it would be difficult to change."

But in January 1940, whether he produced a routine movie or a prestige picture, Welles was at least expected to produce. Under any other circumstances, the collapse of two projects would have been considered routine problems in the often meandering, usually frustrating process of producing a Hollywood film. However, Welles' agreement with RKO and his presence in Hollywood were anything but routine. Welles may have enjoyed Hollywood's most liberal contract, but his powers of creative control were worthless unless he actually started a motion picture.

But now even Welles' strongest supporters began to wonder if he would ever make a film, and his detractors gloated over his prospects for failure. By early 1940, Welles had worked in Hollywood for almost six months, and he did not have a viable story idea to pursue. Given how projects evolved in Hollywood during those years, after that amount of time the studio had fully expected Welles to complete an entire film.

Wilkerson of *The Hollywood Reporter*, perhaps the most vocal opponent of Welles' contract with RKO, spoke for many in the motion picture industry when he publicly speculated that after a half year in Hollywood without results, Welles was finished as a budding filmmaker.

"They are laying bets over on the RKO lot that the Orson Welles deal will end up without Orson ever doing a picture there," Wilkerson said. "The whole thing seems to be so mixed up no one can unravel it."

For Welles, time was running out. His (yet again) revised contract left him with only a few months remaining to get a film under way. Finally, he turned to a project that emerged—not out of inspiration, but from desperation—during his conversations with Herman Mankiewicz, a veteran screenwriter and one of Hollywood's most volatile personalities.

Herman Mankiewicz was a writer for *The New Yorker* and *The New York Times* who switched to the movies in 1926. Mankiewicz was considered a brilliant wit, a valued friend, a writer of extraordinary talent—and perhaps the most infuriating employee in all of Hollywood.

One of the first of the New York print writers to shift to film, Mankiewicz established himself as a solid studio scenarist. It was Mankiewicz who enticed playwright Ben Hecht into writing motion pictures with a telegram now legendary in Hollywood lore: "Will you accept three hundred per week to work for Paramount Pictures?" Mankiewicz wrote. "All expenses paid. The three hundred is peanuts. Millions are to be grabbed out here and your only competition is idiots."

From the closing days of the movies' silent era, Mankiewicz's talent for breezy plots and—when sound films arrived—crackling dialogue earned him choice writing assignments. Mankiewicz's credits included such films as *Girl Crazy, Laughter,* and *Dinner at Eight,* along with dozens of uncredited collaborations. He also served as producer of several films, including the Marx Brothers' *Monkey Business* and *Horse Feathers.*

With a reputation of being one of the stellar wits from the Algonquin Round Table in New York, Mankiewicz was a sought-after companion in Hollywood party circles. Among the frequent invitations accepted by Mankiewicz and his wife, Sara, were festivities hosted by newspaper publisher William Randolph Hearst and his mistress, Marion Davies, as well as weekend jaunts to Hearst's palatial mountaintop estate near San Simeon on the central California coast.

However, Mankiewicz's creative abilities and social charms were marred by a self-destructive nature that diminished his value as either a writer or a social acquaintance. An insecure childhood marred by failure to please an over-demanding father set Mankiewicz on a downward-spiraling path: he could be an uncontrollable drunk capable of ruining an event through overindulgence punctuated by loud outbursts and louder vomiting, a compulsive high-stakes gambler who frequently dragged his family toward financial ruin, and an abrasive studio employee who enraged every production chief in Hollywood. Beneath Mankiewicz's talent and charms was a bipolar personality so caustic that his wife was publicly and routinely referred to as "poor Sara."

Mankiewicz's pendulum-swing behavior, said Houseman, "was a scandal. He was also one of the most intelligent, informed, witty, humane, and charming men I have ever known." Mankiewicz, said Hecht, had "throw-away genius."

By the late 1930s, Mankiewicz's star was badly tarnished. He had been fired by several of the major studios—a sharp contrast to the success of his brother, producer-director Joseph L. Mankiewicz—and between 1935 and 1939, he received screen credit for only two films. In September 1939 he was fired again, this time by MGM for gambling the day after receiving a salary advance to cover his poker losses and solemnly promising studio chief Louis B. Mayer that he would never gamble again.

After that incident, Mankiewicz convinced himself that his future as a writer could be found in New York. He was bound for the East Coast, driving through New Mexico with fellow writer Thomas Phipps at the wheel, when the car skidded on wet pavement and rolled. Phipps suffered a concussion and a broken collarbone in the accident, and Mankiewicz sustained a triple fracture of his left leg, a complicated and painful injury that left him flat on his back for several months.

With most of his body below the waist encased in a cast, as he recalled, "like a boulder holding me down from my navel to my toes," Mankiewicz received a parade of visitors in his hospital room. One of them was Orson Welles.

Welles and Mankiewicz, each friends of writer Alexander Woollcott, had met in New York when Welles was at the height of his success in radio. The young star and the older writer had enjoyed lunch at "21," with John Houseman along as an amused witness.

"I can just see them there at lunch together, magicians and highbinders at work on each other, vying with each other in wit and savoir faire and mutual appreciation," Houseman said. "Both came away enchanted and convinced that, between them, they were the two most dashing and gallantly intelligent gentlemen in the Western world. And they were not far wrong."

In Los Angeles, Welles took pity on the injured and unemployed writer and offered him a job with Mercury Theatre. After recovering in the hospital for a month, in October Mankiewicz—still in a cast—returned home and began adapting classic stories for broadcast on *The Campbell Playhouse,* a subdued successor of *Mercury Theatre on the Air* sponsored by Campbell's soup. He also toyed with Welles' rewrites of *The Smiler with a Knife* before the project was shelved.

Despite Mankiewicz's faults, Welles recognized the writer's abilities and trusted him to produce original material.

"Nobody was more miserable, more bitter, and funnier than Mank—a perfect monument to self-destruction," Welles said. "But when the bitterness wasn't focused straight at you—he was the best company in the world."

Welles was broad-minded about Mankiewicz's conduct, because by January 1940 he was frantic. Welles had to develop a viable project soon or his deal with RKO would collapse. He needed a collaborator who was talented, available, and—perhaps most important—willing to work with a high-profile young Hollywood iconoclast who had radical ideas about filmmaking. So early in 1940, Mankiewicz, desperate for a career break, and Welles, more desperate to make a film, began to talk about their ideas for a motion picture.

The discussions began at Mankiewicz's modest house on Roxbury Drive in Beverly Hills, a property rented from character actor Laird Cregar when Mankiewicz's gambling excesses forced the sublease of his large home on Tower Road above Sunset Boulevard. With Mankiewicz still incapacitated in a cast, he held his initial discussions with Welles in the small bedroom he shared with Sara. For hours, Mankiewicz and Welles would talk, slinging barbs and witticisms at each other as they closed in on the ideas and themes that would become *Citizen Kane.*

"The actual writing," Welles said, "came only after lots of talk. Just the two of us, yelling at each other—not too angrily."

It was an incongruous setting for the creation of a film story: Mankiewicz in bed, pinned in his cast, with Sara frequently a quiet witness to the discussions as she read while lying on her own bed. In the small bedroom, the young, handsome, always charming Welles would simply flop down next to Sara on her bed. As he and Mankiewicz talked, Welles would occasionally massage Sara's neck.

"He was fun," Sara remembered. "Magnetic, absolutely."

The years have fogged the precise source of the original idea for *Citizen Kane.* Welles recalled that he had already developed his own ideas about the exploration of a film character.

"I had been nursing an old notion—the idea of telling the same thing several times—and showing exactly the same thing from wholly different views," Welles said. "Vestiges are left in *Kane* of that, but it was the original gimmick out of which *Kane* grew."

Welles' notions about the central figure of the story may have simmered since his teen years. At sixteen, the spring before he traveled to Ireland, Welles attended one of the few performances of *Alison's House* by Susan Glaspell, the 1931 winner of the Pulitzer Prize for Drama. The play was poorly received and ran only a few weeks, but the story, which begins with a reporter's exploration of a long-dead poet's life as her family empties her house to sell it, could have been one of the sparks that eight years later kindled Welles' interest in creating a film about the mystery of a dead character's background told by the people who knew him.

Mercury assistant Richard Baer later testified in a court case that the idea was brought up by Welles during a lunch meeting at "21" in New York. Welles then discussed the idea with Mankiewicz in Los Angeles.

Houseman said that Mankiewicz, during his convalescence, revived a long-contemplated idea of creating a film biography in which a man's life would be brought to the screen after his death through the recollections and opinions of the people who knew him best. Mankiewicz also put forth the idea of using the newsreel to serve as the catalyst of a character study.

"We discussed an unusual technique," Mankiewicz said, "which was to show an actual guy in a *March of Time* [newsreel] and then find out about the guy."

Geraldine Fitzgerald remembered suggesting a similar method to Welles when his plans were crumbling for *The Smiler with a Knife*. Fitzgerald, in Hollywood to costar in her first American films and staying at Welles' home until her husband arrived in Los Angeles, tried to inspire Welles by offering him one of her long-simmering ideas for a theatrical project: to unfold the story of a central character through the descriptions and accounts of several supporting players.

Welles was enthusiastic about his discussions with Mankiewicz and the broad ideas about power, love, and friendship that were emerging. And even in the early stages of story development, it was clear that a plot focused so tightly on a single character would demand a potent performance, which certainly suited Welles' interest in playing a star-making role for his first film.

As the story developed, Mankiewicz and Welles culled the professions of America's power elite in their search for powerful personalities to showcase.

"We started searching for the man it was going to be about—some big American figure," Welles said. "But it couldn't be a politician, because you'd have to pinpoint him. Howard Hughes was the first idea. But we got around pretty quickly to the press lords."

Welles and Mankiewicz brought together their concepts, themes, and character sketches, and merged them into the kernel of an idea that would become *Citizen Kane*. In days of discussions, they created the basic ideas for a film about the life of a world-shaking newspaper publisher, told from the perspectives of his friends and enemies.

With brainstorming moving forward so successfully, Welles assigned Mankiewicz to write an original screenplay based on their ideas, not an adaptation of existing material as his first two film projects would have been. Welles then contacted Houseman and with a blend of charm and pleading—the specter of flaming dinnerware now behind them—persuaded him to manage Mankiewicz and his writing schedule.

It was hardly an auspicious beginning for *Citizen Kane*, but it was a start nonetheless. On February 19, 1940, Mankiewicz began drawing $1,000 a week to write the script. He would receive an additional $5,000 bonus on delivery of the completed text. Houseman joined Welles and Mankiewicz in Los Angeles.

In this pressured environment, out of an uneasy alliance between a brash new director, an unstable studio, and an erratic writer, *Citizen Kane* was conceived. It was, as Houseman called it, "an absurd venture." The birth of the idea may have seemed strenuous, but all involved would soon realize that the creation of the script and the production of the film would be far more difficult than any of them could imagine.

THE SCRIPT

I don't know—I'm making it up as I go along.
—Herman J. Mankiewicz's response to assistant
Rita Alexander when she asked him how the story
of *Citizen Kane* would end

Two weeks after Mankiewicz joined the RKO payroll, he and Houseman departed Hollywood for Victorville, at the time a small agricultural community in the desert ninety miles east of Hollywood. Victorville was well-known to Hollywood filmmakers; westerns had been shot in the nearby scrub country since the early days of silent films. Two years before, director John Ford had filmed portions of *Stagecoach* on a nearby dry lake, including the climactic Indian chase.

With mutually agreed-upon ideas in mind, the story that would become *Citizen Kane* began to evolve, as Welles recalled, in two separate projects.

"Mankiewicz went to the desert to write his, and I stayed in Hollywood to write mine," said Welles.

Houseman and Mankiewicz settled at the Kemper Campbell Ranch, also known as the Verde Guest Ranch, a small, out-of-the-way resort in Victorville. To Houseman, the location was ideal for a marathon writing session. Welles had agreed that his writers could work undisturbed by him, and the three-hour drive on Route 66 would discourage the director from dropping in unexpectedly to check on their progress.

The location also protected Mankiewicz from the big city and its temptations, especially high-stakes gambling and easy access to alcohol. Preventing Mankiewicz from indulging in his many vices was a difficult task, even with his leg still bound uncomfortably in a cast. While Houseman did some original writing in addition to editing and organizing the material, his most important daily duty was inspecting Mankiewicz's room for hidden stashes of liquor.

Houseman had able assistance from "Litta Belle" Campbell, owner of the ranch and an expert at drying out celebrity guests.

"The only reason Mankiewicz was here was because Mother would keep him sober," said Jean De Blasis, Campbell's daughter and ranch owner, in 2011.

Joining Houseman and Mankiewicz in Victorville was Rita Alexander, a secretary willing to tolerate the professional demands of the pair in their desert writing retreat. In addition to providing secretarial support, Alexander handled less traditional chores, such as helping Mankiewicz with his unique method of consuming regular doses of bicarbonate of soda: Alexander would pour a spoonful of powder into Mankiewicz's mouth, and he washed it down with water as it frothed furiously while he erupted with belches.

For six weeks, Mankiewicz wrote and rewrote the first draft of a script called *American,* forming his story around a reporter's search for the meaning of a publisher's dying word. Mankiewicz did not type or handwrite his original drafts; instead he dictated the story and dialogue to Alexander. The work started in late morning—or when Mankiewicz, ever the procrastinator, would stop playing cribbage with Alexander. Houseman contributed some material, but his principal task was to review the completed pages and edit them as Mankiewicz continued to dictate.

"Mank was so on top of what he was doing," Alexander said, "that Houseman sort of ended up riding herd."

Houseman did offer one concession to Mankiewicz's vices.

"Towards evening around 6 o'clock he was allowed one drink a day," Houseman said of Mankiewicz. "We'd all pile into a limousine and go to the local pub. We had our one drink and came home."

Mankiewicz tried to make light of the alcohol-free policy imposed on him. He wrote a "shopping list" across the first page of an early script draft, requesting:

12 bottles of <u>good</u> scotch *[the double underline is Mankiewicz's]*
4 b. seltzer water
1 box legal pads
Rem Std. 12 *[the Remington Standard 12 is a heavy-duty typewriter]*
and a sexy steno
      Manky

Although Mankiewicz did not leave personal recollections of the creative process that led to his first-draft script for *American,* it is clear that the emerging story featured the ideas developed with Welles in Beverly Hills, real-life issues, historical details, and his own experiences as a journalist and screenwriter. Mankiewicz, pulling no punches, included at least one painful detail from his own career: Jed Leland's inability to write about Susan Alexander's operatic debut because he was drunk was based on an actual incident that occurred when Mankiewicz served as drama critic at *The New York Times* and his drinking delayed his review of *The School for Scandal.*

Mankiewicz used a snow globe with a rural scene to serve as a key plot device and a trigger for Kane's memories of youth. In 1940, Mankiewicz had such a snow globe—a gift from Sara. She remembered that Mankiewicz would often sit in his bedroom, shake the ball, and watch the snow fall while lost in thought.

Mankiewicz and Houseman wrote and edited material at a rapid pace; in little more than ten weeks, they produced hundreds of pages of original and revised script. Each day's writing would conclude—often at midnight or later—with Alexander typing the dictated notes or revisions into script-formatted pages.

While Mankiewicz had the benefit of hours of discussion with Welles about the characters and story elements, he apparently did not have a specific framework for the plot in mind before he started to write. When Alexander asked Mankiewicz how the film would end, he said, "My dear Mrs. Alexander, I don't know—I'm making it up as I go along."

Welles did indeed check in by phone from time to time, but for most of the Victorville writing session, the director let Mankiewicz and Houseman work in peace. (Later, Welles would say that he had already produced three hundred pages of dialogue along with some screen directions that he turned over to Mankiewicz before he left for Victorville, but there is no evidence that this draft existed, nor that Welles wrote extensive new material until after Mankiewicz submitted his first draft.)

As agreed, Welles came to visit in early April; he reviewed nearly one hundred pages of completed script and listened to the writers' plans for the rest of the story. He later saw more material that was sent to him in Hollywood. Apparently satisfied with the progress, Welles told RKO that his first film, titled *American,* would be ready to shoot in July.

The material was acceptable, but much of it was unimpressive; as pages began to arrive from Mankiewicz and Houseman, Welles was not wild about the quality. Welles' assistant Kathryn Trosper remembered that more than once, after reviewing a week's work sent down from Victorville, that Welles said, "This stuff stinks." Mercury assistant Richard Baer also recalled seeing Welles "fume about the pages that arrived from Mankiewicz," and called a lot of the material "dreadful." There would be much work to do.

Mankiewicz and Houseman sent the first major draft to Welles in mid-April—a massive 267-page script containing enough material for at least two films. The script pages were numbered from 1 to 325; between pages 212 and 271 was a fifty-eight-page gap left for material about Kane's developing relationship with his second wife, Susan Alexander.

Two weeks later, another forty-four draft pages were completed, and Mankiewicz and Houseman returned to Los Angeles during the second week in May.

The first public announcement of the project came at RKO's annual meeting on May 27 in New York at the Waldorf-Astoria Hotel, where Welles himself discussed the project. At that time, and only briefly, the film was titled *John Citizen, USA.*

Mankiewicz's script for *American* told the mammoth story of the life of Charles Foster Kane, a newspaper publisher whose struggles to be loved and accepted led to his ruin. While the script did include the most basic story structure that was eventually featured in the film, the plot varied greatly from the finished motion picture (reading this summary after viewing the film offers the best opportunity for comparison).

In its early stages, the script featured a host of twists, bits of Hollywood gimmickry, and lengthy asides—among them murder, corporate espionage, and an assassination attempt on the president of the United States.

(In some draft material, primarily in notes from the discussions in Los Angeles and in some of the Victorville writing sessions as well, the central figure of the film was named Charles Foster Rogers and later Charles Foster Craig. For clarity, "Charles Foster Kane" is used here throughout.)

In *American,* readers are introduced to Kane in a structure similar to the final film: Mankiewicz's script begins with the panorama of the decaying Xanadu and moves into Kane's bedroom and shows his deathbed. As Kane dies, he whispers a single word, "Rosebud." Clutched in his hand is a snow globe containing a rustic cabin scene; the snow globe falls to the floor and shatters.

The action then jumps to a newsreel that covers Kane's life and death (in the original script, this segment is called *The March of Time,* like the actual newsreels of that period). The newsreel captures the highlights and defeats in Kane's life in tremendous detail, including far more information than a film could ever hope to include. "To forty-four million news buyers, more newsworthy than the names in his own headlines, more potent and more bitterly discussed than the world figures he helped to create, was Charles Foster Kane, greatest newspaper tycoon of this or any other generation," reports the newsreel narrator.

Included in the newsreel are scenes of Xanadu, Kane's college pranks, and discussions with wide swings of opinion about the man: as many people called him "pacifist" as "warmonger"; some considered him a patriot, others accused him of treason. The newsreel covers Kane's achievements—such as his papers' muckraking—and also describes the origins of the Kane fortune in a seemingly worthless gold mine left to Kane's mother by a defaulting boarder. Banker Walter Thatcher tells a congressional committee about his first visit to meet the young Kane in Colorado, and he reads a statement that describes Kane as a Communist.

When the newsreel ends, the scene cuts to the projection room of the newsreel company, where the reporters explore the subject of Rosebud. Rawlston, the head of the newsreel company, assigns reporter Thompson to find the meaning of Kane's last word.

As in the final film, Thompson first visits Susan Alexander in Atlantic City, but she is too drunk to talk with him. He moves to the Walter P. Thatcher Library in Philadelphia, where he reads portions of Thatcher's memoirs, as the first flashback begins. Kane's parents hire Thatcher's bank to assume responsibility for the family fortune, and they sign over custody of their son, Charles, to the bank as well. In this version of the script, the terms of the agreement are explained in some detail: the elder Kane can see his son only with the specific permission of Mrs. Kane—if he disobeys even once, he forfeits his $50,000-a-year allowance forever.

Young Charles is, of course, terrified at the prospect of leaving home. He not only hits Thatcher in the stomach with a sled, but kicks him in the ankle. Thatcher takes "little Charles" aboard the train, where he cries himself to sleep while Thatcher watches, incapable of comforting the boy.

The scene then shifts to Rome in 1890, on Kane's twenty-fifth birthday. Thatcher and Jefferson Parker, the American ambassador to Italy, go to Kane's Renaissance palace to pay a call on the young man who, within hours, will become one of the world's richest men.

Kane's drawing room is a model of late-nineteenth-century decadence. Along with a mélange of art treasures, Mankiewicz included among Kane's sophisticated trappings an assortment of pimps, nymphomaniacs, and, in Mankie-wicz's words, "international society tramps." Kane makes his first appearance as an adult in *American* while talking to the Duchess della Cordoni, a woman under five feet tall who weighs three hundred pounds. "Amazing woman," Kane remarks. "Always says what she thinks."

Thatcher has arrived in Rome to officially release Kane's finances from trusteeship and present the young man with a detailed list of his holdings. Kane seems disinterested in the transfer of power, until apparently by accident, he notices that his properties include the *New York Daily Inquirer*, a newspaper Thatcher is trying to sell (in Mankiewicz's draft, the name of the paper is spelled *Enquirer*). Kane demands that Thatcher retain the *Inquirer*, saying, "I think it might be fun to run a newspaper."

Thatcher's memoirs then skip ahead two years, when the banker, shocked by controversial stories published by the *Inquirer*, visits Kane at the newspaper's office. Here, Thatcher meets Bernstein, Kane's business manager. It is Leland (in early scripts called Brad instead of Jed) who wires from Cuba saying that there is no war. Kane, in Thatcher's presence, sends back the message, "Dear Brad: you provide the tropical colors. I'll provide the war." Kane not only publishes rumor and scandal, but also fortifies his Sunday editions with detective stories featuring a new character from Britain named Sherlock Holmes.

Thatcher and Kane spar over the *Inquirer*'s coverage of traction fraud and price gouging ("traction" is the nineteenth-century term for streetcars and electric railways). Kane explains that although he is one of the largest stockholders in the Metropolitan Transfer and Street Railroad, as publisher of the *Inquirer* he is also the protector of the people's interests. When Thatcher reminds Kane that he is losing $1 million a year on the *Inquirer*, Kane replies, "At the rate of a million dollars a year, we'll have to close this place—in sixty years."

Thatcher's memoirs then recall his last conversation with Kane—at least, as Thatcher writes, "I pray the Lord it *will* be my last." Surrounded by anxious associates, including his son, "Thatcher Jr.," the elder Thatcher desperately tries to stop Kane from publishing information that proves that leading investment houses, including Thatcher's, practice unsound business policies.

The story would severely damage the nation's financial enterprises, including Kane's own holdings. Kane, of course, refuses Thatcher's demands, and the banker is mystified. "He's hated me from the moment he set eyes on me," Thatcher tells his colleagues. "You'd think I'd taken things from him—instead of given him things."

Thompson finds nothing about Rosebud in Thatcher's memoirs, so he moves on to meet with Bernstein, the elderly chairman of the board of Kane's organization. Bernstein, like Thatcher, recalls Kane's twenty-fifth birthday in Rome, along with some information that Thatcher did not know: the *Inquirer* was the sole item on Thatcher's list of holdings that Kane wanted, and Bernstein—who gave up the family wholesale jewelry business to work for Kane—had been on Kane's payroll for six months, preparing for the transfer of power.

Kane's interest in the newspaper business is anything but casual. Kane craves the influence that publishing can bring him, and already he is plotting what to do: Bernstein has been buying new printing presses and is planning to print color comics as well. To cover his expenses, Kane has been duping Thatcher with false expense claims for lavish parties and purchases of masterpieces. "There's nothing easier than taking candy from a kid," Kane tells Bernstein, "unless it's holding on to the *Inquirer* without letting Mr. Thatcher know it's the one thing in the world I care about."

A year later, Leland and Kane arrive at the *Inquirer* for the first time, while Bernstein follows close behind with Kane's belongings. Kane meets the staff—a stuffy, old-fashioned bunch—including the editor, Herbert Carter. Kane tells Carter that he will live at the newspaper offices "as long as I have to."

Immediately, Carter and Kane argue about the tone of the paper. "It's not the function of the *Inquirer* to report the gossip of housewives," Carter says.

Kane disagrees. "That's the kind of thing," he says, "that we are going to be interested in from now on."

Kane makes sweeping changes on his first day at the *Inquirer,* but he wants something more. He writes a "Declaration of Principles" for his readers, a pledge "to provide the people of this city with a daily paper that will not only present all the news immediately and honestly," but also serve as "a fighting and tireless champion of their rights as citizens and human beings."

The next morning, Kane reviews editions of all the New York papers and continues to criticize the *Inquirer.* Carter can tolerate no more of the insults and threatens to resign—an offer Kane quickly accepts with "deepest regret."

Kane involves himself in every aspect of the *Inquirer*'s operations. He edits copy, photographs fires, and remakes the paper endlessly. All the while, circulation alternately dips and climbs, growing from twenty-six thousand to sixty-two thousand. F. W. Benton, publisher of the rival *Chronicle,* begins to feel the pressure from his new competitor and offers Kane $500,000 for the *Inquirer.* Kane refuses, saying, "I've never made a penny in my life—maybe I never will—but it's going to be nice to remember that there was someone once who was prepared to give me a profit."

Kane warns Benton that within a year, the *Inquirer*'s circulation will exceed the *Chronicle*'s 430,000 readers. Benton is unimpressed and shows Kane a photograph of the *Chronicle*'s strongest asset: his editorial council, "the outstanding newspapermen of New York City."

Kane retaliates by hiring the entire council. He poses them for a photograph identical to the one that Benton had—except this new image includes Kane beaming in the front row. "None of you has been hired because of his loyalty," Kane tells the new staff. "It's your talent I'm interested in."

The *Inquirer*'s attacks against "the Traction Trust" continue. Kane fights rough: his informants steal carbon copies of letters from wastebaskets in the transit company offices, incriminating notes to city and state officials so inflammatory that Kane's threat to publish them is enough to force the transit company to lower trolley fares and stop pressuring *Inquirer* advertisers. "This new invention—this carbon paper—may prove to be a mixed blessing to the business world," Kane says, sighing.

By now Kane is thirty, and his doctor has persuaded him to take a long vacation in France. On his return, he has a surprise for his staff: he is engaged to Emily Monroe Norton, the niece of the president of the United States. Kane marries Emily at the White House, and they honeymoon in a cabin in the Wisconsin wilderness, accompanied by an army of Kane's servants to tend to them. A yacht has been dismantled, shipped to a nearby lake, and reassembled for their use.

But the honeymoon is short-lived. When Kane sees a newspaper story about three prominent public figures injured in a train wreck, he suspects that the trio's travels together indicate a giant oil swindle is at hand. "If I'm right," Kane tells Emily, "this is the greatest theft that's ever been attempted in America."

Kane wants to cancel the honeymoon, but Emily refuses. The next morning, however, after witnessing Kane's anguish in the night, Emily calls off the honeymoon, and they return to warn the president of the scandal.

The president does not believe that America is being cheated in a fraudulent oil deal and, ignoring Kane's protests, declines to take action. So Kane continues the battle in print for months. As a result of the furor he creates, Kane and his new wife become outcasts from New York society; in the midst of the fray, their son, Howard, is born.

Emily and Kane grow distant. Leland attempts to talk with Kane about Emily without success, and the two friends' relationship grows strained as well. "You can say what you think—and you can fight the whole thing tooth and nail," Leland tells Kane, about the print assault on the oil swindle. There is no reason,

Leland says, for "this savage personal note," pointing to another headline and a vicious cartoon that bitterly attacks the president.

The verbal attacks peak before the president is severely wounded in an assassination attempt; in the gunman's pocket is a Kane editorial blasting the president's policies. The president recovers, but the attack deals a severe blow to the Kane empire. Advertisers cancel, vendors refuse to sell his papers, and Kane is forced to resign from exclusive clubs. The incident is nearly overwhelming for Emily, who stays married to Kane only to ease gossip and to preserve his political aspirations. Leland again tries to intercede on Emily's behalf, again failing.

A year passes before Kane's enterprises begin to revive, and at the same time, his political stature grows. He becomes an independent candidate for governor of New York to fight the corrupt administration backed by political boss Edward P. Rogers. When the campaign begins, Kane is the hopeless underdog; but soon his bandwagon begins to roll, and he has a shot at victory. The election is stolen from him when the Rogers political machine destroys thousands of legitimate ballots to give the election to its stooge candidate. Emily divorces Kane—the election loss and her knowledge of Kane's relationship with singer Susan Alexander are too much to bear (in Mankiewicz's first draft, little is known about Susan's background).

As Bernstein says, Emily is no Rosebud. Thompson agrees; he has already tried to contact Kane's first wife (unlike in the final film, throughout the *American* script she is alive). Thompson tells Bernstein about the response from Emily's lawyer to a request for a meeting: "She regards their brief marriage as a distasteful episode in her life, which she prefers to forget."

Since Bernstein cannot help in the search for Rosebud, the reporter moves on to interview Leland, wheelchair-bound and confined to a convalescent hospital. Leland recalls his early days in New York with Kane—the late dinners, the women, the nights on Broadway. The action flashes back to the 1890s, when against his better judgment, Leland goes to Cuba at Kane's request to cover the war that is brewing.

"It'll be our first foreign war in fifty years," Kane tells Leland. "We'll cover it the way the *Hicksville Gazette* covers the church social."

Leland finds no war, but Kane creates one. Kane papers print headlines and stories under Leland's byline about Spanish atrocities in Cuba, none of which actually occurred. Leland returns to New York, outraged and threatening to resign; Kane makes up excuses for the fabricated stories and charms Leland into remaining on the *Inquirer*. Leland returns to drama criticism, but the warmongering continues. "One of these days," Leland says to Kane, "you're go-ing to find out that all this charm of yours won't be enough."

Leland's uneasy relationship with Kane goes on, and they resume attending plays together. While at a performance, they encounter Kane's father—now a dandy—who is visiting New York accompanied by Miss La Salle, a much younger woman (Kane's mother apparently died years earlier). Kane and his father have not seen each other in years, and it is obvious that the do-nothing elder Kane is not eager to see his son. "I've been meaning to drop in and see you," Kane Sr. tells his son, "but one thing or another . . ."

The group gets together later at Leland's apartment, where father tells son that he is married to Miss La Salle. Kane reacts violently and tries to strangle his father before throwing him out of the apartment.

Leland transfers to Chicago when he refuses to cooperate with a new promo-tion scheme for New York theatrical producers. When Susan Alexander debuts as an opera singer with disastrous results, Leland drinks until he passes out, unable to complete his review. Kane delays the review one day—an unheard-of occurrence—and fires Leland, paying him $25,000 severance.

(Here in the first draft of *American* comes the fifty-eight-page gap, which would later include material about the first meeting of Susan and Kane and her failed operatic career. The story picks up again during Thompson's second inter-view with Susan, sober for this meeting, as she describes her life with Kane at Xanadu, the couple's gigantic Florida estate.)

Among the guests in residence for a Wild West party at Xanadu is Jerry Martin, a man much younger than Kane. Jerry and Susan have an affair; their embrace is witnessed by Kane and Raymond, the butler. Kane suggests that Raymond kill Jerry. "I thought I saw a rat—a rat that ought to be killed," Kane says after spotting Jerry and Susan in a clinch. Jerry is found dead the next morning. Presumably, Raymond does the deed by arranging for Martin to be thrown from his horse. Although Susan does not know for certain that Kane arranged the "accident," she does suspect that something was amiss in Martin's death.

Susan and Kane travel around the world by yacht, a trip that lasts a year. "You always said," Kane reminds his wife, "that you wanted to go around the world." Susan is bored on the voyage and constantly works on her jigsaw puzzles, both on the yacht and as the script shifts back to Xanadu. Kane insists on a "picnic" and camping trip for their Florida guests. During the picnic, Kane and Susan fight, and he slaps her. "You'll never have another chance to hit me again," she vows.

The next day, Susan leaves Kane. When he begs her to stay, she begins to weaken, until he tells her, "You can't do this to me."

Susan's strength returns. "I can't do this to you?" she says as she walks out. "Oh yes, I can."

Susan cannot enlighten Thompson about Rosebud, but she suggests that the reporter talk to Raymond, still in command at Xanadu. Raymond recalls the end of the relationship between Susan and Kane, including a statement that the publisher wrote for all of his papers, which announced that the couple had separated "under the terms of a peaceful and friendly agreement." The butler relates how Kane went to Susan's room before the staff stripped it of her belongings. There he finds the glass snow globe of a rustic winter scene, which he takes as he walks out of the room for the last time.

Now in the depths of the Depression, Kane's fortunes skid downward. The financial calamity that struck the nation—combined with the drain of money from Kane's organization caused by the construction of Xanadu—has depleted his resources, and he approaches Thatcher Jr. for a loan (Thatcher Sr. is presumably dead by this time). Thatcher Jr. agrees to the loan, on the condition that complete financial management of the Kane empire is turned over to his bank.

Although Kane retains editorial control of his newspapers, he does not agree to the financial conditions without a fight. "You'll be somewhat disappointed, Mr. Thatcher, I'm afraid, in how little your business control will affect the editorial policies of my papers," he says.

Thatcher Jr. replies, "I'll be neither disappointed nor surprised, Mr. Kane. My father told me long ago that there was no connection between your own interests and your own behavior."

Kane receives a final blow in the script's closing pages, when he learns that his son, Howard, has been killed in a radical plot to take over the Third Regiment Armory in Washington. Kane's staff tries to downplay the story, but Kane writes the coverage himself. "Deprived of the father's guidance to which he was entitled, neglected by everything except the power of money, Howard Kane, only son of Charles Foster Kane, publisher, last night met with a deplorable end," Kane dictates. At the funeral, Kane and Emily Norton sit side by side without speaking a word to each other.

Then, following a few brief scenes that illustrate Kane's declining health, he dies.

Raymond offers nothing about Rosebud, but he helps Thompson and his staff as they photograph Xanadu and its many treasures. They rummage through the legacy of Kane's life—the art as well as the junk. When Thompson's colleagues ask him about Rosebud, he tells them that he has not found the answers, but he has formed a lot of opinions about Charles Foster Kane.

Kane, Thompson tells his friends, "was the most honest man that ever lived, with a streak of crookedness a yard wide. He was liberal and tolerant. Live and let live, that was his motto. But he had no use for anybody that disagreed with him on any point, no matter how small it was. He was a loving husband and a good father— and both his wives left him and his son got himself killed about as shabbily as you can get it. He had a gift for friendship such as few men have—and he broke his oldest friend's heart like you'd throw away a cigarette you were through with."

The reporters pack to leave, and when one picks up his coat, he does not notice that he has uncovered objects from Kane's youth, including an old sled. After the reporters leave, Raymond's workmen begin to burn the unwanted mementos of Kane's life. One item tossed into the incinerator is the sled—across the front of it, the word *Rosebud* can be read plainly through the flames.

The script ends with an exterior shot of Xanadu, the smoke from the incinerator billowing from a chimney, while the camera pauses on the *K* emblazoned over the main gate of the estate as the scene fades out.

Soon after Mankiewicz completed his first draft, the project was dubbed with a new title. *American* and *John Citizen, USA* lacked screen appeal, but an alternative was difficult to identify; the Mercury staff struggled to produce a suitable substitute title.

"We had sat around trying to think of a name for it," Welles said. "Mankiewicz couldn't, I couldn't, none of the actors—we had a contest. A secretary came up with one that was so bad I'll never forget it: *A Sea of Upturned Faces.*"

The working title *American* was relegated to the archives, and *John Citizen, USA* died after the RKO annual meeting. Finally, an acceptable title was suggested by George Schaefer himself that satisfied Welles. On June 11, 1940, with the first two failed project attempts apparently not counted, a one-line memo was circulated to RKO department heads:

"*Citizen Kane* is the final title of Orson Welles #1."

After working on the initial drafts, Mankiewicz started a new writing assignment at MGM—his firing of a year before temporarily reprieved—and Houseman returned to New York. But before they moved on, Mankiewicz and Houseman met with Welles on May 23 to review their progress on the early draft material.

The meeting, held at Mankiewicz's house, was also attended by Welles' assistant Kathryn Trosper (later Kathryn Popper when she married Martin Popper, who among many accomplishments for the public good was counsel to screenwriters Dalton Trumbo and John Howard Lawson, two among the "Hollywood 10" convicted of contempt of Congress for refusing to tell the committee whether they were communists).

As Trosper reported in a seven-page summary of the writers' conversations, most of the meeting involved discussing the minutiae of script editing, and how to massage dozens of details in the story line—such as when the young Kane is signed over to Thatcher's bank ("this entire sequence has to be worked out to give the scene more personality and character") or Susan's first appearance meeting with Thompson in the El Rancho nightclub ("to be improved and tightened") or Kane's first day at the *Inquirer*, when the new publisher is writing his Declaration of Principles ("the scene calls for a delicacy, a beauty, a gentleness, and a feeling of before dawn").

While Trosper described the atmosphere at the meeting as "friendly," she also noted many disagreements. For instance, when describing the dialogue for the scene at the beginning of Kane's control of the *Inquirer*, and giving orders to investigate the disappearance of a "Mrs. Silverstone," the writers' views about the scene were crystal clear:

SILVERSTONE SEQUENCE

HOUSEMAN: Too long.

WELLES: Loves it.

MANK: It stinks!

And the meeting also exposed some larger issues that would need to be addressed by Welles. One example: at this point in preproduction, the trio leaned toward building up a subplot in which Thatcher kept Kane out of the country and maintained control of the young heir's fortune.

"Thatcher, in order to make him [Kane] a lamb easier for the killing, has kept him away from America," Trosper reported. "Our assumptions must be . . . that Thatcher was in hopes that when his legal tenancy was over, Kane would be in such a muddle and at such a loss that Thatcher would be able to take over full management of the sixty million dollars again."

Plot complications such as this meant that—only a month before Welles hoped to begin shooting—he was still struggling with his vision for the material, and would need not only to revise and refine, but make wholesale cuts and additions. When Mankiewicz and Houseman submitted their first complete draft of *American* in mid-April, Welles had begun the meticulous process of revising and adding to the script. In hindsight, the challenge seems daunting: a first-time director transforming 310 pages of loosely drafted material into a final script ready for production. Quantity, let alone quality, was a significant problem. Later, after a month of edits, studio executive J. R. McDonough told George Schaefer, "It's still 50–60 pages longer than the longest script we have ever shot in this studio."

However, Welles' experience editing theatrical projects, reshaping the plays of Marlowe and Shakespeare into crisp productions for twentieth-century audiences, and writing and editing for radio under the unyielding pressure of broadcast deadlines provided ample training to convert the rough first draft of *American* into the polished script that would become *Citizen Kane*. For much of the late spring, Welles revised the screenplay, either alone or with his Mercury associates, deleting entire sections of the draft, refining the plot, and adding substantial new material that he wrote himself.

Absent from most of the early rewriting sessions was Herman Mankiewicz. Welles and Mankiewicz may have been witty dinner companions, but both headstrong men recognized that close collaboration during the initial slashing of the draft script would not have been productive.

"Herman would rather talk for three days than change two innocuous lines of dialogue," producer Bert Granet would recall of Mankiewicz. "Before you knew it, Plato, Kant, and Mencken were involved in whether the leading lady should open or shut the door."

And Mankiewicz found Welles to be an equally stubborn collaborator—but a convincing one.

"It never occurs to him that there is any solution other than his own," Mankiewicz said of Welles. "Despite yourself, you find yourself accepting this notion."

But once the significant cutting was well under way, Welles realized that Mankiewicz would provide valuable input in completing the project. Mankiewicz returned to the payroll on June 18 and remained on the project until July 27.

Welles and Mankiewicz often worked at the writer's house on Tower Road; his regular paychecks had allowed Sara to reclaim the family home from tenants. Welles and Mankiewicz discussed drafts and wrote together and also produced new material individually. They then exchanged drafts and culled material from each other's versions. The writing pair was often joined by Mercury staff and performers. Joseph Cotten was a regular participant.

"We went to Mank's garden and sat around reading the script and making suggestions," said Cotten in his autobiography. "What Herman was most concerned about was that we might let poor Sara know that the man who came by every day was *not* cleaning the pool. He was a bookie."

With the basic structure of the plot already long established, the writing sessions often focused on refining details that would shape Kane's character. In one session, for example, Welles convinced Mankiewicz that Kane should complete Jed Leland's negative review of Susan Alexander's first operatic performance.

"I always wanted Kane to have that almost self-destructive elegance of attitude which, even when it was self-regarding and vain, was peculiarly chic," Welles said (an explanation that could have described his own personality as much as Kane's). "Mank fought me terribly about that scene: 'Why should he finish the notice? He wouldn't. He just wouldn't print it.' Which would have been true of Hearst. Oh, how Mank hated my version!"

Welles also prevailed when determining how to handle the deterioration of Kane's marriage to Emily. Instead of page after page of Mankiewicz dialogue that illustrated the failure of the relationship, Welles condensed years of declining marriage into a brief montage of conversations at the couple's breakfast table, a now legendary combination of dialogue and editing.

Only after seeing the breakfast table scenes did Welles realize that he had unconsciously lifted the idea for the dining table montage from *The Long Christmas Dinner* by Thornton Wilder, a play that illustrates sixty years of a family's life.

"I did the breakfast table scene thinking I had invented it," Welles said. "And when I was almost finished with it, I suddenly realized that I'd unconsciously stolen it from Thornton and I called him up and admitted to it. He was pleased."

However, Mankiewicz also claimed some script victories. Welles had argued that the interviews with the reporter Thompson's interviews with the eyewitnesses to Kane's life should be used as an opportunity to portray vast disagreements about Kane. Mankiewicz persuaded Welles that the interviews instead should be low-key recollections that would introduce the much harsher material in the flashbacks about Kane's strengths and flaws.

"I wanted the man to seem like a very different man depending on who told it," said Welles. "As the script turned out, he was more ambiguous."

Although Welles heavily trimmed most of the dialogue from the early drafts, he readily credited Mankiewicz for "all the best writing" for the character of Bernstein. "I'd call that *the* most valuable thing he gave us," Welles said.

In fact, Welles' own favorite scene in *Citizen Kane*—part of Thompson's interview with Bernstein—was used nearly word for word as written in Mankiewicz's first-draft script of *American* and in every subsequent draft: in the scene, Bernstein explains to Thompson why Rosebud could have been a woman in Kane's past.

"You take me," Bernstein recalls. "One day back in 1896, I was crossing over to Jersey on the ferry, and as we pulled out, there was another ferry pulling in, and on it there was a girl waiting to get off. A white dress she had on. She was carrying a white parasol. I only saw her for one second. She didn't see me at all. But I'll bet a month hasn't gone by since that I haven't thought of that girl."

To Welles, Bernstein's soliloquy as written by Mankiewicz was perfection.

"If I were in hell and they gave me a day off and said what part of any movie you ever made do you want to see, I'd say that scene of Mank's about Bernstein," Welles said. "All of the rest could have been better, but that was just right."

Some of Welles' own scenes that he added during the rewrite sessions did not survive the final cut—in one case to appease the censors. Mankiewicz's original script for *American* included a party to celebrate the former *Chronicle* staff members joining the *Inquirer*. Mankiewicz envisioned the party to be set solely in the *Inquirer* city room, but Welles capped the party with an additional escapade for Kane and his staff: a trip to a high-class brothel called Georgie's Place.

The brothel setting as envisioned by Welles was cut without hesitation by Joseph Breen, director of the Production Code Administration (PCA) for the Motion Picture Producers and Distributors of America. The PCA served as the film industry's own moral policing organization and looked for questionable content in every script produced by the major studios.

"There is one important detail in the story at hand, which is quite definitely in violation of the Production Code, and consequently, cannot be approved," Breen wrote to RKO on July 15, 1940. "This is the locale, set down for scene 64, which is, inescapably, a brothel. Please have in mind that there is a specific regulation in the Production Code, which prohibits the exhibition of brothels."

The PCA censors were unmovable about including a brothel in a Hollywood film (unless burning it to the ground or some similar "redeeming act" was part of the plot). But Welles ignored the order; he was so eager to use the brothel that he refused to delete the scene and actually filmed it on September 18 and 19—

two months after the PCA edict and when the production was six days behind schedule. Apparently Welles' creative control extended to filming scenes that were forbidden by the PCA, because RKO allowed Welles to proceed with shooting the scene, and the studio absorbed the resulting expense.

The brothel set, assembled mostly of draped Persian rugs, frilly wallpaper, and scattered brocade pillows, also required such Welles-demanded details as $200 worth of glass bead curtains. (The only remaining footage of this set can be seen in the theatrical trailer for the film, which shows the dancers in their rehearsal clothes run onto the brothel set and begin singing.) Only after a second warning from the PCA did Welles relent and remove the brothel footage from consideration for the final edits.

Yet in the days of the Production Code's iron rule, the relatively staid party scene that remained still had to be morally sanitized.

"It will be necessary that you hold to an *absolute minimum* all scenes of drinking and drunkenness," Breen whined. "Have in mind that such scenes are acceptable only when they are necessary for characterization or proper plot motivation."

Welles complied. While the party at the *Inquirer* is loud and bawdy, many champagne bottles are prominently displayed, and glassfuls are poured and raised for toasts, not one of the partyers can be seen actually drinking.

(Welles included a shot that, whether deliberate or not, served as a visual jab at PCA policies that *did* appear in the final film: on July 15, Breen told RKO that the shot near the end of the film of one of the reporters shooting pictures at Xanadu "patting a statue on the fanny" had to be eliminated. In the film, when Jed Leland and Bernstein are shown sorting through antiquities in Kane's office, the arm of a marble statue poked Bernstein in the crotch. The censors did not notice.)

Given the Production Code's untouchable rule about brothels in films, it seems puzzling that Welles fought so hard to include this scene in *Citizen Kane*. Welles may have simply employed a trick often used by screenwriters and directors in the 1930s and 1940s who were forced to bow to the PCA's strict mandates: include a blatantly unacceptable scene in a script to divert attention from other questionable but more important material.

Whether intentional or not, while the PCA focused its criticism of the *Citizen Kane* script on such points as the brothel scene, questions of drunkenness, and other seemingly insignificant points that had little impact on the plot, the censors did not challenge the far more important issue of Kane, a married man, maintaining a relationship—sexual or otherwise—with Susan Alexander and no doubt paying for her lifestyle. With or without realizing it, Welles was quickly picking up the tricks of the screenwriting trade.

RKO forced changes on the script as well, but the studio's own considerations were focused on issues of finance, not 1940s morals. Budget projections based on early versions of the script indicated that production costs would top the $1 million figure. As with *Heart of Darkness,* a budget that exceeded the notorious $1 million mark was again out of the question. Welles may have been a national sensation, but RKO would never have been able to convince its board of directors that such a lavish budget was justified, especially for so risky a venture as an original drama about a subject unproven with the public.

RKO was certainly willing to spend when the studio chiefs believed the project was worth the expense. Other high-budget RKO productions of the period included *Gunga Din,* starring Cary Grant and a cast of thousands, and *The Hunchback of Notre Dame* with Charles Laughton in the title role—sweeping sagas based on well-known stories that featured top box office stars and budgets approaching $2 million. But *Citizen Kane* was no *Gunga Din,* and if RKO had refused to spend more than $1 million on a film adaptation of a renowned book such as *Heart of Darkness,* it would never risk a budget of that size on *Citizen Kane.*

After Welles' experiences with *Heart of Darkness,* he may have deliberately submitted more than three hundred pages of draft script as a padded attempt at budget approval, knowing that RKO would trim expenses for a first-draft script of any length. Indeed, within days of submitting the first script for budget review, Welles' initial edits deleted all of the scenes set in Kane's Roman palace—cuts that immediately reduced construction and labor costs by tens of thousands of dollars. But in spite of the cost savings produced by Welles' first edits, the process of reducing the budget even further dragged on through May, June, and July.

By June 18, a shooting script was ready. This "final" script progressed through several additional revisions, with the last full version dated July 16. But RKO, still nervous about its new young director and his excessive budget, continued to stall the start date and looked for more ways to cut costs.

The RKO bosses would soon discover that Welles was quite willing to deceive them to start the production of his film.

THE CONSEQUENCES
OF HIS ACTIONS

I would say I wrote about 98 percent of the picture.
—HERMAN J. MANKIEWICZ

I did not write any of Mr. Mankiewicz's script, he did not write any of mine.
Combining the two and making a final screenplay from the best elements
of both was, as producer-director, my responsibility.
—ORSON WELLES

Long before *Citizen Kane* was released, the infighting began over who—Mankiewicz or Welles—was responsible for writing the script. That argument grew over the decades as *Citizen Kane*'s stature rose to that of film legend.

The controversy was fueled for decades by conflicting stories: John Houseman credited Welles with the visual presentation of *Citizen Kane* but gave total responsibility for the script to Mankiewicz—saying in his later years that "Welles didn't write a word"—even though evidence in his own files and correspondence proved otherwise. Welles, on the other hand, acknowledged "Mankie" for writing the original draft of the screenplay but also took credit for writing many key scenes.

Film critic Pauline Kael, who in an essay that later became a book heavily favored Mankiewicz well past the point of objectivity, helped continue the debate thirty years after the film was released. (Later, it was learned that Kael declined to interview Welles for her essay, nor did she talk with other people involved in the production. She also ignored opportunities to accurately characterize Welles' involvement by not fact-checking information that was easily available in studio files.) Director–film historian Peter Bogdanovich, as a rebuttal to Kael's writing, produced a more balanced and factually accurate account of each writer's roles in writing the script.

The dispute began in late August 1940, when Mankiewicz became enraged after seeing Welles quoted in Louella Parsons' column: "So I wrote *Citizen Kane*."

Mankiewicz, said publicist Herb Drake to Welles, "is in the biggest fever yet.

"Mr. M. threatens to 'come down on you,'" wrote Drake, "because you are a 'juvenile delinquent credit stealer.'"

Mankiewicz—who was frequently referred to as "Mangel-Wurzel" in correspondence from the Mercury office—said he would run a protest ad in the trade papers and send a story out on the wire services unless Welles gave him his due credit.

Welles, at the very least, did not want Mankiewicz to receive sole credit. Welles said that while Houseman and Mankiewicz were editing their draft, he was writing his own based on their initial discussions; he then merged the two versions.

"My own secretary can show that just as I did not write any of Mr. Mankiewicz's script, he did not write any of mine," Welles wrote to *The Times* of London. "Combining the two and making a final screenplay from the best elements of both was, as producer-director, my responsibility."

Much later, John Houseman backpedaled considerably when he said, "As far as I could judge, the co-billing was correct. The *Citizen Kane* script was the product of both of them."

Looking back at Hollywood policies during the golden age of the studio era, it seems strange that *Citizen Kane*'s authorship became an issue at all. With the motion picture industry near its peak of productivity, screen credit was sometimes not granted to a writer significantly involved in the original creation of the script. Several writers would be rotated through film projects as routinely as auto workers on an assembly line, frequently without knowing that others were assigned to the same project—one writer added dialogue here, another filled in action there—but the on-screen credit was strictly limited. On *The Wizard of Oz*, for example, no fewer than thirteen writers, including Mankiewicz, worked on the project for more than a year, but the final credit was assigned to only three: Noel Langley, Florence Ryerson, and Edgar Allan Woolf.

Mankiewicz, who had written for the studios for almost fourteen years before *Citizen Kane*, knew how the system worked in both film and radio. He did not receive credit for *The Campbell Playhouse;* the programs were "produced, directed, and written by Orson Welles." Mankiewicz had waived his right to any credit for the script when he signed his Mercury contract to write it. A clause stated that for *Citizen Kane,* "Mercury Productions, Inc., for this purpose, shall be deemed the author and creator." It was an odd point for RKO to allow in the contract, given that the Screen Writers Guild would surely demand that at least one individual be given a screen credit for the script.

But even Mankiewicz may have recognized another point in which there was at least a kernel of truth: diverting credit to Mercury or to Welles might have spared the production from being tainted by the participation of a socially dysfunctional writer in a career tailspin.

Later, Welles did not deny Mankiewicz's role in the project. Thirty years after *Citizen Kane,* he described Mankiewicz's contribution as "enormous."

"Without Mank it would have been a totally different picture," Welles said. "It suits my self-esteem to think it might have been almost as good, but I could never have arrived at *Citizen Kane* as it was without Herman."

Welles continued, "There is a quality in the film—much more than a vague perfume—that was Mank and that I treasured. It gave a kind of character to the movie which I could never have thought of."

But today, it seems clear that in the heat of preproduction of *Citizen Kane* in 1940, Mankiewicz thought he deserved sole writing credit.

"Mankiewicz is claiming that he wrote the entire script," Welles' lawyer L. Arnold Weissberger wrote to Mercury assistant Richard Baer on September 9. "He will probably take the position that Orson had not contributed even ten percent to it and is, therefore, not entitled to credit."

Mankiewicz confirmed this view in a letter to Alexander Woollcott:

> *I feel it my modest duty to tell you that the conception of the story,*
> *the plot, the characters, the manner of telling the story and about*
> *99 percent of the words are the exclusive creations of*
> *Yours,*
> *Mank*

Welles was already a veteran of script credit wars. In New York, he had resisted attempts by others to share writing credit on Mercury productions, and when the radio play for *The War of the Worlds* and a study of its impact were prepared for 1940 publication by Princeton University Press, he bickered for weeks with the editors who wanted to identify Howard Koch as the sole writer (in addition to himself, Welles sought credit in the publication for several on the Mercury staff who had contributed to the script).

On *Citizen Kane,* had Mankiewicz not protested, Welles might have sought sole screen credit to complement his work as producer, director, and star—although Weissberger and others, to avoid negative publicity, advised against it.

"It would be unwise to deny Mankiewicz credit on the screen," said Weissberger to Welles, "and have him get credit through the press by publicizing his complaint."

The spat continued for more than four months until the issue of screen credit was resolved by the Screen Writers Guild and a shared credit was granted to both writers. On January 3, 1941, Baer happily reported to Weissberger that "Mankiewicz has conceded to Orson's wishes in the question of credits."

The billing, agreed to by everyone, would be:

```
Original Screen Play
Herman J. Mankiewicz
Orson Welles
```

The Screen Writers Guild's 1940 ruling was indeed appropriate. In 1978, Mankiewicz biographer Richard Meryman asked screenwriter-director Frank Pierson, a member of the guild's arbitration committee, how such a ruling would have been handled under then current rules. Pierson said that if Welles wrote original material during the cutting of *American,* the changes made at that time were more than enough to earn a second credit line.

The scuffle over the creation of *Citizen Kane* will no doubt continue as long as critics, fans, and academics study motion pictures; settling on an answer that satisfies all observers seems unlikely. (Mankiewicz, who died in 1953, did not play a role in the dispute once his own place in the screen credits was established, other than his testimony in a lawsuit filed by a Hearst biographer who claimed the script was derived from his book: "I would say I wrote about 98 percent of the picture," Mankiewicz testified.)

More enlightening in the story of *Citizen Kane* is looking at how the unique talents of Mankiewicz and Welles each contributed to the creation of the film.

As Mankiewicz biographer Meryman put it, "One marvels at the debt those two self-destroyers owe to each other."

The initial ideas were developed by Welles and Mankiewicz before the excursion to Victorville, then the draft by Mankiewicz and Houseman formed the basic structure. The interviews and flashbacks, the opening newsreel, the hunt for Rosebud, the "Declaration of Principles," and the grim concept of a little boy being signed over to the custody of a bank—all originated in script form with Mankiewicz in Victorville. While Mankiewicz and Welles discussed the basic plot points before Mankiewicz began writing, the script that *Citizen Kane* would ultimately become began on paper with Mankiewicz, who created the initial foundation for a film unlike any other.

"The big contribution of Mankiewicz was the Rosebud gimmick," Welles said three decades later. "I'm still not too keen about it, but it manages to work effectively, so I shouldn't be too sour-grapeish about it."

Welles contributed extensively to the original story development in his conversations with Mankiewicz, edited the drafts, and also wrote significant new material of his own. But Welles did much more than add new text and slice out the extraneous scenes: he stripped away unnecessary material to create a lean structure that focused on the major issues that affected Kane's life and career. Although Mankiewicz's original characters said a great deal, they required many pages of dialogue to do so; Welles' rewritten characters communicated much more while saying less.

Welles' early edits alone deleted at least an hour of screen time without damage to the plot. For instance, Mankiewicz wrote page after page of dialogue and anecdotes that described Kane's youthful escapades in Rome and the transfer of power to him from Thatcher's bank—Hollywood shtick that Welles cut in his first large revision of the script.

Welles also replaced many of Mankiewicz's detailed plot points with scenes that describe broad statements about power, personality, and friendship. Mankiewicz wrote that Jed Leland transferred to the *Chicago Inquirer* in protest over a promotion scheme for New York theatrical producers. Welles revised the point so that Leland leaves New York because of his growing concerns over Kane's changing moral and political values. Mankiewicz filled pages with an oil scandal and Kane's conflict with the president as a setback in the publisher's career. Welles removed the scandal and instead used voter hypocrisy as the reason the publisher lost an election to the corrupt New York political machine after being unjustly charged with immoral behavior in his relationship with Susan Alexander. Voters, according to Welles, would rather elect a public thief for their governor than a married man unfairly accused of philandering.

Where Mankiewicz used paragraphs or pages, Welles shortened, tightened, and focused the script, removing long passages and adding new material. Welles made many points with a single line—or sometimes only a look. He left much unsaid, but he also demonstrated frequently how unnecessary it was to say more.

Several scenes involving Kane's wives illustrate Welles' skill at script editing or adding brief new scenes—or sometimes a single shot. The oft described montage of Kane and Emily at their breakfast table was originally intended to be separate scenes. As tightly rewritten by Welles, and then planned in editing with Robert Wise, the montage not only showed the deterioration of their marriage, but also cleverly condensed Emily's anti-Semitism and snobbery into a single conversation (in her attitude about Bernstein's gift to her son and his possible visits to the nursery) and the beginning of the decay in Kane's values into a single phrase (when Emily says, "Really, Charles, people will think—," he cuts her off with a brusque, "What I tell them to think"). Later in the film, when Welles wanted to demonstrate Susan's poor acting ability as an opera performer, he accomplished it visually with a single shot of Susan's leg striding in an exaggerated step, followed by a shot of Matiste, her teacher, wincing.

The draft scripts of *Citizen Kane* have been examined by scholars for decades. The most thorough appraisal was conducted by University of Illinois scholar Robert Carringer, who wrote a masterful analysis of the seven principal scripts and also objectively appraised the roles Mankiewicz and Welles played in the writing and editing.

Another approach to reviewing the evolution of the scripts is exploring the opposite ends of the work: the first and the last versions. Looking at what may be the earliest sketch of the script for *Citizen Kane* side by side with the final official version three months later reveals many differences in the plot, structure, and dialogue. However, given the number of changes during three months of editing and rewriting, first by Mankiewicz and then by Welles, the two documents also contain a surprising number of similarities.

Ninety-two pages of the script from Welles' personal papers—possibly the initial text that Welles reviewed on his first trip to visit Mankiewicz and Houseman in Victorville—are a fragment of a preliminary draft of some scenes written so early in preproduction that the names "Charles Foster Craig" and "Charles Foster Rogers" are used interchangeably. The draft covers many of the plot points that would appear in the first half hour of the final film, and even at this early stage in writing, the script includes the opening with the "No Trespassing" sign, the already decaying Xanadu and its grounds, the camera traveling across the estate to Kane's room, the snow globe, Kane's death, the newsreel, Rawlston and his team talking about Rosebud, and the basic elements of Thatcher's memoirs about Kane as a boy.

Even some of the descriptions used in the scripts remained consistent. For instance, from the first draft to the last, Mankiewicz's depiction of Xanadu never varied. The description would become one of the most memorable script comments in Hollywood history: Xanadu was "the literally incredible domain of Charles Foster Kane."

And though the early draft represents only a small portion of the film, it contains lines that would survive months of rewriting. Among the many appearing in the early pages:

Then . . . as it must to all men, death came to Charles Foster Kane.
That's why he's going to be brought up where you can't get at him.
Is that really your idea of how to run a newspaper?
I don't know how to run a newspaper, Mr. Thatcher. I just try everything
   I can think of.

But at this early stage, this fragment of a first draft includes large chunks of superfluous material that would be quickly refined or cut outright. Thatcher's visit to Kane in Rome to transfer his guardianship, for example, with colorful royalty and bejeweled riffraff, is titillating by 1940 standards but continues for pages without advancing the story at all (this ninety-two-page script ends when Thompson concludes his review of Thatcher's memoirs). As the first material trimmed in editing, Welles not only reduced the budget, but measurably improved the plot.

However, this overly long scene was just a hint of the florid writing to come in the *American* script and in version after version of revised drafts. In the last official version of the script—the "Third Revised Final," dated July 16—the excessive writing and unfocused passages are still obvious. At that late date, the long-windedness that persisted into this "final" script after more than ten weeks of editing is almost embarrassing.

Compared with what the actual film would eventually become, the supposedly final script—less than two weeks before the official start of filming and reduced to less than half the length of the original draft—still included many convoluted discussions and arguments that do not advance the story, not least of which are pages of talk about class struggle, corrupt judges, the potential for war in Cuba, and Thatcher and Kane squabbling about why the young heir wants to be publisher of the *Inquirer*. Also included are some odd plot contrivances, such as Kane offering Leland his own antiwar newspaper column (free of editing by Kane), a subject that never turns up again and serves no purpose.

As written, the Third Revised Final version of the script would have been impossible to use to shoot *Citizen Kane* as we know it. Another session of major edits was needed; for Welles, his best work on the script was about to begin.

Comparing the Third Revised Final script for *Citizen Kane*—still too long and softly focused—with the film as shot shows that Welles' most daring and successful editing and writing occurred after the final version of the script was completed. Already notorious for endlessly but effectively modifying his scripts, Welles had developed last-minute editing instincts that served him well in New York, where he would typically revise theatrical productions the night before a premiere or edit radio programs until minutes before broadcast.

This editing process worked even better for Welles on his first assignment in Hollywood, where the combination of rehearsals that were part of the formal preproduction schedule and the extra time available because of budget delays allowed for frequent cast readings, on-the-spot changes, and more rehearsals. Some of these edits were surely the result of the informal poolside discussions at Mankiewicz's home with Welles and the Mercury cast and crew.

Welles, said scholar Robert Carringer, "was adept at handling last-minute emergencies." In rehearsal, Welles often quickly revised on the spot—at speeds, said Carringer, "that astonished his associates." This type of editing would become routine during the production of *Citizen Kane*, remembered Welles' assistant Kathryn Trosper.

"Orson created much of the film on the fly," Trosper said.

From these sessions, Carringer said, "at last out of trial and error came the master stroke—a way of playing it using tiny bits and pieces from all the previous scenes but forging them into a brilliantly original combination."

Welles' adjustments would produce one of the most impressive but less noted strengths of *Citizen Kane:* the economy of dialogue in every scene. From start to finish, not a line is wasted.

But knowing that these revisions occurred raised a question: What happened to the final shooting script that was used to film *Citizen Kane*?

It would seem logical that a copy—anyone's copy—of the actual shooting script would have turned up in decades of analysis of the film, but no study of *Citizen Kane* mentions any draft that was produced after the Third Revised Final. While copies of every other draft are stored in the RKO production files at UCLA and the other archives that maintain files on *Citizen Kane* (such as Welles' personal papers collection at Indiana University in Bloomington and the Academy of Motion Picture Arts and Sciences' Margaret Herrick Library in Beverly Hills), none of them include new script material after some minor updates were added to the Third Revised Final on July 19. Even more intriguing, no copy of an actual shooting script has ever appeared on the auction market for movie memorabilia, despite the fact that sales of less significant earlier drafts have yielded six-figure prices.

However, two copies of Welles' final version of a script for *Citizen Kane* do exist: at the Museum of Modern Art in New York City, in a file marked simply "Correction Script," and in the personal papers of assistant producer Richard Wilson at the University of Michigan, Ann Arbor, in two folders labeled "Late Draft," are the only known copies of the document that may be the final draft of a shooting script of *Citizen Kane*.

The eighty-five-page script is undated, but based on the contents, it was written after the Third Revised Final was completed. Typed in an atypical two-column format, the Correction Script reveals Welles at his best as the last-minute editor: while work remained, most of the revised scenes and crisp dialogue in this version would be used word for word to shoot the film.

Neither copy of the Correction Script includes a cover page with the title and version description that was standard issue for all RKO scripts. Although those pages could have disappeared over time, their absence from otherwise pristine documents does raise a question: Given that Welles held total creative control of the project, did he prepare the Correction Script without alerting RKO, while the studio assumed he was going to shoot the Third Revised Final as approved? With no records or correspondence about the work after the Third Revised Final on the script by Welles and others on the Mercury team, the answer may forever be a mystery. But the solutions the Correction Script provides are clear.

The Correction Script shows that Welles had deleted almost all of the surplus discussion and unnecessary plot points that appeared in the Third Revised Final—gone is the talk of class struggle, corruption, most of the arguments about Cuba, Kane's defense of his desire to own the *Inquirer,* and the offer to give Leland his own column. *All* of these discussions from the Third Revised Final—and much more—were cut when the Correction Script was created, but the core of every scene in which they appeared was retained. As a result, Welles cut at least fifteen minutes' worth of useless dialogue without losing the intention of each scene and also systematically cleaned up the script, sharpened every point, and clarified each message.

The narration in the newsreel was cut by at least half, including the deletion of some references to beneficial community acts by Kane that had lingered from earlier drafts (relief for victims of the San Francisco earthquake in 1906) and examples of solid journalism (accurately reporting the details of the end of World War I hours before the competition did)—points that, while interesting, stalled the tempo of the newsreel.

Although much of the Correction Script would be shot as is, several scenes would be further refined. One example among many: The difference between the Correction Script and how one shot would ultimately appear on-screen was a transformation of Mankiewicz's focus on words into Welles' complete emphasis on the visuals. To describe Susan's suicide attempt—one of the earliest scenes shot, and only days after the Correction Script must have been completed—Mankiewicz's text, which appears in both the Third Revised Final and the Correction Script, includes a half page of dialogue between Kane and the butler: Kane asks Joseph if he has the keys to Susan's room, Joseph says no, then Kane declares he will break down the door; it was a conversation Welles knew was unnecessary.

Welles deleted the entire conversation between Kane and the butler and instead filmed Susan inside the room, barely breathing, with the door in the background. Welles used only a single shot: Susan is seen breathing, then a knock is heard, then louder knocking, the doorknob rattling, then pounding, and then Kane and the butler break through.

At a point so close to filming, script editing was particularly challenging to maintain Welles' visual plan for *Citizen Kane.* Most of the sequences included in the late scripts that do not appear in the final film were not, as might be supposed, filmed anyway, only to wind up on the proverbial cutting room floor. Editing in postproduction would be of no help to Welles in preserving his original plan to include many long takes with no breaks—especially in the interviews by Thompson with Bernstein, Leland, Susan, and Raymond and in the argument between Kane and Thatcher in the *Inquirer* newsroom. To preserve the single shots used for these conversations—some of which are two to three minutes long without a break—*none* of these scenes could be edited after shooting; Welles had to be certain that his dialogue was precisely the way he wanted it before it was shot. Each of these scenes in the Third Revised Final was edited substantially for the Correction Script and then refined modestly again as filming began.

For instance, in the Correction Script, at the peak of the argument between Kane and Thatcher in the *Inquirer* newsroom about GALLEONS OF SPAIN OFF JERSEY COAST and the possibility of war in Cuba, Kane chooses that moment to remember that he cannot pronounce the word *irrevocable*—a worse-than-useless line that was fortunately left behind before the scene was ultimately shot. Later, Thompson's interview with Jed Leland starts with Leland rambling about getting old and drinking bad bourbon, dull statements that do nothing to establish the character. Welles eventually deleted them and also cut Leland's other comments by one-fourth.

Even Welles' own favorite scene—Bernstein's delicate recounting of his youth and a girl in a white dress whom he saw on the ferry—originally ended with an unneeded exchange: in the script, Bernstein completes his lovely story, then says, "See what I mean?" followed by Thompson's reply before the scene moves on. As shot, Bernstein's story ends with, "I'll bet a month hasn't gone by since that I haven't thought of that girl," with Bernstein then returning to reality and abruptly changing the subject to, "Who else have you been to see?" Not only was the final shot a quicker way to handle the end of the scene, it was more natural as well.

In addition to his cuts for the long takes, Welles edited individual lines from many scenes. Comparing the Correction Script with the actual film shows that Welles deleted either the first line or the last line of many passages before shooting, or in some cases edited them out later, all of which were padding and unnecessary.

For instance, after the Madison Square Garden speech, when Kane asks Emily why she sends their son home while she orders a taxi for their confrontation with "Boss" Jim Gettys, the final script read, "What's this all about, Emily? I've had a very tiring day and . . ." That line became simply, "What's this all about, Emily?" Earlier, in a scene of the newly married Kane and Emily, she says, "Charles, if I didn't trust you—what do you do on a newspaper in the middle of the night?" In the film, the line became simply, "What do you do on a newspaper in the middle of the night?" These one-line edits are small things, certainly, but when multiplied by dozens of cuts, they streamlined many scenes in *Citizen Kane*.

Larger cuts helped as well: near the end of the film, Raymond the butler dictates a long advisory to all Kane papers about the breakup of Kane and Susan's marriage—a scene that is unnecessary because viewers had seen Susan walk out moments before.

In postproduction months later, another overlong scene was trimmed to almost nothing: when Thompson reads about Thatcher's experiences with the young Kane, the sequence was originally intended to begin with a chunk of text on-screen from the memoirs. Thatcher's description of his first meeting with Kane, which appeared largely unchanged in every draft of the script, including the last one, was supposed to be sixty-nine words shown handwritten on the screen—a dreary reading assignment for the audience that would have slowed the film's pace to a crawl. (The text began, "When these lines appear in print, fifty years after my death, I am confident that the whole world will agree with my opinion of Charles Foster Kane," and on and on.) In the final film, bits of the full text can be seen briefly as the camera zooms in on the words *Charles Foster Kane* at the top of the page; but the highlighted text was reduced to a single phrase that reads, "I first encountered Mr. Kane in 1871 . . ."

Other cuts and additions would be necessary as filming dates approached. The Correction Script still included Kane trying to convince Leland to go to Cuba, the *Inquirer* party at Georgie's Place, some of the wordier passages in the argument between Kane and Leland, and a few others. Other scenes would require an injection of energy and realism, such as Susan's recollection of her singing lesson with Signor Matiste. But these were only minor leftovers in the exceptionally long process of editing the script. Welles would cut these passages, trim a few more lines, and change the order of some conversations, and then—finally—the script would be ready to at least start shooting.

Given some of the changes and fine-tuning yet to come, it is possible that the Correction Script was created not only to include a new round of edits, but with its wide typed lines of dialogue that were easier to read than in a conventional script, it may also have served as a more manageable document for Welles to use as he wrote, rewrote, discussed scenes with cast and crew, and rewrote again to create the shooting versions of each scene. There would be much of that type of work during the entire production schedule for the film.

And although it was enough to get started, it was not everything Welles needed. Only weeks before filming began, what may have been the most compelling question about the Correction Script was the material that was not included at all. Welles would soon recognize that from the first draft to the last, the script lacked scenes needed to address major issues that neither he nor Mankiewicz had ever attempted to resolve. Welles would not deal with these questions until much later in production. His solutions would eventually require creating key scenes entirely from scratch—including script, set designs, construction, costumes, and casting—literally at the last minute before they were filmed.

Of all the changes in the *Citizen Kane* script made by Welles, the most important were not his work for brevity or improved plot pacing, but rather his edits of every scene that affected Kane's decisions at critical points in his life. Mankiewicz originally created incidents about Kane and then wrote drawn-out dialogue so the publisher could explain and justify his own behavior. Welles, to explore the essence of Kane as he saw the man, revised those scenes and Kane's behavior so they described *his actions and their consequences*.

The key to portraying Kane, Welles believed, was found not in the reasons *why* Kane did what he did, but in showing *how* his decisions affected himself and others.

Welles saw Kane as a colossal failure—what he called a "damned man"—the first of many central characters in Welles' films who were failed or doomed figures and usually the victims of their own actions. And from the time he started to revise the draft script of *American,* Welles recognized that Mankiewicz was uninterested in, or incapable of, seeing Kane this way.

"In his hatred of Hearst, or whoever Kane was, Mank did not have a clear enough image of who the *man* was," Welles recalled. "Mank saw him simply as an egomaniac monster with all these people around him. So I don't think a portrait of a man was ever present in any of Mank's scripts.

"My *Citizen Kane* would have been much more concerned with the interior corruption of Kane," said Welles. "The script is most like me when the central figure on the screen is Kane. And it is most like Mankiewicz when he's being talked about.

"I don't say that Mank didn't see Kane with clarity—he saw everything with clarity," Welles said. "No matter how odd or how right or how marvelous his point of view was, it was always diamond white. Nothing muzzy. But the truths of the character, Kane, were not what interested him."

Exploring the "truths" about Kane's character may not have interested Mankiewicz, but they were precisely the issues that most intrigued Welles as he created his vision for the film. From Thompson's interviews with the key figures in Kane's life, viewers would learn that Kane was searching for love, acceptance, and friendship. But the audience, like the characters around Kane, is never allowed to understand the reasons that motivated the publisher at the critical junctures in his life: why he alienated his first wife, why he forced his second wife into a career so soul crushing that she is driven to a suicide attempt, why he fired his closest friend, or why he isolated himself in the private world of Xanadu.

In fact, viewers are never completely clear about anything regarding Kane, a point Welles continued to emphasize all the way up to filming the closing scenes. In the final script, at the end of the film, Thompson explains at length about the conflicts in Kane's life, as well as the cruel things he did—a scene that changed little from the first draft of *American,* when Thompson talks about Kane's honesty and his crookedness, his love as a husband who becomes twice divorced, his gift for friendship, and his rejection of his oldest friend "like you'd throw away a cigarette."

Welles removed all of this. In the final film, we hear only the conundrum that was Kane's life: "Mr. Kane was a man who got everything he wanted, and then lost it," Thompson tells his colleagues. "Maybe Rosebud was something he couldn't get or something he lost. Anyway, it wouldn't have explained anything. I don't think any word can explain a man's life. No. I guess Rosebud is just a piece in a jigsaw puzzle—a missing piece."

The explanations of Kane's actions, like the meaning of Rosebud to the reporter Thompson, are the "missing piece" in the story of his life. As Welles saw it, the audience is no more entitled to understand Kane's motivations than are the characters in the film. However, while viewers may not understand Kane's motives, the *results* of his actions and the anguish they cause—the truths that so fascinated Welles—are painfully vivid.

In fact, Welles inverted the entire meaning of a scene to suggest that Kane's personality was a mystery even to himself: in the final script, for Kane's last appearance of the film, he destroys Susan's bedroom, finds the Rosebud snow globe, and walks out of the room and down a corridor. As written in the script, Kane enters a hall of mirrors and stops to look at himself reflected into infinity, contemplating his life as the scene fades out. But in the final film, Welles took the opposite approach: Kane walks through the hall of mirrors, but he never notices his own reflections; only the viewers, as Mankiewicz puts it, "see a thousand Kanes."

Perhaps the most powerful illustration of how Welles developed his lead character appears in the scene that provides a rare moment of self-reflection—although brief—by Kane: Jed Leland's angry outburst after Kane's election defeat. In the original script as written by Mankiewicz, Leland criticizes Kane for his selfish motivations in two separate scenes: the first in the midst of the oil scandal when Kane's relationship with Emily is failing; and later, when the president is wounded. Kane then responds with line after line of dialogue that justifies his actions as a man and as a public figure. As late as the final script, he still talks at length about "stupidity in government" and "crookedness" and "the right of the American people to their own country."

For shooting, however, Welles trimmed Leland's comments to their core by focusing entirely on the futility of Kane's self-centered behavior. After Kane loses the election because of his relationship with Susan, a drunk Leland, in a few brief lines, sums up Kane's motivations.

"You talk about the people as though you own them, as though they belong to you," Leland tells Kane in the newsroom of the *Inquirer*. "As long as I can remember, you've talked about giving the people their rights as if you could make them a present of liberty . . . ."

Later, Leland says, "You don't care about anything except you. You just want to persuade people that you love 'em so much that they ought to love you back. Only you want love on your own terms—something to be played your way, according to your rules."

Kane does not respond directly to Leland's outburst. Instead of the pages of response that Mankiewicz originally wrote, or as trimmed for the final script, Welles lets Kane listen to Leland's tirade without rebuttal and, their friendship over, agrees to Leland's request for a transfer to Chicago.

Then Kane—who has lost his political career, his marriage, and his closest friend—picks up a bottle of whiskey and pours a drink for himself. "A toast, Jedediah, to love on my terms," he tells Leland. "Those are the only terms anybody ever knows—his own." Welles ignored the reasons that explained Kane's disasters; he let their impact tell the story of the publisher's life.

At the time *Citizen Kane* debuted, it was this material left unsaid—the pared-down dialogue and the lack of solidly expressed motivations—that perplexed some viewers and sparked what little criticism was heard about the film.

Mankiewicz and Houseman had been alert to the issue early in preproduction; at their meeting with Welles on May 23, they voiced their concerns that Welles was dealing with a major challenge as he developed Kane's character.

"One of the great troubles with the script," Kathryn Trosper recorded in her meeting notes, "is that we are showing a man who has failed in his ambitions on his own terms, showing a technical matter rather than a tangible thing such as being dispossessed."

A year later, Bosley Crowther, film critic of *The New York Times,* after praising the picture in his initial review, modified his enthusiasm in a second article two days later, in which he cited the "basically vague" characterization of Kane as the primary reason for his somewhat reduced esteem for the motion picture. Welles, said Crowther, created "some disconcerting lapses and strange ambiguities in the creation of the principal character."

He went on to write of Charles Foster Kane, "It fails to provide a clear picture of the character and motives behind the man about whom the whole thing revolves. Just exactly what it is that eats upon him, why it is there, and for that matter, whether Kane is really a villain, a social parasite, is never clearly revealed. At the end, Kubla Kane is still an enigma—a very confusing one."

Film columnist Richard Griffith echoed Crowther's sentiments in his own otherwise positive review, in which Griffith conceded that "we never come close to Kane himself. He remains an imposing, almost a monstrous figure—oblique, morbid, half-understood, and always seen at a great distance, as through the wrong end of a telescope."

For some critics accustomed to straightforward film characters and performances during the golden era of the Hollywood studios, Welles' unconventional approach to exploring Kane's personality no doubt seemed puzzling—and somewhat disturbing. They did not see that Welles was showing how the reasons that explain a man's behavior are often not nearly as important as the consequences of his actions. And a film need not answer every question or solve all problems. As Welles demonstrated with his cinematic journey through Kane's life, just bringing the conflict to the surface has a powerful impact. In his first motion picture, Welles was already using film to examine thought-provoking issues that illuminate the human condition.

RKO PRODUCTION #281

Q: During the shooting of Citizen Kane, *did you have the sensation
of making such an important film?
A: I never doubted it for a single instant.*
—INTERVIEW WITH ORSON WELLES, 1966

While Mankiewicz and Houseman worked on their rewrites in Victorville, Welles orchestrated the approvals for his production. He met with George Schaefer and RKO attorney Harry Edington and performed the entire story of *Citizen Kane,* playing each part while he described the action and the staging. Schaefer approved the idea in concept (at the time, apparently, no one in RKO senior management expressed concern that the central character might be confused with a certain real-life prominent publisher). Schaefer agreed to move *Citizen Kane* into preproduction, with full production pending final resolution of the budget issues.

For weeks, the picture was referred to simply as "Orson Welles #3"; it was also called "Orson Welles #1" in the memo announcing the final name of the film. But when the script was approved, the project gained an additional designation: in the accounting ledgers, production reports, and hundreds of memos that would crisscross the studio during 1940, *Citizen Kane* was identified as "RKO Production #281."

With the failures of *Heart of Darkness* and *The Smiler with a Knife* behind him, throughout the spring and early summer of 1940, Welles began preparing *Citizen Kane* for filming. As work on the script moved forward, preproduction planning for Production #281 proceeded rapidly. Within three months of completion of the Mankiewicz-Houseman drafts, *Citizen Kane* needed to be ready for the cameras. Welles continued to revise the script, but he was also the film's producer. In April 1940, he began to pull together the complex combination of artistry and technology needed to move a film script into production.

Welles was quickly learning the methods of backstage Hollywood. The daily film screenings, the department visits, and his preproduction of *Heart of Darkness*—which had included set design, model building, makeup tests, and photographic planning—fortified Welles with valuable experience collaborating with Hollywood craftsmen that would be applied to *Citizen Kane*.

"Orson had no doubt that he knew it all," said William Alland, who served as assistant producer in addition to appearing as Thompson the reporter. "Yet he was smart enough to appreciate the talent he spotted in others."

RKO, like the other Hollywood studios, employed hundreds of craftsmen and technicians. The corps of specialized experts in all aspects of film production was a primary strength of the Hollywood studio system during its most productive years; this was a period when a studio operating at its peak could routinely release a new feature film every ten days. Welles recognized that the industry's cauldron of talent would be a tremendous benefit to him. He told reporter Alva Johnston, "It's the greatest railroad train a boy ever had!"

Like most forceful creative personalities, Welles certainly had his share of professional liabilities when working with others. As his arguments with Mankiewicz over the script credit showed, not the least of Welles' weak spots was his quenchless thirst for sole recognition and multiple screen billings. But day to day on the set, such flaws were overshadowed by his gift for collaboration. Welles clashed with Mankiewicz because he was a writer himself. However, when preparing unfamiliar aspects of preproduction, Welles eagerly sought collaboration and gladly provided sole credit to those responsible. Welles may not have had experience in a Hollywood studio—a boy's biggest railroad train—but although he did not yet know how to run the locomotive, he certainly knew how to find the right people to lay the track.

The studio backed its new young director with the finest talent available. If Welles could not identify the right person on the RKO lot, he was welcome to look to other studios for staff who could be loaned (for a price) to the Mercury team. It remains an ironic twist of film history that *Citizen Kane*—in spite of its tumultuous evolution, its frantic schedule, the lengthy script revisions, and its unique creative approach—is one of the most thoroughly planned motion pictures of Hollywood's golden era, created with studio methods normally used in much more routine productions. *Citizen Kane* became a collaboration unlike anything ever witnessed in Hollywood before or since: an intensely creative first-time director, one bursting with ideas and without studio interference, working in partnership with the world's finest filmmaking methods and technical staff.

Later in his career, while producing and directing in Europe, Welles longed to direct in the United States again, primarily because he missed that partnership.

"I am dying to work there because of the technicians, who are marvelous," Welles lamented about Hollywood. "They truly represent a director's dream."

Among the first steps in preproduction was casting. Welles was certainly no beginner at choosing performers. With a keen ability to identify the ideal actor for each role, he filled many of the principal parts in *Citizen Kane* by drawing on the talented players in his Mercury Theatre stock company and his other projects in New York.

Several of the principal performers who joined the cast of *Citizen Kane* had already been signed to appear in either *Heart of Darkness, The Smiler with a Knife,* or both. To portray Jed Leland, Kane's best friend, Welles chose Joseph Cotten, a longtime colleague from the Mercury Theatre. In addition to his "starring" role in the footage for *Too Much Johnson,* Cotten had appeared in *Horse Eats Hat, Julius Caesar,* and other Mercury productions, before leaving to appear in the stage version of *The Philadelphia Story,* costarring with Katharine Hepburn. When the company closed for the summer so Hepburn could make the film version with Cary Grant and James Stewart, Cotten traveled to Los Angeles, too.

"I happened to be in *Citizen Kane* purely by chance," Cotten said. "That summer I came out to Hollywood to do a radio show, and that's when I ran into Orson. I was with him a great deal during the preparation of *Citizen Kane,* and it was quite a unique introduction to films for me."

Cotten and Welles would appear in several motion pictures together in addition to *Citizen Kane: Journey into Fear, The Third Man,* and *Touch of Evil;* and Cotten was directed by Welles in *The Magnificent Ambersons.* The two actors remained close friends until Welles' death in 1985.

As Bernstein, Kane's business manager (he has no first name in the film), Welles cast Everett Sloane, whose career had flourished in Mercury radio projects as well as other programs, including a long-running family radio program called *The Goldbergs.* Although not quite thirty-one at the time *Citizen Kane* production began, Sloane had already established himself in a range of character roles on radio—a talent that translated well to film. Sloane, too, would appear with Welles in other projects after *Citizen Kane,* including *Journey into Fear, The Lady from Shanghai,* and *Prince of Foxes.*

Welles selected Ruth Warrick to play Emily Monroe Norton, Kane's first wife. A former model and radio singer, Warrick met Welles when they performed at CBS in New York. In Warrick, Welles found a natural ladylike elegance that was ideally suited to a character who was the niece of the president of the United States.

"Orson told me, 'Emily must be a lady, and there are no ladies in Hollywood,'" Warrick recalled. "'I don't mean someone who can play a lady,' he said; 'I want someone who *is* a lady.'"

Warrick, who turned 24 on June 29, had the ideal bearing to play a dignified lady—and, as viewers would see in the montage of shots that shows the disintegration of her marriage to Kane, one who turns out to be an anti-Semitic snob. But Welles experimented a little and in late June tested her for the role of his second wife, the fragile Susan Alexander, as well. He quickly realized that his first instinct about Warrick's role was correct.

For Susan, Welles instead sought an actress who could be "frightened, whining, pathetic." He tested many actresses, including several strippers from Los Angeles nightclubs, in his search for a "kind of cheapness" that he wanted to instill in Susan. Welles eventually chose from the Hollywood talent pool, casting Dorothy Comingore as Susan. Comingore had only limited experience in films; under her stage name, Linda Winters, she had appeared primarily in short subjects or uncredited roles.

Ray Collins was signed for a brief but pivotal appearance as "Boss" Jim W. Gettys, the corrupt New York political boss who destroys Kane's political ambitions. Collins, who had first appeared in theatrical productions at age thirteen, performed on the stage for some thirty-nine years before his screen debut in *Citizen Kane.* Collins was also a busy radio actor in New York, working frequently with Welles, before coming to Hollywood.

Agnes Moorehead was also selected for a small but significant part, portraying the role of Kane's mother. Moorehead's downplayed performance masked the formidable acting presence she would later show in dozens of character roles (for a snippet of a more typical high-powered Moorehead screen attitude, view the trailer for *Citizen Kane*). Moorehead, like Collins, had been a child performer in theater, beginning her stage career at three and ballet at eleven. Moorehead, thirty-nine at the time of *Citizen Kane*'s production, sang on radio, taught speech and drama, appeared in summer stock, and worked on Mercury broadcasts before her film career began.

George Coulouris, who starred as Mark Antony in Mercury's production of *Julius Caesar,* was cast as Walter P. Thatcher, Kane's humorless banker and guardian. The irascible Coulouris collaborated closely with Welles in several theatrical productions, even though he was frequently irritated by the director's impulsive behavior.

"George was known as 'God's angry man,'" remembered colleague Norman Lloyd. "He was angry about everything, most particularly about Orson, who nevertheless was very fond of Coulouris, and had enormous respect for him as an actor."

Paul Stewart, a Mercuryite who had served as an associate producer for radio programs, was cast as the mysterious and cynical Raymond, the butler "who knows where all the bodies are buried." Stewart had served as rehearsal director of the Mercury radio shows and had also appeared in its productions, including *The War of the Worlds.* He was in New York when Welles sought him out.

"He phoned me in New York and asked me to play a part in a movie he was making," Stewart said. "I said, 'Sure.' Didn't even ask what the part was. I was so pleased to be friends with him again. I'd missed him in my life because every day with him was a day of last-minute preparation and plunging ahead and creating."

Stewart was indeed an ideal choice to play the oily caretaker of Xanadu, and Welles also returned a favor by casting him in his first motion picture. Several years before, Stewart, at the time already an established performer in radio, had helped Welles find some of his first broadcast jobs, which led to the young actor becoming one of radio's biggest stars. (Welles needed all the help he could get when he began his radio career. Joseph Cotten recalled that during Welles' introduction to Knowles Entriken, an important director at CBS Radio, Welles casually emptied his pipe into Entriken's wastebasket and set the trash on fire.)

For Jerry Thompson, the reporter who seeks the meaning of Rosebud—and whose face seems partially obscured from view for most of the film—Welles turned to William Alland, who started his work in Mercury Theatre backstage, doing everything from sweeping floors to managing stage action during performances. Alland maneuvered his way into acting in the Mercury Theatre by literally forcing his talents on Welles, trapping him in his dressing room and reciting the funeral oration from *Julius Caesar.* After the "performance," Welles gave him acting assignments in Mercury productions.

Alland's role as both performer and administrator for Mercury productions continued in Hollywood. Besides acting as Thompson, Alland served as a production aide during the writing and planning of the film, as well as an assistant to Welles when the director appeared in a scene. Alland's soft interview vocal style as the reporter Thompson disguised the fact that he could also speak in thundering tones, which he used with great effectiveness as the narrator of the *News on the March* sequence, imitating the style of real-life *March of Time* commentator Westbrook Van Voorhis.

Alland is sometimes remembered as the character in *Citizen Kane* whose face never appears on-screen, because in most of his scenes he is shown in partial shadow or seen from behind his left shoulder. The idea that Alland's face is not shown at all is the result of *Citizen Kane* for years being screened with the low-quality 16-millimeter prints of the film that began appearing in art houses in the late 1950s and in still lower-quality video transmissions that were broadcast in the 1950s and 1960s (because of this, several film historians stated flatly that Alland's face is *never* seen and analyzed his role in the film from that perspective). However, in crisp prints of the film, and in high-definition video, Alland's face appears quite clearly during the scenes in the projection room when he argues with Rawlston about the importance of Rosebud, as well as in the Thatcher Library when he slams shut the book of the banker's memoirs.

Nevertheless, for almost all of his appearances, Alland is shown from behind and to his left, and he often joked about being the "unknown man" in the *Citizen Kane* cast. When Alland was introduced to the audience after the Los Angeles premiere, he said, "Perhaps you'll recognize me better like this," and turned his back to the crowd.

Another Mercury colleague, character actor Edgar Barrier, holds the dubious distinction of losing two roles in *Citizen Kane* at the last moment. Barrier, a friend of Welles' who had performed in Mercury radio productions as well as in *Too Much Johnson,* appeared in photographic tests as *News on the March* chief Rawlston, the head of the newsreel company who sends Thompson on his futile mission to discover the meaning of Rosebud, before Philip Van Zandt was cast instead. Barrier was also scheduled to play Raymond the butler and was listed in the cast for three months before Paul Stewart was brought in from New York to take on the role. Welles, however, remembered Barrier, and two years later he was hired to appear as Kuvetli in the Mercury production of *Journey into Fear.*

Filling the other featured roles was a versatile team of actors—some of them Hollywood regulars, but most known to Welles because of their reputations in broadcasting or theatrical productions. Erskine Sanford, another colleague from

Mercury Theatre on the Air, appeared as Herbert Carter, the sputtering editor in charge of the *Inquirer* when Kane takes over the newspaper. Fortunio Bonanova, cast as Signor Matiste (called "Matisti" in the script, but not in the screen credits), Susan Alexander's singing teacher, had produced and directed films in Europe and sung with the Paris Opera before coming to America to appear on Broadway in 1930. Welles remembered as a teenager seeing Bonanova onstage in *The Green Hat*.

"I never forgot him," Welles said. "He looked to me like a leading man in a dirty movie."

Another old friend of Welles' from his Broadway days was Georgia Backus, who appeared in the memorable role as Bertha Anderson (her name is never mentioned in the film), the iron-spined keeper of the Thatcher Library ("Mr. Thompson, you will be required to leave this room at four thirty promptly").

Other parts were filled by seasoned performers: Gus Schilling, once a comedian in vaudeville who was remembered from a tryout for one of Welles' Shakespeare productions, took a small part as John, the kindly waiter at Susan's nightclub; Harry Shannon, who had appeared in character roles on film for more than a decade, played Kane's father, a no-good who gave up his son when a lifelong annuity was dangled in front of him; and Philip Van Zandt, who had taken over the role of Rawlston from Edgar Barrier, was another performer from the Broadway and Hollywood ranks.

Chosen from Hollywood youngsters for juvenile roles were Buddy Swan, who played the sled-wielding Kane as a boy, and Sonny Bupp, who appeared as Kane's son. (The two parts were not played by the same performer, as some assumed on first viewing, although the two boys did resemble each other.) Although Swan had been in only one film prior to *Citizen Kane,* Bupp, at twelve, had fourteen pictures to his credit (in *Three Faces West,* Bupp played a character named Welles). RKO publicity reported that Swan got the job playing Kane at age eight because he posed for a gag publicity photo wearing a false beard similar to the real whiskers Welles sported on his Hollywood arrival.

To fill a variety of bit parts and extra roles ranging from stuffy opera patrons to busy newsroom reporters, RKO provided Welles with his pick from the masses in central casting and from extras who specialized in specific recognizable roles. (In a memorable note to the casting office on July 18, associate producer Richard Baer wrote, "We will need Hitler, Goering, and Chamberlain on this day.") Production #281 required hundreds of extras—but not all at once—with daily rates scaled from unrecognizable opera fans ($11) to Theodore Roosevelt ($25) to a man in a gorilla suit ($50, but his scenes did not make the final cut).

Several principal actors played dual roles in *Citizen Kane:* when Welles filmed the projection room sequence where the hunt for Rosebud begins, in addition to William Alland as Thompson and Philip Van Zandt playing Rawlston, some of the nameless chain-smoking reporters are Mercury regulars who happened to be available to shoot a sequence officially labeled as a "test" that was destined to remain in the film: Joseph Cotten, Erskine Sanford, Gus Schilling, Richard Baer, and assistant producer Richard Wilson; Wilson remembered being in the projection room but is not recognizable (the bit players in the shadows of the projection room are Perc Launders, Eddie Dew, Michael Audley, and Vera Winters off camera). Welles said he was also in the projection room shots, but he cannot be seen and his unmistakable voice is not heard among the wisecracking comments from the reporters.

When Rawlston asks his reporters what they think of the Kane newsreel, Sanford can be heard saying, "Well, seventy years in a man's life . . ." Cotten and Sanford are sitting in the background while Rawlston asks, "What were the last words he said on earth?" Later, Cotten laughs and says simply, "Rosebud." Baer is the young reporter in the background between Rawlston and Thompson when Rawlston says, "What were Kane's last words?" Schilling—less than two minutes before his billed role in the film as John the waiter—is sitting at a table in the back of the projection room.

Baer, in addition to appearing in the projection room scene, also played "Hillman," one of the officials accompanying Kane outside of Madison Square Garden. In that scene, Baer makes one of the few notable continuity errors in the film (see page 162).

Wilson played a reporter examining Kane's treasures at Xanadu; he's the one in the background who says, "What's that?" to a colleague, who replies, "Another Venus. Twenty-five thousand bucks—that's a lot of money to pay for a dame without a head." Near the end of the scene, Wilson provides a lead-in to the closing scene by saying, "I wonder—you put all this stuff together, palaces and paintings, toys and everything—what would it spell?"

In addition to Baer and Wilson, another staff member who earned performer's wages above her regular salary was Welles' assistant Kathryn Trosper, who, in her only film credit on camera or off, appeared as a reporter at Xanadu. Trosper has her one moment in the Hollywood sun when she says, "Yeah—all in crates," and then a few seconds later, "What's Rosebud?"

Along with the other reporters at Xanadu was Arthur O'Connell, who became a popular character actor in more than forty-five films, earning Academy Award nominations for his supporting roles in *Picnic* and *Anatomy of a Murder*. In *Citizen Kane*, O'Connell is the skinny reporter at Xanadu in shirtsleeves, sitting in an ornate wooden chair with his leg over one of the arms as he reviews a list. It is O'Connell who says, "He never threw anything away." Later, responding to the reporter (played by Louise Currie) who found one of Susan's puzzles, he says, "We got a lot of those."

Another extra in the Xanadu scenes who received a precious speaking part was Alan Ladd, soon to become one of the biggest stars in Hollywood for his hard-boiled tough-guy roles. In 1940, however, Ladd was a struggling young bit player who bounced around the studios and for a time worked as a stagehand at Warner Bros. For his appearances in the shadows at Xanadu, Ladd was cast not for his looks, but for his soft baritone voice. In the closing moments of *Citizen Kane*, Ladd is the reporter smoking a pipe and wearing a hat with the brim turned up; he's the one who says, "We're supposed to get everything—the junk as well as the art," and a few moments later, "Or Rosebud? How about it, Jerry?" And last: "What did you find out about him, Jerry?"

Citizen Kane would not provide a break for Ladd—his rise to Hollywood stardom would begin in 1942 with his appearance as a killer in *This Gun for Hire*. In *Citizen Kane*, Ladd's face, like those of the other reporters at Xanadu, was mostly lost in the darkness.

Citizen Kane was not only a Mercury family reunion; Welles further personalized the production by filling the script with the names of friends and associates. Susan Alexander's last name was chosen as a tribute to Rita Alexander, secretary to Mankiewicz and Houseman in Victorville. Bernstein, Everett Sloane's character, honored Dr. Maurice Bernstein, Welles' endlessly devoted former guardian and father figure (Bernstein and Welles called each other "Pookles" and "Dadda," even after Welles was an adult).

Jed Leland, the drama critic played by Joseph Cotten, combined the names of theatrical producer Jed Harris and Leland Hayward, agent to many young actors, including Cotten. (Leland's gentle, thoughtful personality was based on Ashton Stevens, a theater critic and one of Welles' childhood friends.)

The name "Boss" Jim Gettys, Ray Collins's character, was selected only days before filming began. The Gettys role had been known as "Edward Rogers" in every version of the script until it was changed shortly before filming started—possibly because the character shared a last name with a real-life New York City political boss of the day: Hugo Rogers, long involved in New York affairs, who in 1948 would become leader of Tammany Hall, the powerful Manhattan political machine. The character's name was changed to Gettys in loving recognition of both Roger Gettys Hill, the son of Welles' friends Hortense and Skipper Hill, and Hortense's father.

At least one prop in *Citizen Kane* featured an insider reference: when Bernstein arrives at the *Inquirer* for the first time and crashes through the doorway with Kane's belongings, one of the crates is marked "Lot 891," no doubt a tribute to "Project 891," the name of the first Federal Theatre Project Welles cofounded with Houseman in New York.

And what of the name for the film's title character? The names Charles Foster Rogers and Charles Foster Craig were abandoned early in the writing sessions, and the last name was changed to Kane—a tribute to Whitford Kane, director of the Goodman Theatre in Chicago and a friend of Welles' who had appeared in the Mercury Theatre production of *The Shoemaker's Holiday*. The director was originally cast to play Kane's father in the film, but he instead chose to appear in Katharine Cornell's stage production of *The Doctor's Dilemma*. While the actor missed his opportunity for screen immortality, his name remained; Charles Foster Craig became Charles Foster Kane.

Immensely talented though Welles' performers were, they also shared a common characteristic that was critical in Welles' plans: most were new to motion pictures. Welles had sought to hire actors without screen experience at all or who were virtual unknowns.

Welles was fond of saying that "not one" of the actors in a major role in *Citizen Kane* had appeared in a Hollywood film. While that description was an exaggeration, he was mostly accurate: Cotten, Sloane, Warrick, Collins, Moorehead, Sanford, Stewart, and Alland had never appeared in feature films. Comingore had acted only sporadically in bit parts, shorts, and Three Stooges episodes; her sole role in a film of note was a brief appearance in Frank Capra's *Mr. Smith Goes to Washington,* in which she played a bright-eyed young socialite who pesters Jimmy Stewart to contribute to a charity milk fund.

Compared with the others, George Coulouris was a Hollywood veteran. He had appeared in a film in 1933 and in 1940 managed to squeeze in appearances in *All This, and Heaven Too* and *The Lady in Question* when he came west to appear in *Citizen Kane*. Fortunio Bonanova had performed in a few silent and sound roles in Spain and the United States.

To Welles, his actors' inexperience in Hollywood was an advantage. Their lack of familiarity with film production provided the director with the latitude he needed to encourage performances that most seasoned Hollywood actors would have found unacceptable from an unconventional first-time director. And Welles had filled his cast with personal friends and close professional associates who trusted his ideas—whether in radio, theater, or motion pictures.

"I could never have made *Citizen Kane* with actors who were old hands at cinema," Welles said, "we thought they would show us up and change the dimension of the film.

"They would have said right off, 'What do you think you're doing?' My being a newcomer would have put them on guard and would have made a mess of the film. It was possible because I had my own family, so to speak."

Or, Welles said bluntly of his actors in a later interview, "they didn't have terrible movie habits."

Welles not only wanted to bring out the best in his stars, he was also adamant about publicly acknowledging their talent. The credits of *Citizen Kane*—all of which appear at the conclusion of the film—include clips of each leading performer in an outtake from the picture (the credits were permitted to appear at the end of the film only after waivers were obtained from several Hollywood unions and guilds). Within the first month after *Citizen Kane*'s premiere, Collins, Comingore, Cotten, and Warrick were all signed to studio contracts; others, such as Bonanova, worked frequently in for-hire screen roles.

Finally, and certainly most important, Welles cast himself to play Charles Foster Kane. Welles could have chosen to not appear in *Citizen Kane;* although his contracts called for him to star in his first two RKO films, Welles-the-producer could have opted to cast someone else in the starring role instead (and as a result lose the notoriety as well as his acting salary and profit percentage). However, there was never a doubt that Welles would play Kane. Long before production began, it was clear that the role was developing into one of the choicest parts in film history.

But with this plum role came a tremendous burden: the success or failure of *Citizen Kane* depended entirely on the effectiveness of that single performance. Welles would have to assume the massive task of preparing to portray an intensely complex personality as it evolved across more than fifty years of the character's life—this in addition to the constant demands of producing, directing, and rewriting his first film.

Understandably, some at RKO were concerned that George Schaefer had gone much too far by allowing Welles to star as well as produce and direct. However, for the man who had established himself as the most dynamic actor in theater and radio—now supported by a talented cast and with the backing of a powerful Hollywood studio—the task of portraying Charles Foster Kane while directing his own performance would be another fascinating artistic challenge.

A GREAT DEAL OF DOING

These unconventional set-ups impose insurmountable difficulties in the path of strictly conventional methods of camerawork. To put things with brutal frankness, they simply cannot be done by conventional means. But they were a basic part of Citizen Kane *and they had to be done!*
—GREGG TOLAND, ON THE FILMING OF *CITIZEN KANE*

While casting and script revision continued, Welles formed the principal behind-the-camera team that would manage the production of *Citizen Kane:* himself, cinematographer Gregg Toland, and designer Perry Ferguson.

Beginning in late spring of 1940, Welles, Toland, Ferguson, and some of their assistants met most mornings during the preproduction of *Citizen Kane* to discuss the photography and set design and to refine the visual plan that would bring the film to the screen. This plan would become the foundation of the project, out of which every shot, the production design, and the postproduction of the film would be established.

The trio reviewed the script scene by scene and developed the camera angles and design requirements. Then they moved to their specific projects: while Welles rehearsed the actors and polished the script, Ferguson coordinated the set design, plans, and construction with RKO production staff, and Toland honed the photographic design with his crew, lighting staff, and Ferguson and his team.

The Welles-Toland-Ferguson meetings produced two results. First, each meeting was an intensified classroom in which Welles was learning from two experts the practical day-to-day business of being a filmmaker. Second, the planning sessions refined the visual plan and the basic look of the film, as well as the mind-boggling level of strategizing they needed for all of the shots.

All motion pictures require planning, but typically much less than Welles needed for *Citizen Kane*. In the assembly-line environment of the Hollywood studio system in the 1940s, most projects had weeks, not months, for preparation; the extended preproduction period granted to Welles was a rare luxury. And for Welles, the cinematography and design were not simply tools to make a movie. For *Citizen Kane,* his goal was for every shot, the entire design, and all of the photographic techniques employed in the film to be integral parts of the story itself.

By the time preproduction progressed to its final stages, the RKO staff as supervised by Welles, Toland, and Ferguson had created storyboards—detailed sketches of scenes, nearly all drawn by studio artist Charles Ohmann—that visually presented most sequences of the production, including not only precise camera angles and shot-by-shot illustrations of complex sequences, but in some cases also the ideas to create transitions between scenes. Welles thus knew how every important sequence of the motion picture would look, weeks before shooting of Production #281 began.

How they would arrive at that point was the challenge for Toland and Ferguson.

Months earlier, Welles knew whom he wanted to shoot his film: Gregg Toland, celebrated in Hollywood for such pictures as *Dead End* and *The Grapes of Wrath,* was known as an artist who brought innovation and imagination to the usually predictable business of motion picture photography. Although Toland worked successfully within the confines of the studio system, he was an outspoken dissenter against predictable Hollywood filmmaking. As a result, he was respected and in demand by the most visionary directors in Hollywood, including William Wyler, Howard Hawks, and John Ford.

Toland was young by cinematographer standards—only thirty-six in the spring of 1940—but he had the aura and authority of a much older artist.

"Toland carries himself with a slight stoop which makes him seem smaller and older than he really is, and probably indicates something of the tremendous burden of responsibility that rests on his shoulders," said Walter Blanchard of *American Cinematographer* magazine. "He gives the impression of being physically tired—until you get him started talking about his work. Then he brightens up, flashes a disarmingly youthful smile, and speaks with almost boyish enthusiasm about this idea or that he is working with."

Welles knew about Toland before the director came to Hollywood.

"Toland was the best director of photography who ever existed," Welles said. "There has never been anyone else in his class."

However, in February 1940 Toland appeared out of reach to Welles. Toland had just won the Academy Award for his cinematography for *Wuthering Heights,* and was under contract to independent producer Sam Goldwyn. But Goldwyn, who made only one or two films a year, kept his principal talent occupied (and profit producing) by lending them—leasing them, actually—to other studios; Toland, in between Goldwyn assignments, was available.

Like everyone else in Hollywood, Toland had heard about Welles and his nonconforming ways. He contacted the Mercury office at RKO and met Welles; it was clear from the start that the creative chemistry was right.

Alexander Kahle, the RKO still photographer who shot almost daily on the *Citizen Kane* set, was a constant observer of the Welles-Toland professional relationship. "The two," said Kahle, "saw eye to eye from the first."

So Goldwyn loaned out Toland to RKO for the film for $700 per week, with the requirement that RKO also hire Toland's team, most of whom had been together for more than a decade: camera operator Bert Shipman, assistant cameraman Edward Garvin, grip Ralph Hoge, and gaffer (lighting supervisor) William J. McClellan. Goldwyn also required RKO to rent Toland's camera and other equipment that was already modified to his personal specifications.

During preproduction, Welles emphasized to Toland that perfecting the cinematography was the critical element in realizing his vision for *Citizen Kane.*

"I thought you could do anything with the camera that the eye can do, that the imagination can do," said Welles. "In the film business you're taught all the things the cameraman doesn't want to attempt for fear he will be criticized for having failed. In this case I had a cameraman who didn't care if he was criticized if he failed, and I didn't know there were things you couldn't do. So anything I could think up in my dreams, I attempted to photograph."

Welles served up an endless stream of ideas about the camera angles and shots he wanted, and Toland developed the visual plan to bring the director's ideas to the screen. The vision for *Citizen Kane* may have originated with Welles, but Toland made Welles' ideas possible and practical.

From Toland's perspective as a cinematographer in 1940 Hollywood, *Citizen Kane* was well timed, not only artistically but technically as well. Recent developments in both lighting and film—in particular the release of Kodak's Super XX black-and-white film in 1938—opened vast new horizons for cinematographers, allowing them to shoot with less light and to achieve greater contrast and depth to the image without an additional grainy look to the film. And when production was completed, copies of the motion picture could be printed on recently developed fine-grain film stock.

Toland preferred a crisp focus to the look of his films, at the time a rarity in Hollywood. As Welles scholar Robert Carringer pointed out, the 1930s cinematographic style, which emphasized soft visual tones and diffused light, had been forced upon the studios in part by the arrival of sound films ten years before: the powerful but noisy arc lights of the silent era were replaced with quieter but less powerful incandescent lamps to accommodate sound recording. However, in the late 1930s the growing use of Technicolor photography, with its voracious appetite for light, had inspired the development of a large selection of new lighting techniques that could also be applied to the black-and-white photography for *Citizen Kane*.

In sum, thanks to better film and new lights, Toland could deepen his focus, create distinctive lighting for his sets, and still deliver a razor-sharp final product—all advancements that were ideal for Welles' visual plan for *Citizen Kane*.

Welles and Toland did not deliberately intend for *Citizen Kane* to be a showcase of filmmaking techniques simply for technique's sake. Instead, they developed their goals for the production, and then—unlike most Hollywood production teams—sought answers to storytelling problems through inventive photographic methods.

"From the moment the production began to take shape in script form," Toland recalled, "everything was planned with reference to what the camera could bring to the eyes of the audience."

Toland recognized Welles' visual understanding of moviemaking even though the director's creative energies had been devoted to theater and radio.

"Welles had a full realization of the great power of the camera in conveying dramatic ideas without words," Toland said.

"Welles was insistent that the story be told most effectively, letting the Hollywood conventions of movie-making go hang if need be," said Toland. "With such whole-hearted backing, I was able to test and prove several ideas generally accepted as being radical in Hollywood circles."

Welles and Toland created a two-part goal for their filming plan.

"Its keynote," said Toland, "is realism. As we worked together over the script and the final preproduction planning, both Welles and I felt this, and felt it was possible that the picture should be brought to the screen in such a way that the audience would feel it was looking at reality, rather than merely looking at a movie."

As important as realism was the second mission for the cinematography: to create a visual flow for the entire film—the seamless blending from one scene to the next.

"Welles instinctively grasped a point which many other far more experienced directors and producers never comprehend: that the scenes and sequences should flow together so smoothly that the audience should not be conscious of the mechanics of picture-making," Toland said.

For *Citizen Kane,* direct cuts would be avoided as often as possible, Toland said. "Instead, we tried to plan action so that the camera could pan or dolly from one angle to another whenever this type of treatment was desirable."

In preproduction, Toland and Welles plotted this seamless quality for almost every scene. "Seamless" did not mean just the simple photographic technique of dissolving from scene to scene. For *Citizen Kane,* Toland created elegant photographic solutions that resulted in seamlessness.

For example, one of the most famous of the seamless transitions in *Citizen Kane* appears early in the film, when Kane, Leland, and Bernstein stand in front of the office of their competitor, the *Chronicle,* and discuss why that publication is "a good idea for a newspaper." Bernstein points to a group photo of the newspaper's reporters, "The Greatest Newspaper Staff in the World." As the camera moves closer to the photograph, the still photo transitions into the next scene, when the photograph becomes a live shot of the same group of men, now on the staff of the *Inquirer,* posing for a new photograph six years later, as a party begins in the newsroom of the paper celebrating the *Inquirer* circulation as the highest in New York.

This seamless look was not always achieved through photographic techniques in the camera alone. In *Citizen Kane,* there is the occasional standard dissolve from one scene to the next. However, in addition to Toland's many planned transitions (such as the photograph of the *Inquirer* staff), seamlessness is achieved through special effects, bridges of sound or music, or onstage movements by the actors that blend from shot to shot.

"These unconventional set-ups impose insurmountable difficulties in the path of strictly conventional methods of camerawork," said Toland. "To put things with brutal frankness, they simply cannot be done by conventional means. But they were a basic part of *Citizen Kane* and they *had* to be done!"

A filmmaking technique critical to achieving Welles' visual goals was Toland's use of deep-focus photography for many shots in *Citizen Kane*. At the height of the Hollywood studio system, many scenes were shot with tight focus, the action arranged to show clearly only a few feet of depth to a set. A typical Hollywood production was limited by film speeds, small studio sets, and (especially) conservative views about lighting and camera placement—all barriers to advances in cinematography that could otherwise complement the storytelling. And those shots that had somewhat deeper focus usually did not make use of the background to enhance the value of the shot.

For Toland, this type of cinematography was unacceptable; he believed his on-screen images should be filmed the same way the eye saw things, as "the perfect universal focus lens."

"Depth of field nearly always is sacrificed in Hollywood productions," Toland said. "The normal human eye sees everything . . . within reasonable distance clearly and sharply. There is no special or single center of visual sharpness in real life. But the Hollywood cameras focus on a center of interest, and allow the other components of a scene to 'fuzz out' in those regions before and beyond the focal point."

Welles put it more simply: "In life you see everything in focus at the same time, so why not in the movies?"

One of Toland's favorite methods to shatter conformity was to create a visual plan that used deep-focus shots. By expanding the distance on the set that was in focus, Toland could increase the visual interest in each scene. And by using deep focus, he also enlarged the physical space on the set that the director could use to plot the action and the movement of actors and that the art director could employ for designs and details—a prospect that delighted Welles and Ferguson.

"It took a great deal of doing," Toland said, "but we proved that it can be done."

Like all photographers, Toland was at the mercy of physics: to get deep depth of field, a lens must be set for a minimum opening, which allows less light into the camera: in short, more depth of field equals less light. Toland's goal for deep focus in *Citizen Kane* was in part made possible by his plan to use lenses treated with new coatings developed to better distribute light through the glass. These coated lenses provided Toland with the light and film speed he needed to use a minimum opening, which increased the depth of the focus in his shots.

To achieve the "human eye" quality that Toland and Welles sought, they planned to use a 24-millimeter wide-angle lens for many scenes in *Citizen Kane* (today, a typical pocket digital camera would have a wide-angle setting of about 28 millimeters). To allow ultraprecise amounts of light into the camera, Toland also used customized lenses that were not adjustable, each fitted with a disk drilled with a hole matching the precise opening he wanted to use.

The combination of wide-angle lenses and small lens openings produced an unusually wide and deep view of the sets. Toland was able to increase the depth of focus from the Hollywood average of less than five feet to twenty-five feet or more.

In fact, for many setups, Toland's planning produced almost unlimited focus. He deduced that by setting the focus at sixty-four inches in front of the camera, everything in his shot eighteen inches from the lens to infinity would be sharp—for *Citizen Kane,* a range that became ideal for many shots in which some actors appear right next to the camera while others are thirty feet away.

None of the principal cinematographers in Hollywood—even those of Toland's stature—were granted the creative freedom to tinker with more than the occasional filmmaking experiment. Toland already received more opportunities than his contemporaries, but in planning with Welles for Production #281, there were no limits.

"During recent years, a great deal has been said and written about the new technical and artistic possibilities offered by such developments as coated lenses [and] super-fast films," Toland wrote in 1941, soon after completing his assignment on *Citizen Kane.* "Some cinematographers have had, as I did in one or two productions, opportunities to make a few cautious, tentative experiments utilizing these technical innovations to produce improved photo-dramatic results.

"In the course of my last assignment, the photography of Orson Welles' picture, *Citizen Kane,* the opportunity for such large-scale experiments came to me. In fact, it was forced upon me. To bring the picture to the screen as both Welles and I saw it, we were compelled to make radical departures from conventional practice."

The second player in forming the visual plan for *Citizen Kane* was Perry Ferguson, a talented designer from the RKO staff who had been assigned to such films as *Bringing Up Baby* and *Gunga Din.*

Welles brought Ferguson to the project not only for his reputation as an innovative designer, but also for his ability to trim costs. With budget cuts of at least 30 percent needed before *Citizen Kane* could move into production, and with many costs impossible to reduce—such as the budget for the cast—set design, construction, and decoration were the categories where the production team could find substantial cost savings.

Ferguson was given a mandate to cut the costs for set construction by almost half. (Ferguson reported to Van Nest Polglase, director of RKO's art department. Polglase, like many other department heads at the major studios, had a contractual agreement that provided him with top billing in screen credits over the art director who did the actual designing for a film. On *Citizen Kane*, Polglase was listed as "art director" while Ferguson was the "associate," although Polglase had almost nothing to do with the production.)

Ferguson, like Toland, was fascinated by the idea of stretching the traditional limits of Hollywood production methods. In *Citizen Kane*—with Welles' commitment to innovation and the studio's mandate to reduce the budget—Ferguson saw an opportunity to push the boundaries of his craft.

Some cost reductions would be simple, such as reusing items from the existing RKO stock of furniture and fixtures, identifying sets from other productions to commandeer, or shooting at real locations on the studio grounds (such as the lawn and pathways at RKO in Culver City, which was used for some of the newsreel shots of the elderly Kane in a wheelchair). But for the dozens of sets needed for *Citizen Kane* that ranged from a nineteenth-century breakfast nook to a current-day projection room to the mammoth Great Hall in Kane's private palace, Ferguson would be challenged—both for his creativity and for his budget sense.

Ferguson was enthusiastic, in part because his work on *Citizen Kane* became an opportunity to address his long-standing complaint about how all of the studios designed their films: set design could look good, but to Ferguson, they simply did not represent reality.

"The classic example, of course, is the movie night-club," said Ferguson. "I have yet to see a real night-club which isn't cramped enough to make one wonder if the human race isn't descended from sardines.

"But a movie night-club generally sprawls over the whole of the studio's biggest sound-stages, and has plenty of room to dolly the camera everywhere between the tables—and for the hero to dance without bumping into the dress extras on the dance-floor."

Ferguson found the same problem with less luxurious sets as well.

"An even better example is the average movie apartment," he said. "We carefully plant our hero as a poor steel-mill worker, or our heroine as an equally poor stenographer—poor enough so that matrimony is an impossible problem for them for six or eight reels. But when the camera follows [each of] them home, we find them living in such spacious apartments we wonder why they don't just take a smaller flat and get married on the savings!"

Ferguson wrote about these complaints in 1942, after the United States entered World War II, when the studios mandated severe restrictions on the use of new material for set construction. For Ferguson, the limitation provided the ideal opportunity to implement more broadly some of the methods he had started using the year before on *Citizen Kane*—in particular, creating greater realism while shrinking construction costs.

"A severe restriction may be turned into an advantage if we only look at it from the right viewpoint," Ferguson said. "To me one of the most interesting is the possibility of a trend toward greater realism in the average set."

Ferguson also lobbied for using the camera's eye to supplement the effectiveness of sets.

"We can minimize actual set construction [by] taking advantage of the camera's powers of suggestion," Ferguson wrote, words that characterize perfectly the visual plan that unfolded with Toland for *Citizen Kane*—especially as the plan applied to the production's largest and most important sets.

By 1942, Ferguson had plenty of evidence that his designs for *Citizen Kane* could address these wartime issues. But in June 1940, he was just getting started on *Citizen Kane,* and his work with Welles and Toland was a challenge to come.

Ferguson started by transforming Welles' ideas into practical film planning tools, first by working with staff artists such as Claude Gillingwater to create detailed sketches; the sketches were later used by Charles Ohmann to produce storyboards. In some cases, Ferguson's craftsmen then created scale models that Welles could view from any angle with a tiny periscope (the periscope had already proved particularly useful when planning *Heart of Darkness;* Welles used a periscope to "travel" through the models).

Once Welles was satisfied with the designs, the sets were constructed on soundstages at RKO's main studio at the corner of Melrose Avenue and Gower Street in Hollywood and on the RKO lot at Washington and Ince Boulevards in Culver

City, now known as the Culver Studios. Also housed at RKO in Culver City were David O. Selznick's offices, his headquarters for filming *Gone with the Wind* the year before. (The offices, in a building that looks more like a white Colonial-style mansion than a studio headquarters, can be seen at the beginning of the opening credits in many Selznick productions of the 1930s and 1940s, including *Gone with the Wind* in a color shot and *Rebecca* in black and white.)

The original production schedule for *Citizen Kane* included filming several major exterior scenes at RKO's outdoor "ranch" in Encino in the San Fernando Valley, fifteen miles north of Culver City. Instead, Welles requested—no doubt to keep production moving quickly when filming and rehearsals shifted between several sets—to shoot all of the principal exterior scenes at RKO in Culver City, either indoors on soundstages or outdoors at the studio's "40 Acres" back lot three blocks to the south. (The back lot itself was really only twenty-eight acres; "40 Acres" represented the approximate combined area for both the outdoor facility and the studios). For example, the scenes set on the New York street where Susan and Kane first meet were filmed on Stage 11. The only significant exterior scene that was actually filmed outdoors—the postwedding departure from Trenton Town Hall—was filmed at 40 Acres.

Eventually, only a few minor shots were completed at the RKO Encino ranch, such as the torchlight "Kane for Governor" rallies, the burning of Kane's effigy, and the intentional "outtake" scenes for the *News on the March* newsreel filmed November 20 that show Kane as an old man dedicating the cornerstone of a building and spilling mortar on his overcoat. (Neither 40 Acres nor the Encino ranch still exist. The ranch's grounds, near the corner of Burbank and Balboa Boulevards, were incorporated into the Sepulveda Basin Recreation Area. In 1976, 40 Acres was bulldozed; an industrial park now occupies the site.)

The sets for *Citizen Kane* would have been a tremendous challenge, even without Welles' elaborate visual plan and RKO's budget restrictions. The film required more than eighty settings spanning nearly eight decades of American history, from middle-nineteenth-century Colorado through pre–World War II urban New York and Florida. The range of sets produced by Ferguson included turn-of-the-century mansions, slum streets, dingy newspaper offices, a gaudy Xanadu bedroom for Kane's second wife (complete with childlike stenciling of little animals), the platform at a political rally, backstage at an opera, doorways, staircases, corridors, and (largest of all) the dark Gothic vision of the Great Hall at Xanadu.

In addition to the traditional three-wall structure that is the standard configuration for Hollywood sets, Welles wanted another feature: ceilings that would be visible in most scenes.

"It's disastrous to let a cameraman light a set without a ceiling—it's artificial," Welles recalled. "You can hardly go into a room without seeing a ceiling, and I believe the camera ought to show what the eyes are normally seeing."

Citizen Kane was not the first motion picture that featured ceilings, but unique to the production were the frequency and variety of ceilings in the film and the many ways Toland exploited the ceilings with his photographic techniques. Ceilings not only contributed to the production's goal for realism, but allowed Welles to shoot up from very low angles, an option he and Toland would use with powerful effects, such as in Susan's Xanadu bedroom or in many of the shots in the *Inquirer* newsroom.

Years later, Welles could not fully explain why he and Toland used low-angle shots in *Citizen Kane*. "I don't know why—I suppose it's because I think the picture looks better down there," he said. "I suppose I had more low angles in *Kane* just because I became fascinated with the way it looked."

The ceilings, most of them fabricated with muslin stretched over frames, were not merely plain, flat surfaces. Ferguson varied the ceiling designs with every manner of texture and treatment—beams, filigree, stained glass, and, for the *Inquirer* newsroom, skylights partially shaded with makeshift curtains, as in the pre–air conditioning era, to shield the reporters in the newsroom from the midday sun. Each ceiling, including the simplest, featured a different design element. For example, when Jed Leland and Bernstein are unpacking statues in Kane's office at the *Inquirer,* the otherwise plain ceiling is slashed by a single long diagonal shadow. But there were also some ceilingless shots in *Citizen Kane.* Curiously, none of the interviews conducted by reporter Thompson have ceilings in them and are the most conventionally shot scenes of the production.

In addition to enhancing artistry and realism, the ceilings provided technical benefits. The muslin ceilings were acoustically transparent, so the sound technicians could place their microphones above the roof and eliminate the constant curse of the cinematographer: a microphone shadow—or, worse, the actual appearance of a microphone in the frame.

Normally, Toland said, "one must always be on the lookout lest the mike or its shadow get into the picture. In this position [above the ceiling], the microphones were always completely out of camera range." However, for the scenes shot with the microphone below the ceiling, with most sets lit from the front by lights mounted on floor stands, microphone shadows were not a problem.

Although microphones were indeed raised above the ceilings when neces-sary, they were not positioned that way for every scene, as some film analysts have assumed. Most of the medium shots and close-ups were recorded with the microphone positioned above the actors but out of the camera's view, as in any other production. For broader shots, RKO sound technicians installed several microphones in and around the set: above the ceiling, off-screen as near as possible to the action, or, if needed, hidden among props. In a period before multi-track sound recording, sound engineer Bailey Fesler switched from microphone to microphone, depending on the location of the actors.

While ceilings presented no concerns for the sound engineers, they did create challenges for Toland and the lighting for each set. Later, as Toland began shooting Production #281, he would find several innovative solutions.

While Welles, Toland, and Ferguson continued to refine their visual plan, the negotiations over the budget did not progress as smoothly. Even as work pro-ceeded, *Citizen Kane* was still at risk: the combination of lost revenue overseas, pressure on Schaefer, and general nervousness at the studio about Welles' abili-ties could have forced RKO to cut its losses and shut down the production.

In June 1940, almost eleven months after Welles signed his contract to produce films for RKO, Toland's visual plotting and Ferguson's set construction had progressed to the point that Welles—if given a green light—could start shoot-ing his picture. But while the director was prepared to begin shooting, RKO was not. Still uncertain about the financial outlay for the project, the studio con-tinued to balk at giving the okay to begin production.

Today, in an era when a Hollywood film can be budgeted for $100 million or more without raising an eyebrow, it may seem hard to understand why studios of the golden era maintained such intense scrutiny over costs that seem laughingly small by comparison; the cost to produce *Citizen Kane* would barely pay the catering budget for some films today. But in 1940, to maintain cash flow as a steady stream of film projects moved through production, tight fiscal control was vital, and the budget pressure was relentless. For Production #281, memos flew back and forth between RKO administration and the Mercury of-fice over questions about costs of every size, with the studio fussing over charges as low as $50 here or $100 there. Charges as small as $10 were itemized and approved; later in the production, RKO accountants would question payments made to composer Bernard Herrmann that varied from the original authorization by $1.

So the budget review continued. Earning the approval of studio management would require a large dose of Welles' chicanery—with encouragement from Perry Ferguson—before the cameras could roll.

Welles had already been rehearsing his principal players for several weeks, both in meetings on RKO soundstages and in less formal gatherings at Mankiewicz's home. Welles conducted extensive off-set rehearsals of every scene, a rarity in the days of factory-like production in the Hollywood studios, and he also made audio recordings of several key passages for his detailed review.

But by early June, Welles was still waiting for a green light, so Perry Ferguson, wise in the ways of studio procedures, proposed how his eager director could get started. Earlier in the spring, with permission from the studio, Welles had shot tests for makeup and costumes: on April 26, RKO cinematographer Russell Metty filmed Welles in costume and makeup as a fifty-year-old, and on May 1 they shot other tests of his makeup as a young man. (Metty would work on actual shots for *Citizen Kane* late in the production and again with Welles in 1946 on *The Stranger* and in 1957 on *Touch of Evil*.)

With Metty, and later with Toland when he arrived from Samuel Goldwyn Productions and assumed cinematographer's duties, Welles directed several other tests in May and June, including makeup experiments and brief scenes with himself, Ruth Warrick, Joseph Cotten, George Coulouris, and William Alland. On June 28, Welles filmed a test of the projection room scene with Edgar Barrier as Rawlston.

Ferguson suggested a simple solution: that Welles continue to shoot "tests," but instead of brief fragments, shoot fully produced scenes. So on June 29, Welles and Toland began to shoot footage that was still logged as "tests" but were actually completed segments used in the final film. The first of these "tests" was the full-cast filming of the projection room sequence in which Rawlston orders Thompson to find the secret of Rosebud.

Ferguson, Toland, and Welles chose an actual RKO screening room—Projection Room 4—to film the meeting of nine *News on the March* staff as they review the newsreel about Kane's life. Thus the first scenes shot were saving money by filming on a location that was free.

On July 3, Welles shot Thompson's first visit to interview Susan Alexander, her suicide attempt, and several related scenes. The shots set in the El Rancho nightclub, with its southwestern theme, were filmed in RKO Hollywood Stage 2B on a set built for a western—yet another location that required no production charges. Toland also filmed Kane and Susan surrounded by reporters on the 40 Acres back lot as they departed from their marriage at Trenton Town Hall. These scenes are listed in the studio's log as "Orson Welles Tests," and all were completed with minimal expense and limited construction.

Other scenes were also shot as "tests" that involved more elaborate sets. On July 1, and between July 22 and July 29, Toland filmed Welles and Comingore in the pivotal argument between Kane and Susan in their Florida picnic tent; several shots for the newsreel (including Kane speaking from a flag-draped platform and being interviewed on a boat deck about the prospects for war; Comingore, Welles, and Bonanova for Susan's singing lesson; Susan confronting Kane in their Chicago apartment after her horrible opera debut; Kane shaking hands with Neville Chamberlain; and Kane standing with Hitler and Goering).

But for one shot, the ruse about tests interfered with Welles' "all new faces" plan, because the RKO casting directors sent longtime extra Gino Corrado to appear as a waiter in the scene at Susan's El Rancho nightclub. (Corrado, in *Citizen Kane* named "Gino," asks Gus Schilling, "Another double?") By assigning Corrado—who had appeared in more than 250 bit parts before 1940 and has the distinction of being the only performer to appear in *Citizen Kane, Casablanca,* and *Gone with the Wind*—RKO inadvertently spoiled Welles' goal of using only film novices.

"My whole idea of having only new faces was ruined by the first day of shooting," Welles remembered. "For the waiter in the nightclub, Casting sent me a tubby little round-faced Italian, who is the waiter in every movie ever made! And I couldn't possibly send him away on the basis that he was too well-known a face because I was claiming to be 'testing.' So there he is—spoiling the whole master plan in one of the first shots." (In recounting this story, Welles conveniently forgot that four days before he filmed the scenes with Corrado, the role of Rawlston had been performed by Philip Van Zandt, who had six films to his credit before *Citizen Kane.*)

These early scenes—the first of Welles' career as a motion picture director— provide viewers with a glimpse of the beginning of his bold start as a filmmaker: in the projection room, for instance, natural overlapping dialogue; actors submerged in darkness or shrouded in a haze of cigarette smoke; intimate, natural photography; and the eerie corona of light from the projection room behind Rawlston when he gives the orders to find out about Rosebud. The camera had barely started to roll, and the visual plan for *Citizen Kane* was working. Welles was already living up to his reputation as an artistic innovator.

Eventually, RKO management realized what Welles was doing with his "tests," but by that time, he appeared to be making steady progress, and—finally—the studio allowed him to proceed with his production. So the actual start date for *Citizen Kane* was June 29, a month before the "official" studio-announced start date. By the time of the official start date, Welles had already completed more than a dozen scenes, almost twelve minutes of the two-hour film.

And while Welles tinkered with his "tests," the budget negotiations mercifully ended. RKO and Welles finalized budget cuts that satisfied both the artist and the accountants, thanks to Welles' judicious editing and rewriting, innovative and inexpensive set designs by Perry Ferguson, and thousands of dollars' worth of savings made possible because special effects would be employed extensively to substitute for expensive shots.

On July 26, 1940, the RKO accounting office and senior studio management signed off on the budget for *Citizen Kane*. The original $1 million–plus estimate had been reduced to $723,800, a total that represented actual production costs of $603,167, plus the studio's 20 percent administrative overhead charge of $120,633. In other words, the largest single charge to the *Citizen Kane* budget was the studio's own administrative costs—the one expense that Welles could not control. But at that point it did not matter. The official first day of shooting was set: July 30, 1940.

NO VISITORS, PLEASE

I said, "There's a lot of stuff here I don't know." And Toland said,
"There's nothing I can't teach you in three hours." It was Toland's idea that
anyone can learn [the fundamentals of direction] in three hours.
Everything else is if you're any good or not.
—Orson Welles

On July 30, the formal start of RKO Production #281, Welles directed one of the most important sequences of the film: the scenes set in the breakfast room of Kane's New York home that depict the nine-year decline of the publisher's marriage to his first wife, Emily. The cast was called for nine A.M.; after extended rehearsals, cameras rolled at three P.M.

The breakfast table sequence—in which Kane and Emily age almost a decade—was shot over two days, with retakes of selected shots completed on August 10, 19, and 27. Makeup artist Maurice Seiderman recalled that the sequence was filmed in reverse order, with Welles and Ruth Warrick in middle age during the first takes, long out of love and virtually ignoring each other as they eat. (As if the mutual silence of Kane and Emily during the final shot of the breakfast room scene were not enough to illustrate their estrangement, Welles and Mankiewicz included a particularly nasty visual slap: in the final shot of the sequence, Kane reads the *Inquirer,* but Emily reads the *Chronicle*.)

As the breakfast room scenes were filmed, Seiderman removed the actors' makeup layer by layer, with the characters becoming progressively younger. Then only the base makeup remained on Welles and Warrick when they appeared in the first scenes set in the breakfast room—innocent, beautiful, and in love. The first official day of shooting concluded at eight P.M.

On August 1, RKO hosted the only formal press gathering held during the production. The reporters saw little—only the scenes of Kane's wedding to Emily Monroe Norton photographed for the *News on the March* newsreel, as filmed on the lawn at RKO in Culver City in front of a backdrop of the White House.

The scenes shot that day revealed nothing of the film's story, and when reporters pressed Welles for details, he evaded their questions. *The New York Times* reported that the film "covers the last 60 years of the American scene," while *The Hollywood Reporter* said Welles would be playing a "robber baron industrialist." However, the film industry trade paper had already moved closer to the truth when it reported three days earlier that "despite denials from the Orson Welles contingent, insiders insist Little Orson Annie's flicker is based on the life of a well-known publisher.

"Treatment of the personality," declared *The Hollywood Reporter,* "is sympathetic throughout."

Throughout the summer and early fall of 1940, Welles rehearsed and filmed *Citizen Kane,* rolling through sixty-three days of shooting that was scheduled to conclude October 11. (The standard Hollywood workweek in 1940 was six days, and the crew would have one holiday off: Labor Day.) At the center of the production was Welles—making requests, answering questions, and generally coaxing, encouraging, and demanding the best possible results from all involved.

"Orson functioned best out of chaos . . . out of disorganization," said assistant producer Richard Wilson. "Disorganization in itself has to have a certain organization beneath it; I furnished that for him, Jack Houseman furnished that for him . . . furnished enough organization for the situation to be chaotic, yet out of it the creative process could function."

RKO Production #281 was, in many ways, an enterprise much like any other Welles project: endlessly frenetic, exhausting, enlivening, and creatively exhilarating. For most of the cast and crew, their time on *Citizen Kane* would be the most productive of their lives.

"I have never observed a director," said William Alland, "who so completely mesmerized, dominated, cajoled, and seduced an entire crew as Welles could do."

Welles loved actors, said his assistant Kathryn Trosper. "He would do anything to help an actor; he'd spend an hour talking with an actor about one line. He felt the same way about technicians; he had deep respect for them."

Agnes Moorehead, who would also appear in Welles' second film, *The Magnificent Ambersons,* said, "There was no one quite like him to create excitement. Orson can get an actor to do things he doesn't know he has it within him to do. He inspires people with an enthusiasm that seems to unlock creative energies that have lain dormant or were hitherto unsuspected."

Welles, said Ruth Warrick, "did everything he could to make you as good as you could possibly be. But he also imbued you with the feeling that you could do anything. So his feeling gave you that support. He had a way of making you feel that you were wonderful and you could do it—and therefore you could."

But effective movie direction requires much more than emotional connection to actors. On the set, it quickly became clear that Welles' lack of practical film-making knowledge was hindering his progress. In spite of his boy genius stature, Welles' transition from stage to film was not always a graceful one.

The problem was Welles' lack of familiarity with the fundamentals of Hollywood filmmaking—those standard on-set working methods that traditionally trained directors learn over months or years as they advance through the production ranks. Once filming began, Welles' early days as a director were marked by some uncertainty and many questions; he had endless vision, but he desperately needed schooling in the basics of Hollywood motion picture production to translate his ideas to film.

Thirty years later, Welles recalled with amused embarrassment that as soon as shooting began, he was befuddled by one of the most basic tools of filmmaking: the logistics of on-set directions to move an actor across the set from left to right or right to left so the action matches when cutting from one shot to another.

"There was one terrible moment about the third day when we had to stop because I couldn't understand why if you went off [the set] one way you had to come in another [in the next scene]," Welles said.

What in theory seems like a simple filmmaking device can be difficult to grasp without the practical experience on a soundstage that Welles lacked. No amount of explanation on the set from Gregg Toland or script supervisor Molly (Amalia) Kent, who was responsible for ensuring that actors' movements were accurate from scene to scene, could enlighten Welles about stage directions, so he shut down production so he could let the concepts sink in overnight.

"I left for the day," Welles recalled. "I said, 'I'm no use; I'll have to go home and think about it.'"

Not long after, Welles walked out again when he was stymied by how to add visual interest to the confrontation in Susan's second apartment, where Gettys threatens to destroy Kane's political career by publicly exposing his relationship to Susan. The long preproduction period and the visual planning had not inspired Welles with ideas on how to move the grim conflict between Kane, Gettys, Susan, and Emily in a section of the set less than ten feet wide.

"I had no idea what to do," Welles said. "That was just a scene in a room, and it seemed to me so boring. I just went away."

Welles may have tried to work out his conundrum by sketching the scene on paper. In a Third Revised Final shooting script from Welles' files, on the blank side of the sheet opposite the page where the confrontation scene begins, is a diagram created in a hand that looks like Welles' that appears to be a rough diamond-shaped plan as viewed from above for staging the scene.

After stewing about the logistics, Welles returned not only knowing how he wanted to handle the scene, but also with a better appreciation of the challenges of camera placement and film direction.

"I think it's like lion taming or being the conductor of an orchestra—you have to come in and know where the camera is, or there are all sorts of evil demons who will attack you, and the doubts will show on the screen," Welles said. "You have to be absolutely on top of it. Or pay no attention to it. One of the two."

The result was one of Welles' least favorite scenes in the film; he described it as "a little overstated." But to anyone other than the overcritical director, the outcome was a smoothly choreographed, tense sequence of eight shots in the apartment—a three-minute, forty-two-second segment anchored by an opening shot featuring all four actors that lasted almost two minutes without a break. Throughout the sequence, Welles, Comingore, Warrick, and Collins move naturally through staging at three distances from the camera as they discuss Kane's impending fate.

Some of Welles' other problems were the result of his not understanding the difference between the role of a director on a Broadway stage and that of a filmmaker in a Hollywood studio. In the theater, for example, lighting is often managed by the director—but not in Hollywood.

"I somehow assumed that movie lighting was supervised by directors," Welles said. "And, like a damn fool, for the first few days, I 'supervised' like crazy. Behind me, of course, Gregg was balancing the lights and telling everybody to shut their faces.

"He was quietly fixing it so as many of my notions as possible would work," Welles said of Toland. "Later, he told me, 'That's the only way to learn anything—from somebody who doesn't know anything.'"

Others on the set were aware that Toland was helping Welles make the transition from theater to cinema.

"Orson would rehearse a scene as he would do it for the stage, then Gregg would explain to him why it could not be done for the screen in the same way," said grip Ralph Hoge. "Gregg was careful to take Orson aside and explain these things in private. Orson was easily convinced on matters he was unfamiliar with—but not in public; you couldn't convince him of anything in front of other people."

Welles soon recognized that his cinematographer was the ideal mentor, and he learned quickly. Day by day, Toland patiently taught the young director lessons about the conventions of filmmaking—and the inside workings of the Hollywood studio system. By guiding Welles through the basics, Toland helped transform him into a practical movie director as well as a visionary.

And Toland also took Welles aside for a specialized lesson.

"I said, 'There's a lot of stuff here I don't know,'" Welles recalled. "And Toland said, 'There's nothing I can't teach you in three hours.' It was Toland's idea that anyone can learn [the fundamentals of direction] in three hours. Everything else is if you're any good or not."

With Welles acting in many scenes while directing at the same time, he could not watch the action from behind the camera. The task fell to William Alland, when he was not rehearsing or appearing as Thompson, to serve as Welles' eyes and ears off camera and ensure that the actor-director was getting the shot he needed.

To rehearse these sequences, Welles hired stand-ins who would walk through the scene while Welles watched from behind the camera. At various times during the production, Charles Hayes, Sid Davis, Bob Crosby, and John Huettner served as Welles' double, earning the studio's regular stand-in rate of $6.50 per day; Crosby, as Welles' double during the dancing sequence, earned $66 per week.

As the production progressed, Huettner handled the bulk of Welles' stand-in assignments. A sailor on the 1932 U.S. Olympic team, Huettner appeared as an extra or in uncredited roles in several films before eventually becoming an attorney. In addition to his stand-in work for *Citizen Kane,* Huettner appeared as one of the anonymous reporters in the shadows at Xanadu. The tallest of the reporters—to match Welles' height for his stand-in work—Huettner is carrying his coat over his arm and says, "There's part of a Scottish castle over there, but we haven't bothered to unwrap it yet."

Said Alland, "Orson would set up a scene and use his stand-in to diagram the physical moves, and then he would get in front of the camera and rehearse the scene himself. When he felt the scene was as it should be, we would shoot it.

"After the take, Orson would then look across the camera to me, and if I smiled, that would be a signal that it was all right. If I looked displeased, he would come behind the camera and look over my shoulder, as though he was checking the script, and say to me, 'What was the matter with that one?'

"My job was not to improve or change the performance—I was to be the mirror of what he already approved in rehearsal," Alland said. "Orson trusted me to not put my own interpretation on the scene, but indeed to not be afraid to tell him, 'Orson, this is not the way you wanted it.'"

Once production began, Welles ran a closed set and strictly limited access to rehearsals and filming. Most of the daily call sheets were inscribed with the firm closing line "No visitors, please." Only cast, crew, and invited guests, such as director John Ford, were welcome; RKO management was not.

Welles' secrecy was not intended to keep details of the film out of the press, regardless of what some later said when the forces of William Randolph Hearst tried to suppress the film; the fact that *Citizen Kane* explored the life of a powerful newspaper publisher was no secret for months before and during production. Instead, Welles was merely ensuring that shooting would move forward at his pace, and on his terms, and with as little interference as possible from the studio. Despite Welles' contract and support from George Schaefer, several dissenting RKO executives would have been only too happy to meddle in Mercury Theatre's operations.

For most of the production, Welles' plan succeeded; RKO executives kept away from his project. But when studio managers did intrude, Welles demonstrated without subtlety that their presence was unwelcome. When studio executives "dropped in" to see how production was proceeding, Welles calmly stopped shooting, divided the group into teams, and played a baseball game until the intruders departed.

Playing softball, according to Welles, was only a practical joke.

"Schaefer came with all the bankers from New York, and they'd all heard, you know, about this crazy Welles," he said. "We thought it would be nice if they came down and found us hard at work—playing baseball."

However, playing catch, even as a joke, was a tactical error for Welles. Said Alland, "It drove the brass absolutely loony."

Welles' secrecy notwithstanding, RKO was never in the dark about progress on *Citizen Kane*. Welles had already performed the entire story for George Schaefer and studio attorney Harry Edington, so the plot was well-known to them. RKO management processed every expense request and received the typical written production reports that were used by all the studios to track a film's progress: start times, end times, notes about problems on the set, explanations of delays, illnesses, injuries, and revisions in production planning.

RKO managers also used another common but less respectable method of on-set information gathering: spies.

The studio received covert reports supplied by RKO technicians assigned to the film. Maurice Seiderman believed that his own assistant, makeup artist Layne "Shotgun" Britton, had been assigned to *Citizen Kane* to inform management about the production. And when John Ford, Welles' idol, visited the set during production, Ford told Welles that assistant director Eddie Donahue was a spy for RKO management.

"Ford's greeting to him was the first hint we had of his real status," Welles said. " 'Well, well,' Ford said, 'how's old snake-in-the-grass Eddie?' "

However, if RKO managers planned to use this knowledge to control Welles, they were out of luck—Welles successfully forged ahead on his own.

The creative pace of production was frantic for all involved, but the physical demands were even more challenging. For instance, when filming scenes of Susan's opera debut on August 16, the initial cast call was nine A.M.; the day's work was completed at three fifty A.M. the next morning.

"Orson," publicist Herb Drake said to attorney Arnold Weissberger in September, "has worked this crew harder than any other crew in the history of motion pictures—according to their own sworn testimony."

And Welles, remembered Paul Stewart, also "shot more film than anyone in the history of the cinema." For one of Joseph Cotten's scenes, Stewart recalled, Welles demanded 108 takes before quitting and starting again the next day.

"One day he shot more than 10,000 feet [nearly two hours] of film," said Stewart. "He got up to the hundredth take, then started again at five, so the studio wouldn't know. He printed nothing from that day's work, then the next day he got the shot in two takes."

Stewart's first day in front of the cameras required fifty-seven takes of the same scene.

"My first line in *Citizen Kane* is: 'Rosebud? I'll tell you about Rosebud. How much is it worth to you?'" Stewart said. "We rehearsed for 2½ hours—just that line. And he'd say, 'Again, again.'"

William Alland suffered through the same ordeal. In the scene in the nightclub when he calls his office and reports to Rawlston that Susan would not speak with him, Welles demanded take after take, with Alland delivering his lines at different speeds—first fast and then slow.

"I was utterly exhausted," said Alland, "but Orson finally got what he wanted from me."

Dorothy Comingore experienced a different kind of pressure and may have been the one actor in the production who was treated badly by Welles—but if so, deliberately. Welles, recalled Ruth Warrick, was rude to Comingore, and when Warrick questioned him about his behavior early in rehearsals, Welles had a director's explanation for his wrath.

"Orson told me, 'That girl isn't an actress—she is *that part;* she is a little waif,'" Warrick said. "'And when she comes to the part when she really has to hate my guts at the end of the picture, she's not going to be able to act it, she's going to have to hate me, and when we get there she'll *really* hate my guts.'"

But if Welles was deliberately trying to kindle flames in Comingore's performance, she felt no malicious heat, recalling instead that "Orson left me completely alone with regard to my lines and characterizations."

What was it like to work with Orson Welles on *Citizen Kane*? According to Welles' assistant Kathryn Trosper, who at the peak of production was often with him eighteen hours a day, "Working for Orson on *Citizen Kane* was exciting and always interesting, and he was often a lot of fun to be around. But sometimes he wasn't fun at all. He could go into a raging fit at the drop of a hat, and scream at some poor klutz in the office. But then it would immediately blow over."

Editor Robert Wise, who as a daily visitor to the set was a constant observer of the director in action, said that Welles' mood depended "on what you walked in on."

"Working with Orson was never very long on an even keel—it was either up or down: exciting and stimulating, or maddening and frustrating," said Wise. "But most of the time, a Welles set was an electric, creative environment."

However, one late morning, while a set was being lit, the atmosphere was less than happy, when Welles—who had probably started his day in the makeup chair at four A.M.—requested lunch for himself.

"About eleven, Orson ordered a tray of food, including a whole chicken," said Wise. "He sat there on the side of the set, observing the work and eating while the lighting was changed."

One P.M. came and went, and then two P.M., with Welles, focused on the technical crew, still not calling for lunch.

"By then, the technicians were ready to drop a lamp on him," Wise said. "Finally, one of his assistants had to whisper to him, 'Hey, Orson, we really should take a break.' Only then did he call, 'Lunch.'

"But that was Orson," Wise said. "He wasn't unfeeling—he was just caught up in the work. One moment he could be guilty of behavior so outrageous that you wanted to tell him to go to hell and walk off the picture, and before you could do it, he'd come up with some idea that was so brilliant it would leave your mouth gaping open. So you never walked."

The tempo of production was, of course, toughest for Welles. For the actor-director-producer, twelve-hour days were constant, and eighteen hours at a stretch were routine. On days when Welles needed heavy makeup and had to meet with the production staff before being called to the set at nine A.M., the director would arrive as early as three A.M., often not leaving until after eleven P.M.

Other than Welles, Joseph Cotten felt the most strain. Cotten faced an inviolate deadline to complete his assignment as Jed Leland: he was scheduled to depart Los Angeles in the third week of September to return to the road tour of *The Philadelphia Story.* Although Cotten was one of the first actors hired for *Citizen Kane,* the complex logistics of filming, set construction, and the early scheduling of brief appearances by other actors eventually pushed many of Cotten's key scenes into late August and the first three weeks of September—including several difficult sequences that required frustratingly long production days.

Three of these sequences involved appearing as Leland when he was supposed to be either drunk or fatigued to the point of complete exhaustion: the postelection argument between Kane and Leland, the discovery of Leland unconscious at the *Chicago Inquirer,* and some of the scenes that showed Kane's first night at the *Inquirer* (when Kane writes his "Declaration of Principles"). To maintain the production schedule, and to add greater realism to acting by wearing down himself and his actors, Welles deliberately chose to shoot late into the night for all three scenes and all night long for two of them.

The most arduous day of the production occurred on August 30, when cast and crew worked into the morning of August 31 on Stage 11 at RKO in Culver City to film the critical sequence in which Jed Leland, drunk, confronts Kane in the newsroom of the *Inquirer* after the gubernatorial election.

"The thing you don't do when faced with a drunk scene is to get drunk," Cotten said. "Orson and I came to the conclusion that fatigue would be akin to the kind of numbness that too much drinking can bring. So we started shooting after dinner, having already completed a full day's work that day. I had nothing to drink, but by three o'clock in the morning, I *was* drunk. I felt so heavy-footed and tired that I didn't have to act drunk at all."

Cotten was so tired that he did a tongue trip in rehearsal.

"I had the line, 'You said yourself you were looking for someone to do dramatic criticism,' but the words came out 'dramatic crimmitism,'" Cotten said. "The line remained in the picture."

The production rolled through the night, bolstered by the routine midnight call for four gallons of coffee and an equal amount of hot chocolate, and continued as morning came.

"I remember that the eight o'clock whistle blew and the soundman cracked, 'That's an interference we don't generally have on a picture,'" Cotten recalled.

"After Orson called an end to the shooting, the propman brought out a silver tray with drinks," Cotten said. "The big stage door was open and we saw the sunshine outside. Someone suggested, 'Why don't we go outside and have our drinks?'

"There we were," said Cotten, "sitting around in the morning sun and having drinks. I'll never forget actors from other pictures walking down the street and seeing us. I can just imagine what they were saying: 'Those actors from New York! Imagine them sitting around in the morning drinking Scotch and sodas off a silver tray!' They didn't know that we had been working for 24 hours straight."

The shooting that night had indeed been productive and resulted in one of the film's most powerful sequences. However, by working all night, the crew received mandatory time off, costing the production a precious day and adding a delay to the production reports.

Not quite as grueling but certainly protracted was the September 3 filming on RKO Hollywood Stage 2B of Kane, Leland, and Bernstein at the *Chicago Inquirer;* shooting began at nine A.M. and halted at five minutes after midnight.

As Cotten's deadline for departure drew near, Welles pushed cast and crew on Friday, September 20, to complete some of the scenes between Kane, Leland, and Bernstein on their first night at the *Inquirer* and their visit to look at the front window of the *Chronicle*—yet another marathon shooting session that ended at eleven P.M. In the day's production report was the anxious note, "Scenes to be shot Saturday *and Sunday* with Joe Cotten," meaning that the studio would be forced to incur the huge overtime charges required for work on Sunday.

Fortunately for the studio budget watchers, Welles finished with Cotten on Saturday, September 21, filming Leland entering a saloon to get drunk after the election, Kane's return to the *Inquirer* after his trip to Europe, and Leland and Bernstein reacting to Kane's campaign speech at Madison Square Garden—completing the day at six A.M. Sunday morning.

As filming progressed, the visual plan so carefully plotted in preproduction began to unfold.

"The greatest gift a young director could ever have is a cameraman who would do anything you ask," Welles said of Gregg Toland. "Anything was possible; he never tried to impress me with the fact that he was doing impossible things, but he was."

Toland's goal of creating a seamless quality for the photography was particularly successful. Throughout *Citizen Kane* are examples of Toland's emphasis on smooth continuity that were accomplished with an imaginative inventory of techniques, each designed to bridge from one scene to the next with minimal disruption and maximum effectiveness in telling the story.

"Orson and Gregg respected each other, and they got along beautifully," said Alland. "No matter what Orson wanted, Gregg would try to get it for him."

Some direct cuts were bridged with a simple but perfectly timed split of a single sentence between two scenes. Early in the film, when Thatcher and Kane's parents tell young Charles he is leaving home, Welles wanted the scene to end with a close-up of Charles. When Kane's father tells Thatcher that Charles needs "a good thrashing," the scene shows all four actors in a medium shot. Mary Kane tells her husband, "That's why he's going to be brought up where you can't get at him." As Mary says "he," the scene cuts to an extreme close-up of Mary and Charles, with the shot ending on young Kane's defiant profile. But the audio of Mary's dialogue plays unbroken between the two scenes and helps ease the transition from a medium shot to a tight close-up.

Changes of angle and simple movements by actors contributed to creating smooth transitions. For example, when Kane and Jed Leland arrive at the *Inquirer* for the first time, Toland created an ingenious bit of continuity between two shots with a deliberate move on the set by Joseph Cotten.

As the scene begins, the camera is behind Leland and Kane as they enter the newsroom. Leland says, "After you, Mr. Kane," and Kane walks forward into the newsroom while Leland follows. Kane walks to the right of a pillar, while Leland passes the pillar on the left. Leland then stops, reverses a step, and circles the pillar to the right while he holds it with his hand. As Leland circles the pillar, the scene cuts to inside the newsroom in front of Kane and Leland, with Leland completing his walk around the pillar—his movement linking the two shots.

In addition to planning well in advance to create smooth transitions in direct cuts, Toland included in his visual plan the use of dissolves (the fade-out of one scene and the fade-in to another) that would be added in postproduction to move the action from one scene to the next. Dissolves, like many other methods used by Toland, are standard filmmaking tools. However, most of the dissolves in *Citizen Kane* were developed as part of the visual plan and created in post-production specifically to improve the links between two scenes.

These smooth dissolves are vivid in *Citizen Kane* from the beginning of the film. As the film opens, and the shots dissolve one after the other from the gates of Xanadu to Kane's deathbed, the lit window in Kane's bedroom remains in the same position—even when Xanadu is shown upside down in a reflection on the estate's Venetian-style canal.

Other dissolves required planning the shot as part of the set design. Late in the film, at the Florida picnic where Kane slaps Susan, the scene ends with a close-up of Susan looking hatefully at Kane. When the shot of Susan dissolves to a stained-glass window at Xanadu, the close-up of Susan's left eye dissolves to a stained-glass eye in the window.

Only a few of the dissolves in *Citizen Kane* were created using the traditional fade-out/fade-in that in 1940 were prepared in an optical printer during post-production. For many scenes, increasing and decreasing the lighting on the set helped to shift the action from shot to shot. For several transitions in *Citizen Kane,* Toland said, "the background dissolves from one scene to the next shortly before the players in the foreground are dissolved. This was accomplished rather simply with two light-dimming outfits, one for the actors and one for the set.

"The dissolve is begun by dimming the lights on the background, eventually fading it out entirely," said Toland. "Then the lights on the people are dimmed to produce a fade-out on them. The fade-in is made the same way, fading in the set lights first, then the lights for the people."

Indeed, this dissolve-with-lights is managed so gracefully that it is almost invisible in some shots as they dissolve from one scene to the next. Note, for example, when Bernstein is talking with Thompson about Leland being "with Mr. Kane and me the first day Mr. Kane took over the *Inquirer*," that the lights on Bernstein don't fade out completely until the dissolve to the *Inquirer* building is almost complete.

The dissolve-with-lights is particularly effective in bridging two scenes involving Dorothy Comingore as Susan Alexander, as Susan sits in the El Rancho nightclub and tells Thompson about her singing career. As the scene ends, all of the lighting in the nightclub slowly dims except the light on Dorothy Comingore, and the shot dissolves to Kane's New York City apartment as Susan rehearses her singing with Signor Matiste and a pianist. As the dissolve continues into the apartment, the sequence of lighting is reversed: the lights first illuminate the background in the apartment, and only when the apartment is fully lit do lights come up on the three characters in the foreground of the shot.

"We actually dimmed down lights on the stage—leaving lit the one key thing you wanted to see longer—and brought up the lights the same way for the incoming scene," Welles said. "In other words, if the last thing you want to see is Susan, that's the last thing you see, because all the other lights are fading out around her by dimmer, just as you would do it in the theater."

This shift between two scenes was also complemented by a subtle musical link: while Susan talked to Thompson, the piano off camera at the nightclub had been playing "In a Mizz," the song that later would be played at Kane's picnic in the Everglades. As the lighting begins to darken, the tune in the nightclub quietly changes to the piano music by Gioachino Rossini for Susan's attempt to sing an aria that is featured in the next scene.

Earlier in the film, a change of lighting—this one abrupt—was combined with a dissolve when Leland, as an old man, reminisces with Thompson about Susan. Leland describes the night Kane and Susan met, then concludes his comment by saying, "That first night, according to Charlie, all she had was a toothache." As Leland says "toothache," the lighting on him is cut, his silhouette lingering on-screen as the scene dissolves to the New York street where Susan and Kane first encounter each other after Kane is splashed with mud.

The shot of Leland talking about Susan begins a sequence in *Citizen Kane* that illustrates how Toland used a catalog of filmmaking techniques—dissolves, dialogue bridges, sound, special effects, and props—to create a seamless flow of cinematic storytelling. The result: a twenty-seven-minute series of scenes that depicts Kane's rise and downfall in politics in the events that surrounded the New York gubernatorial election of 1916.

Susan, who is cured of a toothache by Kane's good-natured antics, is encouraged by the publisher to sing an operatic aria, and she plays an old upright piano in her dingy boardinghouse while Kane listens. The scene dissolves to Kane still listening to Susan singing and playing the same music. Both actors are in about the same positions on-screen, but they are now in a different home that is more lavish. Susan is playing a grand piano, and she is gracefully dressed. This is clearly no boardinghouse; this is Susan's new home—certainly paid for by Kane.

As Susan finishes her performance, she turns to Kane, and he applauds. The sound of Kane clapping for Susan continues into the next scene at a backstreet rally, where the clapping is for Jed Leland campaigning for Kane. Leland describes Kane's merits as a candidate, saying that Kane was the candidate "who entered upon this campaign—"

"With one purpose only," roars Kane in the next scene, which has cut to Madison Square Garden at the climax of his campaign. In only a few seconds of film, Toland and Welles showed the progress of the campaign from a modest grassroots effort to power politics on a massive scale.

Following the speech, Kane and his wife, Emily, are blackmailed into visiting Susan's apartment, where "Boss" Jim W. Gettys tries to force Kane from the campaign. When Kane refuses to withdraw, Gettys and Emily leave, and the scene ends with a shot of the front door of Susan's apartment. The shot of the apartment door freezes and becomes a photograph on the front page of the *Chronicle*, chief competitor to Kane's *Inquirer*, below the headline CANDIDATE KANE CAUGHT IN LOVE NEST WITH "SINGER."

A newsboy offers a copy of the *Chronicle* to Jed Leland, who refuses it as he walks through the swinging double doors of a saloon. The clatter of the saloon doors melds into the roar of the printing presses at the *Inquirer* the night of the election, where Bernstein is forced to choose between two potential headlines for the late evening election edition: KANE ELECTED or FRAUD AT POLLS. Bernstein has no choice: he chooses the second headline.

The shot of the FRAUD AT POLLS headline in the pressroom dissolves to a copy of the actual newspaper a few hours later, already discarded and lying on the muddy cobblestones in front of the *Inquirer* office. (Even in defeat, Kane papers have no credibility; in addition to FRAUD AT POLLS, the subhead on the paper in the mud reads, "Ballot Box Stuffing Robs Kane in Race for Governor's Seat.") Leland, now drunk, steps past the tattered newspaper and into the building to confront Kane in their postelection argument—the entire four-minute, twenty-second confrontation orchestrated in three shots.

After the argument, the next shot shows the headline KANE MARRIES SINGER, which dissolves to the New Jersey courthouse where Kane and Susan are married. They drive off on their honeymoon, with Kane telling reporters that it "won't be necessary" to build an opera house for Susan to get the opportunity to perform. The shot then dissolves to another headline: KANE BUILDS OPERA HOUSE.

The background music and singing as the headline is shown carries over to Susan frantically preparing for her operatic debut. After a disastrous first performance, the action continues in the newsroom of the *Chicago Inquirer,* where Kane discovers Leland, passed out in a drunken binge after trying to write a bad review of Susan's acting (others have already written enthusiastic reviews of her singing). Kane finishes the negative review for Leland and then fires his former friend. As Leland walks out of the *Inquirer* for the last time, the shot dissolves back to Leland as an old man, as he concludes his recollections with Kane's image lingering in the top right side of the frame.

Within this sequence are more examples of the careful planning of continuity and seamlessness: the scenes described earlier of Susan in the mirror; and, in Kane's campaign speech sequence, pops of photographers' flash powder help bridge one scene to the next. Subtle audio cues link scenes as well: after Gettys and Emily depart Susan's apartment building and the doorway shot freezes into the *Chronicle*'s photograph, the newsboy's voice shouting, "Extra, read all about it!" begins before the shot freezes.

To provide the setting Toland required for his deep-focus photography, Ferguson needed to create deep sets. Each set as eventually constructed provided opportunities for deep focus—but that depth was not always shown in the original construction planning. The sketches for several sets originally showed single rooms; as the visual plan evolved and Toland's plans for deep focus began to gel, Ferguson expanded many of the designs into deeper, more complex structures to accommodate Toland's needs for greater depth of field and to increase realism and visual interest.

For example, in the original designs for Susan Alexander's second apartment, the plans showed one room. In the final set as modified to accommodate Toland's photography, Ferguson's production team deepened the apartment into two rooms: the front room where Susan sings at the piano while Kane listens is complemented by the entrance to a detailed bedroom at the rear.

Likewise, the breakfast room where the marriage of Kane and Emily deteriorates was originally designed as a single room. As constructed, the set extends to the outside patio, with a fountain and view of neighboring buildings. Ferguson even used a table setting to add depth: for the final shot of the sequence, the front of the table is covered with a cloth edged with transparent lace panels. But on the back side of the table, the cloth does not hang down; as a result, the background windows and shadows are visible through the lace.

Brief segments were also planned with the same thorough attention to depth. For the film's final scene, in which Paul Stewart as Raymond the butler directs workmen while they burn Kane's mementos, Ferguson created a separate room in the background, also filled with junk, that is behind the furnace and visually separated from the front of the set by a thick stone archway. Raymond, looking bored while he smokes and chews gum at the same time, stands in this back area to supervise the incineration. The back room is visible for only seven seconds, but Stewart's position deep into the set and the entrance of two workmen carrying junk from the back create additional depth and add yet another realistic visual element with impact to what in other films might have been a routine shot.

Fragments of sets were also created with depth in mind. Near the beginning of the film, when Thatcher is dictating a letter to Kane and describing his concerns about Kane assuming his fortune on his approaching twenty-fifth birthday, the shot begins with Thatcher standing in front of a window. The window could have been designed with a simple curtain over it. Instead, Ferguson created a window and background with multiple layers: first the open curtains, then the window (frosted with ice), the edge of the building, a cast-iron fence covered with vines, and a backdrop showing the buildings across the street.

Toland's praise for Ferguson matched his enthusiasm for working with Welles, and the cinematographer made special note of the art director's budget sense.

"His camera-wise designing of the settings not only made it possible to obtain many of the effects Welles and I sought," Toland said of Ferguson, "but also made possible the truly remarkable achievement of building the production's sets for about $60,000, yet gave us sets which look on the screen like a much larger expenditure."

The low cost of sets and decorations for *Citizen Kane* remains one of the more remarkable achievements of the film's production. Careful and detailed planning, not big budgets, was the key. In fact, the budget pressure and resulting cost-conscious planning actually contributed to the visual style of Production #281 by forcing Toland, Ferguson, and Welles to create imaginative visual options that they would not have been required to employ at other, more lavishly funded studios.

One part of the solution to the budget problem was ingeniously simple: several of the larger sets, such as the Great Hall of Xanadu and the reading room at the Thatcher Library, were built in a deliberately stark but striking style. Small sets, such as Susan's room at Xanadu, were packed with props, wallpaper, and structural details for the walls and ceilings that added visual interest and authenticity at a low cost.

Beyond the often discussed ceilings, Ferguson's set designs—achieved in conjunction with set decoration department head Darrell Silvera and his staff—are notable for the extraordinary level of detail and realism that filled every frame of the film. The sets were crammed with paintings, period furniture, and personal mementos—far more props than could be identified in a single viewing—but which reinforce their exceptional realism and visual interest.

Most of the props were plucked from the RKO storehouse or were commonly available and inexpensive personal accessories: mirrors, flowers, cosmetics, photographs, dining utensils, and wallpaper. Even the most inconsequential items were included, such as an atomizer—at the ready to soothe Susan's throat but not used during her rehearsal with Signor Matiste—that can be seen sitting on a pile of sheet music on the piano. Look at any of the small sets in *Citizen Kane*: they are successful because of the attention to detail that created an extremely realistic and visually interesting look, without breaking the budget. The costs for props and accessories in *Citizen Kane*, even by the standards of penny-pinching RKO, were very low; charges for all props and draperies used in the film totaled less than $30,000.

(Silvera had professional experience that may have been useful to the project: he had been involved in decorating the massive beach house in Santa Monica belonging to Marion Davies, mistress to newspaper publisher William Randolph Hearst.)

A good example of this high level of detail is Susan's second apartment, where she sings for Kane. The room is opulent, with folded draperies, a clock, artwork, ornate wallpaper, pottery, rugs, plants, stuffed animals, wood inlay, statues, lamps, and a grand piano. The bedroom in the background was included solely to add depth to the set; in the film, only a glimpse of the bed and the wall behind it is visible. However, reference photographs of Susan's bedroom show that this background area was actually a full room that was completely decorated, including furniture and fixtures that were entirely out of view.

(On this set, and almost all others in the film, Ferguson and Silvera also created the illusion of width in addition to depth: props near the sides of the frame deliberately extend to the right or the left outside of camera range, giving the impression of a wider room.)

Some of the smaller sets were successfully assembled solely with inexpensive detailing—and no structure at all. For instance, in the tent at the Everglades picnic where Kane slaps Susan, the *entire* set is composed of a thick curtain, a typewriter with stand, two lamps, a chair for Kane, a floor bed for Susan, a wardrobe, a trunk, a few scattered books, and side tables (another set enhanced by the added illusion of width produced with furnishings that extend out of the camera frame). The furnishings came from existing stock at RKO or cost next to nothing to purchase, but the set looks like exactly what it is supposed to be: the lush home away from home for a millionaire on a picnic.

For one of the larger sets that was elaborate and costly, the expense was justified by using the space to serve multiple functions: the broad and intricate newsroom for the *New York Inquirer*, with its period furniture and decorated pillars, was one of the priciest sets constructed for *Citizen Kane*. Rather than create additional locations for the *Inquirer* staff party and the Kane election headquarters, those scenes were set in the newsroom. In total, almost 16 minutes of the 119 minutes in the final version of *Citizen Kane* were filmed on this single set.

In the *Chicago Inquirer* newsroom that was used for the scenes of Jed Leland's firing after Susan's opera debut, the mood and look was much different than the New York office, because it represents a different time in the publisher's life. While the *New York Inquirer* is bright and busy at the beginning of the Kane's career, the Chicago office is dark and forbidding while Kane's life and values begin their slow decline. The *Chicago Inquirer* set was constructed with the walls pushed back from the main space and painted heavy gray, so when Kane strides across the newsroom to confront Jed Leland, much of the set is seemingly surrounded by a dark abyss.

With almost no decoration on the background walls, creating an authentic look for the newsroom was achieved primarily by placing the trappings of the journalism trade on top of desks and file cabinets. The set is filled with the mess that was typical of pre-computer newsrooms everywhere: scattered paper, propped-open books, ashtrays, inkwells, card files, typewriters, telephones, and trash.

At the other extreme among the large sets, the reading room at the Thatcher Library, where Thompson reviews the banker's memoirs for his recollections about Kane, was a model of minimalist design—and low cost. Visual impact was produced with simplicity and drama: the entire interior of the library reading room comprises a painting of Thatcher, a backdrop painted to look like stone blocks, a wall vault, a heavy door, a painted floor, a table and chair, and a massive shaft of light blazing in from an unseen window (the window is "visible" because the frame shows up in the shadow cast on the table).

And then there was the biggest set of all: the surrealistic hugeness of the Xanadu estate. "The literally incredible domain of Charles Foster Kane" is implied with great effectiveness in several scenes that show overviews of the grounds, but the sheer size inside is evident in only one interior set: the Great Hall of Xanadu, with its colossal staircase and walk-in fireplace.

Other than the Great Hall, only a model of Xanadu or small rooms or sections are seen, such as Kane's room, Susan's room and the doorways outside, the terrace (with its screeching cockatoo), the walkway above the main staircase, the hall of mirrors, and the furnace room where Rosebud burns. The size and scope of the estate are suggested by photographs in the newsreel, models, special effects, and structural elements, such as the textures of the three type of fences around the Xanadu grounds—chain link, woven wire, and the grim cast iron of the main gate—shown at the beginning of the film (the chain link and cast iron are also shown at the end).

The most stylized (and thrifty) shot designed to suggest Xanadu's size shows Susan leaving Kane, and she walks out of his life down a seemingly endless Xanadu corridor. In fact, the "corridor" is two doorways each built into a portion of a wall. The wall sections and doors, set fifteen feet apart on a dark stage, simulated the corridor, with the emptiness of black in the background. When, a few minutes later, Raymond the butler looks down the hallway to see Kane framed in Susan's doorway, the shot was a special effect.

However, it was clear from the earliest planning that a truly formidable set was needed to represent the Great Hall, controlling expenses wherever possible. The Great Hall, too, is an example of set-building ingenuity, created with a combination of Ferguson's thoughtful, economical design and Toland's camera mastery to give height, depth, and unique visual interest to the huge structure.

Constructed on RKO's mammoth Stage 10—part of a complex of four stages in one huge building that could be opened to include a combination of Stages 7, 8, 9, and 10, creating a maximum space almost 500 feet long and 140 feet wide—the Great Hall does indeed include real wall details, a massive balcony, the stairway, and huge statues. But many of the elements of the Great Hall's structure came from a variety of previous RKO productions, conveniently creating a mix of designs that mesh perfectly with the idea of Kane patching together his home from pieces gathered from structures around the world (as one of the reporters at Xanadu says, "There's a Burmese temple and three Spanish ceilings down the hall"). The only elements of the structure of the Great Hall that were new for *Citizen Kane* were the fireplace, one of the door treatments, and the stairway.

Some expenses for decorating the Great Hall were minimized with the simplest of treatments. For example, on the walkway at Xanadu above the staircase—where Raymond the butler tells Kane that Susan is packing to leave—the floor was constructed out of heavy lumber planks—not the expensive glossy flooring used in the Great Hall below. To enrich the 23-second walkway scene with minimal cost, the designers simply covered the floor with overlapping Persian rugs.

In such a massive set piece as the Great Hall, the cavernous Gothic gloom was created not with detail, but primarily with large, shadowy spaces. Toland lit the set so that hard shadows would fall on the walls and sculptures. To produce the illusion of depth, Toland and Ferguson used the camera's power of suggestion by hanging rolls of black velvet in background corners and through doorways that photographed as impenetrable voids, but with light—no identifiable source—flowing out from them on the floor to suggest depth. Later, when Xanadu is shown in daylight as reporters photograph the leftovers of Kane's life, high stacks of boxes conveniently block those spaces that would, in a real building, lead to other rooms and hallways.

The statues in Xanadu were full-size, but not real; they were replicas gathered from existing studio stock, rented, or fabricated from plaster in the RKO workshops. Several of the statues—especially the Venus seen from the back while a reporter talks about "a lot of money to pay for a dame without a head"—were meticulously scratched and gouged to simulate age; the gouges look like chips broken out of real marble. (More than a half century after *Citizen Kane,* several of the larger statues and crated items sat in storerooms at the Culver Studios, looking as out of place there as they did in Kane's Xanadu, but with the added gleam of each being worth a small fortune on the Hollywood collectibles market when they went to auction.)

The illusion of the Great Hall's size was made more impressive in mid-October, when Ferguson increased the height of the walls to show more of the hall when Kane is walking across the set while Susan plays with her jigsaw puzzles—a $480 expense that could be justified only by eliminating the costs for special effects that would have been required to optically enlarge the set in postproduction (apparently, effects were not always a budget saver). And Ferguson also amplified the immense, sterile look by *not* including furnishings. In the first scene of Xanadu—when Susan says she's lonely and wants to visit New York— the only furniture in the scene is Susan's table and chair; Ferguson does not even include a carpet on the dark polished floor. Later, for Xanadu during the argument about Kane's demand for a picnic, Ferguson has added furniture, but only the barest living room setup: three rugs, a couch, two chairs, and a table.

Later in production, manipulating the sound in the Great Hall would add to the sense of large size: all of the dialogue spoken in the Great Hall was enhanced with echo.

For Ferguson, the goal of planning and building the Great Hall was to create a barren, nightmarish vision as remote as possible from Susan's storybook dreams ("You always said you wanted to live in a palace," Kane reminds her). In partnership with Toland, he succeeded.

"We can make a foreground piece, and background piece, and imaginative lighting suggest a great deal more on the screen than actually exists on the stage," Ferguson said.

Ferguson's work was celebrated in 2003, when his image sketching a set was chosen to represent art design on a thirty-seven-cent U.S. postage stamp in the "American Filmmaking Behind the Scenes" series.

The sets for Production #281 also included subtle details that suggest the passage of time, a requirement of the original visual plan developed by Welles, Toland, and Ferguson. For instance, in Susan Alexander's boardinghouse room—while Susan laughs at Kane wiggling his ears—on the left corner of her dressing table viewers can see the ill-fated snow globe that would later survive Kane's destruction of Susan's room at Xanadu and inspire Kane to remember Rosebud. The snow globe props up a photo of a child, a portrait probably intended to show Susan as a little girl—a decorative tidbit that suggests the importance of youth to Susan, a trait that she and Kane will never know they share.

Citizen Kane was the second RKO picture in production during 1940 that featured a snow globe. In *Kitty Foyle*, starring Ginger Rogers, Foyle's father dropped a snow globe as he died. In *Kitty Foyle*, however, the snow globe did not shatter. Both snow globes were fabricated in the RKO prop shop.

Props and visuals were also used to create visual bridges between unrelated scenes far apart in the film—connections that are almost unnoticeable except after multiple viewings. For instance, halfway through the film, outside Madison Square Garden after Kane's campaign speech, a photographer snaps a photo of Kane holding his son, with wife Emily alongside. Viewers would think nothing of a photo being taken, except that the image taken in that scene had already appeared in the film: early in the newsreel, the photo is shown as a newspaper clip that illustrates the narration about the death of Emily and the boy in an auto accident.

Much later, at Xanadu, in the closing moments of the film, a reporter played by Arthur O'Connell can be seen in a light-colored suit, for no particular reason carrying a large covered basket, which after a few moments he then sets aside. It is the same basket that was one of Kane's original belongings on his first day at the *Inquirer*, first shown on the front of the wagon that drives up to the building and then a few minutes later on the floor of Kane's office.

In Susan's second apartment, set decorators continued the focus on her childhood. Amid the luxury of the Kane-acquired apartment, viewers can see a fancy doll in the center of her bed. A different doll would reinforce this theme in Susan's later life: in her room at Xanadu—before Kane destroys it—is a large doll sitting in the center of her bed, just as in her second apartment; the doll dominates the foreground as Susan is saying good-bye to Kane. That doll later shows up, ready for burning, in the furnace room, in a box of castoffs next to Rosebud, and is being held in the arms of a creepy stuffed monkey. (The monkey had been one of Susan's treasures that sat on a low shelf in the background of her room at Xanadu. It is barely visible except in still photos, but was one of the last items knocked to the floor by Kane about ten seconds before his destructive fury ends.)

On an end table in Susan's second apartment, next to Kane as he sits cozily in a large rattan chair and listens to her hapless singing, stands a foot-high sculpture that is almost identical to the larger-than-life-size statue in Xanadu on the left side of the fireplace while Susan argues with Kane about forcing their guests to go on a picnic in the Everglades.

In the final moments of the film, as Toland's astounding crane shot travels over the fabulous antiques and worthless mementos from Kane's life, the set is crammed with packing crates gathered at the studio as well as from Los Angeles–area junkyards and fruit stands by Silvera's staff of propmen. In the shot, the camera identifies several items that have been seen before—one of them the ornate metal bed frame that Kane brought with him on his first day as publisher of the *Inquirer*. Next to Rosebud on the junk pile is a tattered bundle of decaying newspapers lying on its side, well aged to show the passage of the years, with other bundles like it scattered among the boxes. Viewers cannot see the front of the bundle, but it is without doubt intended to be a stack of *Inquirer*s with Kane's "Declaration of Principles" emblazoned across the front—the same edition that had appeared in a mountain of newsprint early in the film.

Many of the props created specifically for the production include small, nearly invisible details. When Kane and Susan Alexander are married at Trenton Town Hall, a photographer fighting through the crowd of reporters carries a box camera with the word *Inquirer* stenciled across the front; only the closest examination of still photos shot during production reveals such tiny details. Other hard-to-see details offered insight into the personality of a character; viewers never had the opportunity to spot them all. For instance, in the bedroom of the psychologically bruised Susan at Xanadu are no less than nine photographs of her, on the walls and in standing frames in every corner.

Newspapers are featured so prominently in the film that they are practically a character in the production. All of the newspapers in *Citizen Kane* are fabricated props and include headlines, text, and other features created as if for real newspapers. Reporter Elmore Draper "Ed" Blake was hired for $100 a week to create news pages and articles that would appear in the prop newspapers. The papers were produced by Earl Hays Press (EHP), a printer that creates many specialty printing products for movies and television, including individual copies of newspapers.

EHP, in 1941 with offices a half mile from RKO and now twenty minutes north in Sun Valley, printed dozens of individual copies of newspapers from fictional publishers across the United States and (for Kane's death headlines) overseas. Fabricated newspapers—actually the cover page wrapped around a real newspaper—appear throughout *Citizen Kane*, including the *Inquirer* that Kane reads and the *Chronicle* that Emily reads while they ignore each other in the final shot of the breakfast table montage; the catastrophic *Chronicle* front page that trumpeted CANDIDATE KANE CAUGHT IN LOVE NEST WITH "SINGER"; and five front pages of editions of the *Inquirer* in Washington, San Francisco, Detroit, and New York that feature Susan's opera "triumphs." (Blake created at least one headline with a double meaning: after Susan's horrific opera debut, the headline on the *Detroit Inquirer* read, DETROIT HAS "SELL OUT" FOR SUSAN AL-EXANDER.) EHP also printed the thousands of copies of Kane's first edition of the *New York Inquirer* that included his "Declaration of Principles" on the front page.

The content of the newspapers was intensely detailed, even though most of it could not be read on-screen. On Kane's first night at the *Inquirer,* for instance, the story in the *Chronicle* that Kane sees involving a "Mrs. Silverstone," which is shown on-screen upside down for only an instant and is readable only in photos of the scene, has a banner headline, written in the style of 1890s newspapers, which reads:

BROOKLYN WOMAN MISSING!
Police Comb City for Mrs. Silverstone
Great Anxiety

For the montage of newspapers that show the coverage of Kane's death in the *News on the March* newsreel, Blake wrote articles and headlines that reflected the broad range of opinion about the publisher, each of which flashes by in fractions of a second: on the cover of Kane's own *Inquirer,* the banner headline reports, CHARLES FOSTER KANE DIES AFTER LIFETIME OF SERVICE, while a subhead states, "Entire Nation Mourns Great Publisher as Outstanding American," and a photo caption reads, "Finds Place in U.S. Hall of Fame."

However, on the cover of the rival *Chronicle,* the headline simply states, C. F. KANE DIES AT XANADU ESTATE, with the callous subhead "Death of Publisher Finds Few Who Will Mourn for Him." Much harsher is the *Chicago Globe,* which below its banner headline, DEATH CALLS PUBLISHER CHARLES KANE, features a subhead, "Stormy Career Ends for U.S. Fascist No. 1."

The *Minneapolis Record Herald,* which must been have a Kane newspaper, is kinder and states, KANE, SPONSOR OF DEMOCRACY, DIES, with a subhead: "Publisher Gave Life to Nation's Service During Long Career." The *Detroit Star* reports, KANE, LEADER OF NEWS WORLD, CALLED BY DEATH AT XANADU, with a photo caption: "Was Master of Destiny."

The *El Paso Journal* writes, END COMES FOR CHARLES FOSTER KANE, with a subhead: "Editor Who Instigated 'War for Profit' Is Beaten by Death." The *Journal* may have summed up the last half of Kane's life with a smaller third headline: "Loss of Friends, Wives and Prestige Believed to Have Hastened End of Editor Who Built Great News Empire."

For foreign newspapers, Blake's coverage of Kane's death was also translated into several languages by contracted consultants: Ed Sejin wrote the Chinese version for $11.50, Alex Davidoff translated the material into Russian for $25, and C. Margetis created the Greek front page for $10.

Ten years after *Citizen Kane,* life unintentionally imitated art when William Randolph Hearst died on August 14, 1951. Coverage of Hearst's death in *News of the Day,* the newsreel series produced by the Hearst Corporation, showed Hearst newspapers, all with extravagant banner headlines—in some cases painted across more than half of the front page, just as Kane newspapers announced the fictional publisher's death in *News on the March.* For Hearst, competition newspapers played the story more responsibly—and much less lavishly. For example, while Hearst's *Los Angeles Examiner* blared, W. R. HEARST'S DEATH MOURNED BY NATION, with the caption on a huge photo that read, "A Great American," *The New York Times'* modest one-column headline read simply, WILLIAM RANDOLPH HEARST DIES AT 88 IN CALIFORNIA.

By the late summer of 1940, Welles was immersed in production of *Citizen Kane,* but he was already thinking ahead to his next projects. He explored several ideas from classic literature or biography, including *The Master of Ballantrae, The Life of Alexandre Dumas,* and *Jane Eyre;* none of these projects materialized, but later he would star in the 1944 production of *Jane Eyre* for 20th Century-Fox as an actor-for-hire. He also considered a performance of his production of *Julius Caesar* for NBC through a new medium—television, which was then in its infancy.

Welles had also pondered making a film with perhaps the ultimate leading role: a biopic on the life of Christ—with Welles, of course, as the star. Much later, he would tell director Peter Bogdanovich that the story he envisioned would have no original dialogue—"every word from the Bible"—and possibly set in the 1890s in a folk-western theme. In late August, Welles wrote to the religious leadership of many denominations to probe their views on the project (the idea of the western theme was perhaps wisely absent from his correspondence).

"It seems to me that the story of Christ, told without recourse to theatrical sentimentality or to Hollywood overtones—told simply in the spirit of a folk passion play—might accomplish much in these times," Welles said.

Welles sent each cleric near identical letters, with all but one ending with "You are the first to hear" of the project. To Fulton Sheen, a nationally known Catholic bishop who hosted his own network radio program, Welles wrote he was "the *very* first to hear."

The idea of a Christ biopic never got beyond the inquiry stage. But surprisingly, given Welles' reputation for the spectacular, most of the clerics were enthusiastic about his proposal. "You are to be most heartily complimented in your resolve to handle this tremendous theme," said Sheen.

Only Ernest Millington of the Northern Baptist Convention expressed strong opposition to the project, indicting all of Hollywood in the process.

"My opinion of your proposition is definitely and I think unchangeably unfavorable," sniffed Millington. "A picture you speak of would require a delicacy of taste, and a depth of understanding, which are not ordinarily associated with the motion picture industry and its actors."

Through the fall, filming for Production #281 proceeded, and for the moment, at least, Welles was on a roll.

Bernard Herrmann, who received a copy of the script to use while composing the musical score, provided an enthusiastic endorsement of the production. "Script exciting and powerful," Herrmann wired to Welles. "Tremendously gripping . . . at all times one feels this was a real man."

Robert Wise, who as the editor assigned to the production regularly viewed the previous day's footage with Welles, said, "We could see from the rushes coming in day after day that Orson was indeed getting something very special."

In September, associate producer Richard Baer told Arnold Weissberger that "we have just about completed half of the picture with startling good results. We are about on schedule and very close to our budget.

"Orson doesn't say much," said Baer, "but I feel that he is terribly enthusiastic about the results and is really crossing his fingers about the outcome. Everything is functioning smoothly and there is nothing but an optimistic attitude in the air."

That view, incredibly enough, was also shared by some in senior RKO management, including J. J. Nolan, West Coast head of studio operations, when he saw the first month's worth of assembled footage on September 5.

"I couldn't leave for New York today without again telling you that I was simply thrilled last night after viewing your picture," Nolan wrote to Welles, "and again I repeat that I think it is sensational."

The enthusiasm continued. In October, publicist Herb Drake reported to Welles that "as of September 30, there have been 18 major wire service feature stories on you in *Citizen Kane*. . . . According to the best advice I can get from my competitors, this is roughly six times more than any other star or production ever had in a two-month period."

Even Welles' attorney, the ever-cautious Arnold Weissberger, was feeling upbeat.

"There is a slowly rising buzz of anticipation in New York for the arrival of *Citizen Kane*," Weissberger told Welles in November. "The reports about it circulating in from different channels are all good."

GIGGLING LIKE SCHOOLBOYS

Each time, he threw himself into the action with a fervor
I had never seen in him before. It was absolutely electric; you felt
as if you were in the presence of a man coming apart.
—WILLIAM ALLAND, DESCRIBING ORSON WELLES' ACTING
IN THE SCENE WHEN HE DESTROYS SUSAN ALEXANDER'S BEDROOM

As filming for Production #281 continued through the fall of 1940, Gregg To-land showed he was as adept as Ferguson at economizing—and identifying cost-cutting methods that complemented the filmmaking. In fact, some of the most effective scenes in *Citizen Kane* demonstrate budget savings as well as memorable cinematography.

The shrewd use of extras and sly camera placement implied a cast of thou-sands but actually included only a handful of actors in the most elaborate shots. Scenes that seem to feature hundreds or thousands of people were accomplished by using swirls of movement by the extras, carefully chosen camera angles, spe-cial effects, or combinations of all three. Look carefully at the shots of Kane's campaign speech and the aftermath—Kane on the podium, the massive crowd at Madison Square Garden, wildly applauding spectators, Kane's wife and son in the audience, the flurry of action outside the auditorium—and what seems like masses of spectators in a whirlwind of action is really only three to thirty players in any *individual* scene. The huge "audience" at the rally is actually a painting, pricked with holes so light would shine through and create the illusion of motion in the "crowd."

During Susan Alexander's operatic debut as described by Leland, the screen seems filled with mobs of frenzied people from the opera production. The effect is achieved with the intricate choreography of actors rushing across the stage at different speeds in five different distances from the camera, some of whom were only a few feet from the lens and blacked out the shot as they moved. What appears to be hundreds of people filling the frame is actually about twenty; the resulting visual impact of small groups of actors produces a stylized look to the scene that is at least as effective as the more traditional teeming mobs.

RKO's background material on *Citizen Kane* reported that the picture included 28 principal players, 89 bit players, and 796 extras—a statement that implies the film includes scenes involving huge groups of performers. If accurate, those tallies represent the total number of bit players and extras used over the entire eleven-week shooting schedule. While Kane's party in the city room of the *Inquirer* features upward of 60 people (actors and dancers), no other single sequence in *Citizen Kane* includes more than 30 performers, and some of the "crowd shots" show as few as 5.

Another powerful example of Toland's artful yet cost-saving photographic technique is shown in the scene of Susan's devastating debut as she described it to Thompson. A Toland trademark was shooting directly into lights, a challenge to other cinematographers because lights would often show as a halo in a normal lens. But one of Toland's specialized plate inserts would fit into the lens, reduce reflections, and eliminate the halo—an ideal addition for filming the second flashback of Susan's opera premiere.

Welles wanted to show the scene from Susan's perspective, isolated on the stage in her debut. Toland photographed the scene from far behind Susan standing on the stage as she faces the audience while the curtain rises. The scene shows Susan, small and terrified, as she looks out at the abyss of the opera hall and its huge audience, with banks of spotlights shining directly into the camera.

However, the "audience" is not visible and is only suggested by the vast gray expanse and the banks of lights. By implying an audience—unseen and unsympathetic—Toland created a powerful image of Susan's fear and vulnerability; an actual audience was not necessary. So effective is Toland's technique in the filming of this scene that many viewers remember seeing the audience.

The most important result of using deep focus, extended sets, and deliberate staging was the freedom they provided to Welles and Toland to photograph actors from angles, distances, and positions much different from those used for most Hollywood motion pictures. With these tools, they created breakthroughs in the creative boundaries of filmmaking.

Toland's photographic techniques allowed the camera to record objects at a range of a few inches or more than one hundred feet in a single shot with equal sharpness, and Welles capitalized on Toland's methods by placing his performers not according to standard Hollywood practices, but wherever the action should take them.

Toland's plan produced scenes that were not merely inventive for innovation's sake, but powerful demonstrations of how imaginative staging could enhance the action and advance the story. The on-screen movement, combined with extremely long takes, created interesting visual options and also greatly enhanced the realism. As shot by Toland, characters move naturally, and the camera follows; viewers become intimate witnesses—not distant spectators—to all of the action in a scene. In *Citizen Kane,* Toland showed that the camera was an aid, and not a hindrance, to expression on film.

Deep focus helped Toland not only to create realism, but also to support Welles' goal of maintaining the theatrical style of the production. In most Hollywood films of the time, performers in indoor scenes typically moved across the screen, and not often between the front and the back or around the set, as in the theater (or in real life). In several major scenes in *Citizen Kane,* Welles wanted to use deep focus to allow his characters to enter from the rear of a scene, such as when Kane interrupts Susan's singing lesson from a door at the back of the set and walks slowly to the front to confront Signor Matiste.

Toland used these techniques not only to increase realism, but also to provide clarity and emphasis to key scenes by employing what he called "visual simplification."

"Instead of following the usual practice of cutting from a close-up to an 'insert' which explains or elaborates on the close-up, we made a single, straight shot, compressing the whole scene into a single composition," Toland said. "Where the idea is to show an actor reading something, we don't show a close-up of the actor and then follow it with a cut to the reading matter. We simply composed the shot with the actor's head on one side of the frame and the reading matter on the other."

Toland is referring to the scene in which Kane signs over control of his empire to Thatcher's bank during the Depression—a vivid illustration of his goal to simplify the visuals. As the scene begins, Bernstein, on the right side of the screen, reads aloud from the conditions of the agreement, his face inches from the camera. To the left, a few feet away, Thatcher sits across the table. Kane is out of view but soon appears on the right side of the screen.

When Kane walks into the scene while Bernstein reads, he paces toward the rear of the set, walking more than twenty feet from the camera before he turns, returns to the table, sits, and signs the document. The scene—which appears without a break—could have been filmed in the predictable Hollywood style, with cuts to Bernstein, then to Thatcher, then to Kane as each man speaks. Yet staged and filmed as a single, deep-focus shot in *Citizen Kane,* the scene becomes a realistic and intimate illustration of Kane's frustration and disappointment.

The most dramatic of these ultra-deep-focus scenes is the postelection argument between Kane and Leland. Kane's leg in the left corner of the frame next to the camera, the far side of the *Inquirer* newsroom more than fifty feet away, and all of the objects in between remain constantly in focus. Both actors wander across the *Inquirer* newsroom throughout the scene, at some points more than twenty feet from each other, at others only inches apart. One shot begins with the camera lens at floor level and Leland in the far right corner of the screen. What could have been a routine sequence of "over the shoulder" shots showing the actors in conversation instead became a realistic choreography of dialogue and movement that vastly increases the effectiveness of the scene.

Among Toland's favorite examples of his own photography in *Citizen Kane* was not an intensely dramatic scene, but rather a relatively simple sequence when the *Inquirer* staff members prepare to present a trophy to Kane on his return from Europe.

To film Bernstein reading the inscription on the trophy, Toland positioned the camera only sixteen inches from Everett Sloane's face. The trophy and Joseph Cotten are three feet from the camera, and ten other actors—all visible on-screen—surround the trophy at distances from two to ten feet away. Almost hidden by an actor's sleeve next to the handle of the trophy is the tiny figure of a messenger boy more than thirty feet from the camera, also in focus, who yells, "Here he comes!" immediately before Kane enters the room. Despite the extreme depth of the shot, Toland said, "the trophy was in such sharp focus that the audience was able to read the inscription from it."

Toland used this same technique of grouping faces on-screen in several films. One of those fondly remembered is a particularly charming scene in *The Bishop's Wife* that captured the rosy faces of the Robert Mitchell Boys Choir singing a Christmas hymn under the direction of angel Cary Grant.

However, one on-set observer thought that Toland's techniques would inhibit the cinematic storytelling. After Herman Mankiewicz made one of his few visits to the *Citizen Kane* sets, he told Mercury publicist Herbert Drake that the scenes at the El Rancho nightclub should be reshot—especially the lengthy shot of the drunken Susan Alexander struggling to stay conscious while Thompson calls Rawlston in New York to report that she is unwilling to talk.

"There are not enough standard movie conventions being observed," Herb Drake reported about Mankiewicz's reaction to the filming, "including too few close-ups and very little evidence of action. It is too much like a play, says Mr. M."

In spite of his concerns, Mankiewicz also said he thought the scenes were "magnificent," Drake told Welles. "However, if he says it is 'magnificent,'" Drake said, "I'm beginning to worry."

Mankiewicz's reaction as he watched the filming of this single continuous shot was not surprising. From the writer's perspective as a bystander on a film set, the scene—with little character motion and no camera movement at all—did indeed look like a staid theatrical production.

What Mankiewicz could not appreciate was the shot as Toland saw it when he looked through the viewfinder after days of preproduction planning and meticulous staging: the camera positioned to capture the scene inside the phone booth and through its windows into the nightclub; Thompson, in shadow in the foreground on the telephone, talking to Rawlston; Susan in the far background, brightly lit; and John the waiter, in between the two and visible through the glass in the booth's door when Thompson shuts it.

The scene that appeared to Mankiewicz, watching from the sidelines, to be "too much like a play" became on film one of dozens of sequences in *Citizen Kane* that illustrate the exciting and evolving visual possibilities for how the camera could help tell the story. The writer's concerns provide ample illustration of the gulf between the usual Hollywood filmmaking and the visual plan that Welles and Toland created for *Citizen Kane*.

Toland let nothing prevent his use of these techniques, not even the physical structure of the sets. To accommodate low-angle filming, several sets were constructed on elevated platforms. For example, to photograph at floor level on the set of the *Inquirer* office on Stage 11 at RKO in Culver City, Welles requested that the entire set be built on a platform, an $875 expense not anticipated in the early budget planning but approved August 12. (One of the elevated sets is visible in the trailer for *Citizen Kane:* when Ruth Warrick is introduced to viewers, she is shown sitting next to one of the platforms.)

As a result, to photograph some of the film's most dramatic sequences, Toland could position his camera below the floor of the set. Holes were sawed through the set to lower the camera enough to meet Welles' exacting demands; Warrick remembered Welles and Toland "giggling like schoolboys" as they planned the shots and the demolition. The elevated sets that Welles ordered for Stage 11 fell victim to the saw for the low angles needed for the postelection argument between Kane and Leland filmed on August 30 and later for Kane's destruction of Susan Alexander's room at Xanadu on October 22; for the latter scene, the hole was enlarged enough for two cameras that shot simultaneously during the extended takes of Kane's frenzy. (Welles recalled needing such a low angle for one shot that his crew cut through the concrete floor of the soundstage, but the production files show no record of this.)

Toland was not completely immersed in deep focus, economizing, and seamless photography during the production of *Citizen Kane*. His involvement in the production is equally memorable for the sheer imagination of all of the work: delicate close-ups, simulated handheld shots and "candid" footage for the newsreel, and countless other gems. Toland relished the challenge of Welles' approach, even with the hectic pace and the constant demands.

"I must admit," Toland lamented after he wrapped up *Citizen Kane*, "that working this way for 18 or 19 weeks tends to spoil one for more conventional conditions."

Welles never forgot Toland's role in the success of his first motion picture. Thirty years after the film was released, he was still singing Toland's praises.

"It's impossible to say how much I owe to Gregg," Welles recalled in 1971. "He was superb. He was the greatest gift that any director—young or old—could ever, ever have."

In most films, the director's name appears alone in the credits, while the cinematographer appears elsewhere. In *Citizen Kane*, sharing the same screen in the credits are the names of Orson Welles and Gregg Toland.

Not all of the scenes in *Citizen Kane* that seem to be shot with deep focus were actually filmed with that technique. One of the most compelling scenes in *Citizen Kane* that was long assumed to be a single deep-focus shot instead combined two exposures of the same strip of film.

To create Susan Alexander's attempted suicide, Welles and Toland planned the scene with three separate points to observe: in the foreground, only inches from the camera, Susan's medicine and spoon; in middle distance, Susan lying in bed, breathing weakly; and in the far background, the door, which Kane and the butler break through.

To film the scene, the exact length of the shot and the total frames running through the camera were calculated in advance. Then, with Susan and the background dark, the close-up of the medicine and the spoon was lit and filmed. Without moving the camera, the film was rewound back to the point when the scene started. Then, with the foreground dark and Susan and the door lit, the scene was filmed again.

So effective is the photography in Susan's suicide attempt that for many years most observers (including several critics who analyzed the shot) assumed the scene was a single take that had required complex lighting and extremely deep focus. It was not until more than three decades after *Citizen Kane* was produced that film scholars such as Robert Carringer, graduate student Donald Rea, and director Peter Bogdanovich resurrected the methods actually used to create this shot.

Some scenes required complex off-camera choreography to meet the intricate requirements of the staging. When planning the sequence of Mary Kane signing away the guardianship of her son to Thatcher's bank, Welles and Toland wanted to film the entire complex scene in two long, continuous shots. The scene as planned began with young Charles playing in the snow and photographed through the boardinghouse window. The camera would then pull back through the window to show the interior of the boardinghouse with Thatcher, Mary Kane, and Jim Kane inside discussing young Charles's fate while the boy is still seen through the window, playing outside. After Kane's mother signs the papers, the camera would then follow her across the floor as she goes to the window to call to her son.

Filming the one-minute, forty-five-second sequence required the perfect timing of camera movement, actors' performances, and cooperation from a breakaway trick table that was designed to snap into position as a camera dolly rolled back across the set. "It was," said Toland, "a complex mixture of art and mechanics."

The boardinghouse scenes were scheduled to be rehearsed and filmed beginning September 24. In take after take, the shot went awry: either the table failed when the actors performed perfectly, or the table worked but a performer flubbed a line. Four days of rehearsal and shooting were required before Welles and Toland were happy with the result of this single scene. However, the final shot used in the film is not perfect: as Agnes Moorehead walks toward the table and says, "it's going to be done exactly the way I've told Mr. Thatcher," a slight "clunk" can be heard as the camera dolly rolls back and the table moves into position. Eventually, eight days of rehearsal and shooting would be needed to film the six shots that constituted the entire boardinghouse sequence, delaying the production by two days; the sequence was completed October 4.

Driven by both the restrictions of the budget and the enthusiasm of their director, the crew experimented with many techniques that Welles needed to complete the visual plan for *Citizen Kane*.

The unusual sets presented intriguing technical challenges, especially for lighting. The plan for the lighting was complicated in part by the need to coordinate a "psychological look" throughout the production: the first half of the film, when Kane was young and idealistic, was brighter and cheerier; many scenes in the second half grew darker and more somber as Kane's family and values crumbled. (Although some analysts assumed that Welles' ideas for lighting were drawn from moodily lit 1920s German expressionist films such as *The Cabinet of Dr. Caligari* or *Nosferatu*, Welles said he had not seen any films from that period at the time he shot *Citizen Kane* and still had not four decades later, when he discussed the idea with director Peter Bogdanovich.)

The full ceilings on each set excluded using banks of powerful overhead lights, then a basic tool of film production. With the exception of an occasional spotlight, backlighting, or a small overhead fill light, the main illumination for *Citizen Kane* was provided by lights positioned on the floor of the stages—nearly all from the front or the sides of the set.

As Toland originally proposed in the planning meetings, gaffer William Mc-Clellan did indeed use the double-arc broadside lamps developed primarily to shoot Technicolor films as a basic lighting tool for *Citizen Kane*. Viewers can see the effects of these floor-positioned lamps by looking at the crisp lighting on faces in most scenes and at the long shadows across the ceilings and floors that appear as if shot outdoors with the sun low in the sky in early morning or late afternoon—patterns that also added visual interest to many scenes. However, lighting from the front was not always enough, and overhead lighting was sometimes used as a supplement; for example, at the party in the *Inquirer* newsroom celebrating the arrival of the "greatest newspaper staff in the world" that was poached from the *Chronicle*, the party table for the reporters was lit with long sets of small lights suspended under the ceiling.

Close-up lighting was handled with small spotlights. For example, when Kane and Susan Alexander chat in her boardinghouse room, her close-ups were lit by a small spot perched on a floor stand and positioned only a foot above Welles' head. Similarly, when Jed Leland and Bernstein talk about Kane at the party in the *Inquirer* newsroom, Cotten was lit by a lamp directly above the camera, only inches from his face.

For slightly broader shots between five and eight feet wide, Toland used rectangular mailbox-sized box lights mounted directly on the camera, either above or below the lens. For instance, he used one of these box lights mounted above the lens for the Colorado scenes of young Kane in the snow about to be taken away by Thatcher and below the lens to photograph Susan as she performs the closing scene of her operatic debut in *Salammbô* while lying with a pile of pillows. During the filming of this scene, on-set witnesses recalled seeing Toland trying to watch Dorothy Comingore's performance from as close as possible to the lens, contort himself under the camera, his body wrapped around the dolly.

In contrast with the direct light used in many shots, McClellan and Toland lit several scenes to create combinations of light and shadow on the performers that helped emphasize the impact of the dialogue. This use of light, shadow, and words together can be seen when Kane is in his office describing his "Declaration of Principles" to Leland and Bernstein during their first day at the *Inquirer*. As the scene starts, all three characters are shown in full light; when Kane walks across his office, he walks out of the light. Welles is shrouded in shadow as he reads his document, which emphasizes his voice, not his features, as he speaks.

After Susan's horrible debut, sitting on the floor surrounded by newspapers filled with devastating reviews, she screams at Kane that she is through with opera ("I'm the one that gets the razzberries!"). As Kane approaches Susan, his shadow overwhelms her; she is cast into darkness as he orders her, "You will continue with your singing."

In the film's closing scenes, most of the shots of reporters rummaging through Kane's Xanadu treasures are sharp contrasts of light and dark. Generally, the treasures are lit while the reporters are walking shadows or nearly invisible in the darkness. As Thompson takes a jigsaw puzzle from one of his colleagues, all of the characters in the scene are in deep shadow; only the puzzle is lit directly.

An inventive use of lighting makes an intentional on-screen appearance in *Citizen Kane.* For Kane's party in the city room of the *Inquirer,* which cele-brated the publisher's pirating of the *Chronicle*'s "Greatest Newspaper Staff in the World," functioning lights became part of the scene. To light the row of sixteen dancing girls, Toland used a twenty-foot-long bank of footlights lying on the floor between the actors and the performers.

From most angles, viewers can see the row of lights, and the crew did not attempt to hide them. They are make-believe props for Kane's party as well as real-life lighting for shooting the film. When Kane whistles to summon the band, he smoothly steps over the row of lights as they are activated. Later in the scene, the entire row of lights is visible on-screen, and they blaze directly into the camera (a Toland favorite again) while Kane is parading with the dancing girls during the singing of the "Charlie Kane" song.

Logistic problems such as the trick table, extended filming sessions required for complex scenes, and unpredictable personal circumstances all contributed to delays that slowly but steadily dragged Production #281 behind schedule. Set-backs began as soon as the shooting started. *Citizen Kane* fell one day behind during its first week of production because of the time-consuming setups and photography required for Kane's campaign speech. In mid-August, the lengthy sessions needed to shoot Susan's opera debut delayed production another two days. Illness and the mandatory breaks required after the all-night shoots of Cotten's scenes added another week's worth of delays to the "behind schedule" tally on the daily production reports.

On October 11—the day production was originally scheduled to end—Welles filmed Raymond the butler and Thompson on the staircase in the Great Hall of Xanadu, talking about Rosebud. By that time, production was two weeks behind schedule, and at least ten days' worth of key scenes remained, in-cluding virtually all of the shots set in the Great Hall. With catching up no longer possible, the question that remained was how much financial damage the delays would ultimately cause.

A Welles production, whether in a Broadway theater or a Hollywood studio, seemed to have certain prerequisites, one of them being accidental physical dam-age that Welles inflicted on himself—a slip, a gash, or, in one case, a fifteen-foot fall onto his chin through a trapdoor in the Mercury Theatre stage floor. A

Welles injury was a great relief to everyone on the Mercury staff. "We knew," William Alland said, "that a successful Welles production was almost always marked by Orson damaging himself."

Earlier in Welles' career, one accident involving another actor produced near tragic consequences. While directing and starring as Brutus in Mercury's production of *Julius Caesar,* Welles almost killed actor Joseph Holland during the assassination scene. Welles preferred to use a real knife—he liked the sound of the metal when it fell on the stage—and in a moment of colossal artistic misjudgment, he thought that maintaining a razor-sharp edge would add to the veracity of the scene. As a result, the knife he had used without incident to "stab" Holland in dozens of performances slipped cleanly and painlessly between Holland's ribs, the wound bleeding profusely on the stage. The play ended without the audience realizing what had occurred; Holland recovered without permanent damage.

During his work on *Citizen Kane,* Welles injured himself severely only once. On August 10, less than two weeks into production, Welles, in full costume, tripped while rehearsing Kane's confrontation with "Boss" Jim Gettys—the shot in which Kane runs down a staircase while screaming, "I'm going to send you to Sing Sing!" Welles fell heavily on his left ankle, chipping the bone.

It was a painful injury; Welles' assistant Kathryn Trosper, on the set that day, recalled Welles "was in a heap at the bottom of the stairs, howling with pain."

Instead of an ambulance, the crew called Welles' chauffeur, and Trosper accompanied Welles to the hospital in his limousine.

The day began to descend into drunken hijinks when Welles started to self-medicate with liberal doses of alcohol.

"He was drinking brandy out of a flask for the whole trip," Trosper said.

The ride was short, but the alcohol worked quickly. "It didn't take many shots to get him silly," Trosper said. By the time the limousine reached the emergency room, Welles was well along toward drunk—"not blind drunk," Trosper reported, "just sort of cute drunk."

At the hospital, a sozzled Welles was shuttled into a wheelchair and rolled to a room. Still in costume and makeup as a middle-aged Kane, Welles was a sight; drunk, perspiring, and in pain, his finely crafted makeup appliances began to peel off his face, "hanging down in strips," said Trosper. "He was truly frightful looking."

Trosper left Welles momentarily to sign the medical paperwork. When she returned, Welles was gone.

Welles had wheeled himself away on a rolling binge. "With a whoop he went lickety-split down the hallway in his wheelchair, scaring the hell out of people," Trosper said. "He crashed into a couple of patient rooms, yelled 'surprise!' and scared them half to death.

"Orson was pretty wild-eyed when I caught up with him," said Trosper. "I finally got him back in his room, and he was very happy."

Concerned that RKO might use the injury as an excuse to shut down the production (a possibility that was specifically described in his contract), Welles refused to slow down, even after a cast was applied to his foot. Fortunately, the injury occurred on a Saturday; with Sunday off, Welles rested briefly while the production schedule was quickly shuffled. The scenes originally scheduled for Monday, August 12—Kane's arrival at the *Chicago Inquirer* after Susan's operatic catastrophe—were postponed because the shot called for Welles to walk into the office and across the newsroom to find Jed Leland drunk and unconscious. Instead, Welles directed Joseph Cotten's first scenes of Leland appearing as an old man in the convalescent hospital, talking with Thompson about Kane.

For the next few days, Welles directed other characters or filmed scenes of himself while sitting (such as Kane's reactions while in the opera audience, listening to Susan's singing). While his ankle healed, Welles at first directed from a wheelchair. His recovery could be tracked by the assortment of rehabilitation equipment he wore as his ankle improved: first his foot was in a cast, then in a sock and bandage, then in a brace (which he wore on the set during the post-election confrontation between Kane and Leland on August 30), later in a sandal, and then in a shoe again.

On October 22, one day before principal photography ended, Welles was again injured, this time during an actual filmed scene. For Kane's destruction of Susan Alexander's bedroom at Xanadu, and with two cameras rolling, Welles, heavily made up and padded to appear at least sixty-five years old, destroyed most of the set with his bare hands, throwing suitcases, tearing quilts, ripping books from shelves, and breaking a large assortment of makeup and perfume bottles.

The attention to detail in Susan's room was extreme: Ferguson's crew used real perfume in its original bottles—Chanel No. 5 and Joy, among others. Their scents filled the air on the set in the path of Welles' destruction.

"Each time, he threw himself into the action with a fervor I had never seen in him before," Alland said. "It was absolutely electric; you felt as if you were in the presence of a man coming apart."

While shooting the scene, Welles slashed his left hand. "I was bleeding like a pig," he recalled.

The exact moment of the injury is not visible when viewing the scene; no blood can be seen. However, when Kane sees the snow globe and calms himself, Welles abruptly pulls his left hand out of camera view.

Welles' injury may not be visible on-screen, but his energy and anger are unmistakable.

"He literally went berserk," Alland said. "Everyone was holding their breath as Orson destroyed Susan's apartment. As the shot finished, he staggered off the set, and as he walked by me, he said, almost to himself, 'My God, I felt it—I really, really felt it.'"

On the set for the Xanadu furnace room at RKO in Culver City, one other accident was the unintentional result of production demands. On October 21, the *Citizen Kane* production team filmed extras as workmen in the Xanadu cellar, burning Kane's valueless personal mementos, while Paul Stewart as Raymond the butler delivered the film's final line, "Throw that junk in," before Rosebud is tossed on the flames.

Shooting the furnace sequence was a two-step exercise in creating fiery precision: first, to ensure that the extra tossed the sled into the right position at the front of the furnace so the word *Rosebud* could be seen as the camera tracked in; then, in a second shot, filming the front of the sled so the painted word *Rosebud* appeared clearly as the varnish boiled away in the flames.

"Each time, all of us were there," said Richard Wilson, "peering in to see if the word *Rosebud* would surface through the bubbles."

It wasn't long before the Culver City firefighters rushed onto Stage 7. Apparently, the flames had become so hot that the exhaust flue caught fire, and from a distance the studio appeared to be ablaze.

The intensity of this inferno varies greatly depending on the storyteller: descriptions range from a small fire inside the flue to a towering blaze that actually set the roof of the stage on fire. Regardless of its size, however, the firefighters were not taking chances with filmmakers. They remembered twenty-two months before, when David Selznick had filmed the burning of "Atlanta" for *Gone with the Wind*—actually unwanted sets on the 40 Acres back lot, including the main gate from *King Kong*. On December 10, 1938, fire crews watched the largest controlled fire in motion picture history roar hundreds of feet into the Culver City sky, knowing they would be helpless if the inferno burned out of control (a potential tragedy that fortunately did not occur).

The repeated attempts to film the furnace put RKO on alert. When retakes of the cellar scenes were filmed on November 22, the casting call sheet for the day stated tersely, "Firemen for cellar READY at 9 a.m."

Studio visitors who were fortunate enough to witness the filming of Production #281 marveled at the constant physical transformation of the Mercury players, as several of them aged as much as fifty years during the course of the film. The makeup was the product of Maurice Seiderman, whom Welles called "the best makeup man in the world."

"Maurice is an alchemist," said Welles. "Without that medieval Russian, the picture could never have been made."

During a career that would eventually span more than thirty years in Hollywood, Seiderman was not well-known like some of his counterparts at other motion picture studios, such as Ben Nye or the Westmore family. In fact, Seiderman received few screen credits during his career. But working over bubbling experiments in a tiny shop on RKO's back lot, Seiderman created some of the era's most astonishingly realistic makeup.

"No one held my hand on *Citizen Kane* and told me what to do," Seiderman said. "Orson realized that I understood the overall view of the picture, what he was attempting to do, and that I could handle it."

Concocting a combination of latex molds, traditional theatrical body paint, and specialized chemicals of his own creation, Seiderman aged the principal characters of *Citizen Kane* across the span of their adult lives—not merely adding superficial wrinkles, but transforming every aspect of the actors' physical appearance with specially designed wigs, neck wattles, body fat, crabbed hands, and an incredible variety of aged ears, noses, chins, and facial bags.

Seiderman had created scenery and worked in makeup for the theater before arriving in California in 1935. Becoming a studio makeup artist was a challenge, Seiderman recalled, because of difficulty being admitted to the union. However, by persisting, he was hired at RKO as a $25-a-week apprentice in the makeup department, assigned to "sweep up hair" but also finding time to experiment with his own concoctions for innovative makeup.

"I had a little corner all to myself," Seiderman said. "I had clay and my tools, and I would spend as much time as I could creatively."

When Welles visited the makeup department as part of his prowl of the studio departments, he noticed Seiderman in his corner and recognized that the apprentice might have the tools needed to age the players for the production.

"Orson saw me playing with noses and ears and he wanted to know if I could completely change his face," Seiderman said.

"When *Citizen Kane* came out in script form, Orson told all of us about the picture and said that the most important aspect was makeup," said Seiderman. "Straight makeups were done in the makeup department by staff, but all the trick stuff on the principal characters was my personal work; nobody else ever touched them—they could not have handled it."

Seiderman was one of the pioneers in the use of foam, rather than putty, to create facial appliances that simulated the wrinkled skin and sagging flesh of old age—devices that led Mercury publicist Herb Drake to call Seiderman "our wizard of the rubber."

Welles, Cotten, Coulouris, Comingore, and Sloane all aged during the film, and Seiderman built complex makeup systems for each actor. Starting with plaster busts that he cast of the performers, Seiderman added thin layers of modeling clay to create subtle changes.

"When I was satisfied with the appearance, I made models, and cast the clay pieces in plastic foam," Seiderman said. "The resulting plastic pieces would be added directly to the actor's face, forming a new surface: my sculptural image. This elaborate procedure was a completely new approach to makeup."

The requirements of Welles' transformation were the most complicated. Altering Welles' full physical appearance for the film started with a complete body cast, with Welles immobilized in coatings of hydrocolloid (a jelly substance) covered with plaster. While Welles lay frozen in plaster, Seiderman gleefully tortured his subject by reading from books the actor hated.

Then, using the molds, as well as a cast of Welles' head, Seiderman created the array of body pads and seventy-two assorted face pieces for Kane—among them sixteen different chins—as well as ears, cheeks, jowls, hairlines, and eye pouches that aged the publisher from twenty-five to seventy-eight years old in twenty-seven separate stages.

Welles did not wear a padded costume, which at the time was the standard method used to fatten a character. Instead, to simulate the thickening of the body in middle age and the girth of old age, Seiderman used the molds of Welles' body to create a rubber sculpture that the actor wore under his clothes. Such a massive padding project required gallon upon gallon of mixed foam; to handle the job, Seiderman rented an eight-gallon mixer designed to make bread dough.

Modifying the actors' actual features was an integral part of Seiderman's assignment. To age Comingore's face for scenes in which she appears in her late forties, Seiderman applied a mysterious solution to her face that actually wrinkled the skin—although only temporarily.

Sloane's balding head was no simulation. Rather than waste time fitting skullcaps along with wigs to showcase Bernstein's receding hairline and eventual baldness as he aged, Seiderman simply shaved Sloane's head; then various wigs were applied, at first to show his hair thinning and later, in old age, to show him completely bald on top with a narrow wig applied around his ears. The inconvenience of having his head shaved earned Sloane an additional $2,400. Seiderman worked with Charles Wright from Max Factor & Company to create wigs for Sloane and for other characters who required less dramatic hair modifications.

The results of Seiderman's efforts were miraculous and thoroughly convincing, despite the unforgiving glare of Toland's direct lighting. Under close inspection, it was difficult to detect where the makeup ended and the actor's real features began. Seiderman had made casts of his subjects in three different positions—relaxed, contracted, and expanded—to produce what he called his "multidirectional makeup," which created consistently natural facial expressions.

To add more realism, Welles' makeup included Seiderman's painstaking addition of individual pores on the latex surface, each calculated to match its pattern on Welles' own skin. And thanks to Seiderman's body pads, Kane did not look unnaturally fat but appeared to carry the slowly expanding bulk of advancing age.

For Welles-the-director, who was often in costume while he directed or met with technicians, wearing heavy padding and elaborate makeup became second nature; several times he remained in costume and makeup for as long as twenty-seven hours. As editor Robert Wise recalled, he first met Welles while the actor-director was in his makeup and costume as an old man. Not until several days later did Wise see his supervisor as a real-life twenty-five-year-old.

Seiderman's processes were durable but precise. Once, when Welles suffered from a cold while shooting, Seiderman found that his hand-concocted adhesives abruptly stopped sticking to the actor's face. He discovered that because of Welles' illness (or as they had learned earlier, from the effects of pain and alcohol), the acid balance of his perspiration had changed enough to counteract the effectiveness of the adhesive preparation.

Welles' makeup was almost as heavy for the scenes he played at his real age.

Welles' assignment to Seiderman was to create a look of almost surreal youth for Kane as a young man.

"I never looked as young as that," said Welles of his makeup as a twenty-five-year-old Kane. "The idea was to look very young indeed, in fact younger than anyone could look."

Welles was self-conscious about his weight, even at a young age. He had what he called "that terrible round moon face," and most of his official studio portraits show him looking up at a slightly elevated camera, thus tightening his face and neck.

"Note how Orson either never smiles on camera," Joseph Cotten told author Gore Vidal, "or if he has to, how he sucks in his cheeks so as not to look like a Halloween pumpkin."

So Seiderman prepared delicate facial appliances to flatten the roundness of Welles' cheeks and to create a sharper line for his jaw.

"My whole face was yanked up with pieces of fish skin," said Welles. "I was young, but there's a sort of untouched look about that face that's impossible in real life.

"Norman Mailer wrote once that when I was young, I was the most beautiful man anybody had ever seen," Welles said years later. "Yes—made up for *Citizen Kane*!"

Welles also dieted in the weeks before he appeared in scenes of Kane as a young man and wore a corset to shape his torso, particularly for the shots of his first day at the *Inquirer* and his scenes in the newsroom arguing with Thatcher—the only scenes in the film in which he appears approximately his actual age (in the scenes of the party in the *Inquirer* newsroom, Kane has "aged" six years and is thirty-one).

Welles, sensitive that his nose was a bit too pug to complement his otherwise commanding features, also wore a prosthetic nose piece in *Citizen Kane,* as well as in most of his other film appearances, to give his nose a stronger line. Seiderman created three different noses for Kane at different ages.

Impressive though Seiderman's methods may have been, the makeup process was an ordeal for actors and makeup artist alike. Complex applications of old-age makeup required up to four hours for Seiderman to apply, despite help from assistants. (Stripping the makeup at the end of the day was easier—a job accomplished with sponged-on vodka.)

Depending on the extent of the aging required, Welles was sometimes in his makeup chair as early as three A.M., eating a typical Wellesian breakfast of four eggs and a dozen strips of bacon while he watched in the mirror as Seiderman prepped him. Long fascinated by stage makeup, Welles had dabbled in the craft since he was a boy. He was heavily made up in some of his Broadway roles and thoroughly appreciated Seiderman's artistry. Frequently working through the night, and always on call during the shooting day, Seiderman often slept on a cot in his laboratory so he could be ready for the next day's schedule.

Early in production, when Welles' ankle injury forced a shuffling of the shooting schedule, Cotten's scenes playing Jed Leland as an old man were pushed forward. Cotten's makeup was needed with virtually no notice, so Seiderman used face appliances already prepared for Welles.

"Orson and I never had a chance to talk about Cotten's old-age makeup," Seiderman said, "so on the spot I quickly tried a few wigs, and used the pieces that I had already made for Orson's makeup. Cotten was the only principal for whom I had not made any sculptural casts, wigs, or lenses. The bags used under the eyes and chin did not belong to Cotten's facial contours."

Leland's eyeshade was Cotten's own contribution to his appearance. After his first day in makeup and continuing problems with the makeshift bald cap popping up, he bought a tennis visor at a Santa Monica sporting goods store on his way to the studio.

Preparation of principal actors for scenes of characters in old age was complicated by the contact lenses worn to simulate the dull, cloudy-eyed look of the elderly. Cotten's contact lenses, which were fitted on short notice by optometrist R. Greenspoon after Welles' injury, were so uncomfortable that the actor was rendered nearly sightless during the first takes of Leland reminiscing as an old man. (Cotten described the sound of a contact lens being removed as "flurp.")

Later in production, Greenspoon fitted lenses on Welles, Comingore, and Sloane and new lenses for Cotten—complete with a milky surface and tiny veins painted by Seiderman. These lenses fitted somewhat more successfully than the set first used on Cotten, but Welles said they still "drove you mad with pain."

Using complex makeup created logistic issues during shooting. With Welles growing younger or older by decades depending on the scene, the production schedule often revolved around his physical appearance. If the makeup was not planned perfectly, shooting would be delayed by hours while Welles returned to the makeup chair for another session. Seiderman's skills could not reduce the time required to prepare the actors; the daily production reports for *Citizen Kane* are peppered with comments that stated, "45 minutes delay for make-up,"

"30 minutes for wig adjustment," or other related reasons for costly but necessary stoppages.

Seiderman would not receive screen credit for *Citizen Kane*. Seiderman said he was refused credit by makeup department head Mel Berns, based on the RKO policy that authorized screen credits for some supervisors rather than the artist directly responsible for the work on a production. That recollection may have been faulty: for instance, Perry Ferguson was credited as "associate" art director on *Citizen Kane*, even though art department head Van Nest Polglase received credit over him.

In Seiderman's case, the real reason for withholding credit appears to have been its potential effects on his chances for gaining membership in the makeup artists' union. After talking with Berns in November, studio executive Sid Rogell told colleague J. R. McDonough, "We agree that to give credit to Seiderman, an apprentice, might jeopardize his personal situation with the union. Berns is going to discuss this matter with Welles and will attempt to discourage any makeup credit."

However, Welles insisted that Seiderman receive credit, and the issue simmered until January 8, when associate producer Baer ordered the makeup credits for both Berns and Seiderman. But Welles decided not to risk Seiderman's future, and five days later Baer ordered all credit for makeup to be removed.

Instead, when *Citizen Kane* debuted, Welles acknowledged Seiderman's contributions to *Citizen Kane* with full-page advertisements in *The Hollywood Reporter* and *Variety*, tributes in which Welles called Seiderman "the best make-up man in the world." He would work with Welles, again uncredited, on several other productions: *Jane Eyre, Macbeth, Othello, Touch of Evil, Journey into Fear,* and *The Magnificent Ambersons*.

Citizen Kane would nevertheless open Hollywood's doors to Seiderman. His status as an apprentice changed quickly, thanks to Welles and a little federal intervention.

"After *Citizen Kane* was exhibited, Franklin Roosevelt invited Orson to dinner at the White House," said Seiderman. "Frances Perkins, Roosevelt's secretary of labor, was one of the guests. Orson told her the story about this Russian immigrant who did the makeup on *Kane,* but could not get into the union. The following day, the Labor Department called the head of the union and said that it was beginning an investigation into unfair labor practices involving Maurice Seiderman. At four o'clock, a union card was delivered to me at the studio, and I finally was a full-fledged member."

———

Seiderman's makeup was complemented by the costumes created by RKO designer Edward Stevenson and his staff, who produced clothing to reflect the fashion trends of more than seventy years, including thirty-seven changes for Welles alone. During planning of the costumes, Dorothy Comingore and Ruth Warrick represented additional challenges: they were pregnant when they signed to appear as Susan Alexander and Emily Monroe Norton. However, Comingore's condition was a psychological advantage for Welles. "It's all the better," he told her. "If you start in it, it'll really prove to those bums that I'm going to finish the picture on time."

For Warrick, pregnancy did not create difficulties during production. She did not learn she was pregnant until after being cast as Emily, and her appearances were among the first major roles completed. Warrick finished her assignment on August 19, only three weeks into production, and no hints of pregnancy are visible, even when she wore a tightly tailored evening dress.

Comingore, however, remained throughout the production schedule and was shown standing several times, as well as in skimpy opera costumes. Comingore began to work almost immediately after signing her contract, and her first scenes show her meeting Kane for the first time when she was still quite slender. Three months later, when she was noticeably pregnant, Toland relied on discreet camera angles or carefully positioned props to hide her condition.

In the scenes shot October 5 and 7, in which Susan had to be shown standing as she confronts Kane in her Xanadu bedroom, Comingore carried a fur muff and wore a heavy coat over traveling clothes. While playing with jigsaw puzzles in Xanadu's Great Hall during scenes filmed October 19 and 21, Comingore is sprawled across the hearth in a long dressing gown or sitting against a table in a loose-fitting gown. Comingore's daughter was born on January 4, 1941, two and a half months after principal photography was completed.

Even Welles' costuming was planned with economizing in mind; some of his wardrobe was mixed and matched for various scenes. For instance, the outfit he wore to pose for the massive banner used behind the stage for his Madison Square Garden speech (a black pin-striped coat and gray vest) was also used—but with a different necktie—for his confrontation with Matiste during Susan's unsuccessful singing lesson (Welles also may be carrying the same jacket during his postelection argument with Leland at the *Inquirer*).

When developing background for Kane to create the role, Welles apparently included a fascination with Kane's single initial *K*, because the *K*—interestingly, never *C.F.K.*—was visually prominent in Kane's life in many scenes: the overarching *K* on the front gate of Xanadu in the opening sequence and the last shot of the film, the ice-block *K* as a centerpiece at the newsroom party, and the row of *K*s (forward and backward) on the ornate Moroccan-style hanging lamp behind Kane in his tent when he slaps Susan.

The *K* is especially noticeable in the publisher's clothes and personal accessories. Stevenson included the *K* on the pocket of Kane's velvet robe in his apartment after Susan's opera debut, on the gold pin he wears on his cravat in the newsreel scenes from his White House wedding to Emily Monroe Norton, on the even larger tiepin that Kane-the-candidate displays at his speech in Madison Square Garden, as a *K* monogram on the front of Kane's shirt at the picnic tent when he slaps Susan, on Kane's watch chain when he destroys Susan's room, and (almost invisible except in close-up) sewn into the exquisitely embroidered collar and cuffs of the shirt Kane wears when he takes over the *Inquirer* and when he argues with Thatcher about the Public Transit Company.

By mid-September, production of *Citizen Kane* was proceeding smoothly, but Welles was still writing. And writing. Even after the completion of the Correction Script in mid-July, Welles—as he had in New York for his radio and theater productions—continued to revise, create new material, and revise again in a frantic race to keep ahead of the production schedule. Welles' work on the script continued everywhere and at all hours; assistant Kathryn Trosper, who was with Welles every moment he was not shooting or acting, went to the studio each morning for Welles' makeup sessions to conduct business, sometimes arriving as early as 2 a.m., and often taking dictation for script revisions while Welles was being prepped.

Mercury assistant Richard Baer recalled a similar pace to the rewriting. "It is not possible," Baer said, "to fix the actual number of complete redrafts [by Welles], as changes were being continuously made on portions that had previously been written."

Welles would often turn to his cast and crew for participation in the rewrites. Welles was not looking for ad-libs in front of the camera, but rather an exchange between actors and their director in discussions of what worked and what didn't.

"If a shot didn't work, Orson changed it on the set," Trosper said. "If an actor came up with a better line, he used it."

Given the pressured circumstances, some—maybe all—of the final scenes that were rewritten or expanded after the Correction Script was produced may have emerged from Welles' rewriting on the set, and possibly working with the actors involved in a scene. As just one example of what may have been an on-set rewrite is the scene of Susan rehearsing with her teacher, Signor Matiste, played by Fortunio Bonanova: in every version of the script, including the Correction Script prepared only days before filming it, the scene began with Susan singing and Matiste quickly interrupting her by shouting, "Impossible! Impossible!"

One can imagine Welles working with Bonanova—who as a former opera singer no doubt participated in many intense instructional sessions in rehearsals—to develop something much better through discussion, revised dialogue, additional rehearsals, and more writing. But however the scene was rewritten, what resulted was the transformation of two lines into a much longer, seemingly spontaneous, and thoroughly realistic encounter in which Matiste coaches and sings in time with the music while Susan tries to perform. ("Please look at me, Mrs. Kane darling—now, get the voice, out of the throat, place the tone, right in the mask.")

But now halfway through the production schedule, Welles could no longer avoid dealing with the gaps that remained in the script.

The first problem was clear enough: to continue the visual plan, the script needed another seamless transition from scene to scene—this one for the shift from Kane's meeting with Susan Alexander to the start of Kane's gubernatorial campaign.

To script that transition, Welles stole lines from Kane's campaign speech that he converted into remarks for Leland. The two-sentence speech, spoken by Joseph Cotten from the back of a convertible to a small back-alley gathering, lasts only seventeen seconds, as he says "there is only one man who can rid the politics of this state of the evil domination of 'Boss' Jim Gettys"; the remarks then transition directly to Kane's speech in Madison Square Garden. Welles also shortened Kane's speech, with the final text building to a perfect crescendo as Kane concludes his remarks.

Creating the speech for Leland was easy, but the other scenes were not. Correspondence about these sequences does not exist; they may have always been considered problems that should be fixed, or Welles may have shrewdly recognized late in production that he needed to add depth to Kane's character. Even though Welles' goal was to explore Kane's actions and their consequences, he still needed to provide some perspective of the man. Regardless of the reason,

Welles created a sequence of four new scenes, three of which would become some of the most vibrant of the film, followed by another scene that would be one of the most insightful—all produced from start to finish with incredible speed.

The gaps affected critical moments near the beginning of the film. The major deletions from the first few drafts—the scenes in Rome, descriptions of Kane's behavior in college, accounts of corporate espionage to steal material for his paper—were all appropriate cuts, but they removed extensive details about Kane's young adulthood after he inherited his fortune, insights that would have helped audiences appreciate Kane's personality and motives. The newsreel provided an overview of Kane's full life but few details about his early years.

In the Third Revised Final draft, and also in the Correction Script, by the time Kane is seen as a young man for the first time—some twenty-four minutes into the film—the audience knows almost nothing about his life, especially his professional role as both a reckless journalist and a crusading public servant. And Welles also wanted to show more about the impact of the Depression on Kane, which otherwise would have been explored in only a few factual references in the newsreel.

To deal with these issues, Welles focused on the flashbacks in Thatcher's memoirs after young Charles is signed over to the guardianship of Thatcher's bank. In every version of the script, that section had remained the same: Thatcher leaves Colorado with the eight-year-old, and little Charles is shown in his berth on the train, sobbing into his pillow as he cries, "Mom! Mom!" while Thatcher looks on, helpless.

In the draft scripts, that scene then dissolves to Thatcher's handwriting in his memoirs that describes Kane as, among other things, "lucky, spoiled, unscrupulous, and irresponsible," followed by the scene of Thatcher confronting Kane, now twenty-seven, in the newsroom of the *Inquirer* as they argue about the publisher's warmongering and GALLEONS OF SPAIN OFF JERSEY COAST.

For Welles, that was not enough. Sometime in September—the point when a river of new budget requests began to flow and new scenes popped into the shooting schedule—Welles decided to create material to show more about Kane's actions at the beginning and the end of his career: first he would demonstrate how Kane was a dynamic but irresponsible journalist, and then he would show the devastating effects of the loss of Kane's empire on his character and pride, along with some hints of regret in how he had conducted his life.

To do this, Welles wrote four new scenes entirely from scratch. The first three scenes link the start and finish of Thatcher's role as Kane's guardian, and one other shows their relationship late in their lives.

As a start, Welles focused on Thatcher and his frustration dealing with his young ward. He deleted the scene of young Charles crying on the train and in its place used a single shot of his sled covered in snow while the hollow wail of the whistle on the train carrying the boy east can be heard in the distance. In this simple scene, Welles illustrated the boy's loneliness, reinforced the importance of Rosebud in the story (without giving away the secret—the word *Rosebud* is obscured by snow), and set up the chain of scenes that followed.

The white of falling snow dissolves to a completely white screen in the next scene. It is the white wrapping paper that covers a new sled, much fancier than Rosebud, that has been given to young Charles by Thatcher as a Christmas present. (This sled, like Kane's beloved Rosebud, has its name painted across the front, visible only in a freeze frame: "The Crusader.") Surrounded by Thatcher and servants towering over him—yet another extremely low shot by Toland—Charles is visibly unhappy, and the "party" has the dark gloom of the most unfestive Christmas gathering ever.

Looking down on young Kane, Thatcher says, "Well, Charles—Merry Christmas," and the boy replies in a disgusted tone, "Merry Christmas—" The scene then cuts abruptly to an older Thatcher seventeen years later in his office, saying, "And a Happy New Year," as he dictates a letter to the now twenty-five-year-old Kane about his upcoming independence from Thatcher & Company.

Then, in an inspired decision—what scholar Robert Carringer would call "the master stroke"—Welles decided to develop Kane's personality by focusing on Thatcher, who at this point would seem like the least likable character in the entire film and someone who could never inspire sympathy in an audience. Through a series of amusing vignettes, Welles shows Kane's moral character through the banker's growing frustration with Kane's news coverage and by the banker looking *directly* to the audience for understanding.

When Thatcher writes to Kane about the vast holdings he is about to inherit, Kane replies that he is interested solely in the *Inquirer* because "I think it would be fun to run a newspaper." As Thatcher, growing angry but somehow humorous in his deflating pomposity, reads Kane's reply aloud to his staff, he repeats Kane's declaration about running a newspaper, glances at his assistants, and then looks straight into the camera and growls.

This shot kicks off a series of seven brief scenes, each showing Thatcher reading an *Inquirer* headline—including several in which he looks at the audience for support—as he becomes increasingly flustered about Kane's antics in print. The vignettes, each only a few seconds, are accompanied by breezy music by Bernard Herrmann that gallops along to punctuate the brisk pace of the scenes.

In the first vignette, Thatcher sits on a train and whispers the banner headline, TRACTION TRUST EXPOSED, before turning directly to the camera. He reads the next headline, TRACTION TRUST BLEEDS PUBLIC WHITE, with a huff, and the next, TRACTION TRUST SMASHED BY INQUIRER, as he slams his front door, again looking into the camera. When he reads LANDLORDS REFUSE TO CLEAR SLUMS, he throws the newspaper into the fireplace; for the next, INQUIRER WINS SLUM FIGHT, he is outside at night under an arch as he looks straight at the audience and lets out a loud, "Tsk."

For the next headline, WALL STREET BACKS COPPER SWINDLE, Thatcher, whose face is hidden by his chair, is so stunned that he can say nothing; he looks around the side of his chair as his mouth drops open. For this vignette, Toland and Ferguson added a special visual touch: the audience is outside his office, looking through a closed window, with reflections of buildings on the glass. For the next scene, at his breakfast table, Thatcher yells, "Copper Robbers Indicted!" with a mouthful of food before tossing his napkin.

The vignettes are light enough to be comical; the audience cannot help enjoying Thatcher's reactions. And in only thirty seconds, Welles has efficiently characterized the public good done by the *Inquirer* in smashing local trolley monopolies and supporting the poor against tenement owners, as well as the depth of Kane's sensationalist journalism through his exploitative coverage of Wall Street antics and by creating news where there is none—especially when Thatcher then shouts the final and most preposterous headline, "Galleons of Spain off Jersey Coast!" while standing in the *Inquirer* newsroom, slamming down the newspaper and confronting the adult Kane.

Although Thatcher then makes important points about Kane's behavior, and Kane responds with intense eloquence—declaring he would do anything for his readers, even if that meant crushing a company in which Kane himself was a major shareholder—the scene ends on a light note, with Kane pointing out that if he continues to lose $1 million a year, it means "I'll have to close this place in . . . sixty years."

However, in the transition to the next sequence—the fourth of Welles' new scenes—the mood immediately darkens by showing the ominous handwritten line from Thatcher's memoirs, "In the winter of 1929 . . . ," as the scene moves ahead to Kane's final business failure: signing back the custody of his ruined empire to Thatcher's bank.

The result was a scene that, although brief, provided some of the film's few observations by Kane about his own character.

"You know, Charles," Thatcher tells Kane as the publisher signs over control of his companies, "you never made a single investment . . . always used money to—"

"To buy things," Kane recalls sadly as he signs the documents, then mutters again, "To buy things. My mother should have chosen a less reliable banker. Well, I always gagged on that silver spoon.

"You know, Mr. Bernstein," Kane says in the scene's closing moments, while acknowledging Thatcher with a nasty look, "if I hadn't been very rich, I might have been a really great man."

"Don't you think you are?" Thatcher asks.

Kane replies, "I think I did pretty well under the circumstances."

"What would you like to have been?" Thatcher asks.

"Everything you hate," Kane answers as the scene closes.

Considering the brief time in which Welles' new scenes evolved out of nothing, their success in *Citizen Kane* seems particularly astonishing. How the scenes were created may forever be a mystery: there is no discussion in the production files about them, and Welles never talked about how they were written. In fact, today the script does not exist for any of them.

But it is clear that creating the new scenes required a crash schedule. While Welles was writing them, the Mercury team was immersed in the myriad details of film planning that typically requires weeks: conceptualizing and designing *nine* new sets, preparing costumes, selecting extras, and all of the logistic necessities of filmmaking—rehearsals, lighting, and camera placement—all while the regular calendar of production continued. And with zero time for major revisions, Welles' script for the new scenes was used either as originally written or with minimal rewriting.

The prop newspapers alone—so key to the vignettes—were a major project. Like the other newspapers created by Ed Blake to illustrate Kane's death in the newsreels, each of the eight editions of the *Inquirer* that riled Thatcher included not only the fake main headline, but an assortment of related content: smaller headlines, subheads, captions, and political cartoons. Each front page was on-screen for only moments—some for one second—and none of this extra content would have been readable on a theater screen.

The work on the new scenes moved quickly. In late September and early October, many memos requesting approval for budget overages to pay for new sets were sent to RKO management. The explanation was always the same: "This is an added set, not figured in the original budget." The new sets were dirt cheap: creating the partial set of Thatcher's living room cost $200 plus $40 for props; for his breakfast table, the charge was $100 for the set and $20 for props. All of the sets for the vignettes were masterpieces of implied set design, with only fragments of rooms visible; shadows or dark spaces created the illusion of more.

And while the larger sets were also built in a rush, they came together with the same attention to detail—and commitment to the visual plan—that the rest of the production required. For Leland's brief back-alley speech, Perry Ferguson loaded the set with textures and details: grimy walls, campaign posters deliberately askew and overlapping, a soiled cobblestone street, and clotheslines and a fire escape laden with laundry. There's even a touch of depth to the set, with part of the alley and a brick archway positioned behind a streetlight.

For Thatcher's Depression-era office, Ferguson created a spartan chamber with a high ceiling, wood paneling, and tall windows that revealed the New York skyline—the perfect work space for the cold and drab Thatcher. The set was also especially deep, more than twenty-five feet, to accommodate Kane's pacing from the front to the back and then to the front again before he signed his empire back to Thatcher (all while Bernstein, his face filling the right side of the frame, is reading from the agreement as Toland described earlier). Constructed quickly, the set cost $500.

Welles moved just as quickly with the filming. On October 3, he shot the "Merry Christmas" scene with George Coulouris, Buddy Swann, and four extras, the "Happy New Year" scene, and at least two of the vignettes.

With no records of how these scenes developed, only Robert Wise and Richard Wilson may have recalled part of the story. At one point, Wise said in 1990, "Welles sent everyone home, and wrote a scene overnight."

Wise's recollection is oversimplified; he could not remember the scene in question. But Richard Wilson remembered that shooting was stopped while Welles left to rewrite the scene of the signing over of Kane's empire back to Thatcher.

In the first week of October, Welles became ill and was home on October 8, 9, and 10. On October 12, a Saturday, the company was assembled for work but was dismissed when Welles remained sick.

Whether he was actually ill, writing at home, or both, the delay provided time that may have been used to prepare the signing scene, which was mounted with lightning speed.

Welles may have been writing this scene whenever he could spare the time. On the back of a page in a Third Revised Final shooting script from Welles' files, in what appears to be Welles' handwriting, are notes that seem to be the beginning of his draft for this scene: Welles scribbled, and then started to edit: "Well Charles—our foreclosure of your international newspaper syndicate is ~~not~~ only ~~serious~~ business—after all you've been able to print your opinion for over 30 years now. Kane—Yes."

The overage charge for the boardroom was approved on October 9 (whether construction occurred before then or was required to wait for approval is unknown). George Coulouris and Everett Sloane were held past their contracted end dates and paid extra for the time. On Stage 7 at RKO in Culver City, Welles filmed the single-shot, two-minute, twenty-one-second scene on October 16 and 17, thus completing his new sequences and filling the gaps in his script.

Delays and the added scenes continued to extend the production schedule, but in mid-October—in spite of the new scenes—filming of *Citizen Kane* began to wind down. Most motion pictures are typically shot out of sequence, but given the coincidences of the production schedule and the lengthy construction time required for the Great Hall of Xanadu, several of the final scenes of the film were shot as principal photography drew to a close.

On October 14, 16, and 18, Toland shot the reporters rummaging through the vast sea of crates and boxes in the Great Hall of Xanadu as they come to the end of their search for Rosebud. On October 19 and 21, Welles directed himself and Dorothy Comingore in the Great Hall, as Kane and Susan endure the self-imposed boredom of life in their palace.

After filming the demolition of Susan's bedroom and cutting himself on October 22, Welles wrapped up principal photography for *Citizen Kane* on October 23, nearly three months after RKO's official start date—or four months after filming actually began. The last shot of the regular production schedule was Kane's final appearance in the film: his dazed walk through the hall of mirrors after destroying Susan's room and discovering the snow globe that inspired his memories of Rosebud.

For the rest of his life, Welles would *always* say that he completed Production #281 "under budget and under schedule" (he was also known to say that he finished *all* of his films under budget and under schedule), but the official RKO reports list Production #281 as eighteen days behind schedule. While *Citizen Kane* did indeed finish late, the eighteen-day estimate seems questionable, given that principal photography ended only twelve days after the original target closing date. But whether twelve or eighteen days behind, such a relatively short delay was a minor miracle, given Welles' inexperience, the extraordinary nature of the production, injuries on the set, and illnesses.

RKO managers continued to be concerned about finances throughout the production, but the final accounting showed that Welles remained remarkably close to budget during production of *Citizen Kane*. The original budget for direct costs was $603,167; adding in the studio's 20 percent surcharge to recoup administrative expenses brought the total projected budget to $723,800. Welles completed the picture for $686,033; with studio overhead and all postproduction expenses added in, *Citizen Kane* was completed for a total cost of $823,240.05, exceeding the budget target by only 12 percent.

CRYPTIC NOTES AND BIGGER HAMS

*Mark [Robson] and I would be in our cutting room, running pieces
of film through cheesecloth filled with sand to age it for the newsreel.
People who saw us at work and didn't know what was going on
must have been thinking, "These guys are crazy."*
—ROBERT WISE, EDITOR OF *CITIZEN KANE*

A week after principal photography for *Citizen Kane* was completed, filming resumed to finish a variety of retakes and inserts. Among the many snippets needed were a brief clip of Sonny Bupp as Kane's son outside of Madison Square Garden (October 30); Susan and Kane driving in a limousine to the Florida picnic (November 12); retakes of Susan and Kane in the picnic tent, their Chicago apartment, and Susan's now repaired Xanadu bedroom (November 13); and many additional shots of the reporters in the Great Hall.

November 16 marked Gregg Toland's last day on the production. He filmed another round of retakes of the reporters at Xanadu and set up the shots of Kane's death before turning over photography to RKO staff cinematographer Harry Wild. Although Toland began his assignment on *The Outlaw*—on loan by Goldwyn to Howard Hughes—his camera team remained at RKO to help finish the scenes that lingered. Wild shot several scenes for the newsreel, including the protest speaker in Union Square, played by Art Yeoman, who called Kane "a Fascist," and Kane with the foreign generals.

By that time, the only principal players other than Welles with scenes to be filmed were Dorothy Comingore and Paul Stewart. Comingore, little more than a month from giving birth, left the set ill on November 23, her last day on the production (although she recorded one line at home in early February).

To complete the scenes of Susan and her puzzles, extra Ivy Keene substituted her hands for Comingore's on November 26 for the six close-up shots of puzzle construction that were used in the film. Keene had already served as an unidentifiable extra in the background at the *Inquirer* while Kane and Thatcher argue about the paper's credibility, and in a window of the *Inquirer* while the staff waves at Kane and Emily driving away from the building after announcing their engagement.

On November 27, Stewart appeared in the outdoor scenes of the Everglades picnic, which were filmed on Stage 10 at RKO, and then he, too, finished his work. That left only scenes with Welles and Alland to film.

On the call sheet for November 28 was a cryptic note that meant little to anyone unfamiliar with *Citizen Kane* but would mark the filming of what would become one of the most famous scenes in motion picture history: requested on the call sheet that day was a "special effects man to break ball"—a reference to bursting the snow globe when Kane dies and drops it. Then on November 30, Wild filmed Kane's death, and two retakes were completed on December 9 and 20.

On January 4, on Stage 3 at RKO in Hollywood, cinematographer Russell Cully filmed William Alland—again showing his left side—looking up; it was a shot that would be merged with film of the George Washington Bridge as an introduction to the interview with Leland. It was the last shot of the production. On January 6, associate producer Richard Baer reported to set designer Darrell Silvera that "Mr. Welles has completed with the shooting of *Citizen Kane,* so you may release any props which you are holding for that picture." The filming was over.

The shoot was complete, but the myriad details of postproduction—already under way for weeks—would require another month before *Citizen Kane* would become a finished film.

Special Effects

The elements of scenes that could not be created with cleverly designed sets or innovative camera angles were developed in postproduction with special effects. *Citizen Kane*—no action-packed adventure saga or science-fiction thriller— may not seem like a motion picture that required sophisticated special effects, but the film is packed with them. Almost 40 percent of the final footage in *Citizen Kane* includes some form of 1940s effects wizardry, such as matte paintings and back projections for added backgrounds, shots of models, dissolves, and optical printing.

The RKO camera effects department produced the optical processing for *Citizen Kane;* assigned by department head Vernon Walker were effects cameraman Russell Cully, montage effects expert Douglas Travers, matte artist Mario Larrinaga, and, for optical printing, renowned effects expert Linwood Dunn.

Dunn, who created special effects for projects as diverse as *King Kong* in 1933 and the original *Star Trek* series in the 1960s, developed many of the effects techniques needed for *Citizen Kane.* Dunn was already recognized as a filmmaking pioneer for his invention of the Acme-Dunn optical printer, a device that combines a camera and a projector to produce many film effects, such as fades, dissolves, and composites of shots; for his invention, Dunn received an Academy Award in 1944.

Dunn created effects for such seemingly effects-free movies as *Bringing Up Baby,* with its screwball plot involving a pet leopard. Using the optical printer, Dunn merged shots of Katharine Hepburn and Cary Grant with separate footage of a leopard, blending them so seamlessly that the effect is invisible. (Examples of Dunn's effects are available on several Web sites.) Thirty years after *Citizen Kane*—as interest grew in classic films and special effects—Dunn was a popular guest at presentations for film students. Dunn would explain some of his effects by showing several scenes from *Bringing Up Baby* before and after the leopard was added; audiences would roar at the "before" shots of Grant and Hepburn reacting with campy terror to a nonexistent leopard.

For *Citizen Kane,* Dunn used optical printing to combine matte paintings, back projections, and other methods to create doorways, corridors, and entire buildings. Without effects, producing these scenes would have been possible only with many additional sets and backdrops—and far greater expense. Dunn estimated that for some reels of film for *Citizen Kane,* 80 percent of the footage required special effects.

Dunn's optical effects were not only cost-effective substitutes for full-scale construction, they were also more practical than the time-intensive planning Gregg Toland needed to produce in-camera effects such as Susan's suicide attempt. The consequence of using optical printing was loss of visual quality in the final film: an optical effect required copying and recopying elements of the effect on film, with each step producing a small loss of quality. To Toland, this degraded image quality interfered with the cinematographer's goal of creating crisp shots. Even though the budget cuts relied in part on special effects, Toland continued to create his own in-camera effects when he could.

Almost all of the "exterior" scenes in *Citizen Kane*—Xanadu, the *Inquirer* office building, the caravan of cars along the beach going to Kane's picnic, elements of the picnic itself, and several others—required special effects to complete. The departure of Kane and Susan from their wedding at Trenton Town Hall is one of the few exceptions.

Most of the exterior of the *Inquirer* building, for example, was not a constructed set. When Kane returns from his trip to Europe, the *Inquirer* staff looks out the windows to see Kane in a carriage with fiancée Emily Monroe Norton. The scene then shifts to the front of the huge building, with the staff waving out of windows that are partially obscured by large letters that spell out NEW YORK DAILY INQUIRER. The only set pieces needed for the scene were the windows, a horizontal slice of the wall, and the name of the newspaper; the building and the neighboring structure were a matte painting that, in an optical print, was blended into the shots of the actors waving from the real windows.

Another scene involving the *Inquirer* building required not a complex effect, but rather a simple dissolve from a painting to real life: when Kane and Jed Leland arrive at the *Inquirer* for the first time, the scene begins with a shot that seemingly pans down the side of the *Inquirer* building to show Kane and Leland in their carriage, looking up before they enter the offices. To save the expense of constructing the front of a huge office building, most of the *Inquirer* is yet another matte painting; the shot travels down the painting, then dissolves to Kane and Leland in front of the full-size entrance. The effect itself appears natural, and the shift from matte painting to live action is unnoticeable, in part because the dissolve from the previous scene—Bernstein talking about Kane's arrival at the *Inquirer*—continues for several seconds into the shot of the building.

A matte painting was also used to simulate the Florida Gulf coast where Kane invites his Xanadu guests to go on a picnic. The caravan of cars traveling alongside the sand to the picnic was filmed October 19 at a beach near Point Mugu, fifty miles north of Los Angeles; this hilly section of coastline looks nothing like the flat shores of Florida's Gulf coast. In the final film, only the ocean, the cars, and a small section of beach were real. The rest of the Florida sky, the flat beach, and the tropical plants were a matte painting.

Optical printing was also used during the picnic itself: the brief background scenes of birds in flight shown behind the guests' tents were taken from the animated footage prepared in 1933 by RKO for *King Kong*.

The exterior of Xanadu, like the *Inquirer* building, did not exist in full size. The shots of Kane's palace were models in some scenes, matte paintings in others. The model was used most prominently for the close-ups at the end of the film when smoke from Kane's burning mementos pours from the chimney. The rain-swept roof of Susan Alexander's nightclub, the El Rancho, was a combination of set and special effect. As an introduction to the scene early in the film in which Thompson unsuccessfully attempts to interview the drunken Susan, Dunn created an effect that seemingly brought the camera through a skylight and into the nightclub. The segment combines four separate shots of live action and nightclub roof and sign, all linked with strategically timed flashes of lightning. (The "El Rancho" sign, a model, was split so it would pull away from the path of the camera; the cuts in the sign's frame are barely visible between the words *floor* and *show* and after the *x* in "Alexander.")

The final result is a scene that begins with Susan's portrait on the exterior wall of the nightclub; the camera then moves up to the roof and through the framework of the "El Rancho" sign, down to the skylight, and into the club. The sequence, set in a violent storm, is deliberately jarring, but the effects themselves are so smooth that over the decades, several film analysts have remembered the scene as appearing to take the camera directly through the skylight without a break in the action.

Late in the film, before a now sober Susan talks with Thompson, a simpler version of the effect is repeated without the storm. Then, when Susan and Thompson complete their discussion, the camera travels upward, out of the club, and across the roof, this time with only a two-stage effect that links live action to the nightclub roof with a simple dissolve.

Several of Xanadu's interiors were also special effects: after Susan leaves Kane, Raymond the butler looks down a long corridor and sees Kane in the distance, standing in Susan's doorway. In the shot as filmed on the set, only the door in front of Raymond is real; Kane's tiny image is a miniature projection, melded with a matte painting of the Xanadu corridor.

In filmmaking before digital processing, many special effects were created with "wipes" that produced the smooth transition from real action to special effect. When reporter Thompson visits the Thatcher Library, the bombastic statue of Walter Thatcher is a model. As the camera pans down the statue, a nearly invisible wipe creates the transition from the model to the real action below it. (George Coulouris actually posed for the statue and was forced to file a grievance against RKO to collect additional salary for his modeling time.)

A transition from real action to model and back to real action again was also used in one of *Citizen Kane*'s most memorable scenes, when, in Susan's debut as an opera singer, the camera rises through the rafters of the Chicago Opera

House to show two stagehands far above—one pinching his nose in disgust at her performance. To save the expense of building a full-size labyrinth of ropes and beams in the opera house rafters, the scene was completed by merging three separate shots: first is the live action of Susan as the camera starts to move up; the live action then wipes to a model of the rafters; then the shot wipes back to live action for the scene of the stagehands standing in the actual catwalk on an RKO stage.

Even the impact of Rosebud burning was enhanced with optical printing. As the sled is surrounded by real flames in the Xanadu furnace, the camera, of course, could not move too near. Instead, the static shot of Rosebud on fire was run through the optical printer; the projected image moved closer to the recording camera, thus creating the zoom and tight close-up as the letters blister away in the flames.

One frequently discussed effect in *Citizen Kane,* however, was not intentional. When Raymond the butler describes Kane destroying Susan's bedroom, the scene opens with a startling shot of a screeching cockatoo. The cockatoo—which appears on-screen for less than two seconds—has no eye; the background of the Florida coastline shows through where the eye should have been. The missing eye, the meaning of which was long a subject of speculation among film writers and scholars, was, Welles admitted thirty years later, only the result of a mistake in the special effects lab.

Not all of the complex scenes in *Citizen Kane* required special effects. One stunning shot often assumed to be a painting or a model is seen in the film's closing moments, when the camera moves through Xanadu and the vast trove of Kane's treasures and crated mementos. The scene is not an effect; the more than two hundred large wood boxes along with dozens of crates at Xanadu are all real. The crates in particular, ranging from two to eight feet tall, fill large amounts of space, especially with the camera shooting at an angle. Also helping with the illusion were lamps, furniture, suits of armor, and other props interspersed around the containers.

While the sheer volume of objects looks impressive, there are not thousands of containers in the shots as the scene suggests (and RKO publicity touted at the time). The skillful use of camera placement, box positioning, and editing from one shot to the next—using the same boxes but in different positions—gives the impression of a virtual sea of crates and boxes.

The Theatrical Trailer

Welles conceived and wrote a theatrical trailer that was as inventive as the film it touted. Shot by Russell Metty and produced by National Screen Service, the trailer begins with a shot of the door to RKO Stage 10, the call-board on the wall marked "Citizen Kane." The trailer shifts to the interior of the stage, but viewers see nothing but a shaft of light and the silhouette of fingers snapping as Welles' disembodied voice calls for a microphone. A boom mike then swings in from the darkness to the camera, and Welles—never seen in the trailer—begins his description of the film.

"How do you do, ladies and gentlemen. This is Orson Welles. I'm speaking for the Mercury Theatre, and what follows is supposed to advertise our first motion picture. Citizen Kane is the title, and we hope it can correctly be called a coming attraction."

No scenes of the film are shown. Instead, viewers see shots of the stars out of costume as Welles compliments them, followed by several of the actors playing their characters and talking on the telephone about Kane.

The trailer, filmed on RKO soundstages while work on Citizen Kane was under way, includes the only existing film that shows the production behind the scenes: in shots of the actors as their real-life selves, viewers can get a backstage look at some of the sets.

For instance, in the first shot of the trailer, Welles used the dancers from the Inquirer party to run onto a set in their rehearsal shorts—a deliberate bit of 1940s titillation that Welles says in the trailer was included for "purposes of 'ballyhoo.'" As the dancers run in, the trailer shows part of the set for Georgie's Place (the brothel that went unused), with the set for "Mrs. Kane's Boarding House," Kane's childhood home, visible on the left. The clip of Ruth Warrick shows the actress leaning against a set built on one of the raised platforms that allowed Gregg Toland's low-angle shots. The model of Xanadu can be seen when Paul Stewart is introduced, and Everett Sloane is shown hamming it up on RKO's massive Stage 10, where the Great Hall of Xanadu was built. Sloane crashes into one of the mirrors being prepared for Kane's final scene when his reflection is shown into infinity. In the mirror behind Sloane can be seen the fireplace mantel used in the montage of Thatcher's growing disgust over Kane's sensationalistic journalism when he reads, LANDLORDS REFUSE TO CLEAR SLUMS.

Today, the trailer's opening shot of the microphone is shown frequently on the Turner Classic Movies cable channel. For years it was the introductory scene of TCM's "Word of Mouth" program and continues to appear in TCM's regularly broadcast montage of film clips. The full trailer often airs prior to broadcast of *Citizen Kane* and is also available on recent DVDs and the Blu-ray of the film.

Sound

Welles' background in radio taught him how sound can fortify the simplest scenes. In his radio programs, Welles took extraordinary steps to capture the depth and complexity of sounds. For one broadcast, to achieve the ideal echoing tone two actors had to lie down in a bathroom stall at CBS and perform with their heads wedged under a toilet.

From the nearly imperceptible tinkling of crystal wind chimes in the shot of the snow globe at Kane's death, to the booming salvo of Kane's campaign speech, *Citizen Kane* is layered with precisely blended individual sounds, all crafted for the audio track by RKO staff members Bailey Fesler and James G. Stewart, along with Harry Essman from CBS; Welles brought in Essman to assist the sound team with creating the sound effects.

"Sound became for us an integral part of telling the story," said William Alland. "When we walked into the rerecording studios where the soundmen were, we told them what we wanted and how we wanted it. In us, they found people who cared. Previously to that, no one really cared about sound, no one really appreciated what they could do until they were given the opportunity."

Stewart, a veteran of RKO, agreed with Alland's assessment.

"The motion picture business as a whole had no concept for the possibilities for sound," Stewart said. "You fall into a pattern and it's difficult to deviate from that pattern because it costs money, and no one wanted to spend money. For Orson, deviation from the pattern was possible because he demanded it; Orson discovered he could rely on me for anything."

Attentive listening reveals a melding of on-screen action with a rich menu of sounds: among them, early-twentieth-century street noises, train whistles, echo-filled conversations between Kane and Susan Alexander at Xanadu, a woman's scream when Kane slaps Susan, the moan of a solitary steamship whistle during Jed Leland's interview with Thompson, and one of the most famous lines in film history: Kane whispering, "Rosebud," as his dying word, the fading gasp achieved by blending two separate sound tracks of Welles' line. Sound plays such an impactful role in *Citizen Kane* that motion picture appreciation classes have studied the film by "watching" it without a picture and analyzing only the sound.

Without today's digital sound systems and sophisticated playback capabilities, the creation of intricate sound sequences in 1941 using optical recording of sound on film was a painstaking process. Creating the auditory power of Kane's speech—Welles' goal was for the scene to "sound like Madison Square Garden with 10,000 people in it"—took Stewart several weeks. He started with Welles' original footage, which had been shot on a bare Stage 7 at RKO in Culver City.

"Orson adopted the manner of speaking in a reverberant room," said Stewart, "waiting for the echoes to die."

Stewart rerecorded Welles' speech down a long hallway with echo, then added applause, laughter, cheers, and encouraging shouts, all blended smoothly into one sequence.

The result was a "big" sound—but it was too big, Stewart said.

"You're a bigger ham than I am," Welles told Stewart after hearing it. "Who's going to look at me with that sound coming at them? It's great, but give me half as much."

"In my enthusiasm," Stewart recalled twenty-five years after his work on *Citizen Kane*, "I had overdone the effect. I toned it down considerably."

The sound not only complemented the action, but, as coordinated with the cinematography, produced moments of continuity that supported the visual plan. In Leland's office at the Chicago *Inquirer*, when Bernstein tells Leland that Kane is finishing his scathing review of Susan's performance, Kane can be heard typing in the newsroom. When Leland looks into the newsroom, Kane pulls the carriage return to start a new line; the "clunk" of the carriage begins while Leland is looking, and the sound ends when the shot changes to a close-up of Kane, his hand on the carriage return lever.

Sound also enhances the plot. As "Boss" Jim Gettys leaves Susan's apartment building, with Kane screaming, "I'm going to send you to Sing Sing! Sing Sing, Gettys! Sing—," the last word of the sentence is drowned into insignificance by the "beep beep" of a car horn.

Editing

In postproduction of a film as carefully planned and photographed as *Citizen Kane,* an editor's role might seem limited. Despite Welles' penchant for filming multitudinous takes, only select shots were actually printed and held for possible use in the final film. Because so much of *Citizen Kane* was photographed as long master shots, and with few alternate takes printed, Welles and Toland were, in effect, editing in the camera. Nevertheless, assembling all of the diverse elements involved in such an elaborate production into a rough cut required several months of meticulous editing.

RKO staff editor Robert Wise was assigned to unite Welles' footage into a final print. Wise would go on to direct several of the most distinctive films of the 1940s and 1950s—including *The Curse of the Cat People, The Body Snatcher, The Set-Up, The Day the Earth Stood Still,* and *I Want to Live!*—as well as three of Hollywood's biggest blockbusters: *West Side Story, The Sound of Music,* and *Star Trek: The Motion Picture.* Wise broke into the film business at RKO in 1933 as a nineteen-year-old apprentice, and by the summer of 1938, he was an editor at the studio.

Wise's editing began while filming was still under way, and he visited the set at least once a day to see how the work progressed.

"Orson would describe what he wanted to accomplish with a particular segment, and I would take notes and go back into the editing room to cut the scene," Wise said. "I worked with my assistant, Mark Robson, to assemble the footage, and then Orson would review what we had done."

Welles, as was his management style with most of his associates, reviewed the visual plan and the material with Wise, then let his editor proceed unencumbered by a hovering producer-director-star (Welles would, however, later request many changes or revisions as Wise showed him his progress).

"Much of my editing involved merely taking the marvelous material and putting it in proper shape," said Wise. "Orson told me what he wanted to achieve, but he didn't hang on my shoulder."

Welles knew Wise was better off editing *Citizen Kane* with minimal interference. Welles, throughout his career seemingly never completely satisfied with a final film product, was inclined to tinker endlessly. One of the principal reasons he enjoyed creating theatrical productions was that each performance represented yet another dress rehearsal that could be modified for the next day. Watching a final film, Welles said, "always makes me nervous not being able to change anything."

Wise had plenty of work to do to hone a final print, but few full scenes were actually deleted. The brothel scene, filmed even though the censors' had ruled against it, was tossed away before Wise began preparing a rough cut; he did not recall ever seeing footage of it. (All of the material cut from *Citizen Kane,* including the brothel scene and the alternate takes, disappeared long ago. The only existing outtakes are included in the closing credits, the not-quite-perfect unused shots of each Mercury player.)

The full scenes deleted during editing were insignificant: in the longest one, filmed August 28, Kane, Bernstein, and Jed Leland visit the composing room to remake the newspaper pages on their first day at the *Inquirer.* Smathers, the composing room foreman played by character actor Benny Rubin, refuses to cooperate because the paper is scheduled to go to press in five minutes, so Kane scatters the type across the floor. "You can remake them now, can't you, Mr. Smathers?" Kane says. In the final film, the same idea is conveyed in the scene that remains, when Kane writes his "Declaration of Principles" and orders Solly (played by Al Eben) to remake the front page—again.

Given the tight control of each shot, and with a limited selection of printed takes, Welles and Wise were indeed fortunate that nearly all of *Citizen Kane's* usable footage was free of errors in the continuity or other mistakes unnoticed during production. Every film contains modest faults that only the sharp-eyed would see or multiple viewings would disclose, such as a microphone or a camera shadow in the frame. In *Citizen Kane,* there are only a few errors: viewers see one of Susan's puzzles in a state of completion that varies from shot to shot and other such inconsequential lapses.

However, some other errors are a bit more obvious. For instance, when Kane departs Madison Square Garden after his campaign speech, associate producer Richard Baer is appearing as Hillman, the official walking alongside Kane and helping him with his coat. As they turn a corner, Hillman is the official who says, "If the election were held today, you'd be in by a hundred thousand votes." As Kane approaches the street, Hillman, on Kane's left, is wearing a top hat. The scene cuts to Kane's son waving good-bye to him; when the scene shifts back to Kane, Hillman is hatless. The scene cuts to taxis arriving at the auditorium; when the shot returns to Kane and Emily, Hillman is wearing his hat again.

Or another: When Kane returns to the *Inquirer* newsroom after his vacation, a small segment of the track used for the camera dolly can be seen for a moment (photos taken during the filming of this scene show that Welles came within inches of tripping over the rails, nearly causing yet another "Orson accident").

Much later, Welles said that another "error" in *Citizen Kane* provided him with a convenient excuse to not watch the film: in the scene of Susan Alexander's attempted suicide, when Kane breaks into the bedroom, Welles could see his own bracelet on his left wrist.

The bracelet is visible for only a fraction of a second as Kane kneels by the bed, but Welles could not ignore it.

"I had a girlfriend who made me wear it," Welles told Peter Bogdanovich. "Every time I think of that scene, I think of my reaching down and you see this awful love charm. And whenever I think of seeing this picture, the reason I don't want to is because I don't want to see that goddamn bracelet."

Some viewers believe that Kane's death contains an error by omission: Kane appears to be alone when he died, so how could anyone know his last word? Viewers who think they found a hidden "flaw" in *Citizen Kane* fail to remember that, late in the film, Raymond the butler tells Thompson that he was present at Kane's death (although he is not seen on-screen). "He just said 'Rosebud,'" Raymond says to Thompson, "then he dropped the glass ball and it broke on the floor. He didn't say anything after that, and I knew he was dead."

When Welles talked with film fans about this "error," he would playfully tease them about their "discovery," letting them believe that they had exposed a previously unknown mistake and swearing them to secrecy because "only you caught it."

Two of Wise's editing contributions are particularly important to the structure of *Citizen Kane*. The first was his edits for one of the picture's most-talked-about sequences: the breakfast table montage, which in two minutes and thirteen seconds captures the decline of Kane's first marriage. The sequence begins with the innocent mutual adoration of newlyweds and ends years later with the stony silence of the irreconcilable couple. Wise worked intermittently for six weeks to complete the editing of the breakfast table montage, shifting the sequence of film segments, dialogue, and quick pans to achieve just the right tempo for the action and the failure of Kane's marriage.

Wise also collaborated with RKO's own newsreel department to create *News on the March,* the film's convincing imitation of an actual newsreel such as *The March of Time* or *News of the Day.* The sequence meshed 127 pieces of film into a nine-minute, eighteen-second sequence. To assemble the newsreel, the production acquired stock footage from RKO's own Pathé News of striking workers, mass demonstrations, and animals being shipped; General Film Library provided a snippet of U.S. Cavalry in the Spanish-American War. Welles also shot new footage to simulate some events, including Kane's meetings with world leaders such as Adolf Hitler, British prime minister Neville Chamberlain (at 10 Downing Street), and anonymous foreign military officers; and campaigning on a whistle-stop train tour with Theodore Roosevelt.

New footage was also shot for the realistic mob protest ("Don't read Kane papers!") during which Kane is burned in effigy and, a few minutes later, a "Kane for Governor" torchlight parade. Scenes of Kane in a wheelchair as an old man, shot in a jerky, handheld style through fences and between trees as if being captured secretly by paparazzi of the 1940s, were filmed on the front lawn at RKO in Culver City.

Most of the music used in the newsreel was not written for the production but was drawn from other sources: an excerpt from Richard Wagner's overture from *Tannhäuser,* for example, is used when posters for Susan Alexander's performances are shown. Other musical segments were culled from RKO productions: the bouncy theme music for *News on the March* itself was the "Belgian March" by Anthony Collins, composed for the 1939 RKO film *Nurse Edith Cavell.* Other snippets came from more than a dozen RKO films, including *Abe Lincoln in Illinois, Bad Lands, Bringing Up Baby, The Conquerors, Curtain Call, Five Came Back, The Flying Irishman, A Man to Remember, Music for Madame,* and *On Again– Off Again.*

For instance, the romantic sweep of violins that is heard under the description of Xanadu and the montage of shots that illustrate Kane's palace are from *Gunga Din,* when Cary Grant and Sam Jaffe ride Annie the elephant in their pursuit of golden treasure. As Kane responds to charges that he is a Communist and his written statement appears ("I am, have been, and will be only one thing— an American"), the music is the opening theme to *Mother Carey's Chickens.* When viewers see the text about Kane as "the greatest newspaper tycoon of this or any other generation," the music is the main theme from *Reno.* And in the scene of "1941's biggest, strangest funeral," the somber dirge used as Kane's casket is carried from the chapel is the funeral march played during the opening moments of *The Life of Vergie Winters.*

To give some of the footage in the newsreel a tattered, archival quality, Wise and assistant editor Mark Robson copied segments repeatedly to simulate age, dragged negatives across a concrete floor to inflict actual damage on the film, and imposed other horrors not normally associated with careful editing.

"Mark and I would be in our cutting room, running pieces of film through cheesecloth filled with sand to age it for the newsreel," Wise said. "People who saw us at work and didn't know what was going on must have been thinking, 'These guys are crazy.'"

The result of this intentional vandalism was a convincing imitation of an actual newsreel. The smooth intercutting of old and new footage not only thoroughly summarizes the story of Kane's life, but also sets the stage for the use of flashbacks and abrupt shifts of content that fill the rest of the film.

News on the March was perhaps too realistic—when *Citizen Kane* screened in Italy following World War II, Welles recalled that some theater patrons booed, hissed, and shook their fists at the projection booth, because they thought the newsreel material was actually a bad print of the film.

Music

Music was critical to Welles' vision for *Citizen Kane;* forty-five years later, he told his friend Henry Jaglom that the musical score was 50 percent responsible for the film's artistic success.

Welles asked Bernard Herrmann, a colleague from CBS who had served as musical director for *Mercury Theatre on the Air,* to compose the score for *Citizen Kane*. Herrmann was yet another artist involved in *Citizen Kane* who was working on his first film. However, Herrmann's background in radio provided ideal training for his debut Hollywood assignment.

"Here is [a] chance for you to do something witty and amusing," Welles wired to Herrmann, "and now is the time for you to do it."

Welles signed Herrmann for twelve weeks to compose, orchestrate, and record the full score—a luxury in 1940 Hollywood.

"This not only gave me ample time to think about the film and to work out a general artistic plan for the score," Herrmann said, "but also enabled me to do my own orchestration and conducting."

Herrmann was as thoughtful about his musical plan as Toland and Ferguson were about the visual plan for the film. However, the challenges were still extraordinary. For his first Hollywood project, Herrmann had to create not only a musical score of depth and complexity, but one that included authentic moments of grand opera. And the opera was needed for actual filming sessions, so those passages had to be completed much earlier than the rest of the score.

"The problem was to create something that would convey to the audience the feeling of the quicksand into which she is suddenly thrown," Herrmann said forty years later. "It had to be done cinematically. It had to be done fast. We had to have the sound of an enormous orchestra pounding her. There is no opera in existence that opens that way. We had to create one."

Welles, as well versed in opera as in the other arts, reviewed the musical needs for the production with Herrmann throughout July 1940. For Susan's disastrous debut, Welles and Herrmann tentatively discussed using a real opera, in particular *Thaïs* by Jules Massenet because of its exotic Egyptian setting. But *Thaïs* was ruled out, they agreed, because the opera in the film required the added drama of Susan singing as the curtain went up. Herrmann reported back within little more than three weeks, having created *Salammbô*—the short excerpts of an opera needed for Susan's debut that were based on imagery from the novel by Gustave Flaubert set in third-century B.C. Carthage (a real opera on the same subject had been written in 1889 by Ernest Reyer, but it is rarely performed and was not used in *Citizen Kane*). To ensure there were opportunities for highly visual costumes, Herrmann created the segments in the style of the gaudy "nineteenth-century French-Oriental operatic school." John Houseman wrote the lyrics, in French.

Herrmann deliberately wrote the opera segments in a range much too high for Susan Alexander, "so that a girl with a modest voice," he said, "would be completely hopeless in it."

Susan Alexander's performances of operatic arias were sung by Jean Forward, a lyric soprano from Oakland, California. Forward, otherwise a fine performer, deliberately sang weakly and above her normal range, thus intentionally straining the performance so Susan sounded painfully frail. Susan attempts to sing an aria from a real opera—"Una voce poco fa" from Gioachino Rossini's *The Barber of Seville,* with libretto by Cesare Sterbini—which she performs for Kane in the scene that transitions from her boardinghouse to her new apartment and also for her hapless performance during the singing lesson with Signor Matiste that illustrates Kane's stubbornness about forcing her to continue performing (as a comparison, watch any of the fine performances of "Una voce poco fa" or the aria from "*Salammbô"* on YouTube to hear how pathetic Susan was supposed to be).

For the other nonoperatic sections of the score, Herrmann composed one reel of film at a time as they were being edited.

"In this way, I had a sense of the picture being built, and of my own music being part of that building," Herrmann said three weeks after *Citizen Kane* opened. "Most musical scores in Hollywood are written after the film is entirely finished, and the composer must adapt his music to the scenes on the screen. In many scenes of *Citizen Kane,* an entirely different method was used—many of the sequences being tailored to match the music."

Herrmann composed two main musical themes for *Citizen Kane.* The first, a theme for Kane, Herrmann titled "Destiny." This five-note theme is heard as the film begins, when the "No Trespassing" sign at Xanadu appears.

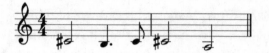

Herrmann also composed a haunting eleven-note theme to identify Rose-bud. This passage is played in several variations during the early scenes of *Citizen Kane*: the first five notes of the Rosebud theme play as the shot dissolves from the woven wire fence around Xanadu to cast iron, and again thirty seconds later when the drawbridge appears; the full eleven-note theme plays after the light goes out in Kane's room before he dies.

Even for an artist with Herrmann's reputation for swift composition, the principal music for *Citizen Kane* evolved with remarkable speed.

"Both themes came to me rather automatically," Herrmann said. "At the very beginning—I was very lucky the first hour—I hit on the two sound sequences that would bear the weight of the film."

The Destiny theme and the Rosebud theme are used in many variations throughout *Citizen Kane.* For instance, the grim rendition of the Destiny theme heard during the opening moments of the film was transformed into a bouncy, upbeat polka style as Kane and Jed Leland arrive at the *Inquirer* for the first time.

"The permutations of this theme are complex," Herrmann said. "Later in the film it becomes a can-can, jazz, all kinds of things."

Herrmann also used the Rosebud theme throughout the film to hint at the identity of the sled.

"The Rosebud theme is heard again and again under various guises," Herrmann said, "and if followed closely, is a clue to the ultimate identity of Rosebud itself."

For example, when young Kane is shown playing on his sled in the snow, the lovely lilting sweep of the Rosebud theme is heard in the background. As Kane leaves Susan's room in Xanadu after destroying it and says, "Rosebud," the theme can be heard playing softly on a solo flute and continues as he walks through the hall of mirrors. When Kane and Susan first meet, a variation of the Rosebud theme is playing softly and continues into Susan's room when we see her reflection in her dressing table mirror—the snow globe sitting to the side in plain view.

No character in *Citizen Kane* ever learns the meaning of Rosebud, and the audience does not learn the truth until the last two minutes of the film. But for those who knew what to listen for, Herrmann kept them informed all along.

Herrmann created different but equally thoughtful melodies used in other key scenes. For the breakfast table sequence with Kane and Emily, Herrmann developed music to correspond with the passing of the years—and the change in the relationship between the couple.

"The popular music of this period corresponding to the images would have been a romantic waltz," Herrmann said. "So each change in mood and each cut was written as another variation on a basic waltz theme. The structure then is very simple: a series of waltz variations in absolutely classic form, giving unity to the otherwise fragmented sequence."

In addition, Herrmann composed some humorous musical moments. When young Kane throws a snowball at the sign above his mother's boardinghouse, the music stops abruptly with the "plunk" of a harp and violins when the snowball hits its target. When Thompson departs the Thatcher Library with the crack "Good-bye, everybody—thanks for the use of the hall," the six-note "wa-wa" of trumpets is as sarcastic as a snicker. When some pompous reviewers criticized Herrmann for the blat of trumpets as a musical close to the scene, Herrmann was steadfast; forty years later, he said, "I would do the same thing again."

Herrmann also composed music that served as sound effects. When Susan is playing with her puzzles, the "tick-tock" of a clock heard within the music is the pluck of violin strings combined with strikes on a woodblock.

Herrmann did not compose the "Charlie Kane" song, which serves as the publisher's theme throughout the picture. The music was taken from the Mexican song "A Poco No," and new lyrics were written by Herman Ruby. The lighthearted song is performed during the party in the *Inquirer* newsroom by Charles Bennett, the actor who appeared in the scene along with the dancing girls. The song is also used as source music (music coming from origins within a scene). For example, as Leland enters the *Inquirer* building to confront Kane after the election, the "Charlie Kane" song is heard playing mournfully nearby on an accordion; the music continues—but softer—inside the building as Bernstein sends the campaign staff home.

Source music can also be heard elsewhere in *Citizen Kane*. When Thompson first visits Susan Alexander at the El Rancho nightclub, a muted trumpet, piano, vibes, and accordion play "In a Mizz" by Charlie Barnet and Haven Johnson. On his second visit, a solo piano plays the same tune. Later, as Susan recovers from her suicide attempt, the street music outside the hotel is a hurdy-gurdy quietly playing "Una voce poco fa"—a reminder of her failures before her singing career began.

When the musical score was completed, Herrmann's background in radio and his familiarity with the split-second requirements of timing a broadcast were indispensable when Welles' frequent tinkering with the film forced changes in the music.

"Most composers go right through the roof if you make any changes in the film after the music is written," recalled editor Robert Wise. "We gave Bernie all of his cues and then later we found out that Orson wanted to make some changes in the film.

"I was expecting big problems, but Bernie would make those adjustments and changes in the score so fast it didn't seem to bother him. That must have come from his days in radio. He would look at the score and say, 'Well, let's see— we can drop from bar four to bar eight, and pick up here,' and it was done."

Herrmann, said sound engineer James G. Stewart, "understood the type of orchestration that would go underneath dialogue.

"That made it possible to have more music underneath dialogue, and very effectively. And then, of course, with Orson's insistence on good original record-ings—so that you had a good intelligible dialogue track, and well-orchestrated music to put underneath it—the combination jelled."

To perform his musical score, Herrmann had access to the entire forty-five-piece RKO studio orchestra, but most of the music for *Citizen Kane* required only a fraction of that number. Herrmann quickly learned that in Hollywood, he could assign or hire musicians playing specific types of instruments for indi-vidual recording sessions. As a result, he had a free hand in composing for any combination of instruments he desired, whether the routine or the uncommon.

For example, in some of the opening scenes of the film, the music is played solely by low woodwinds, including four alto flutes. The music that bridges one scene to the next was often played by no more than two to four instruments.

The brief musical segment performed while Thompson reads the line in Thatcher's memoirs about the onset of the Depression required only a small group of brass and tympani.

One of the few passages that employed the full orchestra is played in the final minutes of the film, during which the Destiny theme and the Rosebud theme are performed with gradually ascending orchestral force: the camera tracks over the relics of Kane's life (primarily variations of the Destiny theme), the sled burns (the Rosebud theme fully reveals the secret of the sled), and smoke pours from Xanadu's chimney (with cymbals crashing that leads into the Destiny theme).

"The ending of *Citizen Kane* gave me a wonderful opportunity to arrive at a complete musical statement," Herrmann said. "Because I wanted to draw all the threads of the film together, this last sequence is played by a conventional symphony orchestra . . . for the simple reason that, from the time the music of the final sequence begins to the end of the film, the music has effectively left the film and become an apotheosis of the entire work."

Although Herrmann was an enthusiastic collaborator and close friend of Welles', he could be hot tempered. His discussions with Welles occasionally escalated into loud clashes.

"I remember Bernie once slammed open the door to the dubbing stage and began telling us what he thought of Orson's manners and methods," said Stewart. "Then he slammed out again, and we all sat there a little stunned.

"Then the door burst open, and Bernie stuck his head in and said, 'Remember, I'm not talking about Orson the artist.'"

Herrmann's composition was hailed as a masterpiece of film scoring. His work on *Citizen Kane* opened Hollywood's doors, and he became one of the most popular and respected film composers.

Herrmann's success with *Citizen Kane,* said David Raksin, the composer of the score for *Laura,* "was just Bernie's particular talent and his gift for doing very simple things. And it immediately made its mark. Everyone knew there was a remarkable new guy in town."

Herrmann would ultimately compose scores for more than thirty motion pictures, including seven of Alfred Hitchcock's best productions, in addition to writing traditional classical compositions and conducting the world's premier orchestras. But *Citizen Kane* was Herrmann's first and—in many ways—best experience in Hollywood.

"I had heard of the many handicaps that exist for a composer in Hollywood," Herrmann said. "One was the great speed with which scores often had to be written—sometimes in as little as two or three weeks. Another was that the composer seldom had time to do his own orchestration. And that once the music was written and conducted, the composer had little to say about the sound levels or dynamics of the score in the finished film.

"Not one of these conditions prevailed during the production of *Citizen Kane.*"

Independent of Herrmann, a key musical segment was performed for the film by some of the top jazz performers of the era. To play excerpts of "In a Mizz" for the picnic in the Florida Everglades, the Mercury company recruited musicians who performed in the thriving jazz scene in Hollywood and the Los Angeles Central Avenue district. The list of performers, which reads like the lineup for an all-star combo, was led by Cee Pee Johnson (guitar and tom-toms), with Kurtland Bradford (alto saxophone), Buddy Banks (tenor saxophone), Buddy Collette (alto saxophone, baritone saxophone, and clarinet), Raymond Tate and Loyal Walker (trumpets), Johnny Miller (bass), and Alton Redd (vocals).

Later, Welles would recall that he used "In a Mizz," and in particular the "It Can't Be Love" section of the lyrics, after seeing the song performed by the King Cole Trio at a Los Angeles nightclub. With Kane and Susan having their final argument in that scene before Susan leaves him the next day, "I kind of based the whole scene around that song," Welles said.

But some film historians interpreted Welles' comment to mean that Nat King Cole actually performs in *Citizen Kane,* presumably playing the piano off camera in Susan's nightclub—an impossible-to-establish point that has crept into many studies and Web sites about the film. Cole, a superb piano player in addition to his prowess as a vocalist, would have been a welcome addition to the performances in *Citizen Kane,* but there are no records in the correspondence or accounting reports from Production #281 indicating that Cole was hired or otherwise involved in the film.

Early in January 1941, after five months of planning and writing, four months of shooting, and nearly twelve weeks of postproduction, the first rough prints of

Citizen Kane were ready to view. The film was, indeed, still rough—it was shy some special effects, bits of music, and a few lines of dialogue that needed to be rerecorded. Nevertheless, the studio was ready to schedule the release date of its newest picture. The premiere for RKO Production #281 was set for February 14, 1941.

Orson Welles at the center of the media storm, adroitly handling reporters at the morning-after press conference held during the national uproar over his October 30, 1938, broadcast of *The War of the Worlds*. At the time, Welles was already an accomplished painter, writer, radio performer, and emerging Broadway director and star. "Were Welles's 23 years set forth in fiction form," *Time* magazine reported in 1938, "any self-respecting critic would damn the story as too implausible for serious consideration."

The Hearts of Age, an eight-minute film that the nineteen-year-old Welles coproduced in 1934 *(top)*, offered little insight into the abilities of the future filmmaker. However, the footage Welles directed in 1938 to accompany his stage production of the farce *Too Much Johnson (bottom)* provided some hints of the camera angles, placement of actors, and film style he was beginning to develop—such as this scene with Joseph Cotten *(center,* see the top of his straw hat) chasing Edgar Barrier *(lower right,* see the other straw hat) that foreshadowed shots of Kane's mementos at Xanadu at the end of *Citizen Kane.* Little more than a year later, Welles would be prowling RKO studio.

Welles's sense of the visual—a potent creative tool in the planning for *Citizen Kane*—was vividly apparent in his early stage productions, such as the stark fascist imagery for *Julius Caesar (top)*, or the voodoo-themed designs for *Macbeth (bottom)*.

RKO studio president George Schaefer after a successful fishing trip aboard his boat, *Jack and Jill*. Schaefer started work in the film industry in 1914 as a secretary, moving up through the Hollywood hierarchy before joining RKO as chief executive in 1938. Mastermind behind a plan for "Quality Pictures at a Premium Price," Schaefer sold the RKO board on this direction for the company that brought new filmmakers to the studio, some with no experience in Hollywood—like Orson Welles.

The announcement from the 1940–41 RKO report to shareholders on the studio's upcoming films, which revealed the name of Welles's first production—a rare description of the project as *John Citizen USA*.

ORSON WELLES
in
JOHN CITIZEN, U. S. A.
and
ONE OTHER PRODUCTION

Herman Mankiewicz (cowriter of *Citizen Kane*). "Nobody was more miserable, more bitter, and funnier than Mank," said Welles. "A perfect monument to self-destruction."

> ### A New "School for Scandal."
> "The School for Scandal," with Mrs. Insull as Lady Teazle, was produced at the Little Theatre last night. It will be reviewed in tomorrow's TIMES.

On October 22, 1925, then-theatrical critic Herman Mankiewicz was too drunk to write his review of *The School for Scandal*, so *The New York Times* was forced to publish this humiliating announcement. For Mankiewicz, the painful personal incident translated perfectly to the script of *Citizen Kane*.

Mankiewicz *(center)* and Houseman *(right)* wrote in Victorville—far from Hollywood's temptations. Welles *(left)* made the three-hour trek at least once to review progress, but otherwise let the pair work undisturbed. (This is the only known photograph of the trio working on the *Citizen Kane* script.) The woman applying suntan lotion to Mankiewicz's head is either Rita Alexander or an unidentified nurse.

The *Citizen Kane* production, on Stage 3 at RKO in Culver City in mid-August 1940, rehearsing the closing moments of Susan Alexander's operatic debut. Welles had injured his left ankle on August 10 and was temporarily confined to a wheelchair. Cinematographer Gregg Toland is wrapped around the tripod under the camera, checking the lighting on Dorothy Comingore. With overhead lighting not possible for most shots in *Citizen Kane* because of ceilings constructed over the sets, head-on lighting like this, either above or below the camera, was a necessity.

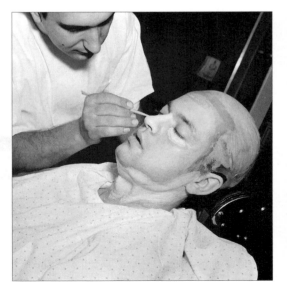

Makeup artist Maurice Seiderman adds bags under Welles's eyes for one of the 27 setups of makeup that aged Welles from 27 to 78 for *Citizen Kane*. Already applied are a neck wattle and a fine mesh net over his hair in preparation for the addition of a bald cap. Publicity shots such as this one required RKO staff photographer Alex (Sandy) Kahle to be available for the four hours or more required to apply makeup for Kane at age 70; Kahle, like Seiderman and Welles, likely reported to the studio as early as 3 A.M.

Perry Ferguson—who looked more like a Hollywood leading man than a pioneering art director—was an invaluable contributor to the visual plan for *Citizen Kane*, and even more important to the production's survival for his economizing when the budget had to be cut by 30 percent. "A severe restriction may be turned into an advantage if we only look at it from the right viewpoint," Ferguson said. "We can minimize actual set construction by taking advantage of the camera's powers of suggestion."

This shot of Ruth Warrick (Emily Monroe Norton) shown in the theatrical trailer provides a brief glimpse of one of the sets built several feet above the stage floor that allowed Gregg Toland to shoot from extremely low angles, a key element in the visual goals for the film. (Theatrical trailer frame still: 00:01:16)

(a)

(b)

This sequence of four frames shows one of the many dissolves in *Citizen Kane*—this one a complex series of shots requiring special effects—that were planned well in advance of shooting to support Gregg Toland's goal of seamless, visually interesting transitions from one shot to the next. (a) When Bernstein talks about Kane's first visit to the *Inquirer*, the shot dissolves slowly from Bernstein to (b)

(c)

(d)

a matte painting of the top floors of the *Inquirer* building—note the lingering image of Bernstein's windows—which then dissolves again to (c) the full-size set of the *Inquirer* entrance as the camera moves lower to show (d) Welles and Joseph Cotten looking at the building. (Frame stills beginning 0:32:37)

An extreme example of deep focus combined with a deep set: Kane prepares to sign away control of his failing empire. Everett Sloane (Bernstein) sits only inches from the camera, with George Coulouris (Walter Thatcher) three feet from him across the table, and Welles more than twenty feet away at the back of the set—all in sharp focus. The shot is also a prime example of Gregg Toland's goal of simplifying the visuals: "Instead of following the usual practice of cutting from a close-up to an 'insert' which elaborates on the close-up, we made a single, straight shot, compressing the whole scene into a single composition," Toland said. (Frame still: 27:57)

The scene of Susan Alexander singing for Kane in her second apartment shows how detailed set decoration, intricate lighting, and supplemental space at the back of the set all combine to increase the realism—a primary goal of the visual plan for *Citizen Kane*. The bedroom in Susan's apartment was not in the original designs for *Citizen Kane*—nor were separate spaces at the back of many other sets—but were added as the visual plan for the film evolved. (Frame still: 1:00:22)

Bernard Herrmann *(top right)*, composer of the musical score for *Citizen Kane*, here with Welles *(left)* in November 1939 during rehearsal for the *Campbell Playhouse* radio program on CBS. "Most composers go right through the roof if you make any changes in the film after the music is written," recalled editor Robert Wise. "We gave Bernie all of his cues and then later found out that Orson wanted to make changes. Bernie made those changes in the score so fast it didn't seem to bother him. He looked at a score and said, 'Well, let's see—we can drop from bar four to bar eight, and pick up here,' and it was done."

The theatrical trailer for *Citizen Kane* includes the only known backstage footage from the film, including this shot "for purposes of ballyhoo" of the dancers from the *Inquirer* party singing on the set used for Georgie's Place—the scenes cut by the censors because the locale was "inescapably a brothel." Note the set for Mary Kane's boarding house *(left, rear)*, also on Stage 8 at RKO in Culver City. (Theatrical trailer frame still, 00:00:44)

Archrival gossip columnists Hedda Hopper and Louella Parsons pretend to pal it up at the Mocambo nightclub in Hollywood in 1948; Hopper was able to generate fabricated charm better than Parsons ever could. "Mr. Hearst would have ignored *Citizen Kane* had he been given the chance," said Herman Mankiewicz to Alexander Woollcott, "but this behavior was denied him chiefly because of an idiot named Louella Parsons and a very smart woman named Hedda Hopper."

William Randolph Hearst was a ruthless media giant; when actor Douglas Fairbanks asked Hearst why he built his empire on newspapers and not by making movies, Hearst replied, "You can crush a man with journalism, but you can't with motion pictures."

Marion Davies, a talented film actress and for more than thirty years Hearst's devoted mistress, was no flop in motion pictures as Susan Alexander was in her nightmarish experience as an opera singer.

Hearst Castle, the sunny estate in the foothills of Central California *(top)*. The warm woody interiors—the morning room is shown here *(left)*— and bright flowery grounds at Hearst's real-life mountaintop palace are the polar opposite of the gloomy Gothic vision of Xanadu *(bottom)* in *Citizen Kane*. (Frame still 1:38:33.)

After months of delays, *Citizen Kane* premiered at New York's Palace Theater on May 1, 1941, followed by near-unanimous acclaim from America's film critics—and large doses of crow-eating by Welles's detractors, who said success for the first-time director would be impossible.

THANK YOU, Orson Welles!

CITIZEN KANE

IS A VERY FINE PRODUCTION, THE RESULT OF GREAT INITIATIVE AND COURAGE, ESPECIALLY UNDER THE MOST TRYING OF CIRCUMSTANCES.

The essence of show business is to present the new, the novel and the unusual to the public.

You were not given the chance to present your ideas, but were severely criticized for daring even to have an idea!

You were condemned before being tried!

Your triumph is one of the great accomplishments in motion picture history, and proof that America is still the land of opportunity, where there will always be room for those with dreams and courage to bring them to reality.

RKO RADIO PICTURES, INC.

GEORGE J. SCHAEFER, President

In the May 1, 1941, editions of *Variety* and the *Hollywood Reporter*, George Schaefer published eight-page supplements that acknowledged Welles and *Citizen Kane*, and also gave a backhand slap to those in Hollywood who had criticized the studio for hiring the young director (the final page is shown here).

The first "mention" of *Citizen Kane* in Hearst newspapers after the film was banned from their pages appeared in October 1941 in this advertisement for a "Big Screen Attraction"; five months after the film was released, its name was still not published in Hearst papers.

Decades after the filming of *Citizen Kane*, some of the statues used on the set of the great hall of Xanadu were stored in a warehouse near the lot that once housed RKO's studios in Culver City. Still visible were tags that read XANADU, FLORIDA.

Orson Welles, basking in the adulation after receiving his Life Achievement Award from the American Film Institute on February 9, 1975. Although always in demand as an actor, Welles, at this point almost sixty, was endlessly on a quest to fund the next film project he wanted to direct.

PART
TWO

CONFLICT

What I saw appalled me. It was an impudent, murderous trick, even for
the boy genius, to perpetrate on a newspaper giant.
—HEDDA HOPPER

The rumor mill spins endlessly in Hollywood. In 1940, as now, the motion picture business conceals few secrets, and late in the year many of the insider whisperings involved the filming on Orson Welles' closed set.

The gossip started shortly after filming commenced. Welles had not hidden that his picture portrayed the life of a fictional newspaper publisher, but as production progressed, the word began to spread that the film was a near factual exposé of one of the most powerful men in America: William Randolph Hearst, a media giant whose corporate web at its height included twenty-six newspapers, sixteen magazines, eleven radio stations, and five news services.

As usually recalled, the story of the conspiracy against *Citizen Kane*, because of its supposed parallels to Hearst, began with Welles caught in the festering power struggle between movie columnists Hedda Hopper and Louella Parsons, two ruthless competitors in the Hollywood gossip factory. As the story goes, Hopper, after seeing a rough cut during the first week of January, alerted the Hearst organization to the "dangers" of *Citizen Kane,* and Parsons then saw the film and took up the Hearst cause with an unprecedented pressure campaign by a journalist against the film industry. Although Parsons (who wrote for Hearst) and Hopper (a syndicated columnist at the Chandler family–controlled *Los Angeles Times* and Parsons' main competitor) had been among the most vocal of Welles' supporters when he arrived in Hollywood, they would later exercise their considerable influence within the film industry to try to ruin his film.

But the plot against Welles, RKO, and *Citizen Kane* was much darker and more insidious than the results of a feud between two gossip columnists. Before Hopper and Parsons seemingly started the war against *Citizen Kane,* the Hearst organization—working under the direction of the corporation's senior leadership and with the knowledge of Hearst himself—was already planning to disrupt the film. The Hearst organization coordinated a national effort to crush *Citizen Kane* and discredit Orson Welles, first by trying to prevent the film's release and then by blackmailing Hollywood's leadership, Red-baiting Welles and his associates, publishing a blitz of distorted articles about the director, and ultimately scheming to force RKO to destroy the film.

The full story of *Citizen Kane* and Hearst remains a black cloud over this period in American journalism: a newspaper organization that described itself as standing for "Genuine Democracy," with words like *Character, Quality,* and *An American Paper for the American People* featured prominently at the top of most editions, considered itself so menaced that it tore up the First Amendment and ignored the right to free expression in its efforts to destroy the film.

In the first few weeks of 1941, whether *Citizen Kane* actually depicted the life of William Randolph Hearst or not was irrelevant; Louella Parsons believed it, Hedda Hopper believed it, and Hearst's legion of lawyers, editors, and informants most certainly believed it. The pressure applied by the Hearst organization grew to such extremes that early in 1941, there were moments when *Citizen Kane* was in grave danger of never being seen by the public and instead winding up in the incinerator, negative and all.

The trouble had several possible origins. From the beginning of *Citizen Kane*'s production, the Hollywood press knew an unusual story was brewing on the Welles set. With reports of Welles' flair for the incredible preceding him, film industry insiders began to speculate that the fictional story Orson Welles was producing at RKO might not be so fictional after all.

As early as September 1940, rumors about *Citizen Kane*'s possible links to Hearst appeared in the national press. The September 16 edition of *Newsweek* reported that "the script of Orson Welles' first movie, *Citizen Kane,* was sent to William Randolph Hearst for perusal after columnists had hinted it dealt with his life. Hearst approved it without comment."

But the *Newsweek* brief may have been an error; there are no records in the RKO production files, Welles' Mercury papers, or the Hearst archives that this "perusal" occurred. And the original rumors about Hearst's link to Kane may have developed when those reporters who were allowed a rare visit to the set from time to time began to piece together bits of the plot. Based on this sketchy information, some writers may have concluded that the film was solely about Hearst.

Or the idea may have first traveled other paths. Herman Mankiewicz, in an extraordinarily unwise move, gave a copy of the script to fellow screenwriter Charles Lederer, nephew of Marion Davies, Hearst's mistress. Mankiewicz, never a long-range planner, was concerned the script would offend Davies and as a result adversely affect his future as a screenwriter—a potential problem he should have considered before he co-wrote a script about a fictional publisher.

Some accounts, with no factual foundation, have reported that Lederer passed along the script to his aunt Marion, who showed it to Hearst and then to their lawyers. But for those who actually asked Lederer what happened, his answer was simple and direct: Lederer said he read the script and then returned it to Mankiewicz without showing it to anyone else.

"[Mankiewicz] asked me if I thought Marion would be offended and I said I didn't think so," Lederer told director Peter Bogdanovich. "The script I read didn't have the flavor of Marion and Hearst."

Most likely, the actual responsibility for the rising concern did not fall on Lederer, Mankiewicz, or *Newsweek*. The leaks about the script and the rumors that followed probably occurred because of RKO executive J. R. McDonough, who Welles said was openly an opponent of the young director, his production, and the Mercury company. McDonough, without permission from Welles, sent a copy of the *Citizen Kane* script to RKO's New York office with no restriction on its distribution. The script was copied and leaked to reporters—"exactly," Welles said later in a list of grievances about mistreatment by RKO managers, "what we were trying to prevent."

Whatever the source, between the *Newsweek* item and the bubbling rumors, in the autumn of 1940 the Hearst organization was alerted that the young upstart making news in Hollywood was, in their view, threatening "the Chief" (as he was called by those who knew him or pretended to know him). Hearst had built an organization that was a bastion of self-righteous sensationalist journalism. Hearst sought readership rather than credibility, publishing without discretion to create national agendas for his own purposes while working to suppress others like Welles from expressing their own views.

With *Citizen Kane* only weeks into production, Parsons was ordered to contact Welles and confront him with one question: Was Kane really Hearst?

"When I heard that the film Welles was making was about Mr. Hearst," Parsons wrote in her memoirs, "I called him to ask if this was so.

" 'Take my word for it,' he said. 'It isn't. It's about a completely fictional publisher.'

"I took his word, and so informed the Hearst editors, who kept insisting that it did concern Mr. Hearst."

Hearst leadership ignored Parsons' assurances; as a result, late in 1940 a quiet investigation began within the organization. Eventually, three objectives would develop: first, to find out everything about Welles' liberal leanings and political involvement; second, to learn if Hearst could suppress the film by marshaling enough support among the studio chiefs and theater owners to keep the film off the screens; and later, to try to drum up enough support in Hollywood to buy the film and destroy it.

Hearst had plenty of resources at his disposal: the anti-Welles planning was anchored by his personal assistant Joseph Willicombe in California and bolstered by Richard Berlin, a well-connected twenty-two-year company veteran and a climber within the organization who in 1941 headed Hearst's magazine division in New York (Berlin was Hearst's personal choice to succeed him; Berlin was named president in 1942 and CEO after Hearst's death in 1951). Also involved in the fight was the entire Hearst legal team, as well as the hundreds of editors and reporters at Hearst newspapers, magazines, and wire services who were eager to make points with the Chief and could turn their attention to any subject that was passed down to them from on high— as they would do many times concerning Welles and RKO in the first half of 1941.

RKO was first alerted to the problem on January 2—before Hopper or Parsons knew that a screening would occur—when the studio learned that its request to purchase a $5,000 advertisement in *Cosmopolitan* to tout *Citizen Kane* had been declined by Berlin himself. Clearly, the Hearst leadership was already convinced that the film was a blast directly at Hearst; its publications were declining ads for *Citizen Kane* before the film was finished or before anyone from the organization was clear about what the film explored.

"I was refusing the advertisement for *Cosmopolitan* purely on the grounds that it was an unkind gesture against Mr. Hearst," Berlin told Willicombe on January 2. Berlin reported that he told the RKO representative to report back to

Schaefer that "*Cosmopolitan* does not wish to carry advertising on pictures that endeavor to destroy people's character."

A polite rejection is one thing; active suppression of a film is another. What RKO did *not* know was that Berlin had already been busy contacting the other major studio heads to see how they could stop *Citizen Kane*—in particular Harry Warner (the New York–based president of Warner Bros.) and Spyros Skouras (who was in charge of theaters at 20th Century–Fox and whose family owned one of the large independent theater chains in America). Together, the pair represented hundreds of theaters that might have screened *Citizen Kane*.

In the same letter that described his rejection of the ad for *Cosmopolitan*, Berlin noted his efforts to collude with some of the studios to keep *Citizen Kane* out of theaters. On New Year's Day, Brad Sears, the general manager of Warner Bros., told Berlin that Harry Warner had already directed that *Citizen Kane* would be banned from the company's national chain of theaters.

Berlin also spoke directly to Skouras, who was a personal friend, and received the same assurances.

"Spyros," Berlin said, "was going to make it his job to talk to every important independent theater chain operator and see that they boycotted the picture."

Berlin said that Skouras would do everything possible to stop what he called "this vicious picture." "It looks to me," said Berlin, "as if *Citizen Kane* will not have much of a showing."

It was the end of a very bad week for Orson Welles, RKO, and *Citizen Kane*. Three days earlier, on a gloomy Monday, December 30, *The Hollywood Reporter* broke the news that *Friday* magazine, a sensationalized scandal sheet, was set to print a story that linked *Citizen Kane* directly to Hearst.

"The Orson Welles interests are concerned about it," wrote *Hollywood Reporter* publisher W. R. Wilkerson. "Seems most of the dope on this hushed-up yarn was dug up in New York by *Friday* editors who knew Mercury players returning from parts in the flicker."

Welles and his staff had good reason to be concerned. *Friday,* with sensational headlines splashed across its cover and little regard for accuracy, may be remembered solely for its contribution to damaging *Citizen Kane*. Calling itself "The Weekly Magazine That Dares to Tell the Truth," and with headlines such as "Does Basketball Kill?" and "Ford's Secret Gestapo Exposed," the weekly magazine, during its short run in the early 1940s, chewed up and spit out whomever it chose. In January 1941, without provocation, *Friday's* writers did everything possible to ruin Orson Welles.

Friday did not carry its story about *Citizen Kane* until its issue dated January 17, 1941 (it was on newsstands about a week earlier), so it was not the first publication to disclose points about the plot of the film. What the magazine did print was a photo feature about *Citizen Kane*—but instead of showcasing the film and its stars, it published a hatchet job in a point-by-point "exposé comparison" between Welles' story and the life of William Randolph Hearst; the article was written by a reporter who had not seen the film or read the script.

Friday printed seven photographs and captions that "revealed" how plot points of *Citizen Kane* were a virtual match for Hearst's life, and the reporter created most of his "facts" about the film and the real-life publisher out of thin air. The story that accompanied the photos was even worse and was loaded with slurs about Welles and his work habits.

"Orson Welles' first motion picture, *Citizen Kane,* had better be strictly colossal, or Hollywood will give him the old heave-ho back to Mars where he came from," the story began. "He came two years ago and it has taken him that long to produce a picture. Most of the time, Orson was amusing himself. His imported cast grew beards and cut them off, or dyed their blonde hair black, as Orson's newest idea succeeded its predecessor."

When *Friday* focused on *Citizen Kane* itself, the magazine drilled home the point that Welles had maintained a closed set specifically because he had something to hide—namely, that the film was about Hearst. "There was only one script," *Friday* stated. "Orson wrote it and has been sleeping with it under his pillow."

Friday saved the worst for last. The article closed with this bombshell: "Louella Parsons, Hollywood's correspondent for Hearst, has been praising Welles lavishly, giving *Citizen Kane* a terrific advance build-up. When informed of these outbursts of praise, Welles said, 'This is something I cannot understand. Wait until the woman finds out that the picture's about her boss.'" *Friday* carried the story, even though, as editor Dan Gillmor later confessed to Welles, his source for the alleged statement about Parsons was "fallible."

The article reinforced what Hollywood observers were already starting to believe—that *Citizen Kane* was about Hearst. But even before *Friday* appeared, controversy was rushing straight at *Citizen Kane.*

On January 3, Welles previewed the film for the first time to viewers outside the studio. The trade press called the audience "a small group of friends," but the audience also included one extremely interested and angry reporter: columnist Hedda Hopper. Welles had not invited Hopper to the screening, even though months before he had promised that she would be included in the first audience.

Hopper and Parsons had not gone along with the crowd's early disdain of Welles when he signed his contract, possibly because the young, handsome, charismatic star had taken plenty of time to charm the influential middle-aged columnists. From the time Welles arrived in Hollywood, Hopper had been one of those who publicly and actively supported the young director. More than a year before, she had stoutly defended Welles when the rest of the motion picture industry was screaming about the mistake RKO had made by signing him.

"Too bad Orson Welles isn't an Englishman," Hopper wrote in September 1939. "If he had been, Hollywood would never have given him such a runaround. We reserve that for our own citizens. Mr. Welles doesn't scare easily and I'm thinking he'll make Hollywood sit up and beg for mercy."

By some estimates, Hopper mentioned Welles in her columns twice as much as any other Hollywood personality—publicity that was acknowledged with lavish floral gifts in December 1939.

"I wish you could have seen my little home at Christmas time," Hopper wrote to Welles in January 1940 after he sent her baskets of flowers. "I'll be darned if it didn't look like a florist's shop. Yours were so beautiful. I want you to know how much I appreciate your thinking of me, and thank God, my flowers came before I'm dead."

But all of that was a year gone by. The January 3 screening was supposed to have been, said Mercury publicist Herb Drake, "a dread secret," but word squeezed out from the main RKO press department, and *The Hollywood Reporter* got the word and published a news brief. When Hopper saw the note, she demanded to attend—a command no doubt buttressed by a separate news brief in *Variety* that poured gasoline on the already simmering flames:

"Nationally-distributed magazines and even house organs are carrying the story, which merely report what *Variety* reported several months ago: *Citizen Kane* is patterned somewhat after the biog of none other than William Randolph Hearst."

Hopper had not been invited to the screening because Welles was showing not the final film, but rather an incomplete rough cut intended only to accommodate the long-lead deadlines of the weekly and monthly magazines, especially *Life, Look,* and *Redbook.* Nevertheless, her angry phone call to Drake generated an immediate and apologetic telegram, in which Welles reinvited the columnist to attend.

"Dearest Hedda," Welles began, "I owe you the biggest apology of my life and here it comes. Drake said, 'The magazine people—*Look* and *Life*—have to make their deadline, so we must show them the picture no matter how bad or incomplete very soon.' I said, 'Must we?' He said, 'We must.'

". . . fully realize I have broken a solemn promise that you'd be the first to see *Kane*. Please understand and forgive. Come tonight if you must, but it still stinks. Many shots are missing or only tests are cut in and we need music like Britain needs planes. Love, Orson."

That night, Hopper and five others became the first people outside of Welles' inner circle and RKO management to see *Citizen Kane*. Among the magazine reporters, the reaction, said Drake, was "terrific."

"James Francis Crow, a reviewer for *Look,* said it was one of the most unusual pictures and one of the finest pictures he'd ever seen," Drake said. "Dick Pollard went even further. Doug Churchill was enormously impressed but discovered that his normal critical clichés were not sufficient to deal with the subject."

But not Hopper. To the columnist—always eager to rush to a hasty judgment—there was no question that Charles Foster Kane was in reality William Randolph Hearst.

"She was . . . violently angry at the 'vicious and irresponsible attack on a great man,'" reported Drake.

"What I saw appalled me," Hopper said years later. "It was an impudent, murderous trick, even for the boy genius, to perpetrate on a newspaper giant."

Hopper warned Welles that he would not get away with what she believed was an obvious attack on Hearst. Welles insisted that his film would stand on its merits, regardless of what Hopper assumed. Then Hopper took the first step in ruining whatever chance for early financial success *Citizen Kane* might have achieved. Even though Hearst was chief executive of the newspaper that was her organization's main competition, she called Oscar Lawler, one of Hearst's attorneys, to alert him that *Citizen Kane* was all about Hearst.

Hopper maintained a friendly relationship with Hearst as well as Lawler. But for Hopper, the call accomplished something much more important than warning a friend: not only did Hopper inform on Welles, but at the same time she discredited her principal rival, Louella Parsons, motion picture editor and columnist for Hearst's International News Service.

"Hedda has for some time been letting it be known that she would be much better in Louella's job than Louella is—which is true," Mankiewicz wrote to Alexander Woollcott. "It is not impossible that her call was connected with her ambitions."

Parsons was often considered America's first movie columnist and a writer with considerable influence in Hollywood. At her peak, her column appeared in more than four hundred newspapers worldwide. Parsons had supported Welles at the beginning of his filmmaking career. From the day Welles arrived in Hollywood, she used her column to track his moves and provided plenty of solid backing for the young director when he was on tenuous footing during the failures of *Heart of Darkness* and *The Smiler with a Knife*.

"If Mr. Welles makes a great picture, I'll be the first to say so," Parsons wrote in a column on October 13, 1939. "If he makes money we will all have to eat our words, and I for one will do it gladly, for we need good pictures. Furthermore, we cannot deny that Welles is a brilliant young man." On New Year's Eve 1939, in her summary of a year considered the best in motion picture history, Parsons said, "Orson Welles wins the honor of being the most discussed personality to come to the films in 1939." Later, when Welles told Parsons that he had lived near her childhood town of Dixon, Illinois, she soon reported him as a "home town boy making good."

When Parsons was invited to the August 1 press day on the *Citizen Kane* set, she gushed, "I can hardly wait until tomorrow at 5 p.m., to see the great Orson Welles in action." When she missed the press event because of other commitments, she caught up with Welles three weeks later on the set during the filming of the opera scenes. Parsons devoted a full column to Welles, which in the *Los Angeles Examiner* was topped with a photo of Welles in costume as the middle-aged Kane. Parsons described him as a "remarkable young man," "a brilliant youth," and "a genius." In the months *Citizen Kane* was in production, Welles appeared in Parsons' column more than any other Hollywood performer.

Parsons probably did not see the news item in *The Hollywood Reporter* about the screening and certainly must have missed the brief in *Variety* that declared Kane was based on Hearst—otherwise her squawks of protest to Welles would have come sooner and been louder than Hopper's. Parsons was unaware that trouble was brewing until, while attending a dinner party, she was informed of Hopper's call.

Parsons was not only personally upset by Hopper's call to Lawler, she was also jeopardized professionally. Parsons was an eighteen-year employee of the Hearst organization who also considered herself a close friend of the publisher's—

"the devoted slave of Mr. Hearst," recalled Douglas Fairbanks, Jr. Even worse for Parsons, Hopper's alert demonstrated to Hearst that Parsons had apparently been duped by the young director.

"As the story was reported to me," Parsons said, "Hopper said, 'Mr. Hearst, I don't know why Louella hasn't told you that this picture is about you.' Mr. Hearst thanked her."

Then Hearst himself talked to Parsons, an event that Hopper described with this florid phrasing: "Across the cerulean Hollywood sky, the clouds obscured the sun, yes, and the moon, too. Mr. Hearst called Louella, and when she gathered that I had seen the picture and that it did, in fact, have much to do with her boss' life, her sky fell right down around her ears."

Parsons did not remember the conversation as having quite the same melodramatic tone. She recalled simply, "Mr. Hearst called me and asked that arrangements be made for me and two of his lawyers to see *Citizen Kane*."

For Welles, the timing could not have been worse. In the second week of 1941, not only were the two most prominent columnists in Hollywood on the warpath, but the *Friday* magazine attack on *Citizen Kane* was arriving on newsstands. Welles had to respond quickly; he sent an urgent letter to Parsons on January 8.

"*Friday Magazine* this week carries a vicious lie," Welles wrote. "I hope I'm the first to tell you about it."

Welles told Parsons that *Citizen Kane* was not about Hearst and that the publisher of *Friday* was going to publish a full retraction.

"A good deal of nonsense has been appearing lately about *Kane*," Welles said. "Since it has been learned that the picture concerns itself with a fighting publisher, who lives in a big country house, it has been assumed that *Kane* is about Mr. Hearst. People seem to have forgotten Bennett, Munsey, Pulitzer and McCormick, to mention only a few you could name. Not that it matters, *Kane* isn't any of them."

But Hopper's phone call had already planted the seed; Parsons was alert to the idea that Kane was Hearst. Parsons demanded a screening the next day, which she attended with Lawler and A. Laurence Mitchell, another Hearst attorney.

The trio watched the film in silence—the only sounds reported were "several audible gasps."

Reports vary about how much of *Citizen Kane* Parsons could tolerate. Some said she stayed to the end, others said she walked out partway through. However, all witnesses reported that Hollywood's most powerful journalist was fuming about the film, felt betrayed by Welles, and was humiliated by her chief rival. "She was purple and her wattles were wobbling like a turkey," said Ruth Warrick.

Twenty years later, Parsons was still bitter about both Welles and his film. Writing in her memoirs in 1961, Parsons said that by allowing Hopper to attend the first screening of *Citizen Kane,* Welles "pulled one of the classic double crosses of Hollywood." (What Welles might have gained by double-crossing Parsons remains impossible to explain.)

"I must say now, so many years later, that I am still horrified by the picture," Parsons wrote in her memoirs. "It was a cruel, dishonest caricature. It was done in the worst of taste. The boy genius certainly used all his talents to do a hatchet job."

Parsons never spoke to Welles again. Her relationship with the "brilliant young man" was over.

Parsons, however, was just getting started with Welles' picture. The same day that she saw *Citizen Kane,* she called George Schaefer's office at RKO in New York demanding that he shelve the film and threatening, noted a nervous secretary, "one of the most beautiful lawsuits in history if they release *Citizen Kane.*"

Within days, Parsons called, among many others, Louis Mayer at MGM, Darryl Zanuck at 20th Century-Fox, producer David O. Selznick, and Jack Warner. Some refused to talk with her. She continued to lash out for months, trying to strong-arm everyone of importance in the motion picture industry at the Hollywood studios and at the industry's corporate headquarters offices in New York—including the Rockefellers, who were major stockholders in RKO—demanding that they suppress the film and prevent it from being screened.

Parsons told Will Hays, president of the Motion Picture Producers and Distributors of America (which under his leadership established the film industry's Production Code Administration), that *Citizen Kane* should be banned because the code forbade making a picture about a living person (it did not). And she called W. G. Van Schmus, managing director of Radio City Music Hall, America's premier theater and the intended venue for the premiere of *Citizen Kane,* ordering him to not run the picture; the penalty would be a "total press blackout."

Parsons, wrote Mercury publicist Herb Drake, "called everybody but St. Peter."

Lawler and Mitchell moved even faster, setting the Hearst organization into motion with brutal speed that night. Later accounts which claimed that Hearst was a silent, innocent witness to his staff's attempts to suppress the film were clearly erroneous; within hours of the screening, on Hearst's direct order, his entire organization was alerted and taking action against RKO, Welles, and *Citizen Kane.*

"[The] Chief requests that you omit from any of our magazines any reference in text or illustration relating to any moving picture produced by RKO," Willicombe wired to Berlin on the night of January 8. "Similar instruction has gone to the papers."

On January 9, every mention of Welles, *Citizen Kane,* and all other RKO films was removed from Hearst papers, and the studio's advertising was dropped from the papers as well. In some cities, the order to kill all coverage of RKO took effect with ruthless speed. Many Hearst papers, including the *Los Angeles Examiner,* dropped reviews of *Kitty Foyle*—a Ginger Rogers hit and a film crucial to RKO's financial stability—from late editions that same day.

And Parsons wasted no time informing the trade papers of her pressure against RKO. On January 10, *Variety* carried the details of the attack under the headline HEARST BANS RKO FROM PAPERS. To further strengthen the assault, all of the motion picture studios were put on notice that they, too, would be punished because of Welles' offenses.

"As a result of the fury, Hearst papers will keep up a continuous shellfire against the entire industry, using employment of foreigners instead of 'idle Americans' as ammunition," wrote *Variety*. Indeed, the planning for these attacks started quickly. *Time* magazine had received a report from a radio commentator in Hollywood who had been approached "by Hearst interests" on January 11. Five days later, *Variety* moaned that "all film companies may suffer because of Hearst's peeve at Welles' *Kane*."

When the Hearst ban slammed down on RKO, Welles was momentarily stunned. "It looks," he told a reporter for *Newsweek,* "like my throat has been cut."

Other threats were more personal—and more offensive. Parsons called every member of the RKO board of directors and promised that if *Citizen Kane* was released, fictionalized (but recognizable) stories about each of them would appear in Hearst publications. She also warned that long-suppressed stories about the sexual escapades and other indiscretions of stars and prominent Hollywood personalities—stories originally withheld from print as favors to the studios—would suddenly appear. More specifically, she promised Nelson Rockefeller that *The American Weekly* would run a "double-page spread" on him if the film was released.

"Mr. Hearst told me to tell you," Parsons said, "that if you boys want private lives, he'll give you private lives."

On January 14, Parsons reported on her progress to Willicombe and Hearst. The plan to stop *Citizen Kane* had descended into a conspiracy to stop RKO.

"Mr. Hearst might like to know that L. B. Mayer [MGM], Joseph Schenck [20th Century-Fox], Nicholas Schenck [president of Loew's, MGM's parent company], and Jack Warner have all refused to book *Citizen Kane*," Parsons said. "Joe Schenck told me that if RKO books the picture the companies will book no more RKO movies in their theaters."

This was serious business. These studio executives alone who committed to not showing *Citizen Kane* represented thousands of theaters across the country.

Parsons also sent a copy of a telegram from Nelson Rockefeller that hinted of an even more dire fate for the film:

"Had long talk with George Schaffer [*sic*] on telephone last night," Rockefeller's telegram read. "He is giving the matter serious consideration."

At this point, "serious consideration" could have meant only one thing: RKO had a decision to make about the fate of *Citizen Kane*.

And the problems continued with the Hollywood press as well. The same day that Parsons wrote her progress report for Hearst, W. R. Wilkerson of *The Hollywood Reporter* spoke out again about Schaefer and Welles in his column. If Wilkerson knew about the enthusiastic reports from *Life, Look,* and *Redbook* at the January 3 screening, he did not include that knowledge in his broadest indictment yet of Schaefer and his deal with Welles.

"You can't blame a fellow for trying," Wilkerson wrote in his "Tradeviews" column on the front page. "There's no question but that George Schaefer was trying, and trying hard, when he slipped Orson Welles a contract that gave him carte blanche for RKO.

"It was not a good effort for his company or for this business to give a young fellow who had never seen the inside of a studio, who had never looked at a picture script, had never directed or acted in a picture nor had anything whatever to do with picture production the leeway in a contract that Mr. Schaefer gave Mr. Welles.

"This comment is not written for the purpose of recording an 'I told you so,' but rather in an effort to place the blame for any harm that may accrue from the Welles effort of almost two years, to the tune of one million two hundred thousand of RKO's dollars.

"So far they have never uncovered a genius capable of writing, directing, acting, and producing a picture; contributing all those necessary picture ingredients at the same time. Every one else in the picture business knew it but George Schaefer, and now he knows—it can't be done. And he knows too that every production outfit MUST have supervision over its stories that are to be made into pictures, which Schaefer tossed away in his Welles deal."

January 1941 had become the critical month for the survival of *Citizen Kane*, as the pressure mounted from the Hearst organization. The fight may have seemed one-sided: against the vast nationwide Hearst forces were Welles, Schaefer, and the RKO staff—at least those staff who supported the young director and the controversial studio chief. Welles' allies also included his lawyer-manager, Arnold Weissberger, who was communicating almost daily with Drake, Welles, and others in the Mercury company.

Weissberger, a New York–based attorney and agent, represented many performers. He was also an accomplished—and later published—photographer who specialized in informal portraits of high-profile friends and clients. (And as a lawyer whose full name was L. Arnold Weissberger, he was kidded for having the initials *L.A.W.*)

Weissberger had spent much of his time in the late 1930s extricating Welles and Mercury Theatre from financial difficulties. In early 1941, he was a principal player in the fight to save *Citizen Kane*, negotiating and mediating with RKO studio executives in Los Angeles and the company's board and corporate leadership in New York.

January would be filled with peaks and valleys: at the top, the rave early reports received from the long-lead publications; at the bottom, the rapidly escalating fight with Hearst. But the early reports from *Life, Look,* and others who had seen the film were keeping spirits up in the Mercury camp, even as the pressure from Hearst increased.

"I do not see how Orson can lose, no matter what happens," Drake told Weissberger on January 10. "This morning I persuaded *Life* and *Look* magazines to call Schaefer and give him assurance of their opinion that *Kane* is one of the great pictures of all time, and that they think it would be foolish not to release it. We are the biggest story today."

Like Weissberger, Drake was prominent in the struggle. Formerly the assistant drama editor and critic at the *New York Herald Tribune*, Drake was, in early 1941, chafing and ready to go on the offensive, knowing he could build support with the non-Hearst media while the discussions about *Citizen Kane* were held behind closed doors by the studio leadership. Instead, RKO's response to the early Hearst actions was simple: no public statements, no interviews, and no decisions.

"We have been asked by Mr. Schaefer to say nothing," Drake told a friend on January 15, "so we are not giving interviews to the press nor showing them the movie as we would like to. Welles says we are all behaving like characters in a melodrama. . . .

"I am going slowly mad because my hands are tied," Drake said. "I want to lead a crusade, I want to get the whole independent and liberal Hollywood element behind us. But the big battle, apparently, is being fought among the money boys. Meanwhile all we can do is play ball with [Schaefer] who has been our very great friend and protector."

Drake had been told how the offensive against the whole film industry might unfold: like *Variety,* he had heard about the proposed assault by Hearst papers against employment of aliens in the movie industry. And like everyone in Hollywood, he knew about possible attacks on the private lives of Hollywood notables. "The man," Drake said of Hearst, "is consistently inconsistent as ever."

The Hearst plans for the film industry never materialized, but there would be no letup on *Citizen Kane,* and neither RKO nor the Mercury camp knew the depth of the assault that was already under way. They would soon learn how low Hearst could go.

NEGOTIATING AND PLACATING

This is not a tempest in a tea pot, it will not calm down, and the forces opposed to us are constantly at work and will not stop until they succeed in having the picture withdrawn.
—ATTORNEY ARNOLD WEISSBERGER TO ORSON WELLES

While Welles waited, Weissberger planned for the worst and considered the tangible civil actions Hearst might realistically take. Some thought *Citizen Kane* libeled Hearst, but Weissberger believed that Hearst did not have a case for libel, and the facts were on Welles' side.

"We have not used Hearst's name, portrait, or picture," Weissberger told Welles. "On the contrary, we have done everything possible to avoid using Hearst."

Weissberger's opinions were reinforced by the views of RKO's own lawyers, who had, of course, long before reviewed and cleared the script for potentially litigious content. When the Hearst attacks began, they screened the film along with Hollywood attorney and power broker Mendel Silberberg and reconfirmed that there was nothing in the film that was actionable.

However, Weissberger also warned of a danger even greater than actual legal proceedings.

"There is nothing to prevent Hearst from starting actions to cause as much trouble as possible, even though he does not expect to be and is not ultimately successful," Weissberger told Welles. "If he is bent upon doing all he can to have the picture withdrawn, he may decide to use all his legal machinery to harass RKO in order to bring pressure."

Weissberger was right: the Hearst organization neither filed for an injunction to stop the film's release nor brought an actual lawsuit. However, the hints that Hearst would seek an injunction against the picture and stop its distribution were rumored endlessly, further reinforcing the stress.

Hearst's staff knew that the mere suggestion of a lawsuit was as effective as actual legal action and much less risky, because a lawsuit involving Hearst and RKO would have been problematic for either side. To win, the Hearst companies would have been forced to prove both that Kane was specifically modeled on Hearst with malice, and that actual damages had occurred—extremely unlikely prospects, all.

Deliberate malice by RKO would have been especially difficult to prove by Hearst, one of the most public of public men, long a controversial figure with extremist views and a man who lived openly with Marion Davies while he was still married to another woman. In the unbiased appraisal of a courtroom, Hearst lawyers would have faced a difficult struggle to convince a jury that there was actionable material in *Citizen Kane*. And Hearst had to face the hard facts that if they sued and lost, RKO could countersue.

But RKO could hardly afford to be involved in a legal action that, if lost, would have worsened the company's already shaky financial footing. Just as damaging to the studio would have been an injunction that prevented the release of the film while the legal wrangling played out.

Thus, a far more effective weapon against RKO was the continuing threat of a lawsuit over *Citizen Kane,* which dangled over the studio and any exhibitor who wanted to screen the film long after *Citizen Kane* premiered.

Parsons recalled in her memoirs that Hearst himself prevented his company from taking actual legal action. "I don't believe in lawsuits," Parsons reported Hearst telling her. "Besides, I have no desire to give the picture any more publicity."

In spite of the lengthy public coverage about the suppression of *Citizen Kane,* this conversation between Parsons and Hearst regarding a lawsuit was the only published acknowledgment (until now) that Hearst himself knew his organization was retaliating against the Hollywood filmmaking community over *Citizen Kane*. No one else has ever admitted publicly that Hearst discussed the issue, nor did the Hearst organization issue a statement about *Citizen Kane*. "But then," said a Hearst associate, who nearly a half century later still requested anonymity, "making a direct request wasn't how Mr. Hearst would have done it."

Regardless, with the *Citizen Kane* problem covered extensively by film industry publications and the general-interest press, even if Hearst was not directly involved, he could hardly have failed to notice that his own organization was attacking the creator of a film and Hollywood in general—thus, approval by his silence would have amounted to an endorsement of his company's actions. But there is, in fact, no question that Hearst knew what was happening; among several items of Hearst correspondence that showed Hearst was being kept informed was Joseph Willicombe's February 1 reply to one of Parsons' frequent progress reports about actions against *Citizen Kane:* Willicombe replied, "Dear Louella—this is a note to tell you that the Chief received your letter of January 29th."

In mid-January, Weissberger continued to meet with Schaefer and the RKO attorneys and reinforced his view that an actual lawsuit was unlikely, hoping that his confidence would reassure the nervous studio executives.

But assurances about the future of *Citizen Kane* from Welles' "very great friend and protector" did not come. Welles received reports that the decision to release *Citizen Kane*—or not—was being considered by the RKO board of directors in New York, and views on the board were divided.

"Schaefer is not phased [*sic*]," Weissberger told Drake, "but we must remember that he is bound to come to Orson's defense to make a stand on our behalf, inasmuch as he gave Orson carte blanche and has really stuck his own neck out."

On one point, Weissberger was insistent: no one should admit "in the slightest way" that *Citizen Kane* had anything to do with Hearst. Weissberger had become concerned when, in a *New York Times* interview, Welles denied that Kane was Hearst but also said, "Had Mr. Hearst and similar financial barons not lived during the period we discuss, *Citizen Kane* could not have been made."

"It is essential," Weissberger ordered, "that we maintain consistently, emphatically and unequivocally that Hearst has nothing to do with this picture."

Weissberger, like Drake, was eager to go on the offensive and on several occasions urged Schaefer to release a public statement in support of the film. However, the best the RKO president could do was issue a mild comment to reporters: "There is no serious consideration," Schaefer had told *Variety* for January 13 publication, "to withholding *Citizen Kane* from release."

The one point about which everyone agreed was that the existing prints of *Citizen Kane* needed to be kept under tight control. On January 17, J. R. McDonough—no friend of the Mercury company, but an executive who knew a valuable company asset when he saw it—sent out the word: "No one on or off this lot should be allowed to see *Citizen Kane* without the prior approval of Mr. Schaefer, Mr. Nolan, or Mr. Welles. I haven't heard of any running of the picture in violation of the foregoing but I nevertheless believe it important at this time that you have this written instruction."

Even a public preview screening, normally a routine step to gauge public reaction before finalizing a film, was not permitted, although Welles almost got away with one. Late in January and with approval from the studio, Welles and colleagues traveled in secret to Salt Lake City to preview the film for the first time in front of a public audience. However, by the time Welles and his group arrived, the approval had been rescinded, and the preview was canceled.

In mid-January, no definitive statement came from RKO. A week passed after the Hearst papers banned RKO from their pages, and the studio chief still had not taken public action. The low-key Schaefer, who always sought to please everyone but seemed to be satisfying no one involved in this predicament, may have been doing what he often considered the best thing: assume that a problem would go away by not doing anything.

"I asked Schaefer whether there were any developments, and he said there were none," Weissberger told Welles on January 17. "I asked him what the RKO policy would be, and he said that he thought nothing would be done. He felt that the whole matter was a tempest in a tea pot, and that after Hearst had blown off steam, the thing would settle down and nothing would happen."

But things were happening that Schaefer may have been reluctant to discuss: the RKO board was considering the issue. And Schaefer was likely working on the board members, one by one, to build their commitment to release *Citizen Kane*—or at the very least make clear that the consequences of shelving the film would be much worse than any possible repercussions from releasing it.

But Weissberger was also concerned that the board might make a decision without Schaefer's involvement.

"The controlling stockholders must be aware that Schaefer is on your side," Weissberger told Welles, "and they may very well reach their decisions without taking him into their confidence."

Hearst was not the only one talking about legal action. With RKO hesitating and limited options available to them, Welles and Weissberger began to explore the possibility of using their own threat to sue the studio as a crowbar to release *Citizen Kane*.

But Weissberger also wanted to proceed if he could provide some protection for Schaefer.

"If they fail to release the picture . . . you could legally force the picture to be shown," Weissberger told Welles on January 17. "Since Schaefer is on your side, he should be informally apprised of your legal right, so that he can tell his board of directors and stockholders that they have no alternative to releasing the picture."

Incredibly, discussions continued into the third week of January without action by RKO. With so many forces at play—Hearst's attacks, Welles' demands for action, RKO board members who supported the film, and others who were against it, Weissberger began to think that Schaefer may have bent past the point of rebounding.

"The more I regard the situation, the more I am inclined to feel that Schaefer, with the best of intentions, may prove to be a broken reed," Weissberger told Welles on January 20. "The current insecurity of his position with RKO, his own easy-going disposition, and his natural proclivity towards adopting a 'laissez-faire' attitude are all factors that will prevent him from functioning as he must if the picture is to be saved. . . .

"The one thing that is clear is that Schaefer must be urged not to sit back and await developments," Weissberger said. "This is not a tempest in a tea pot, it will not calm down, and the forces opposed to us are constantly at work and will not stop until they succeed in having the picture withdrawn."

Finally, some good news came: on January 21, RKO announced a mammoth advertising campaign for *Citizen Kane,* a blitz that Schaefer called "one of the most far-reaching ever launched for an attraction by RKO Radio Pictures."

The campaign included full-page advertisements in, among other magazines, *Life, Look,* and *The Saturday Evening Post.* All three publications would later publish large features about the film as well. RKO planned to reach fifty million readers with its promotion. The film would premiere on February 14 at Radio City Music Hall.

It should have seemed like a major victory and a final solution to Welles' problems. But after the January 21 announcement came a general silence about the future of *Citizen Kane,* other than the notice that the release would be postponed. And then postponed again.

The silence would continue for weeks.

To further convolute the problem, the *Citizen Kane* controversy brought to the surface other business issues at RKO beyond the future of a single film.

Two of the studio's largest shareholders were the Rockefeller family and industrialist Floyd Odlum, chairman of his holding company, the Atlas Corporation.

Odlum in particular was active in RKO's corporate affairs; a shrewd investor and brilliant financial strategist, Odlum had built the foundation of his fortune during the 1920s financial boom. He had been one of the few investors who had recognized that the boom would be followed by an even bigger bust. As a result, Odlum sold half his holdings in the months before the 1929 crash and was cash rich when the bottom fell out of the stock market in October. Then, during the Depression, Odlum bought large positions in several major companies at post-Depression low prices. By the time the darkest days came in the early 1930s, Odlum was one of America's ten richest men, with major investments in airlines, retail, banking, and RKO.

Like the Rockefeller family, Odlum also held a significant stake in Chase National Bank, which was a principal lender to the Hearst organization. Therefore, as *Variety* pointed out, "the owners of RKO have an interest in the financial stability and solvency of Hearst."

It also meant that the Rockefellers and Odlum were handed more than their share of involvement in the *Citizen Kane* problem. While no one considered the film to be damaging to the financial stability of the Hearst organization, the intertwined business relationships meant that unlike the participants in the fray who had clear opposing viewpoints, Odlum and the Rockefellers would need to consider the issue from all sides.

Odlum in particular became involved. *Variety* reported that he was neutral on the issue of *Citizen Kane* and would leave the decision to Schaefer. Odlum may have been neutral in public, but privately he was, at the very least, open to options about the fate of *Citizen Kane* if in his view they served the interests of the shareholders, especially during the darkest incident to come that would threaten the survival of the film.

George Schaefer may not have been speaking out publicly, but he was busy behind the scenes, meeting with the board at its regular sessions, soothing individual board members at informal conferences, and placating his counterparts at other studios. But in the last weeks of January, none of his involvement resulted in public statements or even in reports back to Welles about progress.

Welles wanted to take action that would support Schaefer, because from the viewpoint of the Mercury team, the studio chief could not stand alone. When Weissberger asked Schaefer what he thought the RKO board was likely to decide, he replied, "How can you tell what a board of directors may do?"

Meanwhile, Welles reacted with fury to the article in *Friday* magazine and called publisher Dan Gillmor to demand space to reply. The conversation must have sizzled. In Welles' letter to Gillmor, which accompanied the rebuttal, Welles cracked, "As you can see, I'm just as ill-tempered as I promised to be."

Welles' reply, titled "*Citizen Kane* Is Not About Louella Parsons' Boss," was brief but scathing, and featured captions on the photographs in Welles' own words.

"*Citizen Kane* is the portrait of a public man's private life," Welles wrote. "I have met some publishers, but I know none of them well enough to make them possible as models.

"*Friday* ran a series of stills from *Kane,* whose captions were inaccurate descriptions of the action of the picture. Constant reference was made to the career of William Randolph Hearst. This is unfair to Hearst and to Kane.

"Worst of all," Welles continued, referring to comments about Louella Parsons, "*Friday* put these words into my mouth: 'Wait until the woman finds out that the picture's about her boss.' This is not a misquotation. *Friday*'s source invented it. *Citizen Kane* is not about Louella Parsons' boss. It is the portrait of a fictional newspaper tycoon, and I have never said or implied to anyone that it is anything else. The easiest way to draw parallels between Kane and other famous publishers is to not see the picture."

But his response was too little too late. Welles' reply did not appear until February 14, a month after *Friday*'s original story. By then, the distortions had already done their worst. And as Welles himself pointed out in his rebuttal, "Retractions are notoriously valueless."

Late in January, the Hearst attack on *Citizen Kane* continued to unfold with a threat even more foul than legal action or journalistic blackmail. One of the first calls Parsons made after viewing *Citizen Kane* had been to Louis B. Mayer, production chief at MGM, head of the most formidable studio in Hollywood, and arguably the most powerful man in motion pictures. Mayer bluntly suggested a solution to the *Citizen Kane* problem that would end the irritant forever: through his corporate management in New York, Mayer proposed that the Hollywood studios should form a fund to buy the negative and prints of *Citizen Kane* from RKO and destroy them.

Mayer asked Nicholas Schenck, president of Loew's, MGM's parent company, to meet with Schaefer in New York.

"Louie asked me to speak to you about this picture," Schenck told Schaefer.

"He is prepared to pay you what it cost, which he understands is $800,000, if you will destroy the negative and all of the prints."

Schaefer did not say yes, but, ever the diplomat, he did not refuse outright.

"Such an extraordinary suggestion coming from a man in your position must be carefully considered," he replied.

But Schenck, always cautious, corrected him for the record. "The request comes from Louie," Schenck said. "Not me."

Instead of taking the issue to his own board for formal consideration, Schaefer took a huge risk with his peers: on January 22, he screened *Citizen Kane* for the chief executives of the studio holding companies and their attorneys, with Welles in attendance, the goal being to drum up support for the film. RKO's president knew that regardless of his public announcement of the plans for advertising and release announced the day before the screening, one result of the meeting was that the picture might still be scuttled.

Editor Robert Wise flew to New York with a work print of the film—a harrowing, frequently delayed journey through blizzards that required sixty hours in a two-engine plane.

"The idea of the screening was to show the picture to all of the big bosses so they could make a judgment as to whether they should tell RKO to shelve it or release it," Wise recalled.

Before the screening in the private projection room at Radio City Music Hall, Wise said, Schaefer let Welles argue for his film's release.

"Orson talked to them first, and presented his case for the film," Wise said. "I've never seen him give a better performance—with talk of fighting tyranny in the world, freedom of speech, and the bill of rights, he really charmed the hell out of them."

Welles "performance," combined with what surely must have been stunned surprise among the executives over the quality of the film, produced the effect that Schaefer had hoped for. Judgment came the next day: the film could be released—but with some judicious editing. Louis Mayer's plan to buy and burn *Citizen Kane* had been neutralized.

"The next day I got a list of changes that they all felt were necessary," Wise said. "The changes were all minor—a little trim here, a new line of dialogue there. Orson didn't mind the changes—he was relieved."

The "minor changes" took several weeks to complete, with Wise coordinating the editing by telephone with assistant Mark Robson in Los Angeles. Wise recorded new dialogue with actors who had already returned to New York.

The resulting compromise trimmed a scant three minutes and twenty-four seconds from the final print. The deletions included several references to Hearst in the opening newsreel (although one comment about Hearst remains in the projection room scene), an assortment of statements by Jed Leland and others about Kane's irresponsible journalism and Susan Alexander's drinking, part of Thompson's summary statement at Xanadu about Kane, and allusions to presidential assassinations. (Material about Kane's support of political assassination had featured prominently in Mankiewicz's early drafts of *American* and had been pared down to a brief mention in the final print before the last fragments were deleted.)

The tally of cuts would seem to consume much less than three minutes, so it is possible that Welles, ever the whittler, also used the opportunity to shave other unwanted footage.

Paul Stewart recorded two replacement lines of dialogue: where Raymond the butler told Thompson on two occasions that the old man was "a little gone in the head," the dubbed-in lines were changed to Kane "acted kind of funny sometimes." Oddly, while the studio executives and their lawyers decided that "a little gone in the head" had to be deleted, the line that followed—"He did crazy things sometimes"—was apparently acceptable and remained in the film.

When the changes were completed, Robson cut a new work print and shipped it to Wise for a second showing for the studio representatives.

"The second time we screened it only for the lawyers," Wise said. "They said okay, and that was it."

Years later, Welles recalled his own relief.

"We *didn't* expect that the film might be destroyed," he said. "And that was nip and tuck; it was very close."

It may have been closer than he thought. Parsons told Willicombe on January 29 that Floyd Odlum and his attorney would meet with Louis Mayer that day to discuss the fate of the film—a week after the screening for the studio executives. Mayer, as head of production at MGM, was not CEO of the company; he reported to Nicholas Schenck in New York, and it was no secret in Hollywood that Mayer and Schenck hated each other. Mayer, a longtime friend of Hearst's, was certainly capable of acting independently of his boss if it served his—and Hearst's—interests.

"If they are sincere they will either remake the picture or not release it," said Parsons, who had nothing on which to base her appraisal, "but of course you never can tell about people and their promises."

The fight was far from over.

Agreement within the film industry leadership about the survival of *Citizen Kane* did nothing to appease Hearst. On January 21, 1941, Hearst papers lifted their ban on mentions of RKO, but the order remained in effect against *Citizen Kane*. The Hearst edict against mentions of *Citizen Kane* continued for more than eight months. As a result, a film that even in 1941 was already recognized as a landmark achievement was not reviewed and did not receive news coverage in any of Hearst's publications.

In late January, Schaefer faced the problem head-on. After the studio chiefs viewed *Citizen Kane*, Schaefer sought a meeting with the opposition: he invited Richard Berlin to lunch.

Berlin reported the invitation to Hearst management and was advised not to talk with the RKO chief. However, the always ambitious Berlin must have considered a lunch meeting with the enemy as an opportunity to further ingratiate himself with Hearst, because he was conveniently unavailable when the directive came to avoid the meeting.

Berlin and Schaefer met on January 24, but with no clear result.

"I did the listening and he did the talking," Berlin reported to Joseph Willicombe.

Berlin said Schaefer tried to explain that there were many references to Kane that had nothing to do with Hearst.

"Then," Berlin said, "he admitted that there are a number of episodes that could be construed as biographical with reference to the Chief."

Schaefer, of course, was eager to hear what Hearst himself thought about *Citizen Kane,* but Berlin ducked the issue.

"I told him that I had not discussed this with Mr. Hearst so I could not answer that question," Berlin said.

According to Berlin, Schaefer denied that Welles had created *Citizen Kane* with Hearst's life as background. But Berlin came well prepared. The previous day, he had met with advertising executive Ward Wheelock, who had represented Welles for his Campbell's soup–sponsored radio programs and would have seemed—based on his attempts at chummy correspondence with Welles in previous years—to be a pal of the radio star. But in January 1941, Wheelock was more than willing to sell out his client.

"Mr. Wheelock informed me that *Citizen Kane* had been submitted to him for possible use and he had rejected the idea on account of the fact that it was the life of Mr. Hearst," Berlin said. Wheelock, said Berlin, had specifically said he could be quoted to others on this point.

But off the record, Wheelock was even more frank and possibly less than accurate: he told Berlin that three months earlier, John Houseman "had spoken to Welles and warned him to be careful about this picture as Mr. Hearst was too powerful and too strong—Welles' reply being, 'To hell with it.'" If true, what Houseman really could have been trying to warn Welles about, long after production began, is hard to fathom.

There was one result of the meeting about which Berlin spoke for both himself and George Schaefer: "There was nothing said that in any way would clarify the situation."

If the controversy over *Citizen Kane* had not been strange enough during the first month of 1941, it took a truly bizarre turn in late January when CBS announced that beginning February 3 Hedda Hopper would be hosting a six-part radio series on the life of Orson Welles—with Welles interviewed in the program.

Welles had never faulted Hopper for her role in alerting Hearst, later saying, "I couldn't blame her" for passing along such a choice piece of gossip. In fact, a month later, Hopper practically endorsed *Citizen Kane* by including a nugget in her column that reported when "a well-known producer" offered to buy *Citizen Kane* for cost, George Schaefer said, "I wouldn't sell it for $3 million." And in 1944, Hopper would perform in *The Orson Welles Almanac* radio program on CBS.

But in February 1941, the timing of Hopper's radio series—only weeks after she attempted to build her own stature at the expense of Welles and RKO—did seem hypocritical, even by the standards of Hollywood gossip columnists. Parsons could not have agreed more, as she later said in a note to Joseph Willicombe about other antics by Hopper: "I think she's a louse."

Welles, the consummate storyteller, recalled yet another meeting that he said saved his film—this time by capitalizing on the religious beliefs of Hollywood's head censor. Welles said that Joseph Breen, administrator of the motion picture industry's Production Code, screened the film to pass his own judgment (in recounting this story, Welles suggested that Breen had the final say about *Citizen Kane*'s physical survival, a point that was great for storytelling drama but was not accurate).

"I got a rosary and put it in my pocket," Welles told Peter Bogdanovich. "When the running was over, in front of Joe Breen, a good Irish Catholic, I stood up and dropped my rosary on the floor and said, 'Oh, excuse me,' and picked it up and put it back in my pocket.

"If I hadn't done that, there would be no *Citizen Kane*," Welles said. "It was only *not* burned because I dropped a rosary."

But still *Citizen Kane* was not released, nor was a final release date set, even after RKO's announcement about a February 14 premiere. What actually occurred in the privacy of the RKO boardroom and in executive meetings at the studio will never be known; records of those conversations do not exist. What little was reported about the board's view comes from conversations between Arnold Weissberger and RKO attorney Gordon Youngman, which does not include specifics of the discussions, only some suggestions on how they could proceed.

The board's regular sessions, as well as the informal discussions between meetings for politicking and consensus building, certainly must have served as opportunities to clarify the members' positions. There were several options to consider: the board could have formally voted to either release the film or decide to shelve it—either way ending the discussion. Or the members could have publicly recognized that Welles' contracts protected the film, "forcing" RKO to release it—thus making a decision without a decision. Or, most likely of all, the board could have chosen not to take a formal position of its own, leaving the final decision—and the responsibility for what came later—to Schaefer.

RKO had strong financial and legal reasons to release *Citizen Kane* as soon as possible. With nearly $1 million in production costs, administrative charges, advertising, pre-*Kane* salaries for the Mercury team, and other expenses, the studio desperately needed to get its high-profile picture into theaters. As one of the studio's most expensive productions of the year, and certainly its most publicized, RKO hoped to generate blockbuster box office receipts from its controversial project.

Further, RKO probably could not have destroyed the negative, even if the board had insisted. It certainly could have been said at the time that Welles' contract would have prevented such a desperate measure. If RKO refused to release *Citizen Kane,* Welles could have bought the film and distributed it himself—a step that, if necessary, he most certainly would have taken. (Forty-eight years later, Welles' control of his film would extend beyond his death to protect it from a new form of tampering: colorization.)

Fortunately, the January 29 meeting between Floyd Odlum and Louis B. Mayer did not produce a serious offer to destroy the film. The visit to Mayer may only have been a courtesy or to test the waters to see if the high-strung executive could be appeased with alternatives to the incinerator. One can hope that the sensible Odlum realized that destroying the film would have been a corporate embarrassment of unprecedented proportions in the film industry. Regardless of the final reasons, the idea of destroying the film for a price was finally over.

But the final verdict, whatever it would turn out to be, was still weeks away. Even after the studio executives saw the film, Schaefer would not commit to a firm release date. By the last week of January, it was clear that the February 14 release date was off.

At the end of January, Welles was itching to sue, and Weissberger outlined his options: he could bring legal action against RKO and force the studio to release the film; he could sue Hearst for interference with contractual relations; or he could file a federal action if he could show that the producers and exhibitors had conspired to prevent *Citizen Kane* from being shown.

As with Hearst, it was intimidation rather than actual legal action that may have produced results for Welles. "The threat of action on your part," Weissberger told Welles on January 31, "might have considerable weight in persuading the powers that be."

But despite the pressure and the bullying, the momentum was beginning to swing in *Citizen Kane*'s direction; every private screening produced new advocates for the film. Ironically, the reaction within the Hollywood establishment—once so hostile to Welles—may have been the best catalyst to convince Schaefer and his board that the time had come to release *Citizen Kane.*

With Welles in New York preparing his theatrical production of *Native Son* on Broadway, on February 14—the original release date—Schaefer screened the film for an audience of Hollywood luminaries.

The reaction was beyond Schaefer's most optimistic expectations.

"Never in my experience in the business have I screened a picture before such a tough and professional audience as I did last night and received such [a] wonderful reaction," Schaefer wired Welles the next day.

"[The] picture not only received a wonderful round of applause, but each and every [guest was] most enthusiastic [about] one of the great motion pictures that had ever come out of Hollywood. Most every one was so impressed that they were virtually speechless and some came back the second and third time after the picture was concluded and told me how much they were impressed."

Welles and Schaefer continued to build a broad base of popular support in Hollywood that would help ensure the survival of the film. During some weeks, they showed *Citizen Kane* several nights in a row or even twice a night.

A reporter from the *Hollywood Citizen-News* kept a head count of movie industry VIPs who saw *Citizen Kane*. *Variety* reported that at one March 6 screening, guests included Cary Grant; producers David O. Selznick and Walter Wanger; studio executives Harry Cohn, Roy Disney, and Sam Goldwyn; and directors Leo McCarey and William Wyler.

"*Citizen Kane* has the longest projection room engagement of any picture to come out of Hollywood," reported *Variety*.

Even D. W. Griffith, originally so sour about Welles' arrival in Hollywood, reacted favorably to the young director's first product.

"I loved *Citizen Kane*," Griffith said, "and particularly loved the ideas he took from me."

After the studio chiefs had previewed *Citizen Kane*, RKO attorney Gordon Youngman hoped to neutralize one concern that had emerged: because Kane was shown to be, in Youngman's words, "half-crazy in his declining years," the film should be legally protected via an all-purpose on-screen disclaimer preceding the film.

Without telling Welles, Schaefer added such a disclaimer to the beginning of the print shown at his screenings. "This is not the story of any man be he living or dead," it read. "This is the story of the power and strength which impels the lives of many great men seen through the eyes of little men."

Schaefer eventually confessed to Welles what he had done with the disclaimer, sending him the wording on March 11, the same day Welles announced his lawsuit to force the release of the film.

When Welles learned of the statement, he exploded. "Cannot express my disapproval of revised title concerning fictitious nature of the picture," he wired to Schaefer of the disclaimer, "in no way matches the picture and I do not believe it expresses my intentions. Am working on a similar one to which you can object."

Welles' version was somewhat better: "*Citizen Kane* is an examination of the personal character of a public man—a portrait according to the testimony of the intimates of his life. These, and Kane himself, are wholly fictitious."

Welles and Schaefer exchanged several drafts of the title card but eventually gave up. The end result was that *Citizen Kane* has no disclaimer at all—neither at the beginning, as proposed by Schaefer, nor in the credits at the end of the film. Instead, the opening credits were used as seen today: the RKO tower and corporate name, followed by "A Mercury Production by Orson Welles" and then the bold white outline letters *CITIZEN KANE.*

When Welles went east to drum up support for *Citizen Kane* with the studio leadership, he screened the film to others in New York as well. Among the prominent guests were Henry Luce, publisher of *Time* and *Life,* and several of his editors. Luce was reported to have thoroughly enjoyed the *News on the March* sequence, fully appreciating the re-creation of his own *March of Time.*

Luce then helped Welles defend his film. With disdain for Hearst, his politics, and his pressure tactics, Luce ordered his staff, as *Variety* put it, "to unleash their guns to get the film released." In mid-March, stories appeared in *Time* in support of Welles, and a photo-feature about *Citizen Kane* ran across four pages in the March 17 issue of *Life,* where the film was showcased as the magazine's Movie of the Week (an even longer feature would appear in *Life* in May).

Although the *Life* coverage in March was a photo-feature article, the article included plenty of hints about the quality of the film.

"Few movies have ever come from Hollywood with such powerful narrative, such original technique, such exciting photography," *Life* wrote. "Skeptics about Mr. Welles may now relax. His 18 months in Hollywood have not been wasted."

The attempts by the Hearst organization to blackmail America's eighth-largest industry were watched closely by the national press.

For the film industry publications especially, the opportunity to show Hearst's true colors was welcomed. Because of his attempts to blackmail the entire motion picture industry over the *Citizen Kane* issue (as well as many other heavy-handed tactics in print over the years), the film industry press hated Hearst more than they had ever disliked Welles when he arrived in Hollywood. *Variety* and *The Hollywood Reporter* followed the story for months, often with front-page coverage.

The mainstream national media were also alert to the story. On January 11, in the lead story on its entertainment page, *The New York Times* covered the demand that *Citizen Kane* be shelved and the Hearst ban of RKO films in the company's publications—a disclosure of the company's petty behavior in America's paper of record. The *Times* also hinted that the film was the cause of problems at the studio as well: "The situation is also said to have created a sharp division in the RKO forces."

But in other coverage, the *Times'* Douglas Churchill pointed out that if *Citizen Kane* was shelved, Welles' contract would haunt RKO in ways some at the studio had dreaded from the start.

"The judgment of its executives can be questioned," Churchill said, "if, as a result of signing an unproven man as writer, producer, director, and actor, to make a picture without supervision, the investment has to be written off."

However, some major news outlets besides the Hearst publications soon withdrew their coverage. The Associated Press and the United Press stopped writing about the story; the official reason offered by the AP was that the service "didn't carry private fights between two gentlemen," but some observers speculated that both companies feared losing Hearst's business if the coverage continued.

Several publications did continue the discussion. In John O'Hara's preview of *Citizen Kane* in the March 17, 1941, issue of *Newsweek,* the writer used the article as much to slam Hopper and Parsons as he did to praise the film.

"A few obsequious and/or bulbous middle-aged ladies think the picture ought not to be shown," O'Hara wrote. ". . . Sycophancy of that kind, like curt-seying, is deliberate. The ladies merely wait for a chance to show they can still do it, even if it means cracking a femur. This time I think they may have cracked off more than they can chew. I hope."

In an essay in the *New Republic,* author Michael Sage saw the issue as transcending Hearst; instead, Sage explored the broader question of Hollywood's artistic courage.

"Will Hollywood stand up to William Randolph Hearst over the matter of Orson Welles' film *Citizen Kane*?" wrote Sage. "Many people find it hard to believe the producers really intend to defy the lord of San Simeon.

"Hollywood is oozing with synthetic geniuses; an authentic one would be a menace," Sage continued. "Welles did no boot-licking. He defied the Hollywood caste system, ate with his aides and was even seen publicly with people who made less than $1,000 a week. Instead of casting shopworn stars, he brought his

Mercury Players from New York for the picture. Now, in certain quarters, he is the greatest villain in Hollywood.

"Instead of praising him for his forthright determination to make an interesting character study, even if it did offend Hearst, instead of condemning the effrontery of anyone who tries to suppress a creative work, some leaders of the industry say privately that Orson Welles must be stopped," wrote Sage. "Whether they will join hands with William Randolph Hearst remains to be seen."

But the most disturbing issue in the Hearst conspiracy to destroy *Citizen Kane* was that the actions by the publisher and his organization did not inspire broader public dialogue about censorship, corporate manipulation, or the trampling of First Amendment rights in 1941 America. One can only imagine the flood of national news coverage and highly charged commentary that would pour forth today if a twenty-first-century media mogul such as Rupert Murdoch, for purely personal reasons, banned all mention of a motion picture by his organization's outlets, and then actively tried to suppress or destroy the film. While a few stories about Hearst's attempts to ruin *Citizen Kane* continued to appear throughout the first half of 1941, the minor coverage of journalistic integrity and business ethics that had emerged early in the affair drifted away before the film premiered.

By the middle of February, the survival of *Citizen Kane* seemed assured, but where was the release date? RKO still would not commit to one. The original February 14 release had long passed, as had the revised date of February 28. When the new release date of March 11 was canceled, the early March advertising was wasted, as was the golden opportunity to capitalize on the publicity in *Time, Life, Newsweek, Variety, The Hollywood Reporter,* and other publications that printed features and reviews in March.

The problem may have been simple but distressing: RKO may have been trying to find enough theaters that would screen the film. The threats from Hearst continued to be effective, and in spite of support in some corners of Hollywood for *Citizen Kane,* most of the major theater chains were controlled by studios that refused to show the film. When, in late February, *The New York Times* asked RKO why a release date had not been set, the paper reported that "according to a spokesman for the studio, the company is still trying to decide whether to road-show the picture [meaning in a very small number of major theaters] or put it out through regular channels."

It was a critical decision, and one that would later prove disastrous to the financial success of *Citizen Kane*.

The delays continued, and Welles was growing frustrated with his boss and benefactor. After a particularly frustrating phone call to Schaefer on March 6, Welles sent him a long stream-of-consciousness follow-up letter.

"I managed to say very little of what I wanted to today on the phone," Welles wrote. "Your answers to my questions were themselves unanswerable even if they weren't good answers. When I ask you when the picture will be released, you say you hope to be able to tell me Monday or Tuesday. I ask you to tell me more about it and you simply repeat answer number one."

Referring to the canceled February release dates, Welles pointed out that "no real reasons were offered for either postponement. I never questioned your wisdom and I don't now. I did ask for your reasons and I never got them. Almost two weeks ago you told me that you thought the picture would be released in two weeks. Again, a few days ago, you assured me you expected final word late that night or early the next morning."

In early January, when the Hearst ban hit RKO and *Citizen Kane*, Welles and Schaefer often spoke twice daily by phone. "Now," Welles wrote, "I have to sit up until four o'clock in the morning trying to get in touch with you and failing to do so. I cannot think you are deliberately avoiding me. I can only suppose that you are pursuing some policy the nature of which must be kept secret."

Welles was expecting a typical upbeat but unhelpful response from Schaefer.

"Don't tell me to get a good night's rest and keep my chin up," he wrote. "Don't bother to communicate if that's all you have to say. There's no more rest for me until I know something concrete, and as for my chin, I've been leading with it for more than a year and a half. . . . I'll know better how to think and what to do when I have your answer."

Schaefer, trying to lighten the mood, sent a somewhat misguided reply.

"Have been trying to get you on the telephone all day, it seems that you are 'ducking me.' Now laugh that off. Seriously speaking you probably have just cause to complain but please be assured you have nothing to worry about."

Welles indeed had "just cause," and assurances of "nothing to worry about" did not yield an announcement of a release date. Welles was fed up; on March 11, he called reporters to his suite at the Ambassador Hotel in New York and announced he would sue RKO for breach of contract if the studio did not release *Citizen Kane* within three months.

"I believe that the public is entitled to see *Citizen Kane,*" Welles wrote in a statement. "For me to stand by while this picture is being suppressed would constitute a breach of faith with the public on my part as a producer. I have at this moment sufficient financial backing to buy *Citizen Kane* from RKO and release it myself.

"Under my contract with RKO, I have the right to demand that the picture be released and to bring legal action to force its release. If it does not do so immediately, I have instructed my attorney to commence proceedings."

Finally, Welles was able to directly confront the Hearst issue.

"I have been advised that strong pressure is being brought to bear to cause the withdrawal of *Citizen Kane* because of an alleged resemblance between incidents in the picture and incidents in the life of Mr. William Hearst," he said. "Any attempts at suppression would involve a serious interference with freedom of speech and with the integrity of the moving-picture industry.

"There is nothing to warrant the situation that has arisen," Welles concluded. "*Citizen Kane* was not intended to have nor has it any reference to Mr. Hearst or to any other living person."

Welles did not state where this "sufficient backing" to buy the film would come from. However, a powerful backer was available: *Time* and *Life* publisher Henry Luce would have been a likely candidate. Although Welles recalled that Luce never offered to buy *Citizen Kane* but would have if he had been asked, the *Motion Picture Herald* reported that Luce was indeed willing to pay $1 million for the film.

For the moment, Schaefer and Welles had won—*Citizen Kane* survived. But Hearst was succeeding as well. The promises by some of the studio chiefs to not screen *Citizen Kane,* combined with the threats of action by Hearst against any theater that showed the film, were successfully hampering RKO in its search for venues. But the film had not yet been released when the Hearst organization set in motion a different kind of attack: first had come suppression, then came attempts at destruction; now Hearst turned to revenge—first against the studio and then against Welles himself.

As if demanding penance for RKO's sins, Hearst newspapers attacked the studio for the most insignificant issues to keep the battle in the public eye and ensure that theater owners would remember the risk if they screened the film.

Even after the original release dates in February passed, the Hearst newspapers continued the trumped-up attack against RKO. When the studio found itself entangled in a trivial lawsuit for breach of contract, with a mere $7,000 awarded to producer Joseph Ermolieff, the court decision was splashed across the front pages of Hearst dailies nationwide. "Under ordinary circumstances," said *Variety* of the lawsuit, "it would not have rated a mention."

In the *New York Daily Mirror,* one of Hearst's flagship papers, film critic Lee Mortimer blasted Hollywood in general and RKO in particular for its business practices, primarily an alleged unethical practice called "the Hollywood Runaround" that Mortimer never fully explained. The film industry press coverage of the Hearst organization's wrath continued to report rumblings about lawsuits and pressure on theater owners.

Welles' draft status was reviewed by Hearst reporters, who were eager to stain him with charges of draft dodging. They were stymied by reality, learning that Welles, although appearing generally healthy, was indeed thoroughly unfit for military service because of many lifelong maladies, including severe allergies, asthma, and chronic back issues.

Even after the personal attacks and smear campaign, Welles always felt that Hearst himself was blameless for the attacks on him and *Citizen Kane;* Welles would say that "Hearst wouldn't have stooped to such a thing," or that Hearst's staff "intervened on his behalf," or that the minions "in the Hearst organization were after me, to show the boss that they were on the ball." But even Welles had to admit that some of the covert actions by those minions took on truly sinister tones. While on a lecture tour before *Citizen Kane*'s release, Welles was at dinner when he was approached by a local police investigator.

"Don't go back to your hotel," the detective told Welles. "They've got a 14-year-old girl in the closet and two photographers waiting for you to come in."

"Of course, I would have gone to jail," Welles said. "There would have been no way out of it. I never went back to the hotel. I just waited until the train in the morning. I've often wondered what happened to the cameramen and the girl waiting all night for me to arrive. But that wasn't Hearst. That was a hatchet man from the local Hearst paper who thought he would advance by doing it."

Welles was magnanimous in acknowledging that the leadership of the Hearst organization probably did not order the ambush. But the idea that an employee of the Hearst organization might achieve career advancement through staged entrapment and fraud spoke volumes about the character of the corporation.

However, the worst of the attacks was no crude plot cooked up by the troops;

it was a Communist witch hunt that was planned and managed at the top level of the Hearst organization, with Welles as the target.

Congressional investigations of communism in the motion picture industry and the notorious blacklisting of the Hollywood Ten were not just phenomena of the late 1940s. The House Un-American Activities Committee launched its first investigation of Communists in Hollywood in 1940, when committee chairman Martin Dies, Jr., took testimony in Los Angeles in conjunction with a local grand jury. The topic was still an open sore in 1941—for liberals who denounced the inquisition and for conservatives who believed that the movie industry was vulnerable to "the Red Menace."

The subject, of course, was especially ripe for coverage by sensationalist media outlets like the Hearst papers. Welles was no Communist, but he was politically liberal and supported leftist causes. In January 1941, Welles directed a new play, *Native Son,* working once again with John Houseman. *Native Son* was based on the novel by Richard Wright, who freely acknowledged that he was a member of the Communist Party and explored Communist ideas in his writings. Welles also participated in the Free Company, a group of liberal-leaning writers and performers who produced programs on CBS about fundamental freedoms and rights.

In the spring, Welles said he was asked directly by federal investigators if he was a Communist. When Welles told his inquisitor to define his terms, he replied that a Communist was someone who gives his money to the government.

"In that case," Welles joked, referring to his high tax bracket, "I'm 87 percent Communist. The other 13 percent of me is pure Capitalist."

But it was no joke. When Hearst executives such as Berlin and Willicombe began looking for Welles' potential weak spots to poke, they turned to his politics.

"Our friend, Welles, is a pretty bad boy and is mixed up with the Leftists," Berlin wrote to Joseph Willicombe on January 21 (the same day the ban against RKO was lifted for Hearst papers). "Hollywood is due for a good purging as the picture industry, I am sure, has a healthy representation from the Communist Party."

Berlin sent to Hearst "a preliminary, and rather hasty" investigation of Welles in a summary that Berlin believed showed how Welles "acted as a front for the Community Party, if not an actual member."

In Welles' case, Berlin defined "acting as a front" as, among other supposedly notorious activities, appearing in *Ten Million Ghosts* by Pulitzer Prize–winning author Sidney Kingsley (an antiwar play that attacked munitions manufacturers with links to a powerful newspaper publisher), a speaking appearance at a liberal bookstore, and lectures at the New School for Social Research (which was "known for its left-wing teachers," Berlin said). Welles was also a member of the Negro Cultural Committee, which Berlin indicted because "further investigation of this committee probably would reveal radicals as its inspiration." Berlin noted other activities that to him indicated Communist sympathies, such as being the judge of the New Theatre League play contest.

Berlin's letter also reinforced that the Hearst organization was in bed with the Congressional investigators who had hunted Communists in Hollywood.

"We have the complete assurance from our friends in Washington that the result of the investigation made by them over a period of a year-and-a-half of the motion picture industry is available to us," Berlin told Willicombe. "This should be extremely valuable."

Berlin was aided in his "hasty" investigation with information gathered by Howard Rushmore. Berlin could hardly have chosen a more disreputable ally: in 1941, Rushmore was a former writer for the Communist Party's *Daily Worker* (he was fired when his review of *Gone with the Wind* was not critical enough); Rushmore then did a 180-degree political swing and in 1941 was gaining recognition for writing anti-Communist articles. He would soon become a high-profile right-wing editor, a witness for the House Un-American Activities Committee who vastly exaggerated the involvement of Communists in Hollywood, an investigator who fabricated evidence about Communist infiltration in the U.S. Navy, and the director of research for Joseph McCarthy during the senator's paranoia-driven investigation beginning in 1950 of supposed Communist involvement in the U.S. government.

All of this would provide ideal training for Rushmore to become editor of *Confidential,* one of the original models for scandal and exposé journalism. Rushmore would later turn on his own publication and become a star witness against *Confidential* in a massive libel suit. (Rushmore's career came to a horrifying end in 1958 when, in the backseat of a traveling New York taxi, he shot and murdered his wife and then killed himself.)

In spite of Rushmore's already notorious reputation, Berlin proposed that he be brought to Hollywood as an undercover operative to continue his investigation of Welles. The plot to launch undercover investigations by Rushmore did not hatch, but the investigation of Welles' politics by others in the Hearst organization proceeded. Welles' background, character, and political beliefs were scrutinized. Mysterious "government investigators" poked around the studio to check on whisperings of his alleged Communist sympathies. With initial input from Hearst supporters, the FBI opened a file on Welles and began an investigation that continued for years, with some reports sent directly to director J. Edgar Hoover.

It was all too simple: if the Hearst investigation had indeed proved that Welles was a Communist, the news would have been fodder for weeks of front-page coverage. But just as effective was Hearst reporters finding links between Welles and his liberal causes and projects such as *Native Son* and then encouraging anti-Communist organizations to speak out against his involvement; the resulting "protests" were then covered in prominent articles. Hearst publications were not only covering the news—they were creating it.

The Hearst team drummed up support among members of the American Legion, Veterans of Foreign Wars, and other groups against Welles' radio programs and stage productions, then featured the protests in news coverage. Hearst newspapers extended their ban on Welles to include coverage of *Native Son*. Hearst publications also attacked Welles' radio programs, implying that they had Communist overtones and opposed "the American way of life." The Hearst offensive against the broadcasts continued until listener surveys showed that the repeated assaults were generating public awareness of the broadcasts and actually helping to *increase* their ratings.

"The Hearst press is under strict orders to ignore Welles," reported *The New Yorker,* "except for a series of articles pointing out that he is a menace to American motherhood, freedom of speech and assembly, and the pursuit of happiness."

Later, Welles compiled a list of articles criticizing his work that appeared in Hearst publications. With headlines such as ORSON WELLES PLAYS DENOUNCED and THREE MORE LEGION CHIEFS RAP WELLES PLAY, Hearst publications were employing the same philosophy ("if the headline is big enough, it makes the news big enough") embraced by Charles Foster Kane in the *Inquirer.*

In a statement written in July—no joking this time—Welles responded to the harassment.

"I have stood silently by in the hope that this vicious attack against me would be spent in the passing of a few weeks. I had hoped that I would not continue to be the target of patriotic organizations who are accepting false statements and condemning me without knowing the facts.

"But I cannot remain silent any longer. The Hearst papers have repeatedly described me as a Communist. I am not a Communist. I am grateful for our constitutional form of government, and I rejoice in our great tradition of democracy. Needless to say, it is not necessarily unpatriotic to disagree with Mr. Hearst. On the contrary, it is a privilege guaranteed me as an American citizen by the Bill of Rights."

But in March, all of the harassment tactics employed by Hearst for more than two months continued to send a clear message to the theater chains: an operator who screened *Citizen Kane* would feel the effect of some action, unspecified though that action might be.

The pressure continued to weigh heavily, and in early March, Schaefer and RKO remained silent about *Citizen Kane*'s future, leading many Hollywood watchers to assume the lack of action was a clear signal—even after the industry-sanctioned edits—that the film might still be destroyed.

Variety, at this point in the fight perhaps trying too hard to keep the story bubbling more than was accurate, reported, "Optimism of a few weeks ago has greatly subsided, and a lot of insiders are willing to believe that an $800,000 bonfire of prints and negatives is not impossible."

Schaefer may have been silent only because he still had nothing new to report. The balancing act of placating his board, negotiating with the other studios, and soothing Welles was endless and complicated by the still unsuccessful hunt to identify enough theaters for a profitable run. Most likely, the discussion about choosing between a road show and a wide release that was described to *The New York Times* in late January produced the decision to distribute the film as broadly as possible—if theaters were willing to screen it. Unfortunately, the response was not good, thanks to Hearst, and the studio backed away from its early plans for wide release, instead opting for an extremely narrow schedule. Eventually, *Citizen Kane* would open in only a handful of premium theaters in seven cities.

Welles, too, was doing his best to promote his film's cause, including speaking about *Citizen Kane* during a national lecture tour. And there were some signs that he enjoyed the commotion—to a point. On January 27, he told an authors' club luncheon in Los Angeles, "When I get *Citizen Kane* off my mind, I'm going to work on an idea for a great picture based on the life of William Randolph Hearst." His friends printed a fake newspaper called *The Daily Press,* topped with an intentionally misspelled banner headline that read:

HEARST INDORSES CITIZEN KANE
Urges Sheaeffer to Release It

And Welles continued to play his strongest card: *Citizen Kane* itself, holding private screenings in New York and Los Angeles. The screenings in Los Angeles were especially effective, helping to convert the original disdain for the boy genius into genuine admiration for Welles as a filmmaker and respect for his brilliant cinematic achievement. Although Welles was denied his own print by Schaefer—placing a copy of the film in Welles' hands was considered by many at RKO as an open opportunity for the director to begin his own public screenings—the studio chief gladly arranged showings for Welles to host.

Thanks to the screenings and prerelease publicity, the word began to spread: *Citizen Kane* was a special picture—a *very* special picture—word that was no doubt eagerly delivered by Schaefer to the RKO board and his other detractors. *Time* captured the sentiment felt in much of Hollywood when the magazine reported that "to most of the several hundred people who have seen the film at private showings, *Citizen Kane* is the most sensational product of the U.S. movie industry."

By late March, many of Hollywood's top talents had seen *Citizen Kane,* as had most of the film industry press, and they knew the film delivered everything Welles had promised. Destroying or shelving the film, if there was even a chance at that late hour of either occurring, would have caused the biggest uproar in Hollywood history. Had the threat to *Citizen Kane*'s survival continued, Hearst would have been barraged by every major publication other than his own, along with most of the prominent figures in the motion picture industry, many of whom Hearst considered his friends. The Hearst organization had initially tried to position itself as a wronged company trying to prevent a slur against its chief executive. By March the corporation was viewed, rightly, as a conspiratorial suppressor of a stunning artistic achievement.

As spring 1941 drew near, Schaefer was feeling less of the negative pressure from Hearst and more of the positive encouragement from those at the screenings who urged him to release the film. Schaefer could no longer find a reason to wait; whatever the catalyst—*Kane*'s early lavish coverage in the weekly magazines, realizing that he could no longer avoid his contractual obligation to Welles, or the overwhelmingly positive audience responses—Schaefer relented. Perhaps, too, at this point the board simply gave up worrying about the *Citizen Kane* problem, realizing that RKO had much more to lose by shelving the film than it ever could by releasing it to theaters.

Welles and Schaefer met, and—finally and firmly—the release date was set: *Citizen Kane* would be shown to critics in formal press screenings on April 9, and its public premiere was scheduled for May 1 at the Palace Theatre in New York.

MR. HEARST

You furnish the pictures and I'll furnish the war.
—Cable from William Randolph Hearst to correspondent
illustrator Frederic Remington, when the artist wrote
that Cuba was at peace

You provide the prose poems, I'll provide the war.
—Charles Foster Kane's response to Wheeler, the *Inquirer*
reporter who writes that he can find no war in Cuba

Was Charles Foster Kane a fictionalized portrayal of William Randolph Hearst? That question has been discussed and analyzed as much as any issue in film history. For several uncertain weeks in early 1941, the question of Kane's links to Hearst was one of vital importance to the survival of *Citizen Kane*. Although *Citizen Kane* was ultimately saved from destruction, Hearst's actions not only severely damaged the film's chances for success, but derailed the grand plan by RKO president George Schaefer to produce high-quality films at his struggling studio—a step forward that could have had far-reaching ramifications in Hollywood. And Orson Welles' future as a potentially bankable producer-director was damaged as well—a setback that altered the course of his career.

For those reasons, Kane's relationship to Hearst continues to fascinate. However, exploring why influential people were driven to near hysterical, unethical attempts to destroy a motion picture makes an even more intriguing story.

Clearly, many parallels exist between the fictional Kane and the real-life Hearst. As a start, the fortunes of both Kane and Hearst were built on the discovery of precious metals: Kane's mother unexpectedly acquired the supposedly worthless deed to the "Colorado Lode" gold mine from a defaulting boarder;

real-life fortune came to Hearst's father, George, when he discovered a major vein of silver in Nevada in 1859. (There was also a curious similarity between the fictional Kane and the real-life Welles regarding inheritance. In one of several odd parallels in the Kane saga, in June 1940, Welles—then twenty-five—received the final distribution of his family trust fund, just as Kane at the same age did in the script Welles was preparing to film. However, Welles' trust fund distribution of $33,438.18—which after taxes, loan payments, and other expenses shrank to $2,692.41—was anything but "the world's sixth-largest private fortune" that Kane received.)

In his youth, Hearst, like Kane, was expelled from Harvard; administrators were not amused when Hearst delivered chamber pots to several professors, each vessel containing a photo of the recipient. Kane was also expelled from several other colleges, according to Bernstein, including Yale, Princeton, Cornell, and unnamed schools in Switzerland.

As a young man, Hearst, like Kane, assumed control of a struggling newspaper; in Hearst's case, it was the *San Francisco Examiner,* which was given to him by his father. Hearst turned the *Examiner* into a profitable entity in only two years. When Hearst entered the New York newspaper business with the *Morning Journal,* he raided the competition's staff just as Kane did, stealing talented reporters away from no less than Joseph Pulitzer and his *New York World.*

In 1935, Hearst published his own "Declaration of Principles"—but unlike Kane's, the declaration did not appear in his own papers. In retaliation against a proposed boycott of his newspapers, Hearst purchased advertising space in rival papers and published an ad that stated, "The Hearst Papers Stand for Americanism and Genuine Democracy."

The film includes a fictional nemesis for Kane who was similar to an actual political enemy of Hearst's: the character of "Boss" Jim W. Gettys resembles Charles F. Murphy, in the early 1900s the leader of the Tammany Hall political machine in New York. In Gettys' confrontation with Kane in Susan's apartment, he describes to Emily how the *Inquirer* printed a political cartoon of Gettys wearing prison stripes, as Hearst had done to Murphy in 1903.

Hearst insiders also would have noticed the similarities between two other characters in *Citizen Kane* and real-life confidants of Hearst's: to the Hearst factions, Bernstein would have seemed like a near match with Solomon Carvalho, general manager of Hearst's newspapers who came to the organization from the *New York World* and was one of the few Jews in the Hearst senior management; Leland must have been perceived as the Hollywood version of Eugene Lent, Hearst's longtime personal friend, his companion in European travels, and a fellow student at Harvard and colleague on the *Harvard Lampoon* who went west with Hearst to work on the *San Francisco Examiner*.

Hearst, like Kane, did strongly support in print—with screaming headlines and partially fabricated stories—the declaration of war by the United States against Spain, and he was a leader among those who verbally attacked President William McKinley for being a pawn of corporate trusts. Kane, instead of opposing a president as was written in early drafts of the script, chose to attack Wall Street monopolies and his banker-guardian, Walter Thatcher.

In 1905, Hearst lost the New York mayoral election, not as the result of a personal scandal like the one that brought down Kane's candidacy for governor, but because corrupt political bosses stole victory from him by dumping legitimate ballot boxes from pro-Hearst neighborhoods into New York Harbor. In the early drafts of *Citizen Kane,* Mankiewicz used this same reason to explain why Kane lost the gubernatorial election, but the circumstances of Kane's political failure were changed to the situation involving Susan Alexander as soon as Welles began to revise the script.

Hearst newspapers carried editorials supportive of political assassination only a few months before President McKinley was killed in Buffalo. Similarly, in early versions of *American,* Kane papers launched a print assault against "President James Norton" before he was wounded—although not fatally. This ongoing feud between Kane and the president of the United States was featured prominently in early versions of *American* and *Citizen Kane* but dwindled to a few brief references in the final draft and eventually became only a two-sentence sidelight in the breakfast table montage, when Kane and Emily talk about "this whole oil scandal." Other modest references to presidents, corruption, and assassination were deleted in New York when the lawyers for RKO and the other studios reached a compromise on the final cut.

During Hearst's most severe financial crisis, his banks and a "Conservation Committee" assumed partial control of his organization, a less severe version of how Thatcher assumed complete control of Kane enterprises during the depths of the Depression. Although Hearst retained some control of his organization, like Kane he lost much of his power and influence and in his declining years was primarily a figurehead.

Kane and Hearst each had an insatiable appetite for old-world treasures, and they filled warehouses with expensive but mostly unappreciated antiques. When, in his later years, Hearst sold hundreds of art items, auction crews discovered that many of the original shipping crates had never been opened.

Beyond factual similarities, however, those close to Hearst noticed personality traits in Kane that they believed mocked "the old man." In Kane on-screen, they saw Hearst's overbearing behavior, his misuse of power, the extravagant spending that led him to the brink of ruin, and—perhaps most revealing— the transformation of Hearst from a publisher perceived as a champion of the workingman into a narrow-minded elitist who irresponsibly used his publications for his own unethical purposes, such as to suppress *Citizen Kane*.

Welles recalled thinking that Hearst would appreciate the characterization of Kane because as callous and self-centered as the fictional publisher may have been, he was still a better person than the real-life one—an interesting rationalization and hard to imagine as a method to placate "the Chief."

"I made Charles Foster Kane a more sympathetic character than Hearst ever was in real life," Welles said. "I always surmised that Hearst would be pleased."

There were many in the Hollywood community who would have agreed with Welles' assessment of Hearst. When actor Douglas Fairbanks, Sr., asked Hearst why he built his empire on newspapers and not by making movies, Hearst replied, "You can crush a man with journalism, but you can't with motion pictures."

But even harder for the Hearst factions to stomach were comments in the *News on the March* newsreel about the declining credibility of Kane and his crumbling financial kingdom—views that mirrored the real-world opinion of Hearst. "Kane's world now is history," reported the newsreel about Kane's death in a statement that applied equally well to the still living Hearst, "and the great yellow journalist himself lived to be history, outlived his power to make it . . . an emperor of newsprint continued to direct his failing empire, vainly attempted to sway as he once did, the destinies of a nation that had ceased to listen to him, ceased to trust him."

Other, more personal issues must have been as difficult to endure, such as Kane's discovery of a bottle of booze hidden in a bookcase while he is destroying Susan's bedroom. To Parsons, who must have been aware that Marion Davies had a serious drinking problem that was rapidly descending into alcoholism, one can easily imagine that one of those "audible gasps" heard during Parsons' screening could have occurred when Kane finds the bottle and flings it across the room.

But the most damning visual similarity between life and cinema was that Kane, like Hearst, constructed a gigantic private hilltop hideaway that served as both a pleasure palace for guests and an inaccessible refuge—as well as a financial drain. Kane built his Xanadu on a man-made mountain along Florida's Gulf coast; Hearst constructed a castle he always referred to as "the Ranch" in the hills of central California.

Located on what Hearst called "La Cuesta Encantada" (the Enchanted Hill), the Mediterranean Revival–style citadel looked more like a nineteenth-century church than a home, with two swimming pools, 250,000 acres of surrounding range land, and a menagerie of animals from around the world. Now the estate, which is generally referred to as "Hearst Castle" or "San Simeon" (for the tiny town nearby), is part of the California State Parks system—the Hearst San Simeon State Historical Monument—and is a popular tourist destination.

Hearst inherited most of the land that would surround his castle, and for decades he continued to add to the property by buying small parcels from local farmers. One legend recalls that Hearst was obsessed with the prospect of owning all the land for as far as he could see from his estate—no easy feat when the house is built sixteen hundred feet above sea level—and he supposedly dickered for years with one local farmer who would never sell the final piece needed to fulfill the publisher's baronial dream.

Some small details about Xanadu would have been noticed by Hearst confidantes such as Parsons, who prided herself on being a frequent guest at San Simeon, and perceived as intentional slaps at Hearst: in the first scene of the breakfast table sequence, shown prominently sitting on the Kanes' elegant table next to Emily were retail bottles of condiments; Hearst was famous for serving Heinz ketchup and French's mustard in their original bottles, sitting on the dining table alongside priceless china and silver. Such table settings, with the bottles, can be seen today in displays at Hearst Castle.

However, there were at least as many differences as there were similarities between Hearst and Kane. The principal distinction between them, of course, was that in 1941, Hearst was alive and Kane was dead. Hearst, seventy-eight at the time of *Citizen Kane*'s release, lived until 1951. Nevertheless, Hearst cronies who closely scrutinized *Citizen Kane* could not have failed to notice that Hearst and Kane were the same age; although Kane's age is never specifically stated in the film, Buddy Swan is listed in the credits as playing "Kane, age 8." If Thatcher "first encountered Mr. Kane in 1871," as he stated in his memoirs, then Kane would have been born in 1863—just as Hearst was.

Looking at the drafts of the script, the ages for Hearst and Kane raise a question: In the first draft, Mankiewicz wrote that Thatcher meets Kane in 1870 and not 1871, and Kane was six years old and not eight—a combination that would have made him a different age from Hearst. The reference to 1870 persisted in every version of the script, including the last one, before Welles inexplicably changed the date to 1871 for the on-screen text in Thatcher's memoirs; the reference to the young Kane's age as eight years is mentioned only in the credits. Why Welles changed the age and the date—revisions that did not affect the plot but either intentionally or accidentally reinforced that Kane was Hearst—is a mystery.

Hearst, unlike Kane, had indeed been elected to public office and served two uneventful terms in Congress before he encountered the New York political machine in his unsuccessful bid for mayor. Hearst had a happy life as a child and later in the company of Marion Davies, his devoted mistress for more than thirty years; another reason Charles Lederer may have been convinced that Kane and Susan were not Hearst and Marion was that the real-life couple cared deeply about each other.

While Hearst's single marriage soured—Kane's two relationships ended badly—he maintained contact with his wife, Millicent, and was a devoted father to his five sons. In fact, it may have been the devotion of the second son that stirred up the trouble over *Citizen Kane*: Charles Lederer, who as Marion Davies's nephew was in a position to know about Hearst family affairs, said that while he thought Hearst and Miss Davies were "completely unconcerned" about *Citizen Kane* and that "neither had any rancor or resentment" about the film or Welles, he also believed that Hearst's second son, William Randolph Hearst, Jr., a family company executive, was "completely concerned" about the potential effects of the film on the family name and led the assault.

Lederer's view was no doubt sincere. However, considering the corporate correspondence that shows Hearst's full knowledge of the attacks on Welles and *Citizen Kane,* Lederer could not have been correct. But regardless of the catalyst, as things turned out, of course, the family name was tarnished much more by the unethical journalistic practices and disreputable behavior involved in suppressing *Citizen Kane* than it ever would have been by the film itself.

Millicent refused to divorce Hearst, and they remained married, if only legally, for forty-seven years. During Hearst's financial crises, it was in part money from Davies's personal fortune (and her offer to sell some of her jewelry) that helped keep the publisher afloat. Had Millicent divorced Hearst, Davies, although thirty-four years younger than Hearst, would have married him.

Davies, whom Hearst supported in a long acting career, was not a flop in

Hollywood, as was Susan Alexander in her brief, nightmarish experience with grand opera. Some Hollywood observers noted that Davies, who made more than forty films between 1917 and 1937, might have enjoyed greater success had Hearst not meddled in her career by demanding that the gifted comedic actress play more dramatic roles. Mankiewicz's idea to write Susan as a failure was drawn not from Davies, but from the sagging career of nightclub singer Evelyn Nesbit; the idea to set Susan's interview in a nightclub came from a backstage interview with Nesbit that appeared in the "Broadway" column by New York *Daily News* reporter Dan Walker.

And whether or not Kane was modeled exclusively on Hearst, there is no doubt that Marion Davies played a key role in how to *not* model the character of Susan. Kathryn Trosper recalled that one topic in the script under constant scrutiny was the dialogue for Susan Alexander, because "no one really wanted to hurt Marion Davies."

"A number of times, Orson was told things like, 'This line is something Marion might say—we better rewrite it,'" recalled Trosper. "Or, 'We're getting a little too close to Marion in this scene.'"

In spite of their caution, "we were terribly unfair to Marion Davies," Welles said. "Marion was an extraordinary woman—nothing like the character Dorothy Comingore played in the movie.

"I always felt Hearst had the right to be upset," said Welles about those drawing the parallel between Susan and Marion. "She gave him everything, stayed by him—just the opposite of Susan. *That* was the libel. Kane was better than Hearst, and Marion was much better than Susan—whom people wrongly equated with her."

Publicity photos showed Marion working on large wooden jigsaw puzzles, as Susan did in Xanadu. But, said Welles, her experience at Hearst homes was anything but lonely, and she enjoyed serving as the palace hostess.

"Hearst built more than one castle, and Marion was the hostess in all of them," Welles said. "They were pleasure domes indeed, and the Beautiful People of the day fought for invitations. Xanadu was a lonely fortress, and Susan was quite right to escape from it. [Davies] was never one of Hearst's possessions: he was always her suitor, and she was the precious treasure of his heart for more than thirty years, until his last breath of life. Theirs is truly a love story."

However, a much more intimate subject involving Davies could have played a role in generating speculation that Hearst was Kane: "Rosebud" may have been Hearst's personal nickname for Davies' genitalia—a bit of gossip that

Mankiewicz supposedly learned from silent screen star Louise Brooks. If true, it would have been the worst possible example of Mankiewicz's self-destructive nature to reveal such a personal detail in a script. There would have been no question among Hearst's closest friends that Kane's character was a direct assault on the publisher and his mistress. However, author Louis Pizzitola said that "Rosebud" was the nickname that Orrin Peck, a friend of William Randolph Hearst's, gave to Hearst's mother, Phoebe. But either origin for the name would have connections to Hearst that would not have been missed by the publisher, Davies, or the people who knew them.

And there were other possible explanations for the origin of the Rosebud name: for instance, author Patrick McGilligan wrote that Mankiewicz himself reported, in the heat of lawsuit testimony (see page 227), only a few years before he died from the ravages of alcoholism and drug abuse, that the name was taken from "Old Rosebud," the winner of the 1914 Kentucky Derby, on which Mankiewicz bet and won. However, Mankiewicz biographer Richard Meryman said that Rosebud was Mankiewicz's bicycle, a gift stolen from him when he was ten—a story confirmed by his son Frank in a 2011 interview.

As for Welles, his view of the Rosebud name was simple—perhaps too simple: "It didn't mean a damn thing," he said. "We inserted that as a dramatic gimmick, nothing more." But if Rosebud was indeed "nothing more" than a gimmick, and the name actually had other meanings, anatomical or otherwise, the coincidence would be beyond extraordinary.

Outside of the Hearst organization, however, some observers were certain that Kane was modeled after someone other than the publisher. For every example of evidence that demonstrated Kane was modeled after Hearst, an equally solid explanation pointed to another person.

The list of prospects was lengthy: some cited newspaper executives other than Hearst as better models for Kane, such as the *World*'s Joseph Pulitzer, or James Gordon Bennett, Jr., editor and publisher of the *New York Herald*—two controversial publishers in the late nineteenth and early twentieth centuries. Other candidates from the world of journalism included *New York Sun* publisher Charles A. Dana and newspaper chain owner Frank Munsey.

Even Charles Lederer thought Kane's character more closely resembled Robert McCormick and Joseph Patterson, former publishers of the *Chicago Tribune*, than Hearst. In fact, Harold McCormick, from another branch of the *Tribune* publishing family, actually did finance the opera career of his wife, Ganna Walska. McCormick devoted a small fortune to attempting to develop Walska's voice, and she appeared in several failed productions.

Other executives outside the world of journalism were also nominated as models for Kane. Kodak chairman Jules Brulatour funded the operatic aspirations of both his second wife, Dorothy Gibson, and his third wife, Hope Hampton; they, like Susan Alexander, did not fare very well, but they certainly sang better than Susan did.

Executive Samuel Insull was instrumental in building the Chicago Civic Opera House. Insull also supported the acting career of his wife, Gladys; her debut performance was reviewed by none other than Herman Mankiewicz.

While some pointed to Xanadu as evidence of the link between Hearst and Kane, others suggested that the Florentine Renaissance estate built in Florida by John Ringling North (the founder of Ringling Bros. and Barnum & Bailey Circus) offered a suitable alternative inspiration to Hearst's castle. During the *News on the March* newsreel, other real-life estates also served as stand-ins for Xanadu, including Oheka Castle, the early-twentieth-century home to investment banker Otto Kahn. Built on the north shore of Long Island and still the second-largest private home in America, Oheka Castle appears in the first aerial shot in the newsreel.

Many viewers of *Citizen Kane* are surprised to learn that the exteriors of Xanadu shown in the newsreel and elsewhere in the film were not clips of Hearst's actual home. The images of Xanadu flash across the screen so quickly during *News on the March* that some simply assumed Welles had shot covert footage to serve as Kane's on-screen palace. But no one from the design team had been to Hearst Castle at the time of *Citizen Kane*'s production. (Mankiewicz had, of course, stayed at the house as a weekend guest several times.) According to makeup artist Maurice Seiderman, Welles, Toland, and Ferguson visited the Hearst grounds during preproduction—an unlikely story, given the security at the Hearst estate, but if true, a fact that certainly was *not* discussed during the prerelease controversy. (Although Seiderman described the visit in several interviews, Welles never confirmed that it occurred.)

The scenes that depict Kane's home used in *News on the March* or other sequences in the film were models, paintings, stock footage acquired from newsreel companies, footage taken on the RKO back lot, or (most prominently) buildings in Balboa Park in San Diego that were constructed for the 1915 Panama-California International Exposition; the San Diego buildings today look the same as they did when filmed for *Citizen Kane* in 1941. Several brief glimpses of Kane's Xanadu animal collections, such as the large bird sanctuary, were filmed at the San Diego Zoo, adjacent to Balboa Park. Unfortunately for the defenders of *Citizen Kane* in 1941, the exposition buildings, shown early in the newsreel, are constructed in the same Mediterranean Revival style as Hearst Castle. The Casa Del Prado, with its twin towers, although shown only briefly in the newsreel, looks enough like the main building at San Simeon to provide added ammunition for the Hearst-is-Kane factions.

Photos of the Hearst estate were indeed referenced by RKO designers as a model for the exteriors of Xanadu—examples of privately owned hilltop castles in twentieth-century America are, after all, hard to find—and photos of the property can be found in the Mercury Theatre archives. However, the images of the Hearst estate were used primarily to help RKO artists determine the physical position of a large house on a hillside setting; with its bright stucco façades and well-manicured grounds, the mansion itself would have served little purpose in creating the dark and Gothic Xanadu. The exterior designs for Xanadu were inspired by a combination of real and fantasy buildings, such as Mont-Saint-Michel and the Queen's castle in *Snow White and the Seven Dwarfs*.

A visit to Hearst Castle shows a high regard for intimacy and a comfortable, wood-lined warmth, even in the largest rooms of the mansion, which are nothing like the stark, foreboding abyss that art director Perry Ferguson created for the Great Hall at Xanadu. While Greek sculptures and medieval tapestries give Hearst Castle a stately quality, the rooms are not bleak or overwhelming like those of Xanadu.

The presentation of Xanadu in the film was cinematically dramatic and effective, but Xanadu was no Hearst Castle. If Hearst loyalists assumed that Xanadu was the Chief's house, it was only because they accepted Kane's grim edifice as the grossest caricature of Hearst Castle.

Perhaps the greatest irony in the battle between the Hearst organization and Orson Welles remains that the central figure in the dispute may never have seen the film that he tried to destroy. Over the years, Hearst's biographers, associates, and family members have reported that either he absolutely saw the film or he absolutely did not—both with equal certainty.

The one certain point is that Hearst was offered the opportunity to view *Citizen Kane.* As an attempted peace gesture, George Schaefer himself sent a print of *Citizen Kane* to Hearst; when the film was returned to RKO, the protective seals on the cans were not broken. And Hearst did not attend any of the early screenings (consider the media uproar *that* would have created). When *Daily News* film columnist John Chapman wrote to Hearst to ask him about the film, Hearst wired him on April 12 saying he was "the only other guy in Hollywood who has not seen CK. So I cannot discuss the picture."

Hearst's son William Randolph Hearst, Jr., says his father never saw the film. Charles Lederer, too, was positive that neither Hearst nor his aunt Marion Davies ever saw it. Lederer and his wife, Virginia, may have been some of the best sources of inside information on the subject from that period. In yet another peculiar coincidence in the *Citizen Kane* story, Lederer married Welles' ex-wife Virginia Nicolson soon after Welles and Nicolson divorced in 1940. Charles and Virginia often visited Aunt Marion and "Uncle" William, bringing along Welles' daughter Christopher.

While Lederer was positive that his aunt and Hearst had never seen *Citizen Kane,* his own wife remembered otherwise. Virginia Nicolson told Welles biographer Frank Brady that a group hosted by Hearst and Davies viewed the film at the estate.

"When the film ended and the lights came up, we all looked over in Hearst's direction," Nicolson said. "He had a slightly scampish smile but didn't say anything. We were all afraid to utter a word. Then, he and Marion simply got up and went upstairs in his private elevator to retire. Although I saw him many times after that, I never heard him mention a word about the film."

John Tebbel, who wrote a biography about Hearst in 1952, says that Hearst and Davies saw *Citizen Kane* at the Geary Theatre in San Francisco, soon after the film opened there. While no proof exists that Hearst saw the film then, the publisher was indeed in San Francisco at the time (as Welles himself would later recall). Tebbel wrote that when a friend of Hearst's asked him how he liked *Citizen Kane,* "He looked away thoughtfully and replied, 'We thought it was a little too long.'"

Marion Davies' own recollections about seeing *Citizen Kane* were absolute: either she definitely did not see the film or she saw it multiple times, depending on the source—clouded memories that may have been the result of alcoholism that plagued Davies for years.

Davies said in her memoirs, *The Times We Had,* that she never saw *Citizen*

Kane, and neither had Hearst, "but my sister Rose did," said Marion. "She said, 'I'll call him. It's terrible. You can't even see the picture, because it's all dark.'"

However, columnist James Bacon remembered the opposite and said that Davies supplied many details.

"Marion once told me that she and W.R. saw the famous Orson Welles movie seven or eight times," Bacon said. "[She said] 'We screened it in Beverly Hills, Wyntoon [the Hearst lodge in the Northern California woods], and San Simeon. Once we even went into a theatre in San Francisco, ate popcorn, and watched it with an audience. W.R. loved it, and we laughed at the reference to Rosebud.' Then she told me that Rosebud was Hearst's pet name for her genitalia."

At one time Hearst may have owned a copy of *Citizen Kane,* and the print might have been kept in his motion picture collection at the estate; first-run film screenings were standard evening fare for Hearst and his guests. W. A. Swanberg, another biographer of Hearst, wrote that a year after *Citizen Kane* was released, Hearst noted the film's existence in his collection. Hearst reportedly told Louis Shainmark, the managing editor of Hearst's *Chicago Herald-American* and a guest at Hearst Castle, "We have [*Citizen Kane*] here. I must run it off again sometime."

Hearst may have been joking about owning a copy of the film. The inventory of the estate's contents conducted in 1957 after the property was given to the state of California—a yearlong real-life project not unlike the reporters' rummaging at Xanadu—showed that several motion pictures remained in Hearst's vaults, but not *Citizen Kane.*

If Hearst never saw the film, it would have been a loss, according to one of Hearst's oldest associates. Ashton Stevens, the real-life model for Jed Leland, was often called the dean of American drama critics and worked for Hearst's papers for more than fifty years. Stevens knew Welles from childhood and later gave positive reviews to the young director's Mercury productions and other projects. Welles showed Stevens the script for *Citizen Kane,* and the critic visited the set. When Stevens saw the film, Welles said, he "thought the old man would be thrilled by it."

Whether or not Hearst saw *Citizen Kane* may never be known for certain. However, Welles, as usual, had a colorful story on the subject: Welles said that in a chance encounter in a San Francisco hotel elevator, he actually invited Hearst to see *Citizen Kane.* Welles told several different versions of this story, but in each, the basic facts were the same.

"I found myself alone with Hearst in an elevator in the Fairmont Hotel on the night *Citizen Kane* was opening in San Francisco," Welles recalled. "So I introduced myself and asked him if he'd like to come to the opening of the picture. He didn't answer. And as he was getting off at his floor, I said, 'Charles Foster Kane would have accepted.' No reply. And Kane would have, you know. That was his style—just as he finished Jed Leland's bad review of Susan Alexander as an opera singer."

Over the decades, Welles frequently reshaped his statements about Hearst's connection to Kane. He always denied that Kane was Hearst, meaning that Kane was not modeled *solely* on Hearst. At one point in January 1941, Welles talked about how Kane was the product of many personalities and would include Hearst among them—such as his comment to *The New York Times,* at the height of the Hearst assault, about how if Hearst and others like him had not lived, "Kane could not have been made." It was this statement that had inspired his lawyer, Arnold Weissberger, to insist that no one should admit "in the slightest way" that *Citizen Kane* had anything to do with Hearst.

As the years passed, Welles was willing to state that Hearst played a larger role in the composite of personalities that became Kane than he had earlier admitted, but he remained steadfast that the "Kane is Hearst" explanation was far too simple.

When, in 1941, he was asked to describe how Kane's character was created, Welles wrote, "I wished to make a motion picture which was not a narrative of action so much as an examination of character. For this, I desired a man of many sides and many aspects. I immediately decided that my character should be a public man—an extremely public man.

"For a time I considered making him a fictitious American president. Deciding against this, I could find no other position in public life besides that of a newspaper publisher in which a man of enormous wealth exercises what might be called real power in a democracy." Years later, Welles said that if the film had been about Howard Hughes, Joseph Cotten would have starred in the title role.

Six years after *Citizen Kane* was released, Welles and RKO were sued for allegedly using Ferdinand Lundberg's book *Imperial Hearst* as the basis for *Citizen Kane.* When the case came to trial in 1950, Welles testified under oath about where the inspiration for Kane came from.

"As in the case of a great deal of fiction, we drew to some extent on our observations of certain aspects of American life, and our knowledge of certain types of influential Americans," Welles testified. "It was intended to be the study of the character and psychological motivations of a fictional character who, of course, could never have been invented had not certain types of personalities of an equal position appeared in the American scene."

When Welles' radio programs were attacked by Hearst papers, he responded with his own statement: "William Randolph Hearst is conducting a series of brutal attacks on me in his newspapers. It seems he doesn't like my picture *Citizen Kane*. I understand he hasn't seen it. I am sure he hasn't. If he had, I think he would agree with me that those who have advised him that Kane is Hearst have done us both an injustice."

Mankiewicz was equally emphatic that Kane was not based solely on Hearst. Even before *Citizen Kane* was released, fellow screenwriter Ben Hecht said that Mankiewicz did not intend to caricature Hearst.

"Do you think . . . Willie Hearst will figure it's about him?" Mankiewicz asked Hecht in March 1941. "I didn't write it about him, but about some of our other mutual friends—sort of a compendium."

Hecht's recollection of Mankiewicz's mystified comment about Hearst stands in sharp contrast to a later and bolder statement, when Mankiewicz said that he specifically mentioned Hearst early in his script planning discussions with Welles.

"I told Welles that I would be interested in doing a picture based on Hearst and Marion Davies," said Mankiewicz. "I just kept on telling him everything about them. I was interested in them, and I went into all kinds of details."

Whether Kane was a compendium of several people or a specific attack on Hearst, Mankiewicz bizarrely argued to retain highly charged fictional elements in the script, specifically to demonstrate that Kane was *not* Hearst. When revising the original draft script with Welles, Mankiewicz suggested that they use the scene in which Kane orders Raymond the butler to kill Susan's lover at Xanadu. By including the scene, Mankiewicz reasoned, Hearst would never protest, because by suggesting that he was the model for Kane, Hearst would also be admitting to murder.

"If we keep it in," Mankiewicz told Welles of the murder scene, "we'll never have any trouble with Hearst."

Considering how many true anecdotes about "Willie" were included in early drafts of the script, it seems that Mankiewicz's "compendium" emphasized Hearst far more than the writer realized. Or more likely was that the alcoholic, self-destructive Mankiewicz—who in the 1930s moved in Hearst's social circles and had been a welcome guest at the publisher's home—subconsciously created another new route to his own social and professional suicide by deliberately attacking Hearst. If indeed "Rosebud" was Hearst's private sexual nickname for Davies, that prospect seems even more probable.

A point missed during the early controversy over *Citizen Kane* was that Hearst is actually *mentioned* in the film as a real-life figure in Kane's fictional world. During the scene in the projection room after the screening of *News on the March,* Rawlston, the head of the newsreel company, asks his staff about Kane, "But how is he different from Ford? *Or Hearst, for that matter?* Or John Doe?" Rawlston's line flies by so fast in Welles' swift pacing of the screening room dialogue that on first viewing few hear the reference to Hearst. (The script originally included a reference in this scene to Nelson Rockefeller as well, but mentioning a tycoon who served on the studio's own board of directors was too much even for Welles to get away with.)

However, two true and well-known incidents appear in *Citizen Kane* that were unquestionably linked directly to Hearst. Early in the film, when Kane's banker-guardian, Walter Thatcher, warns the young publisher that he is losing $1 million a year by operating the *New York Inquirer,* Kane quips, "At the rate of a million dollars a year, I'll have to close this place in . . . sixty years." The line, famous in newspaper circles, came from a comment by Hearst's mother, Phoebe, who was asked about her son losing $1 million a year on his *San Francisco Examiner* and *New York Journal* and replied, "At that rate, he'll last thirty years."

Even more damaging was dialogue in the same scene that included Kane's response to a cable from Wheeler, his correspondent in Cuba, who could not find signs of a military uprising against Spanish rule. "You provide the prose poems," Kane replied, "I'll provide the war." It reprised a much-cited exchange between Hearst and artist Frederic Remington, who before the Spanish-American War was Hearst's correspondent in Cuba. When Remington did not find bloodshed or atrocities, he wired to Hearst, "Everything quiet. There is no trouble here. There will be no more. I wish to return." Instead of recalling him, Hearst wired back, "Please remain. You furnish the pictures and I'll furnish the war."

Thirty-five years after he and Mankiewicz wrote *Citizen Kane,* Welles admitted that they created dialogue for the film based on the exchange between Remington and Hearst. "In fact," Welles said, "it is the only purely Hearstian element in *Citizen Kane*. Except for the telegram and the crazy art collection—much too good to resist—in *Kane* everything was invented." (Given the long list of other similarities, Welles had an intriguing definition of "only.")

Herman Mankiewicz's wife, Sara, who witnessed the Hearst lawyers' review of her husband's copy of the Third Revised Final version of the script when they came to the Mankiewicz home, said they found other true-life references: in Kane's first appearance in the film, he is interviewed in the newsreel about the prospects for World War II. Kane promises that there will be no war. Sara said the lawyers wrote, "This happens to be the gist of an authentic interview with WRH—occasion his last trip to Europe."

The lawyers also noted other references that hinted of Hearst. For instance, in a line not in the final film, when at the *Inquirer* party Kane promises that while on vacation he "will forget all about the new features sections—the Sunday supplement—and not try to think up any ideas for comic sections," the lawyers wrote, "Who else?" (The lawyers did not have the opportunity to note another true-life similarity that appeared later: in Hearst's own Metrotone News, in a newsreel titled "A Talk on Liberty by W. R. Hearst," after a trip to Europe Hearst said, "Every American is glad to be home, and glad to see the Statue of Liberty as he enters New York Harbor"—a statement very much like Kane's response to a reporter in the newsreel that wasn't finalized until production began. When asked if he was glad to be back from a trip to Europe, Kane replies, "I'm always glad to be back, young man. I'm an American. Always been an American.")

In spite of his own claims that Kane was primarily invention, Welles also acknowledged that Hearst was correct when he defended himself.

"He was right," Welles told Peter Bogdanovich. "He was dead right. Why not fight? I expected that. I didn't expect that everyone would run as scared as they did."

In January 1941, Welles had indeed told Parsons and Hopper the truth—or at least the truth as he viewed it: from Welles' perspective, Kane *was* a fictional publisher, except that his definition of "fictional" was a character based on many real and imaginary people, Hearst among them. The tragic mistake Welles made dealing with Parsons and Hopper was not acknowledging early in production that Hearst was one of several models for the fictional publisher—an explanation that might have lessened the blow when they saw the film.

When Charles Lederer read the script and told Mankiewicz that Hearst and Marion Davies would not be alarmed, his response may have been based on a screenwriter's understandable focus on dialogue and plot. But when Hedda Hopper and Louella Parsons viewed the film itself, they must have been shocked by the visual details that from their perspective pointed directly at Hearst.

The evidence visible early in *Citizen Kane* caused the most damage. Consider how Hopper and Parsons—who were already assuming that Kane was Hearst—must have reacted at their screenings when they saw scenes of a newspaper publisher who owns an incredible hilltop palace with its own private zoo, who acquired a huge art collection, and who urged his country into the Spanish-American War—followed by the brutally frank depiction of the declining credibility of the once powerful executive. Then minutes later came the conversation between the young Kane and Thatcher, which included the "I'll provide the war" dialogue about Cuba and the comment about the *Inquirer* losing $1 million a year for sixty years.

Given all of this "evidence," it is no wonder that Hopper alerted Hearst about the film and there were "audible gasps" at Parsons' screening before she walked out. Both columnists, always swift to jump to conclusions and play up controversy, were blinded to other alternatives. In their minds, Charles Foster Kane was indeed William Randolph Hearst and only Hearst. Given their introduction to Kane, how could they have thought anything else?

A wry commentary by *The New York Times*' Hollywood correspondent Douglas Churchill summed up precisely what Hopper and Parsons must have been thinking:

"Mr. Welles says the film, which deals with the life of a fictional figure who owns a chain of newspapers, who unsuccessfully runs for the governor of New York, who boasts that he started the Spanish-American War, who marries an obscure singer and attempts to gain recognition for her as an opera star through his publications, and who retires to a fabulous castle to die when his newspaper empire crumbles, is in no sense biographical. Representatives of William Randolph Hearst, the publisher, have advised the producer that they believe another interpretation can be put on the story."

The sad epilogue is that Parsons and Hopper are probably best recalled—if they are recalled at all outside of discussions of gossip and scandal journalism—for their role in attempting to destroy *Citizen Kane*. Parsons in particular lost credibility when her seemingly endless attempts to crush the film were well publicized in the non-Hearst press.

"It is my opinion that Mr. Hearst, who is smart about these things, would have ignored *Citizen Kane,* positively and negatively, had he been given the chance," Mankiewicz wrote to Alexander Woollcott. "But this behavior was denied him chiefly because of an idiot named Louella Parsons and a very smart woman named Hedda Hopper."

Hopper would go on to cover Hollywood almost until her death in 1966. She continued to write about Welles from time to time—in October 1941, after *Citizen Kane* had opened in local theaters, she prattled on about a cage of birds in Welles' Mercury office—and never recognized her role as one of the catalysts in derailing the young director's early career. Always promoting her own reputation as a manipulative dirt digger, she attributed her own success to "bitchery, sheer bitchery."

Louella Parsons never stopped blaming Welles for what she saw in *Citizen Kane*.

"Many years back, I heard that Welles was making a picture about someone I love very much," she wrote in 1951 in *Modern Screen*. ". . . And from that day to this, I have never forgiven him."

Parsons continued her column until 1965—by then an anachronistic curiosity—more than a decade after her influence began to wane in the early 1950s. When in her 1961 memoirs she referred to *Citizen Kane* as a "hatchet job" that was "done in the worst of taste"—at that point long after the film had been recognized as a pinnacle of cinema achievement—her comments no doubt helped further erode her already crumbled reputation. And through it all, not for a moment did it occur to Parsons that even if Welles had deliberately created *Citizen Kane* as an attack on Hearst, the director had the same right to express his views on film as the publisher had to rant about people and issues in his own newspapers.

Parsons officially gave up her column in 1965, more than a year after her assistant, Dorothy Manners, had begun writing it. When Parsons died in 1972, the few stars who attended her funeral were shocked by the sparse attendance of the celebrities she had once covered; most of those in the church were autograph hounds.

The conspiracy to destroy *Citizen Kane* damaged the film's popularity and financial success during its initial release, and the principal casualty was Welles' long-term prospects as a producer and director in Hollywood. But it was those attempts that spawned far greater interest in the relationship between Hearst and Kane than ever would have been generated if the film had been released without interference. Hearst, who had been one of the most powerful and well-known personalities of early-twentieth-century America, is now remembered primarily for his manipulative media control and his role in the emergence of American tabloid journalism—prime examples being his organization's attempts to destroy *Citizen Kane* and blackmail the motion picture industry. When *Citizen Kane* is described as "a fictionalized biography of William Randolph Hearst," that characterization is in large measure due to the highly publicized attempts to stop the film rather than the story itself. Hearst's own organization, more than anything on-screen created by Orson Welles, was responsible for the links between Hearst and Kane.

RELEASE

Seeing [Citizen Kane], *it's as if you never really saw a movie before; no movie has ever grabbed you, pummeled you, socked you on the button with the vitality, the accuracy, the impact, the professional aim, that this one does.*
—CECELIA AGER'S REVIEW OF *CITIZEN KANE* IN *PM*

The Hearst organization banned *Citizen Kane* from its own pages, but the company's efforts to suppress the film stimulated tremendous interest at every other news organization in the country. RKO received a flood of requests for passes to press screenings. In April 1941, admission to an advance screening of the film was the hottest ticket in New York.

"Newspapermen wanting ducats seem to be climbing out from under every table," said one RKO press aide.

The April 9 preview at the Broadway Theatre in New York was attended by four hundred reporters and critics. However, the press interest did nothing to motivate theater owners to show *Citizen Kane* to a paying audience; in New York and Los Angeles, one theater after another refused.

"Show it in tents," Welles wrote to Schaefer. "It will make millions—'the film your local theater won't let you see.'"

Eventually the Palace Theatre in New York was enlisted, but not without RKO paying for massive renovation costs to outfit the facility for a showcase engagement. In Hollywood, the El Capitan Theatre was converted from a venue for stage productions to host the Los Angeles premiere.

Some newspapers, perhaps as a response to Hearst's interference, responded with pseudo-blackouts of their own by deliberately not mentioning his name in their coverage of *Citizen Kane,* instead referring to "a certain publisher" or other characterizations. While Hearst's *Los Angeles Examiner* boycotted the film, the rival

Los Angeles Times included news briefs or photographs about *Citizen Kane* in every issue for the six days prior to its local debut.

On May 1, *Citizen Kane* finally premiered at the Palace in New York City. The film debuted in Chicago at the Woods Theatre and Palace Theatre on May 6—Orson Welles' twenty-sixth birthday—and in Los Angeles at the El Capitan on May 8.

Conflicts forgotten, at the Los Angeles premiere Welles told reporters, "I'm usually criticized for talking too much, but right now I hardly know what to say. If it had not been for George J. Schaefer, there would not be a *Citizen Kane*."

The last of the threats from the Hearst organization came in the form of rumors circulated when *Citizen Kane* opened in Los Angeles: that celebrities who attended the opening would somehow "incur the wrath" of the Hearst organization. Whatever doom was suggested never materialized; instead the Los Angeles premiere was sold out, and was attended, reported the *Los Angeles Times,* by "one of the largest representative gatherings of the motion picture industry" ever assembled for a screening. Among the film luminaries in the first-night Hollywood audience were Bob Hope, John Barrymore, Gloria Swanson, directors King Vidor and Busby Berkeley, Mickey Rooney, Olivia de Havilland, Charles Laughton, and—perhaps no surprise in an industry where seemingly anything can happen—Hedda Hopper.

And with the premieres came an outpouring of accolades and enthusiastic commentary unlike anything ever before written about a film—not simply positive reviews, but acclaim for *Citizen Kane* as a groundbreaking production. By any measure, *Citizen Kane* was an astounding critical success, one of the great films in Hollywood history, and a milestone in the development of the motion picture.

"Now that the wraps are off," said *New York Times* critic Bosley Crowther, "it can be safely stated that suppression of this film would have been a crime. *Citizen Kane* is far and away the most surprising and cinematically exciting motion picture to be seen here in many a moon. As a matter of fact, it comes close to being the most sensational film ever made in Hollywood."

Time wrote, "*Citizen Kane* has found important new techniques in picture making and story-telling. Artful and artfully artless, it is not afraid to say the same thing twice if twice-telling reveals a fourfold truth."

William Boehnel of the *New York World-Telegram* summed up the feelings of most in the film business who were disgusted with the manipulations by the Hearst organization.

"After you've seen Orson Welles' first film, you'll wonder what all the contro-

versy is about," said Boehnel. "Because it doesn't make the slightest bit of difference whether it is or isn't about William Randolph Hearst or any other
individual. What matters is that *Citizen Kane* is a cinema masterpiece."

Leo Mishkin of the *New York Morning Telegraph* predicted the film's destiny
when he wrote, "*Citizen Kane* will be around, will be remembered, will be followed and copied and imitated and reprinted, so long as the movies, as we now
know them, exist."

Cecelia Ager in New York's newspaper *PM* was one of the first to note that
beyond the film's singular excellence, *Citizen Kane* was a benchmark by which
the coming generations of film would be measured.

"Before *Citizen Kane*," Ager wrote, "it's as if the motion picture was a
slumbering monster, a mighty force stupidly sleeping, lying there sleek, torpid,
complacent—awaiting a fierce young man to kick it to life, to rouse it, shake
it, awaken it to its potentialities, to show it what it's got. Seeing [*Citizen Kane*],
it's as if you never really saw a movie before; no movie has ever grabbed you,
pummeled you, socked you on the button with the vitality, the accuracy, the
impact, the professional aim, that this one does."

Genee Kobacker Lesser, who wrote for her hometown *Columbus* [Ohio]
Citizen, phrased her approval more succinctly: "Tonight I was present at the
birth of a new art form—The Motion Picture."

Absent from the coverage, of course, were reviews by any of the Hearst publications.

Even more important than the general-interest press were notices from film
industry trade papers, which reported not only on the quality of a motion picture,
but also on its potential earning power at the box office. *Variety*'s critic raved about
the film and predicted that it would be a ticket-selling smash as well; he called the
film "a box office explosion establishing Orson Welles as an overnight film click.

"*Citizen Kane* is a film possessing the sure dollar mark, which distinguishes
every daring entertainment venture that is created by a workman who is master
of the technique and mechanics of the medium," *Variety* reported. "*Citizen Kane*
is a triumph for Orson Welles, who overnight, so to speak, joins the top ranks
of box-office film personalities."

To *Variety,* "Arson Annie" had become "Mr. Genius."

At the offices of *The Hollywood Reporter,* publisher W. R. Wilkerson—author
of the harshest denunciation of Welles and Schaefer—was happily apologizing
for his early criticism.

"When George Schaefer came along with Orson Welles and the latter's authority to produce, write, direct and star, we believed it too much to ask of any individual and suggested that Mr. Schaefer was just plain nuts," Wilkerson wrote in his column. "However, the nearest approach that anyone ever came to a batting average of one thousand in the delivery of entertainment for the screen, Orson Welles accomplished with *Citizen Kane*.

"We criticized George Schaefer, we condemned Orson Welles, we ridiculed even the thought of what they attempted to do; we must now retract much of it. Where there was criticism, we now come to praise. Where there was condemnation, we now feel compelled to eulogize."

The reviews were not unanimous; a few critics called the picture, among other things, "cold," "unemotional," and "unsatisfying." However, the vast majority were lavish in their praise of *Citizen Kane*.

In May 1941, Hedda Hopper's readers would never have known that only four months earlier she had been one of those who unleashed the Hearst hounds on Welles and more than twenty years later would still describe *Citizen Kane* as a "murderous trick" that "appalled" her. Perhaps waiting to hear what the New York daily press would say about *Citizen Kane,* Hopper sidestepped a positive comment about the film in her Sunday, May 4, roundup of releases that month (in 1941, the Sunday feature sections would have been printed before the reviews from the New York premiere appeared), instead saying, "There's been so much written about *Citizen Kane* that I won't add to it. It's a story told through a technique and photography new to the screen and at last you'll see Orson Welles and his Mercury players."

But after acclaim was showered on Welles and the film, Hopper jumped on the *Citizen Kane* bandwagon with the lead item in her May 10 column.

"The Kid . . . I'm speaking about 'Kid' Orson Kane—has finally arrived," Hopper wrote. "And the boy who was spat upon, jeered, and ridiculed, has made the town swallow its words. So we're hailing 'King Kane'—terrific!"

RKO president George Schaefer, who despite the release delays was the unsung hero of the *Citizen Kane* ordeal, felt thoroughly vindicated by the accolades. Responding to a complimentary letter, Schaefer replied, "Letters such as this have amply repaid me for the heartaches and the 'predicted' failure of the proposed 'Welles picture.'

"They were making bets out here that Welles would never even get started, and then again, bets to the effect that after he had been shooting 10 days he would fold up," Schaefer wrote. "Every important producer and director in Hollywood have now seen the picture, and they are unanimous in their praise.

"They all say it is one of the finest things that has ever been done, not excepting the most important pictures that have been released in recent years."

The positive reviews in the trade press came as good news to film exhibitors across the country, who were still nervous about the film's box office appeal and the potential rage of the Hearst papers. And at first, *Citizen Kane* appeared to be a big winner. In New York, the Palace Theatre was nearly sold out for every performance during the first week.

Unfortunately, the success of the limited first run did not continue. In limited release, the early returns in New York were good—at one point early in the run, the Palace had booked advance ticket sales for four weeks. But the film was not profitable; the engagements in New York at the Palace and at the El Capitan in Los Angeles were not long enough to make money after accounting for the costs associated with a major theatrical presentation, such as publicity, premiere parties, and (especially) retrofit expenses. Theaters in other large cities reported good ticket sales at first, but the momentum could not be sustained. By the end of a week's run in Los Angeles, *Citizen Kane* was pulled from RKO's Hillstreet Theatre. Early receipts at the El Capitan, reported *Variety,* were "very disappointing."

One possible contributor to the low returns was the policy at the time of limited daily screenings. While today a two-hour major release will show five times a day or more to maximize the per-screen revenue, in 1941 the road show philosophy used a much more constrained schedule. At the El Capitan in Los Angeles, for instance, *Citizen Kane* screened only three times a day: twice in the afternoon (twelve thirty and three thirty) and only once in the evening at eight thirty—both too early and too late for most working weekday filmgoers. Only after the film went into general release in Fall 1941 did it play in a more efficient five-times-a-day schedule.

The threats by the Hearst organization and terrible timing for the marketing combined to stall *Citizen Kane*'s chance for success. Although RKO produced a massive advertising campaign to support *Citizen Kane,* most of the publicity appeared in a March blitz planned to coincide with the release that was then canceled. By the time *Citizen Kane* was released two months later, the momentum was gone.

When the film received rave reviews after its premiere, more coverage appeared in major magazines, such as a lavish nine-page feature in *Life* on Welles and *Citizen Kane* published in the May 26 issue. But the coverage appeared while the film was still showing in just a small number of theaters in seven cities, not in the broad national release that RKO had contemplated in January but could not orchestrate because of the pressure from Hearst and the subsequent refusal by some theater chains to screen the film. Given the enthusiastic reviews, if the studio had been able to distribute *Citizen Kane* to the hundreds of theaters that no doubt would have been clamoring to screen it had Hearst not intervened, its success would have been assured. That problem would crop up again in the fall, when the film eventually went into general release.

Compounding the problem was the studio's promotion, which did not capture the spirit of the film or excite its potential audience. If *Citizen Kane* opened today, the advertisements would be packed with glowing quotes from the reviews. In 1941, some small ads included quotes from critics, but the core marketing philosophy called for snappy slogans to sell a film; the best RKO's advertising department could manage for *Citizen Kane* was, "It's Terrific!" Paired with the slogan on much of the advertising material was a portrait of Kane as a young man, standing tall and defiant but bearing little resemblance to Welles.

Sample ads distributed to theater owners showed the young Kane surrounded by other characters, each uttering a comment about him—none of which were direct quotes from the movie: "I Hate Him!" (Susan), "He's a Dirty Dog" (Gettys), "He's Crazy" (Thatcher), "I Love Him!" (Emily), "He's a Saint!" (Leland), "He's a Genius!" (Bernstein).

The same painting of Welles as Kane used in the print advertising was employed in an animated sign above the marquee of the Palace Theatre in New York City when the film premiered. The display included nine neon-rimmed images of the standing Kane stacked one in back of the other, each slightly larger than the one before it. The sign was a dazzling presentation, but it disclosed nothing about the significance of the motion picture and pushed up expense costs for the New York run.

Not surprisingly, RKO chose to ignore the Hearst controversy in its advertising, but neither did the studio capitalize on the cinematic innovation that Welles, his cast, and his crew worked so hard to achieve. Instead, RKO left the film without a hook for the public to grab, and the early box office returns showed it. The picture continued to play in limited run for several months, with only mild success. The interest raised by the Hearst controversy, expensive advertising purchased by RKO, and mountains of free publicity generated by the nation's critics could not be converted into big returns at the box office.

Yet in spite of the disappointing early run, in broader release in Fall 1941 to smaller theaters across the country—with the threats from Hearst discredited or at least overshadowed by the superb reviews and a growing realization that Hearst was all bark and no bite—*Citizen Kane* did moderately well. The limited number of theaters in larger cities that dared Hearst by screening the film reported stable business, and in some cosmopolitan areas, *Citizen Kane* played with great success for several months. But it was not enough.

In smaller communities, the results weren't as favorable. Theaters in some towns reported an endless series of horror stories about dismal turnouts. Their woes were featured in the "What the Picture Did for Me" section of *Motion Picture Herald* magazine, and *Citizen Kane* was the favorite subject for gripes in late 1941 and early 1942.

Nevertheless, RKO must have been somewhat encouraged to note that most of the theater owners who complained about *Citizen Kane*'s poor box office performances also said that the film was a creative masterpiece—even in remote towns not known for their appreciation of unusual film fare.

"An artistic triumph, but not a small town picture," said one correspondent from the Paramount Theatre in Dewey, Oklahoma. "It may be a classic, but it's plumb nuts to your show-going public," reported the manager of the Iris Theatre in Velva, North Dakota. "While this picture was pleasing to me and to a few of our better-informed patrons, it was very disappointing from the box office viewpoint," came a comment from the State Theatre in Big Timber, Montana.

Unfortunately, theater owners who declined to show *Citizen Kane* did not appreciate that a local controversy sparked by a Hearst paper could have increased patron interest in the film. Apparently, Welles' potential drawing power was not sufficient to overcome the harassment—even with the national notoriety inspired by his radio career and *The War of the Worlds*. "After all," said one theater owner, "the star of *Citizen Kane* may be *the* Orson Welles, but he's no Clark Gable."

And still the pressure from Hearst loomed. Film industry trade papers reported that theaters—or, in one case, an entire theater chain—still believed that potential litigation dangled over any exhibitor who dared show *Citizen Kane*. For some, even the mere suggestion of Hearst action (or perhaps it was just willingness to cooperate with the press tycoon) was disastrous for *Citizen Kane*. The Fox West Coast theater chain paid the distribution fee for *Citizen Kane* but refused to show the film when it was included in an RKO bloc of pictures for general release in Fall 1941. The studio earned its base rental fee for distributing *Citizen Kane,* but because the film languished unviewed, no additional receipts could be collected from Fox West Coast theaters. The results from those theaters alone—40 percent of the profits from ticket sales in 515 Fox West Coast theaters on the Pacific coast, in the Rocky Mountain states, and throughout the Midwest—would have been enough to ensure that *Citizen Kane* showed a profit.

The Hearst ban in print continued. The first time that *Citizen Kane* would "appear" in Hearst papers was in RKO advertisements in mid-October of 1941. Even then, the title of the film was excluded from advertisements in Hearst papers; beginning on October 15, Hearst readers saw only that a "Big Screen Attraction" would be opening in local theaters.

Ironically, the first time Hearst papers mentioned *Citizen Kane* was when they were compelled to do so for news coverage that reflected positively on the film. In February 1942, when *Citizen Kane* was nominated for Academy Awards, Hearst papers printed the name of the film in the coverage—and then only because they had to list the title as part of their reporting of the Oscar news.

In the first month of release, the praise was sufficient to inspire George Schaefer to purchase multiple pages of advertisements in *Variety* and *The Hollywood Reporter* that served as both a lavish acknowledgment of Welles and an "I told you so" to the early detractors. The eight-page insert, which Schaefer signed in print, served as a mini-history of Welles' time in Hollywood, including—strangely— quotes of the early negative coverage as well as later excerpts from the enthusiastic reviews of the film.

The final page of the ad was a letter from George Schaefer.

"Citizen Kane is a very fine production, the result of great initiative and courage, especially under the most trying of circumstances," Schaefer's letter began. It closed with a thank-you directly to Welles:

"You were not given the chance to present your ideas, but were severely crit- icized for daring even to have an idea. You were condemned before being tried! Your triumph is one of the great accomplishments in motion picture his- tory, and proof that America is still the land of opportunity, where there will always be room for those with dreams and courage to bring them to reality."

The limited public enthusiasm for buying tickets did not diminish the continu- ing tributes for *Citizen Kane*. At the end of 1941, *The New York Times* ranked *Citizen Kane* in its top ten motion pictures of the year. The National Board of Review named the film its Best Picture, with Welles and George Coulouris receiving "Best Acting" awards. And on the last day of the year, *Citizen Kane* was voted the outstanding production of 1941 by the New York Film Critics Circle, during the shortest voting session in the organization's history.

Welles also featured strongly in the New York critics' balloting for best director; through five ballots, he was tied with John Ford, who won on the sixth vote for his sensitive direction of *How Green Was My Valley*. Curiously, Welles' astounding acting performance—now considered among the best ever played on film—was one of the less noticed merits of *Citizen Kane*. But Welles, along with Cary Grant, Henry Fonda, Humphrey Bogart, and a host of other fine actors with first-rate film appearances in 1941, was overlooked in votes for acting awards; the runaway favorite role of the year in the critics' vote was Gary Cooper's low-key portrayal of Medal of Honor winner Alvin York in Howard Hawks' production of *Sergeant York*.

While *Citizen Kane* continued to play sporadically across the nation, the last hope to turn the film into a financial success was the Academy Awards, where a strong showing would have injected new life into the film's box office potential. *Citizen Kane* was nominated for nine Academy Awards: Picture; Directing (Welles); Actor (Welles); Writing: Original Screenplay (Mankiewicz and Welles); Art Direction: Black and White (Perry Ferguson, Van Nest Polglase); Interior Decoration (Al Fields, Darrell Silvera); Cinematography: Black and White (Toland); Music Score of a Dramatic Picture (Herrmann); Film Editing (Wise); and Sound Recording (RKO Studio Sound Department, John Aalberg, sound director). In 1941, the Academy of Motion Picture Arts and Sciences did not award an Oscar for achievement in makeup, or Maurice Seiderman would have been a certain nominee.

Incredibly, the superb performances by Dorothy Comingore, Joseph Cotten, and Everett Sloane went unrecognized in the Supporting Actor categories. And had the extent of the special effects in the film been known, it might have been nominated in that category as well.

It must have been tremendously gratifying to Welles—who still burned from his early grilling by the Hollywood establishment—to see his first film receive such broad acknowledgment from the nominating committees. Nevertheless, the final results of the voting were no doubt a blow. With most of the Hollywood powers and virtually all of the press backing Welles, *Citizen Kane* seemed like a sure bet to win a bushel of statuettes. But when Oscar night came on February 26, 1942, other films took most of the top honors.

While Welles did share an Academy Award victory with Mankiewicz for

Best Original Screenplay—in the process becoming the youngest writer to win the screenplay Oscar until the even younger Ben Affleck co-won with Matt Damon in 1998—*Citizen Kane* was beaten in all of the other categories.

As expected after the New York critics' vote, crowd favorite Gary Cooper received the Best Actor award for *Sergeant York.* John Ford again surpassed Welles for Best Direction on *How Green Was My Valley,* and the same film beat Perry Ferguson in the Art Direction category and Gregg Toland for Cinematography. *Citizen Kane*'s spectacular achievement in sound was surpassed by *That Hamilton Woman,* an Alexander Korda production, and Robert Wise's editing lost to William Holmes' work on *Sergeant York.*

Bernard Herrmann also lost—but to himself; nominated for two musical scores, he won the Oscar for *The Devil and Daniel Webster* (at the time called *All That Money Can Buy*). And then, after already winning four other Academy Awards, *How Green Was My Valley* was named Best Picture of 1941.

Neither Mankiewicz nor Welles was on hand to accept his Oscar. Welles was in South America, filming *It's All True,* a disaster-in-the-making documentary project intended to encourage Pan-American goodwill; Mankiewicz stayed home and listened to the ceremony on the radio, afraid that if he attended and lost, he would be unable to control himself from erupting in a public outburst. George Schaefer accepted Mankiewicz's Oscar and sent it to Mank with, "Congratulations and best wishes from a high-priced office boy."

After the ceremony, Welles sent congratulations to Mankiewicz: "Dear Mankie: Here's what I wanted to wire you after the Academy Dinner: 'You can kiss my half.' I dare to send it through the mails only now that I find it possible to enclose a ready-made retort. I don't presume to write your jokes for you, but you ought to like this: 'Dear Orson: You don't know your half from a whole in the ground.' Affectionately, Orson."

Instead, Mankiewicz provided a joke of his own—the acceptance speech he never delivered: "I am very happy to accept this award in Mr. Welles' absence because the script was written in Mr. Welles' absence."

Welles certainly enjoyed earning an Academy Award for his first film, but his defeat in other categories—and some booing at the ceremony when his name or *Citizen Kane* was mentioned—clearly demonstrated that he remained a Hollywood outsider. At the time, the film industry press fixed the blame on the screen extras who voted their disapproval of Orson Welles by casting their ballots for films other than his; but that explanation raises more questions than it answers.

The voting rules for the Academy Awards in the 1940s were different from those in force today. At the time, the Academy of Motion Picture Arts and Sciences opened a large number of voting categories not only to its own membership, but to screen extras and union guilds as well. At various times in the academy's history, the policy covering who could vote has changed. In 1941, more than six thousand screen extras were eligible to vote for Best Picture, all of the acting categories, and Best Song. The extras held a strong hand in six categories; almost ten thousand ballots were mailed, and more than 80 percent were returned with votes.

Welles figured strongly in the nominations because the committees that chose the nominees included directors and leading actors who had rallied to support him when the Hearst papers closed in. However, according to *Variety,* that backing was not enough to earn victories when thousands of final ballots were counted. The extras, reported the film industry press, took up the anti-Welles cause that had festered since his arrival in Hollywood and, by sheer weight of numbers, destroyed his Oscar hopes. Why extras would have disliked Welles was not explained in the coverage, but "there is no dissent," *Variety* said of Welles' losses, "that the extra vote scuttled him. The mob didn't like the guy personally, and took it out on him at the polls."

In retrospect, this analysis by *Variety* of the vote—which now represents the conventional wisdom in film study for why *Citizen Kane* was not a multiple Oscar winner—seems flawed. Although the extras' votes could certainly have affected the odds of *Citizen Kane* winning Best Picture and Welles winning Best Actor, their votes could not have influenced the results of the off-camera categories, such as the nomination for a popular artist like Perry Ferguson from establishment Hollywood. And, of course, if the "mob didn't like the guy personally," then how did Welles and the increasingly antisocial Herman Mankiewicz win the film's only Oscar?

Just as likely an explanation of the anti-*Kane* vote was bitterness that festered from Welles' high-profile arrival and the resentment over the "innovation" (as *Variety* called it) that Welles would use only actors from outside the studio ranks and was bringing his own acting corps with him from New York. As *Variety* tersely reported in its initial 1939 coverage of Welles' contract, "No players from the studio personnel will be used in the picture." Or the truth might be even simpler: *How Green Was My Valley* may have won Best Director and Best Picture because John Ford was a Hollywood favorite and voters may have liked his film more than they liked Orson Welles and *Citizen Kane*.

Not until 1957 were Academy Award nominations and final voting limited solely to academy members—a rule that stands today. Given strong support of Welles and *Citizen Kane* among the Hollywood elite, there can be little doubt that had current voting rules been in force in 1941, the Academy Award winners that year would have been quite different. If *Citizen Kane* won several Oscars, or at least received the Academy Award for Best Picture, the film would have earned a longer and more successful theatrical run, which would have bolstered Welles' already weakening position at RKO.

In the spring of 1942, *Citizen Kane* was withdrawn from general circulation without fanfare. After its first run, the film was listed on RKO's books at a loss of more than $150,000—all things considered, not a bad showing, when the problems of timing the release to the publicity and the impact of hundreds of theaters refusing to show the film are figured into the accounting. But even such a seemingly insignificant loss was considered a step backward for George Schaefer and his grand plans for RKO.

Film history may recall that *Citizen Kane* was not profitable in its initial release as a result of the plot orchestrated by the Hearst organization, while some would say that it was destined for failure by being too highbrow for popular appeal. The reality is somewhere in between, for if even some of the theaters that refused to show the film, especially in large cities, had instead stood up to Hearst and screened *Citizen Kane* for a short time during the height of the publicity, the film would have been available to more people, including a broader, more sophisticated audience. Screenings at theaters in college towns, for example, could have been a ripe source of revenue. As a result, the film would have shown a profit, which would have changed considerably the future prospects for Welles, Schaefer, and RKO.

After *Citizen Kane*, Welles' tenure at RKO was fraught with even more controversy. Control of the final cut for his next production, *The Magnificent Ambersons,* was wrested from him after horrible previews, its eventual release buried as the second half of a double feature. The third Mercury production for RKO,

Journey into Fear, made with limited off-screen involvement from Welles and only a token screen appearance, inspired little enthusiasm among critics, audiences, and the studio. Welles' work on *It's All True* in South America became an unfinished financial catastrophe for RKO. When his operations in the field became unmanageable, the project was canceled and the entire crew withdrawn.

With the accolades for *Citizen Kane* in the distant past (by Hollywood standards) and Welles mired in the category of "what have you done for me lately," the RKO board gave up. The agreement between Welles and RKO became an embarrassment that produced more casualties than the modest financial loss of $150,000 for *Citizen Kane* ever could: for many reasons involving Schaefer's management of RKO—but with Welles near the top of the list—the studio chief was forced to resign in June 1942, little more than a year after *Citizen Kane*'s premiere.

With strong backing from investor Floyd Odlum, the new RKO executives led by Charles Koerner deliberately swiped at Welles when they unveiled the studio's lineup for 1943 with the slogan "Showmanship in Place of Genius." Two weeks after Schaefer's ouster, the Mercury staff was summarily ejected from the RKO lot. The reason, according to a studio memo, was that "the space was urgently needed for those engaged on current productions."

Through the rest of the 1940s, *Citizen Kane* sank into obscurity. As the decade closed, the film played only sporadically in the few revival theaters in larger cities that showed "oldies." But that was all. By 1950, *Citizen Kane* had disappeared from America and did not come into view again for more than five years.

TRIUMPH

With the changes that mark the distance between the last poll and this one, it is remarkable that Citizen Kane, *which has topped the last three polls, should reign supreme for both critics and filmmakers.*
—SIGHT & SOUND MAGAZINE, IN ITS 1992 ARTICLE ANNOUNCING THAT
CITIZEN KANE WAS NAMED THE BEST FILM OF ALL TIME IN ITS POLL
OF CRITICS AND DIRECTORS

In the 1950s, *Citizen Kane* began to emerge as a milestone film—but not, at first, in the United States. In France, where the postwar study of cinema as an art form was flourishing, the first serious appreciation of *Citizen Kane* acknowledged the film as a cinematic achievement.

The Nazi occupation of Europe during World War II prevented importation of American films, so *Citizen Kane* did not reach France until 1946, where it played with great success. There, during the 1950s, a cadre of young film writers, including André Bazin and later François Truffaut, appraised *Citizen Kane* with a blend of appreciation for the film itself, combined with a near euphoric hero worship for the man who had produced so extraordinary a film so early in his career.

"To shoot *Citizen Kane* at 25 years of age," wrote Truffaut of Welles in 1959. "Is this not the dream of all the young habitués of the *cinématèques?*"

Several French film magazines printed reviews and articles about Welles and his film, but it was *La Revue du Cinéma* (now *Cahiers du Cinéma*) that led the acclaim for *Citizen Kane*. In a number of issues, the magazine printed articles that analyzed Welles' direction, Toland's photography, and, most important, the overall influence of *Citizen Kane* on film as an artistic medium rather than as a purely commercial enterprise. Thanks in large measure to film writers in

France, the film world again began to see *Citizen Kane* as a masterpiece, just as it had done when the motion picture debuted in 1941.

That view had not yet been revived in the United States. At the height of the American studio system, motion pictures—even the most popular films—were only fodder for the endless mill of production, distribution, and exhibition. With few revival theaters in operation, and the convenience (and profit potential) of videotape and discs still decades away, the vast majority of films disappeared: the negative went into the studio vaults (if the studio was responsible enough to maintain proper storage), most prints were destroyed, and the movie never returned to the screen. For more than a decade, such was the case with *Citizen Kane;* praised though it was, the film did not have the golden box office performance that would ensure regular rerelease to America's theaters.

For the first half of the 1950s, *Citizen Kane* was not shown *anywhere* in America where a ticket-buying audience could see it. RKO had declined to reissue *Citizen Kane* in August 1951 to take advantage of the publicity surrounding the death of William Randolph Hearst. "We're not that hard up for a buck," said RKO president Ned E. Depinet. Not until May 1956, exactly fifteen years after the film's initial release, was *Citizen Kane* reissued, in part to capitalize on Orson Welles' rousing return to Broadway in *King Lear*. RKO had no better success choosing a slogan for the picture the second time around than it had for the original release. "It's Terrific!" was replaced with "Some Called Him a Hero . . . Others Called Him a Heel."

At about the same time, the study of film in the United States evolved, as emerging university film schools and institutions such as New York City's Museum of Modern Art led the appreciation of classic cinema. When American historians and academics began to explore the rise and fall of the Hollywood studio system, high on the list of motion pictures to appraise was *Citizen Kane*.

Ironically, it was the steady stream of films available on television—a principal villain in the fall of the Hollywood studios—that helped resurrect classic motion pictures with a new audience of young postwar viewers. When the studios began to sell or lease their film catalogs for broadcast, RKO's products were among the first to go on the market. In December 1955, 740 RKO films were sold to C&C Super Corporation. Within months, *Citizen Kane* aired on television for the first time.

By the mid-1950s, *Citizen Kane*'s reputation was beginning to solidify. As early as 1952, a poll of film critics conducted by British film magazine *Sight & Sound*—a once-each-decade survey that has become one of the benchmarks of cinematic achievement—ranked *Citizen Kane* as first runner-up in its listing of the top ten best films. In 1962, the *Sight & Sound* poll voted *Citizen Kane* the best film of all time. While most other films included in the survey have dropped off with the passing decades, *Citizen Kane* has remained at or near the top of the *Sight & Sound* poll since then.

"With the changes that mark the distance between the last poll and this one," wrote *Sight & Sound* in its 1992 poll, "it is remarkable that *Citizen Kane,* which has topped the last three polls, should reign supreme for both critics and filmmakers."

After *Citizen Kane* was rereleased in May 1956, a Brussels poll of international cinema historians in September 1958 selected the film as one of the twelve best motion pictures of all time. Since then, *Citizen Kane* has also been ranked number one in an array of other international polls, including the FIAF Centenary List, France Critics Top 10, *Cahiers du Cinéma 100 films pour une cinémathèque idéale, Kinovedcheskie* Russia Top 10, and Romanian Critics Top 10.

What must have been particularly satisfying for Welles was that *Citizen Kane* had not only risen to the top of surveys of critics and academics, but also acquired an equally lofty position with the public. In 1989, the U.S. Library of Congress designated *Citizen Kane* as "culturally, historically, or aesthetically significant" when it selected the film for preservation in the National Film Registry. Several polls of film fans placed *Citizen Kane* at the top of their picks of screen favorites. And in 1998, in perhaps the most highly publicized tally yet compiled of cinematic popularity, a survey by the American Film Institute voted *Citizen Kane* number one on its list of the top one hundred American films of all time—a ranking that was repeated on the tenth anniversary of the original poll in 2007.

The film that routinely tops critical polls, the motion picture used most frequently in cinema studies to show young filmmakers how to create their art, is also first among film viewers who have grown to love it. For Orson Welles and *Citizen Kane,* the triumph was complete.

WALKING ON THE EDGE OF A CLIFF

I had luck as no one had; afterwards, I had the worst luck in the history of cinema. But that is in the order of things. I had to pay for having had the best luck in the history of cinema. Never has a man been given so much power in the Hollywood system. And absolute power. And artistic control.
—ORSON WELLES, ON HIS FIRST HOLLYWOOD CONTRACT

After *Citizen Kane,* Orson Welles embarked on a career checkered with brilliant achievements, miserable failures, and seemingly unending artistic challenges during nearly forty-five years of filmmaking.

"I passionately hate the idea of being 'with it,'" Welles said. "I think an artist has always to be out of step with his time."

Welles may have been a maverick who received little financial support from studios in the United States and Europe, but the film world at least learned to acknowledge his artistry. The motion picture industry bestowed on Welles its highest awards: he received an honorary Oscar in 1971 for lifelong contributions to the art of cinema, the Life Achievement Award of the American Film Institute in 1975, and the D. W. Griffith Award from the Directors Guild of America in 1984—a rogue visionary honored by the establishment.

Welles appeared in a motion picture for the final time in a captivating role as the commentator of Henry Jaglom's *Someone to Love.* The film, shot in 1985 shortly before Welles' death but not released until three years later, provides a bittersweet memorial to Welles—a last opportunity for him to probe once more the questions of life, love, and relationships.

Welles' appearance in *Someone to Love,* however, would not mark the last time he would make news after he died. Welles turned out to be something of a psychic, because in his last days, he fully understood that a new threat loomed for his greatest work.

Welles knew that an emerging technology, video colorization, might be used one day to alter *Citizen Kane*. Colorization, which with a computer palette adds color to a video transfer of a black-and-white film, provides what some marketers consider a necessary boost to entice new viewers to buy classic motion pictures. Although the use of colorization was still in its infancy—only four feature films had been digitally colorized by 1985—the process had received national attention and inspired alarm in Hollywood among filmmakers who were concerned the process would deface their original artistic intentions.

Recalled director Henry Jaglom, "Orson said to me, about two weeks before he died—I remember this vividly—'Please do this for me: don't let Ted Turner deface my movie with his crayons.'"

Welles' plea was an impressive bit of clairvoyance. The conversation between Welles and Jaglom in September 1985 occurred nearly a year before Turner Entertainment acquired MGM/United Artists, the studio that at the time owned the video rights to *Citizen Kane*. In 1986, cable mogul Ted Turner sought only the fabulous celluloid treasure in the studio vaults; he sold the company itself but retained the broadcast rights to more than thirty-six hundred motion pictures and other properties. Then, despite protests from every level of the motion picture industry, Turner Entertainment began to colorize some of Hollywood's most popular films.

Colorization affects only the video version of a motion picture; the original film is not altered. However, for DVD, Blu-ray, and television viewing, colorization obscures the original artistic intentions carefully planned by directors, production designers, cinematographers, costumers, and lighting experts.

With such film classics as *Casablanca, It's a Wonderful Life,* and *The Maltese Falcon* already colorized, the announcement on January 29, 1989, that *Citizen Kane* would fall victim to the same computerized treatment became a battle cry to gather Hollywood's most powerful forces to stop the colorization. Many motion picture artisans rallied in support, including directors who were weaned on *Citizen Kane;* the protest over colorizing *Citizen Kane* became one of the major film industry stories of 1989.

"This is sickening that people would take the finest products of the film world and treat them so casually, so contemptuously," said director Elliot Silverstein, chair of a committee formed by the Directors Guild of America to investigate the artistic issues raised by colorization. "Colorizing *Citizen Kane* is a gross misrepresentation of Welles' work." ·

The uproar lasted barely two weeks. On February 14, Turner Entertainment canceled its plans to colorize *Citizen Kane*. The reason was not artistic or aesthetic—rather, it was legal: with the Welles estate and the Directors Guild of America promising court action to stop the colorization of *Citizen Kane,* and with the company no doubt looking for a graceful exit, Turner Entertainment acknowledged that *Citizen Kane* had been protected by Orson Welles' original 1939 contract with RKO. In addition to providing Welles with complete creative control—presumably in perpetuity—the contract specifically stated that the product of the RKO-Mercury relationship "shall be black and white pictures."

"Our attorneys looked at the contract between RKO Pictures, Inc., and Orson Welles and his production company, Mercury Productions, Inc., and, on the basis of their review, we have decided not to proceed with colorization of the movie," said Roger Mayer, president of Turner Entertainment. "While a court test might uphold our legal right to colorize the film, provisions of the contract could be read to prohibit colorization without permission of the Welles estate."

For Welles, *Time* reported, "it was a victory from the grave."

In spite of the threat from colorization, the video versions of *Citizen Kane* have had a better fate than the original film that spun through Gregg Toland's camera: the irreplaceable film negative originally shot in 1940 was destroyed in a studio vault fire (the exact date of the loss is not clear; published and online sources constantly recirculate references to the fire without a confirmed source, describing the "date" of the fire as being in either the 1950s or the 1970s).

Fortunately for the long-term salvation of *Citizen Kane,* in April 1941, George Schaefer—agreeing to a request from Gregg Toland—ordered that the entire original print run of the production be processed on Fine Grain Duplicating Positive Film, at the time a relatively new product from Kodak that ensured the initial distribution of the film would be shown with beautiful, grain-free prints.

"This is one of the outstanding photographic jobs of the decade," wrote RKO executive Reg Armour to studio manager Sid Rogell in April 1941. "I feel that every effort should be made to give it the benefit of the superior quality offered by the new material."

However, at the time, Fine Grain Duplicating Positive, like all other 35-millimeter films of the era, was based on nitrate stock—an unstable, highly flammable material that was dangerous to use and subject to irreversible deterioration (today, only theaters with certified fire prevention equipment, mostly at archives or universities with film schools, can run nitrate films).

Kodak ceased production of nitrate stock in 1951, so the rerelease of *Citizen Kane* in 1956 was printed on safety film stock. However, the passage of time, wear and tear from repeated projection, degeneration of nitrate copies, and the film industry–wide view that release prints were useless leftovers to discard after their theatrical run radically reduced the number of pristine prints of *Citizen Kane* available today from either release of the film.

Since the 1970s, when video versions of *Citizen Kane* were first produced on VHS and Betamax tapes, and later on laser disc, official studio releases have been acceptable, but a fair number of inferior versions duplicated from lesser prints made their way into the market. And one early release of *Citizen Kane* on DVD was problematic, with criticism for some inappropriate light levels in a few scenes and with some details inexplicably digitally "painted out."

But even the best video transfer, if shown on a low-resolution television prior to HD or 4K (UHD) TV, would provide only a fraction of the quality needed to showcase the crisp imagery that Welles and Toland worked to create. *Citizen Kane* was ripe for conversion to high-quality video; the film was featured on several online "top ten" lists of films most wanted on Blu-ray.

As the seventieth anniversary of *Citizen Kane* approached, and with significant advances in digital image processing being applied routinely to video conversion of classic motion pictures, in 2009 Warner Bros. (owner of the video rights to *Citizen Kane*) took up the challenge of creating new DVD and Blu-ray releases that were worthy of the original film. The Warner Bros. Technical Operations team used scans of three of the precious original nitrate fine-grain prints to record a single new high-definition video master, using the best elements of each print selected one frame at a time.

"The three prints had different strengths and weaknesses," said Ned Price, head of the technical team. "For instance, one of them had less flicker in one reel but coarser grain in another reel. So we put together the best bits and pieces of all three."

After a video master was assembled, the team digitally cleaned each of the more than 171,000 frames in *Citizen Kane*, removing dirt, blemishes, and white spots (but *not*, the team emphasized, the deliberate scratches and worn film in some shots in the newsreel). They also corrected slight misalignments in some frames—a process that was particularly important given the film's painstakingly planned special effects and complex dissolves.

The result of the restoration process, which took more than a year, was a high-resolution video that transcended any previous digital version of *Citizen Kane.* The Blu-ray disc produced from the new video master was acclaimed as a near perfect duplication of the motion picture as it appears in a pristine original print, now preserved forever for generations of classic film audiences to come.

Part of the epilogue to *Citizen Kane* has emerged from the news coverage of the ever-escalating auction prices for relics from the film. The memorabilia market first focused on *Citizen Kane* in June 1982, when a Rosebud sled constructed for the filming of the furnace scenes was purchased by director Steven Spielberg at a Sotheby's auction for $60,500 (including commission). The sled, one of three made out of balsa wood available for burning in the final shot of the film, survived because only two were needed; it is likely that the surviving version of Rosebud was not seen in the film.

At the time of the sale, Spielberg said he bought the sled for inspiration.

"Rosebud will go over my typewriter to remind me that quality in movies comes first," Spielberg said.

But what of the Rosebud that *did* appear prominently in the film, the precious sled that young Charles used to defend himself from lawyer Thatcher and was left behind in the snow as Kane was torn from his childhood life? That version of Rosebud, which surely ranks with the ruby slippers from *The Wizard of Oz,* Sam's piano from *Casablanca,* and the black bird from *The Maltese Falcon* as one of film's premier icons, seemed to have disappeared without a trace.

But lost over the decades was the quite public story of what actually happened to Rosebud: RKO had offered the sled as a prize in a 1942 contest, which was won by twelve-year-old Robert Bauer, a student in Brooklyn and president of his school's film club, who won based on how closely his choices for film honors matched those made that year by the New York film critics. The pine sled with the painted Rosebud logo was presented to Bauer by RKO star Bonita Granville in the New York office of Will Hays, president of the Motion Picture Producers and Distributors of America (while this sled was indeed the prop presented to Bauer in 1942, there are some physical differences between that sled and Rosebud as it appeared on screen). In 1996, Bauer's family offered Rosebud for sale through an auction by Christie's. On December 16, the sled, which had an original auction estimate of $50,000 to $70,000, sold to an anonymous buyer for $233,500.

Apparently, Bauer's mother had originally suggested painting the sled and using it as a plant stand—a thought that no doubt caused shivers among conservationists five decades later. "Instead," reported Bauer's son, "my dad said, 'No—just save it and put it in the closet.'"

Interest in Kane memorabilia continues to grow. In November 1999, Herman Mankiewicz's family sold the Oscar statuette he won for *Citizen Kane* at a Christie's auction for $244,500, more than ten times what Mankiewicz was paid in 1940 to write the script. In 2012, the Oscar sold again—this time for $588,455. In 2011, Welles' own Oscar for co-writing *Citizen Kane* drew a winning auction bid of $861,542, a sum that would have paid the film's entire budget seventy years before. In 2012, another type of trophy—the large cup given to Kane by his staff when he returns from Europe ("Welcome home Mr. Kane from 467 employees of the *New York Inquirer*")—sold for $275,544.

Clothing from the film (what little remains) has sold particularly well in the collectors' market. The gray three-piece suit that Welles wore in Kane's final scenes as he destroyed Susan's bedroom, found the snow globe, and then walked past the hall of mirrors sold in December 2013 for $132,000—more than double the preauction estimate. Ten months later, a single article of clothing—the jacket that Welles wore most prominently during Susan's disappointing singing lesson—sold for $102,000.

The dress that Ruth Warrick wore while sitting in a carriage below the *Inquirer* offices while Kane delivered their wedding announcement—visible onscreen for seven seconds—sold in 2011 for $2,500. And in May 2014, the mink coat that Kane wore when he arrived at the *Chicago Inquirer* after Susan's opera debut sold for $100,000 at the Debbie Reynolds Film Memorabilia Auction. The calf-length coat had been expected to sell for $40,000 to $60,000.

Even equipment used to film *Citizen Kane* inspires interest from collectors. In the same auction that featured Emily's dress, the RKO camera crane employed to shoot *Citizen Kane,* including the closing shots in Xanadu, sold for $75,000. (A 35-millimeter camera was included, but not the one used to film *Citizen Kane*.)

Original copies of the scripts used by the cast and crew have proven, to be particularly valuable and prices continue to climb, especially for Welles' own copies. For example, his second-draft script—not even one of the last versions, but with some notes from Welles recorded by assistant Kathryn Trosper—sold in

March 2014 for $164,000. In April, twenty-four pages from a later version of Welles' script sold for $15,000, miles above the $2,000 presale estimate. Script material related to Mankiewicz sells well, too. The cover page of a script scrawled with Herman Mankiewicz's amusing shopping list that included "good scotch" and "a sexy steno"—a single sheet of paper—sold at a Profiles in History auction in September 2015 for $4,800.

"These items are treasures from the past," said one eager bidder. "It's like touching something real that came from a fairy tale."

The Hearst organization's assault on Orson Welles, *Citizen Kane,* and the film industry faded away after the film was withdrawn from release in 1942; it was soon business as usual for Louella Parsons and the Hearst media coverage of Hollywood. The unprincipled methods that William Randolph Hearst encouraged in his newspapers gradually changed after his passing and as his cronies retired. Today, the Hearst Corporation is one of the world's largest communications companies, with holdings in newspapers, magazines, television, digital distribution, and nonmedia businesses.

In the current generation of the Hearst family, there are no grudges held about *Citizen Kane,* and more than seventy years after the film debuted, the family held events that were widely portrayed in the media as "forgiving" Orson Welles: *Citizen Kane* finally screened at Hearst Castle.

On March 13, 2015, *Citizen Kane* was shown in the same fifty-seat private theater used by William Randolph Hearst for his guests. The screening was organized for the San Luis Obispo International Film Festival as a benefit for the Friends of Hearst Castle. The $1,000 ticket price included a private tour of the estate and an introduction to the film by Ben Mankiewicz, host on Turner Classic Movies and grandson of Herman Mankiewicz.

While the 2015 screening was the first time *Citizen Kane* was shown in Hearst Castle—for certain, anyway—it was not the first time the film was shown on the grounds: in 2012, *Citizen Kane* screened in the visitors' center as another fund-raiser for the film festival.

"I tossed out the idea of screening *Citizen Kane* there as a joke, and they didn't laugh," said festival director Wendy Eidson in 2012. "I was sort of floored."

Steve Hearst, the publisher's great-grandson and manager of many of the family's interests, said each screening was "a great opportunity to draw a clear distinction between W.R. and Orson Welles, between the medieval, gloomy-looking castle shown in *Citizen Kane*, and the light, beautiful, architecturally superior reality."

Hearst reminded reporters of something that would have served the family well in 1941: while there were some similarities between Kane and his great-grandfather, there were also many differences.

"*Citizen Kane* is a classic American film, but is in no way a historically accurate description of W.R.H. or his favorite place in the world, his ranch," Hearst said.

"The character Orson Welles depicted was quite a bit more flamboyant and outgoing than W.R.H. was," he said. "W.R. wasn't the kind of guy who would be dancing in the editorial room with his staffers."

But would "the Chief" have appreciated the screenings at his beloved estate?

When a reporter asked Steve Hearst if showing *Citizen Kane* on the grounds would have his great-grandfather spinning in his grave, Hearst said, "I recently found out that I'm also in charge of the mausoleum. I can check."

Orson Welles died in the early morning hours of October 10, 1985. To the end, he was still the plotting producer, planning to create another film. At his death, he was working on several projects, including a film production of *King Lear*—with himself in the title role.

Welles was always in demand as an actor, but he was reluctant to devote his energies solely to performance when he also wanted to produce and direct. Although he was constantly busy in ventures other than his film projects—first in radio and theater and later in television—his life was a constant quest to create motion pictures and secure the financing to produce them. And when an investor was willing to back him, or on those rare occasions when a studio let him direct, Welles' motion pictures after RKO—*Macbeth, The Lady from Shanghai, Othello, Chimes at Midnight, Touch of Evil, The Stranger,* and *The Trial,* among many—always pushed the cinematic boundaries, exploring new directions and bold ideas in filmmaking. His legacy to cinema remains the unique creativity in all of his productions, the successes and failures.

Welles, said director Martin Scorsese, "was a beacon in a way. He was someone I could keep looking towards, someone whose work constantly surprised me and enriched me."

Did Welles ever lament that he received good fortune so early in his career?

"I don't regret that in *Kane*," Welles said twenty years after the film was produced, "because it was the only chance I had of that kind. I'm glad I had it at any time in my life."

The extraordinary alliance forged between an imaginative young director and a progressive studio chief did not produce the long-term benefits that all had sought when the relationship began in the summer of 1939. Nevertheless, *Citizen Kane* has become the most compelling example of the tremendous achievement possible when a filmmaker defied the Hollywood routine. By receiving such broad control and succeeding so spectacularly with his first film, Welles created a singular experience in Hollywood history.

The motion picture industry was not inherently flawed by its ironclad control over film production. The studios developed what they considered the most practical methods to produce a steady flow of product through their assembly-line methods, and for decades the system operated superbly to produce entertainment loved worldwide. However, the price paid for that homogenized product was the sacrifice of some of the creativity, innovation, and individual expression that could have been possible had the studios been willing to take more risks.

For a few brief months during 1940, Orson Welles possessed the unshackled power to create a motion picture, and he shared the artistic freedom with his cast and crew. *Citizen Kane* remains a fabulous aberration, the potent proof that a film of greatness could be produced—even within the studio system—if led by an individual whose ideas and methods clashed with the conventional thinking. How many more *Citizen Kane*s might have been produced if those who ran Hollywood in its heyday had been willing to grant their artists even a portion of the control that Orson Welles had received?

It is the inspiration *Citizen Kane* continues to provide, as much as the summit the film has reached, that ensures its place in cinema history. *Citizen Kane* may forever rank high on the lists of great motion pictures, but its true importance is found in the film's enduring ability to inspire new generations of artists to become filmmakers. Today, *Citizen Kane* continues to demonstrate the tremendous power of expression with the same impact it delivered in 1941, and many directors, writers, cinematographers, and actors point to the lessons they learned from *Citizen Kane* as the milestone revelations of their careers.

"I think it was the first time that I realized I was watching a film in which the actual art of film was being played with," director Sydney Pollack recalled of his initial viewing of *Citizen Kane*. "It was the first time I saw this real feeling of passion about moviemaking itself. . . . I was aware that the filmmaking process itself was a vivid part of the storytelling. I kept thinking, 'Wait a minute—you mean you can do *that*? Well, then you could do anything you wanted.'"

Said François Truffaut about *Citizen Kane,* "This film has inspired more vocations to the cinema than any other."

Recalled Martin Scorsese, "I really discovered what a director does when I saw *Citizen Kane.*"

Welles' colleague Henry Jaglom said of *Citizen Kane,* "I simply think of it as a film that made me want to make films."

And summed up Steven Spielberg, "*Citizen Kane* means everything to me. It is an icon of the courage of the filmmaker. It is one of the great American experiences in the cinema."

Citizen Kane will no doubt continue to provide such inspiration. To budding artists, perhaps the most enlightening point of all is recognizing that the motion picture was produced not by an experienced Hollywood director trained in the traditional methods of the studio system, but by a twenty-five-year-old novice eager to tear down barriers to creativity during his first filmmaking journey.

Asked two decades after *Citizen Kane* where he found the confidence to become a filmmaker, Welles replied, "It was ignorance—sheer ignorance. There's no confidence to equal it.

"I had the confidence of ignorance," Welles said. "Not knowing anything about [filmmaking], there was no basis for fear. If you're walking along the edge of a cliff, and you don't know it's the edge of a cliff, you have perfect confidence."

VIEWER'S GUIDE TO *CITIZEN KANE*

Cast and Production Credits

The list of the cast in *Citizen Kane* is shown here in two parts. The first offers the credits that appeared in the film itself. The second lists performers who are not shown in the credits on-screen. Some explanatory notes are included, such as for Georgia Backus' Bertha Anderson; a note describes who she is in the film because her name is never mentioned.

The first ten actors in the cast are listed here in the order in which they were showcased in brief scenes in the credits at the end of *Citizen Kane*. The scenes—each a few seconds of outtake footage—were part of Welles' efforts to highlight his players. "Most of the principal actors in *Citizen Kane* are new to motion pictures," the film's credits read. "The Mercury Theatre is proud to introduce them."

One quirk of the film's credits has been left here unchanged: Sonny Bupp, who played Kane's son at the campaign rally in Madison Square Garden, is listed in the credits as "Kane III"—meaning, of course, that his full name was "Charles Foster Kane III." However in the scenes set in Colorado, when Mary Kane speaks to her husband, the boy's grandfather and presumably the first Charles Foster Kane, she calls him "Jim." Adding to the puzzle is the fact that as late as the July 15, 1940, script, Kane's father was identified as "Thomas Foster Kane."

The second list presents bit players and extras in roughly their order of appearance. Part of this list comes from RKO's roster of "small parts and bits," extracted from the expense records for hires between April and November 1940 for Production #281. Individuals from the RKO list are marked with a ‡.

The rest of the list of bit players accounts for everyone identifiable who was part of the production, including many of the extras. These names were painstakingly gathered by the research team at the American Film Institute's *AFI Catalog of Feature Films*. This invaluable online database describes itself as "the most authoritative filmographic database on the web," and that characterization may be an understatement. Among the treasures of the *AFI Catalog of Feature Films* are entries for nearly sixty thousand American feature-length motion pictures and seventeen thousand shorts produced since 1893, including extraordinarily comprehensive lists of casts and crew, as well as plot summaries, historical notes, and a trove of other material—all intensely researched, verified, and searchable online.

For example, the listing for *Citizen Kane* includes not only the additional credits included here, but also a lengthy plot summary, genres and subgenres, major and minor subjects explored in the film, fifty-six hundred words of production notes, and bibliographic sources.

You can see the *AFI Catalog of Feature Films* at afi.com; select "catalog."

The Cast of *Citizen Kane*

Joseph Cotten	Jed Leland/reporter in screening room
Dorothy Comingore	Susan Alexander
Agnes Moorehead	Mary Kane
Ruth Warrick	Emily Norton
Ray Collins	"Boss" Jim W. Gettys
Erskine Sanford	Carter/reporter in screening room
Everett Sloane	Bernstein
William Alland	Jerry Thompson/narrator of *News on the March*
Paul Stewart	Raymond
George Coulouris	Thatcher
Fortunio Bonanova	Matiste
Gus Schilling	Headwaiter/reporter in screening room
Philip Van Zandt	Rawlston
Georgia Backus	Miss Anderson (Thatcher Library)
Harry Shannon	Kane's father
Sonny Bupp	Kane III
Buddy Swan	Kane, age eight
Orson Welles	Kane

Small Parts and Bits in *Citizen Kane*

Peter Allen .... Man in Senate investigating committee

Landers Stevens ‡ .... Senate investigator

Norman Taylor .... Man in Senate investigating committee

Tom Curran ‡ .... Theodore Roosevelt

E. G. Miller .... Neville Chamberlain/reporter at Trenton Town Hall

Carl Ekberg ‡ .... Adolf Hitler

Carl Faulkner .... Hermann Goering

Captain Garcia ‡ .... General in newsreel

Art Yeoman ‡ .... Union Square speaker

Guy Repp ‡ .... Radio reporter on ship

Terrance Ray .... Reporter on ship deck/Man at Madison Square Garden

Sam Ash .... Reporter on ship deck in newsreel

Buddy Messinger .... Reporter on ship deck in newsreel

Buck Mack ‡ .... Reporter on ship deck in newsreel

Evelyn Mackert .... Reporter on ship deck in newsreel

Sally Walker .... Reporter on ship deck in newsreel

Petra De Silva ‡ .... Reporter

Baudena Alva .... Extra in newsreel

James Brouht .... Extra in newsreel

Gene Chervow .... Extra in newsreel

Jack Jahries .... Extra in newsreel

Dave Ledner .... Extra in newsreel

Bob Terry .... Extra in newsreel

Jack Robins .... Extra in newsreel

Demetrious Alexis .... Extra in newsreel

Victor Romito .... Extra in newsreel

Lou Young .... Extra in newsreel

Art Dupuis .... Extra in newsreel

Rudolph Germaine .... Extra in newsreel

Robert Samven .... Extra in newsreel

T. Lockwood Arbright .... Extra in newsreel

Walter Lawrence .... Extra in newsreel

Guy Smith .... Extra in newsreel

Brent Shugar .... Extra in newsreel

Dimas Sutteno .... Extra in newsreel

Gene Coogan	Extra in newsreel
Lee McCluskey	Extra in newsreel
John Northpole	Extra in newsreel
Jack Taylor	Extra in newsreel
Tim Wallace	Extra in newsreel
Vince Speaker	Extra in newsreel
Major Sam Harris	Extra in newsreel
Mike Lally	Extra in newsreel
Dick Elmore	Extra in newsreel
Michael Audley ‡	Reporter in projection room
Richard Baer ‡	Reporter in projection room/ Hillman (official at Madison Square Garden)
Eddie Dew ‡	Reporter in projection room
Perc Launders ‡	Reporter in projection room
Richard Wilson ‡	Reporter in projection room
Vera Winters	Reporter in projection room
Gino Corrado ‡	Waiter
Joe Manz ‡	Jennings
William O'Brien ‡	Thatcher's secretary
Joe North ‡	Thatcher's secretary
Donna Dax ‡	Maid at Thatcher's Christmas party
Myrtle Rischell ‡	Kane's governess at Thatcher's Christmas party
John Dilson	Man in Thatcher montage
Walter James	Man in Thatcher montage
Olin Francis	Expressman
Walter Bacon	*Inquirer* employee
Ray Flynn	*Inquirer* employee
Frank Haney	*Inquirer* employee
Bob Lawson	*Inquirer* employee
Verne Richards	*Inquirer* employee
George Sperry	*Inquirer* employee
Olin Francis	Expressman
Ed Ryan	*Inquirer* employee
Tim Davis ‡	Copy boy
Jesse Graves	Joseph (butler in Kane's *Inquirer* office)
Al Eben ‡	Solly
Benny Rubin	Smathers (printer's assistant in cut scene)

Edward Hemmer ‡ .... Printer's assistant in cut scene

Lillian O'Malley .... Person in front of *Chronicle*

Dot Cleveland .... Person in front of *Chronicle*

E. Kerrigan .... Person in front of *Chronicle*

John Eckert .... Driver of car

Ivy Keene .... Driver of car/Woman in loggia scene/
.... Susan's hands in jigsaw puzzle scenes

Bob Dudley ‡ .... Photographer at *Inquirer* party

Charles Bennett ‡ .... Singer at *Inquirer* party

Joan Blair .... Dancer at *Inquirer*

Irene Crosby .... Dancer at *Inquirer*

Margaret Davis .... Dancer at *Inquirer*

Frances Deets .... Dancer at *Inquirer*

Pauline Easterday .... Dancer at *Inquirer*

Juanita Field .... Dancer at *Inquirer*

Gloria Gale .... Dancer at *Inquirer*

Jerry Gordon .... Dancer at *Inquirer*

Edna Mae Jones .... Dancer at *Inquirer*

Laura Knight .... Dancer at *Inquirer*

Mary Lorraine .... Dancer at *Inquirer*

Loretta Marsh .... Dancer at *Inquirer*

Frances Neal ‡ .... Dancer at *Inquirer*

Leda Nicova .... Dancer at *Inquirer*

Suzanne Ridgeway .... Dancer at *Inquirer*

Joleen Reynolds .... Dancer at *Inquirer*

Ruth Seeley .... Dancer at *Inquirer*

Vivian Wilson .... Dancer at *Inquirer*

Dan Borzage .... Reporter at *Inquirer* party

Robert Brent .... Reporter at *Inquirer* party

Jack Egan .... Reporter at *Inquirer* party

Guy Gada .... Reporter at *Inquirer* party

Bob Gladman .... Reporter at *Inquirer* party

Harlan Hoagland .... Reporter at *Inquirer* party

J. D. Lockhart .... Reporter at *Inquirer* party

John McCormack .... Reporter at *Inquirer* party

Roy Smith .... Reporter at *Inquirer* party

Monty Ford .... Reporter at *Inquirer* party

B. B. Tobin .... Reporter at *Inquirer* party
Larry Wheat .... Reporter at *Inquirer* party
Bobby Haines .... Reporter at *Inquirer* party
William Reed .... Reporter at *Inquirer* party
Don Roberts .... Reporter at *Inquirer* party
Fred Trowbridge .... Reporter at *Inquirer* party
Harry Bailey .... Reporter at *Inquirer* party
William Calkins .... Reporter at *Inquirer* party
J. J. Clark .... Reporter at *Inquirer* party
Harry Harris .... Reporter at *Inquirer* party
Paddy O'Flynn .... Reporter at *Inquirer* party
J. R. Ralston .... Reporter at *Inquirer* party
Sam Rice .... Reporter at *Inquirer* party
Larry Williams .... Reporter at *Inquirer* party
Porter Chase .... Reporter at *Inquirer* party
Tom Coleman .... Reporter at *Inquirer* party
Gayle De Camp .... Reporter at *Inquirer* party
Clayton Jones .... Reporter at *Inquirer* party
Alexander Julian .... Reporter at *Inquirer* party
Jack Manolas .... Reporter at *Inquirer* party
Carl De Loro .... Reporter at *Inquirer* party
Hercules Mendez .... Reporter at *Inquirer* party
Ludwig Lowry .... Reporter at *Inquirer* party
George Jiminez .... Waiter at *Inquirer* party
Karl Thomas ‡ .... Jetsam (entertainer cut from *Inquirer* party scenes)
Glen Turnbull ‡ .... Flotsam (entertainer cut from the *Inquirer* party scenes)
George Noisom ‡ .... Copy boy
Ellen Lowe ‡ .... Miss Townsend (*Inquirer* society editor)
Ernest Gruney .... Man on hospital roof
Bill Kane .... Man on hospital roof
Teddy Mangean .... Man on roof
Bill Wilkins .... Man on roof
Jack Wynn .... Man on hospital roof
A. Linke .... Druggist
Coy Danz .... Nurse on hospital roof
Edith Evanson ‡ .... Nurse on hospital roof
Slim Hightower .... Fish driver

Major George C. McBride ‡ .... Shadowgraph man/Man at *Inquirer* office
Mitchell Ingraham ‡ .... Politician
James Itay .... Man at Madison Square Garden
Charles Meakin ‡ .... Politician at Madison Square Garden
Phillip Morris ‡ .... Politician at Madison Square Garden
Frank O'Connor .... Man at Madison Square Garden
Ed Peil ‡ .... Civic leader at Madison Square
Jack Ryan .... Man at Madison Square Garden
Bert Stevens .... Man at Madison Square Garden
Francis Sayles ‡ .... Politician at Madison Square Garden
John Dilson ‡ .... Ward heeler
Walter James ‡ .... Ward heeler
Louise Franklin ‡ .... Susan's maid in New York
Jack Curtis ‡ .... Boss printer
Mickey Martin ‡ .... Newsboy at saloon
Ed Dahlen .... Reporter at Trenton Town Hall
George DeNormand .... Reporter at Trenton Town Hall
Bud Geary .... Reporter at Trenton Town Hall
Lew Harvey ‡ .... Reporter at Trenton Town Hall
Cliff Herd .... Reporter at Trenton Town Hall
Harry Jones .... Reporter at Trenton Town Hall
Albert Le Baron .... Reporter at Trenton Town Hall
Clyde McAtee .... Reporter at Trenton Town Hall
Jim Merritt .... Reporter at Trenton Town Hall
Louis Natheaux ‡ .... Reporter at Trenton Town Hall
Cy Ring .... Reporter at Trenton Town Hall
George Rogers .... Reporter at Trenton Town Hall
Bruce Sidney ‡ .... Reporter at Trenton Town Hall
Sam Steele .... Reporter at Trenton Town Hall
Ken Weaver .... Reporter at Trenton Town Hall
Roland Winters .... Reporter at Trenton Town Hall
Milton Kibbee ‡ .... Reporter
Jean Forward .... Singing for Dorothy Comingore
Arthur Kay ‡ .... Orchestra conductor
Charles West .... Stage manager
Tudor William ‡ .... Chorus master
James Mack ‡ .... Prompter

Gohr Van Vleck ‡ .... Stagehand on catwalk at opera

Jack Raymond ‡ .... Stagehand on catwalk at opera

Gerald Pierce ‡ .... Delivery boy with message from Leland for Kane

Lillian Nicholson .... Woman at opera

Charles Cross .... Man at opera

Lou Duello .... Man at opera

Herbert Corthell ‡ .... City editor, *Chicago Inquirer*

Eddie Cobb ‡ .... Hireling, *Chicago Inquirer*

Ernie Daniels .... Hireling, *Chicago Inquirer*

Jack Floyd .... Hireling, *Chicago Inquirer*

Shimen Ruskin ‡ .... Hireling, *Chicago Inquirer*

George Sherwood ‡ .... Hireling, *Chicago Inquirer*

Ralph Stein .... Hireling, *Chicago Inquirer*

Jack Morton .... Butler in Susan's bedroom

Irving Mitchell ‡ .... Dr. Corey

Vera Haal ‡ .... Nurse to Susan

Don Ackerman .... Man at party in Everglades

Jimmy Grant .... Man at party in Everglades

Suzanne Dulier ‡ .... Marie (Susan's maid at Xanadu)

Carmen La Roux ‡ .... Maid in corridor at Xanadu

William Alston .... Reporter at Xanadu

Harriet Branden ‡ .... Reporter at Xanadu

Eddie Coke ‡ .... Reporter at Xanadu

Louise Currie ‡ .... Reporter at Xanadu

Jack Gargan .... Reporter at Xanadu

John Huettner ‡ .... Reporter at Xanadu/stand-in for Orson Welles

Alan Ladd ‡ .... Reporter at Xanadu

Arthur O'Connell ‡ .... Reporter at Xanadu

Bert Moorhouse .... Reporter at Xanadu

Walter Sande ‡ .... Reporter at Xanadu

Jack Santoro .... Reporter at Xanadu

Kathryn Trosper ‡ .... Reporter at Xanadu

Richard Wilson ‡ .... Reporter at Xanadu

Harry Vejar ‡ .... Portuguese laborer in Xanadu furnace room

Marie Day ‡ .... Unspecified bit

Albert Frazier ‡ .... Gorilla suit man (not used)

Charles Hayes .... Stand-in for Orson Welles

Sid Davis ....Stand-in for Orson Welles
Bob Crosby ....Dancing double for Orson Welles
Vicki Anderson ....Stand-in for Dorothy Comingore
Catherine Stanley ....Stand-in
Roberta Johnson ....Stand-in
Marie Osborne ....Stand-in
Ralph Stein ....Stand-in
Ed Ryan ....Stand-in
William Knutson ....Stand-in
George Havens ....Stand-in
P. Campbell ....Stand-in

Production Staff of *Citizen Kane*

(* indicates on-screen credit)

Production Company ....Mercury Productions, Inc.
Distribution Company ....RKO Radio Pictures, Inc.

Director ....Orson Welles*
Assistant Directors ....Eddie Donahue
Freddie Fleck
Producer ....Orson Welles*
Associate Producer ....Richard Baer
Assistant Producers ....William Alland
Richard Wilson

Screenplay ....Herman J. Mankiewicz*
Orson Welles*
Editorial Supervision ....John Houseman

Cinematography ....Gregg Toland*
Camera Operator ....Bert Shipman
Assistant Cameraman ....Edward Garvin
Gaffer ....William J. McClellan
Grip ....Ralph Hoge

Cameraman for Makeup, Wardrobe Tests, One Retake .... Russell Metty
Retakes and Additional Shots .... Harry Wild

Musical Score (Composed, Arranged,
and Conducted) .... Bernard Herrmann*
Music Copyist .... Mischa Violin
Music for *News on the March* .... Excerpts of music from the films: *Abe*
Lincoln in Illinois, Bad Lands, Bringing Up
Baby, The Conquerors, Curtain Call, Five Came
Back, The Flying Irishman, Gunga Din, A
Man to Remember, Mother Carey's Chickens,
Music for Madame, Nurse Edith Cavell, On
Again–Off Again, and *Reno;* and excerpts
from classical compositions
"Charlie Kane" Song .... Music from "A Poco No" by Pepe Guizar
Lyrics by Herman Ruby
Sung by Charles Bennett
Opera Aria .... "Una voce poco fa" from
The Barber of Seville
Music by Gioachino Rossini
Libretto by Cesare Sterbini
Opera Dubbing for Dorothy Comingore .... Jean Forward
"In a Mizz" .... Music by Charlie Barnet
Lyrics by Haven Johnson

The Jazz Band

In 2004, Welles scholar Ron Gottesman contacted musician Buddy Collette to iden-
tify the performers who appeared in the scenes from the picnic at Xanadu. The list of
performers reads like the lineup for an all-star combo:

Guitar & Tom-Toms .... Cee Pee Johnson
Drums & Singer .... Alton Redd
Alto Sax .... Kurtland Bradford
Tenor Sax .... Buddy Banks

Alto Sax, Baritone Sax, Clarinet .... Buddy Collette
Trumpet .... Raymond Tate
Loyal Walker (high notes)
Bass .... Johnny Miller

Music Editor .... Ralph Bekher
Dance Choreography .... Arthur Appel
Art Director .... Perry Ferguson*
Assistant Art Director .... Hilyard Brown
Principal Sketch Artist .... Charles Ohmann
Sketches and Graphics .... Al Abbott
Claude Gillingwater
Albert Pyke
Maurice Zuberano
Art Department Head .... Van Nest Polglase*
Set Decoration .... Darrell Silvera
Assistant Set Decorator .... Al Fields
Drapery Department .... Tom Peer
Prop Manager .... Charles Sayers
Newspaper Headlines and Articles .... Edward Blake
Prop Newspapers .... Earl Hayes Press
Makeup .... Maurice Seiderman
Assistant Makeup Artist .... Layne Britton
Wigs .... Charles Wright
Costume Design .... Edward Stevenson*
Men's Wardrobe .... Earl Leas
Women's Wardrobe .... Margaret Van Horn
Claire Cramer
Optical Printing .... Linwood G. Dunn
Effects Cameraman .... Russell Cully
Montage Effects .... Douglas Travers
Matte Artist .... Mario Larrinaga
Special Effects Department Head .... Vernon L. Walker*
Editor .... Robert Wise*
Assistant Editor .... Mark Robson
Sound Production Mixer .... Bailey Fesler*

Boom Operator .... Jimmy Thompson
Rerecording .... James G. Stewart*
                                                            Hugh McDowell
Sound for Tests .... T. Kilburn
                                                            J. Tribby
                                                            John C. Grubb
                                                            Earl B. Mounce
Sound for Rerecording .... G. Portman
Sound Effects .... Harry Essman
Sound Effects Editor .... T. K. Wood
Sound Department Head .... John Aalberg
Script Continuity and Supervision .... Molly Kent
Still Photography .... Alexander Kahle
Mercury Theatre Publicity .... Herbert Drake
Secretary to Orson Welles .... Kathryn Trosper
Producer Manager .... J. R. Crone
Secretary .... Fleta Preston
Secretary to John Houseman and
Herman Mankiewicz in Victorville .... Rita Alexander
Secretary for Preproduction .... Blanche Walters
Lab Technician .... Johnny Swain
Automobile Supplier for Everglades Picnic .... Jack Rubens
Auditing Department .... H. Schilling

GREGG TOLAND: "I BROKE THE RULES IN 'CITIZEN KANE'"

I BROKE THE RULES IN "CITIZEN KANE"

by GREGG TOLAND, A.S.C.

Photos Courtesy RKO Radio Pictures, from "Citizen Kane"

The author, whose revolutionary technique in Orson Welles' new picture created a sensation, tells how he startled moviedom.

THERE'S been a good deal of gratifying discussion recently about the photography of Orson Welles' first movie, *Citizen Kane*. The gist of the talk has been that the cinematography in that film was "daring" and "advanced," and that I violated all the photographic commandments and conventions in shooting the picture.

Right away I want to make a distinction between "commandment" and "convention." Photographically speaking, I understand a commandment to be a rule, axiom, or principle, an incontrovertible fact of photographic procedure which is unchangeable for physical and chemical reasons. On the other hand, a convention, to me, is a usage which has become acceptable through repetition. It is a tradition rather than a rule. With time the convention becomes a commandment, through force of habit. I feel that the limiting effect is both obvious and unfortunate.

With these definitions in mind, I'll admit that I defied a good many conventions in filming *Citizen Kane*. Orson Welles was insistent that the story be told most effectively, letting the Hollywood conventions of movie making go hang if need be. With such whole-hearted backing I was able to test and prove several ideas generally accepted as being radical in Hollywood circles.

Welles' use of the cinematographer as a real aid to him in telling the story, and his appreciation of the camera's storytelling potentialities helped me immeasurably. He was willing—and this is very

rare in Hollywood—that I take weeks to achieve a desired photographic effect.

The photographic approach to *Citizen Kane* was planned and considered long before the first camera turned. That is also unconventional in Hollywood, where most cinematographers learn of their next assignments only a few days before the scheduled shooting starts. Altogether, I was on this job for a half year, including preparation and actual shooting.

Although it was Welles' first effort in movies, he came to the job with a rare vision and understanding of camera purpose and direction. It was his idea that the technique of filming should never be ev-

ident to the audience. He wanted to avoid the established Hollywood conventions, most of which are accepted by audiences because of their frequent use. And this frequent use of conventions is dictated

(Continued on page 90)

Fast film, coated lenses, and twin-arc broadside lamps made it possible to stop down and get the tremendous depth seen here.

This one scene tells a story which might require consecutive shots from several angles if handled in the orthodox way. Great depth of field renders everything sharp, from the reading matter in the foreground to the panels in the far corner.

Realism results from filming an entire group like this instead of making closeups. Note the use of a ceilinged set, in defiance of movie traditions.

I Broke the Rules in "Citizen Kane"

(Continued from page 55)

by pressure of time and reluctance to deviate from the accepted.

As a case in point, depth of field nearly always is sacrificed in Hollywood productions. The normal human eye sees everything before it (within reasonable distance) clearly and sharply. There is no special or single center of visual sharpness in real life. But the Hollywood cameras focus on a center of interest, and allow the other components of a scene to "fuzz out" in those regions before and beyond the focal point.

The attainment of an approximate human-eye focus was one of our fundamental aims in *Citizen Kane*. It took a great deal of doing, but we proved that it can be done.

We solved the depth-of-field problem by means of pre-production testing and experiment. We built our system of "visual reality" on the well-known fact that lenses of shorter focal length are characterized by comparatively greater depth, and that stopping down a lens increases the depth even further.

The tendency in Hollywood has been to stop down to *f* 3.5 occasionally in filming interiors. More often the working aperture is between *f* 2.3 and *f* 3.2. The use of the *f* 3.5 aperture is still uncommon enough to be cause for conversation in the film capital. Yet any professional or amateur who has used short-focus lenses knows that the increase in depth obtained by stopping down from *f* 2.3 to *f* 3.5 can make quite a difference.

But we wanted to stop down considerably further. By experimenting with high-speed films we discovered that lens aperture could be reduced appreciably, but that we still weren't able to stop down enough for our purposes. This meant that an increased illumination level had to be obtained. And since we were already violating Hollywood tradition by using ceilinged sets, we were unable to step up illumination by means of extra lights mounted on catwalks or strung above the scene.

The Vard "Opticoating" system, developed at the California Institute of Technology, proved to be one factor in the eventual solution of our lighting problem. Being essentially a method of treating lens surfaces, Opticoating eliminates refraction, permits light to penetrate instead of scattering, and thus increases lens speed by as much as a full stop. Our coated lenses also permitted us to shoot directly into lights without anything like the dire results usually encountered.

Another aid in solving our small-aperture problem was the twin-arc broadside lamp, developed for Technicolor work. We began to employ these lamps before we hit upon the use of the high-speed film which we eventually chose. The combination of coated lenses, arc broadside lamps, and the fastest available film made it possible to photograph nearly all interior scenes at an aperture of *f* 8 or even smaller. I shot several scenes at *f* 11 and *f* 16. That's a big jump from

f 2.3 and it's certainly unconventional in Hollywood filming.

Even the standard 47 and 50 mm lenses afford great depth of field when stopped down to *f* 11 or *f* 16. And the shorter-focus wide-angle lenses act virtually like human eyes, providing almost universal focus at such small apertures. In some cases we were able to hold sharp focus over a depth of 200 feet.

I referred previously to the unconventional use of ceilinged sets. The *Citizen Kane* sets have ceilings because we wanted reality, and we felt that it would be easier to believe a room was a room if its ceiling could be seen in the picture. Furthermore, lighting effects in unceilinged rooms generally are not realistic because the illumination comes from unnatural angles.

We planned most of our camera setups to take advantage of the ceilings, in some cases even building the sets so as to permit shooting upward from floor level. None of the sets was rigged for overhead lighting, although occasionally necessary backlighting was arranged by lifting a small section of ceiling and using a light through the opening. The deep sets called for unusually penetrating lamps, and the twin-arc broadsides mentioned earlier filled the bill. The ceilings gave us another advantage in addition to realism—freedom from worry about microphone shadow, the bugaboo of all sound filming. We were able to place our mikes above the muslin ceiling, which allowed them to pick up sound but not to throw shadows.

There were other violations of Hollywood tradition in the photographic details of *Citizen Kane*. One of them resulted from Welles' insistence that scenes should flow together smoothly and imperceptibly. Accordingly, before actual shooting began, everything had been planned with full realization of what the camera could bring to the audience. We arranged our action so as to avoid direct cuts, to permit panning or dollying from one angle to another whenever that type of camera action fitted the continuity. By way of example, scenes which conventionally would require a shift from close-up to full shot were planned so that the action would take place simultaneously in extreme foreground and extreme background.

Our constant efforts toward increasing realism and making mechanical details imperceptible led eventually to the solution of all the problems we had created for ourselves. As we avoided direct cuts, so we steered clear of traditional transitions. Most of the transitions in *Citizen Kane* are lap-dissolves in which the background dissolves from one scene to the next shortly before the players in the foreground are dissolved. This was accomplished rather simply with two light-dimming outfits, one for the actors and one for the set.

The dissolve is begun by dimming the lights on the background, eventually fad-

ing it out entirely. Then the lights on the people are dimmed to produce a fade-out on them. The fade-in is made the same way, fading in the set lights first, then the lights for the people.

Intercutting was eliminated wherever possible, with the idea of achieving further visual simplification. Instead of following the usual practice of cutting from a closeup to an "insert" (which explains or elaborates upon the closeup), we made a single, straight shot, compressing the whole scene into a single composition.

Here's an example. Where the idea is to show an actor reading something, we don't show a closeup of the actor and then follow it with a cut to the reading matter "insert." We simply compose the shot with the actor's head on one side of the frame and the reading matter on the other. In one such case in the filming of *Citizen Kane* the actor's head was less than 16 inches from the lens, the reading matter was about three feet away, and a group of men in the background was 12 to 18 feet away. Yet all three components of this scene—actor in foreground, reading matter, and group—are sharp and clear to the audience.

My focusing was based on the principle of depth of field. Knowing the focal length and other characteristics of the lenses we were using, I worked out the various focal points as I came to them. By following a depth-of-field table in using any lens, you can always tell just where to set your focus in order to attain overall sharpness within required limits. It's an important fact, however, that much depends upon the properties of the lens in use at the time—and its characteristics should be determined carefully before any attempt is made to use this zone-focusing technique.

Such differences as exist between the cinematography in *Citizen Kane* and the camera work on the average Hollywood product are based on the rare opportunity provided me by Orson Welles, who was in complete sympathy with my theory that the photography should fit the story. I have been trying to follow that principle for some time in an effort to provide visual variety as well as a proper photographic vehicle for the plot. Fitting *Wuthering Heights* and *Grapes of Wrath* and *Long Voyage Home* to an identical photographic pattern would be unfair to director, writer, actors, and audience.

Style too often becomes deadly sameness. In my opinion, the day of highly stylized cinematography is passing, and is being superseded by a candid, realistic technique and an individual approach to each new film subject.

You will accomplish much more by fitting your photography to the story instead of limiting the story to the narrow confines of conventional photographic practice. And as you do so you'll learn that the movie camera is a flexible instrument, many of its possibilities still unexplored. New realms remain to be discovered by amateurs and professionals who are willing to think about it and take the necessary time to make the thought a reality.—▶

BERNARD HERRMANN: A CONVERSATION AT THE GEORGE EASTMAN HOUSE

Thirty-three years after Bernard Herrmann composed the musical score for Citizen Kane, *he recalled the experience in a 1973 lecture and Q&A session at the George Eastman House. Here are excerpts from that presentation.*

The use of music in film is completely unknown territory. The most sensitive directors can be completely ignorant about the use of music, while an inferior director can have a great instinct for it—largely because film music has a certain mystical quality. The camera can only do so much; the actors and the direction can only do so much. But the music can tell you what people are thinking and feeling—that is the real function of music.

When speaking of music in the cinema, it is also important to remember that the ear often deludes the eye. It can change time values: what appears very long may only be four seconds and vice versa. There is no rule, but once again music has this mysterious quality.

There is nothing in the nature of a film that requires the use of an orchestra. The "orchestra" was developed over several hundred years—an agreed representation of certain instruments to play a certain repertoire. But music for film is a single unique entity. You are creating for one performance, for that film, and there is no law that says it has to be related to concert music. Film allows a composer the unique opportunity to shift the complete spectrum of sound within one piece— something hitherto unknown in the history of music. You can't do that in an opera house! Each film can create its own color.

Imagine the opening shots of *Citizen Kane* without music. That was the way it was turned over to me. I began with that sequence. I had neither the idea of a "Rosebud" theme nor a "Destiny" theme. But both themes came to me rather automatically.

You don't write music with the top of your head, you write it from a part you don't know anything about. At the very beginning (I was very lucky the first hour) I hit on the two sound sequences that would bear the weight of the film. The picture opens with the first, the motif of Destiny—Kane's destiny. The permutations of this theme are complex. Later in the film it becomes a can-can, jazz, all kinds of things.

When Kane sees the flickering snow, we hear the second—the Rosebud motif—around which the whole picture pivots. The second theme also immediately reveals what Rosebud is, but it is soon forgotten! This opening sequence uses an orchestra of eight flutes (four alto, four bass), very deep contrabass clarinets, tubas, trombones, a vibraphone, and deep lower percussion.

Now imagine the sound track to the opening sequence without the visuals. I think the music is too long. Of course, I had no choice about length. Sometimes you can discuss changes with a director, but certainly not in a film like this! Finally, imagine the full opening sequence, visuals and sound track together. Is the sequence still too long? I think not—and that is one of the great mysteries of the power of music in cinema. Without that music that sequence is not complete, and the time scale is skewed.

The opera sequence in *Citizen Kane* presented a unique set of problems. The problem was to create something that would convey to the audience the feeling of the quicksand into which Susan is suddenly thrown (by Kane's inflated estimation of her musical talent and by his obsession with her becoming a success as an opera singer). It had to be done cinematically. It had to be done fast. We had to have the sound of an enormous orchestra pounding her. There is no opera in existence that opens that way. We had to create one.

I wrote the piece in a very high tessitura, so that a girl with a modest voice would be completely hopeless in it. I didn't particularly care to write an opera sequence like this, but *Citizen Kane* demanded it—not Welles, *Citizen Kane*. And it is my contention that no other approach could have solved the problem. Had we played the last scene of *Salome* we would have gotten the same effect, but it would not have shown Susan starting an opera (the beginning of *Salome* anybody can sing). The problem was: can she survive this beginning?

The next part of *Citizen Kane* to consider is the little breakfast sequence in Kane's first marriage. Imagine the visuals alone, without the music. That is what I was given. The popular music of this period corresponding to the images would have been a romantic waltz. So each change in mood and each cut was written as another variation on a basic waltz theme. The structure then is very simple: a series of waltz variations in absolutely classic form, giving unity to the otherwise fragmented sequence.

The ending of *Citizen Kane* gave me a wonderful opportunity to arrive at a complete musical statement (it contains no dialogue with the exception of perhaps one or two lines). Because I wanted to draw all the threads of the film together, this last sequence is played by a conventional symphony orchestra. I used a full orchestra for the simple reason that, from the time the music of the final sequence begins until the end of the film, the music has effectively left the film and become an apotheosis of the entire work.

I was very fortunate that I started my cinema career with *Citizen Kane*. People always tell me how difficult Orson Welles is. The only people I have ever met worth working for were difficult people—because they are interested in achieving something. Just spare me the charmers. Welles in every other way might be difficult, but when it comes to making artistic decisions he is like the Rock of Gibraltar.

* * * * * * * *

Q: The music in Citizen Kane *seems so romantic. Could you have eliminated music entirely and used percussive or rhythmic effects instead?*

BERNARD HERRMANN: Yes, of course you could, but not with this subject. This is a romantic picture. It is about something called Rosebud. A percussive effect would not work in the opening, and it would not work later in the film.

When Kane meets Susan in the street, he says, "I was on my way to the warehouse to look at the things my mother left me." The reason that he responds to her is that she faintly resembles his mother and the orchestra faintly repeats the Rosebud theme. But nobody's ever caught it. Nobody's ever written about it. They don't have to; it's there!

So sometimes with a subject this romantic you must do romantic things. Every picture is unique. I'm not saying there's only one way, there are many ways, providing imagination is used. But I doubt whether one could eliminate all music from a picture like *Citizen Kane,* a kaleidoscopic picture. A certain grayness would settle over it.

Q: Usually a composer does not have the final say on a film, the director does.

BH: I have the final say, or I don't do the music. The reason for insisting on this is simply, compared to Orson Welles, a man of great musical culture, most other directors are just babes in the woods. If you were to follow their taste, the music would be awful.

There are exceptions. I did a film *The Devil and Daniel Webster* (1941) with a wonderful director, William Dieterle. He was also a man of great musical culture. And Hitchcock, you know, is very sensitive; he leaves me alone. It depends on the person. But if I have to take what a director says, I'd rather not do the film. I find it's impossible to work that way.

Q: Despite the almost universal acclaim for Citizen Kane, *I have read one recurring criticism—the "waw-waw" effect at the end of the library scene. How do you feel about that now, after all these years?*

BH: I would do the same thing again.

CITIZEN KANE:
SCENE-BY-SCENE GUIDE

This scene-by-scene guide, compiled to complement your viewing, was timed using the 2011 Blu-Ray digital transfer of *Citizen Kane,* which is included in the seventieth-anniversary release packages of the film (both single disc and "ultimate collector's edition").

The official release length of *Citizen Kane* is 10,734 feet of film, or one hour, fifty-nine minutes, sixteen seconds. The total displayed length of the 2011 Blu-ray and in this scene-by-scene guide is seven seconds longer because of the addition of three seconds of black leader at the beginning of the film, two seconds of black at the end, plus two seconds that have crept into the length because of minuscule differences over the span of a two-hour film in the transfer between the analog film and the digital disc. Thus the total running time of the Blu-ray is one hour, fifty-nine minutes, twenty-three seconds.

The conventional DVD runs one hour, fifty-nine minutes, and 18 seconds because of the addition of two seconds of black leader at the beginning of the film.

Because of differences in the performance of disc players, the times below may vary by a few seconds during your review.

Opening Credits

0:00:00 Black.
0:00:03 RKO logo.
0:00:14 Fade to black.

0:00:16   Opening credits: A Mercury Production by Orson Welles.

0:00:23   Title: *Citizen Kane.*

0:00:29   Fade to black.

The Death of Charles Foster Kane, Xanadu, Florida Gulf Coast

0:00:36   "No Trespassing" sign and chain-link fence.

0:00:55   Wire fence.

0:01:02   Decorative fence.

0:01:08   Main gate with *K* at top (Xanadu in background).

0:01:14   Monkeys in cage (Xanadu in background).

0:01:24   Gondolas on an artificial canal (Xanadu shown in reflection upside down).

0:01:36   Bridge (Xanadu in background).

0:01:44   Golf course, sixteenth hole (Xanadu in background).

0:01:53   Decaying swimming pool (Xanadu in background).

0:01:59   Xanadu (close-up).

0:02:06   Kane's bedroom window (shot from outside); the bedroom light goes out at 0:02:09.

0:02:14   Kane in bed (shot from inside the room).

0:02:23   Snowstorm (close-up).

0:02:30   Snow globe in Kane's hand.

0:02:32   "Rosebud."

0:02:34   Snow globe falls from Kane's hand and breaks.

0:02:39   Nurse enters.

0:02:47   Nurse puts Kane's hands on his chest, covers Kane's body.

0:03:01   Kane's covered body and window.

0:03:10   Fade to black.

The *News on the March* Newsreel

0:03:12   *News on the March* title screen.

0:03:18   Text: ("Obituary: Xanadu's Landlord")

0:03:22   Montage of Xanadu buildings (seven shots).

0:03:41   Overview of Xanadu grounds (two shots).

0:03:45   Xanadu swimming pool and guests.

0:03:48   Florida Gulf coast.

0:03:51   Xanadu under construction.

0:03:56   Construction workers build Xanadu (four shots).

0:04:01   Statue of knight on horseback.

0:04:04   Statues in crates.

0:04:06   Xanadu close-ups (two shots).

0:04:09   Camels carrying Kane crates.

0:04:11   Kane crates loaded onto trains and ships (three shots).

0:04:16   Kane crates in storage.

0:04:19   Racehorses in stables.

0:04:21   Giraffes in zoo.

0:04:23   Birds in aviary.

0:04:25   Octopus in tank.

0:04:27   Elephant loaded onto ship.

0:04:29   Mules unloaded from ship.

0:04:31   Aviary.

0:04:34   Xanadu gardens.

0:04:35   Xanadu fountain.

0:04:36   Montage of Xanadu buildings and grounds (six shots).

0:04:51   Text: Kane's funeral description ("In Xanadu last week . . .").

0:04:57   Kane's funeral procession.

0:05:13   Kane's photo on newspaper; montage of headlines on eleven news papers announcing Kane's death.

0:05:32   Text: description of Kane ("To forty-four million U.S. news buyers . . .").

0:05:43   *New York Inquirer* building.

0:05:51   U.S. map: Kane's empire.

0:06:00   Montage of Kane investments: grocery store, paper mill, apartment buildings, factory, lumber cutting, ocean liner (six shots).

0:06:10   Photo: Colorado Lode Mine Co.

0:06:13   Montage of gold refining (four shots).

0:06:20   Photo: sign at Colorado state line indicating three miles to Little Salem.

0:06:22   Photo: young Kane and Mary Kane.

0:06:27   Painting: Mrs. Kane's Boarding House.

0:06:33   Gold poured into bars.

0:06:37   U.S. Capitol building.

0:06:40   Walter Thatcher testifies before a congressional committee; calls Kane a Communist (five shots).

0:07:35   Shots of outdoor crowd (two shots).

0:07:44   Speaker calls Kane "a Fascist."

0:07:50   Kane at press conference.

0:07:53   Text: quote from Kane ("I am . . . an American").

0:07:57   Kane congratulated at press conference.

0:08:04   Text: ("1895 to 1941—All of these years he covered . . .").

0:08:09   Old newsreel footage: Spanish-American War.

0:08:12   World War I cemetery.

0:08:15   Kane with Theodore Roosevelt on train.

0:08:18   Anti-Kane rally.

0:08:23   Kane effigy burning (two shots).

0:08:26   Newspaper presses.

0:08:33   Montage of Kane with political leaders: Theodore Roosevelt, Neville Chamberlain, Latin American military officers, Hitler (four shots).

0:08:48   Text: ("Few private lives were more public . . .").

0:08:52   Kane marries Emily Monroe Norton at the White House (two shots).

0:09:02   Newspaper photo: Kane, Emily, Kane III.

0:09:07   Newsreel footage: Kane marries Susan Alexander at Trenton Town Hall (two shots).

0:09:20   Poster: Susan Alexander opera performance.

0:09:22   Opera program for *Salammbô*.

0:09:26   Drawing: Chicago Opera House.

0:09:31   Photo: Kane, Susan, and guests on Xanadu terrace.

0:09:39   Photo: Xanadu exterior.

0:09:44   Text: ("In politics—always a bridesmaid . . .").

0:09:47   Newsreel footage: Kane campaign speech.

0:09:52   Exterior shot of Madison Square Garden, 1916.

0:09:55   Newspaper presses (two shots).

0:10:01   "Kane for Governor" campaign rally.

0:10:07   Newsreel footage: Kane congratulated after speech.

0:10:09   Outdoor political rally.

0:10:10   Fireworks.

0:10:11   Newsreel footage: Kane shakes hands with audience.

0:10:15   *Chronicle* headline: CANDIDATE KANE CAUGHT IN LOVE NEST WITH "SINGER" (two shots).

0:10:29 1929 photo: Factory closed.

0:10:31 Closed gate with water tower in background.

0:10:33 *St. Louis Inquirer* entrance with CLOSED sign.

0:10:38 CLOSED sign painted on warehouse door.

0:10:40 U.S. map: the Kane empire collapses.

0:10:47 Text: ("But America still reads Kane newspapers . . .").

0:10:52 Kane gives shipboard newsreel interview, 1935; "there'll be no war" (two shots).

0:11:40 Newsreel outtakes: Kane lays cornerstone (two shots).

0:11:55 Candid: Kane writing by Xanadu swimming pool.

0:12:02 Candid: Kane in wheelchair on Xanadu grounds (four shots).

0:12:19 New York news ticker ("Charles Foster Kane Is Dead").

0:12:26 *News on the March* end title; the film ends (four shots).

The Projection Room—Interior, New York City

0:12:33 Rawlston talks about the newsreel with his reporters; discusses Kane's life; looks for an angle; wonders about the importance of Kane's dying words; assigns Thompson to learn the identity of Rosebud (eight shots).

El Rancho Nightclub—Exterior, Atlantic City

0:14:22 The nightclub wall, roof, and skylight in the rain; the shot descends through the skylight into the club.

El Rancho Nightclub—Interior
(Thompson's first meeting with Susan Alexander)

0:14:48 Thompson arrives; Susan, drunk, orders him out.

0:16:09 Thompson reports to Rawlston; talks to John the waiter about Rosebud; learns from John that Susan knows nothing about Rosebud.

Thatcher Library—Interior, Philadelphia
(Walter P. Thatcher's memoirs and his recollections of Kane)

0:17:19   Statue of Walter Parks Thatcher.

0:17:28   Miss Anderson instructs Thompson about using Thatcher's memoirs.

0:17:53   Thompson enters the vault room.

0:18:35   Thompson reads Thatcher's memoirs.

0:18:41   Handwriting: ("I first encountered Mr. Kane in 1871 . . .").

Mary Kane's Boarding House—Exterior, Little Salem, Colorado

0:18:58   Young Kane in the snow.

0:19:05   Snowball hits the boardinghouse sign.

Mary Kane's Boarding House—Interior and Exterior

0:19:07   Young Kane plays in the snow, seen through the window; Jim Kane
          argues with Mary Kane and Thatcher about assigning guardianship of
          Charles to a bank; Mary signs the guardianship papers.

0:20:53   Mary calls to young Kane through the window; Thatcher meets Kane,
          and the boy learns about his future; Kane strikes Thatcher with his
          sled; Jim Kane says Charles "needs a good thrashing"; Mary declares
          that she is sending away young Kane to keep his father from "getting
          at him" (two shots).

Mary Kane's Boarding House—Exterior

0:22:53   The sled lies in a snowstorm; the train whistles in the distance (two
          shots).

Kane's New Home, Christmas—Interior, New York

0:23:07   With Thatcher, young Kane unwraps a new sled.

Thatcher's Office, seventeen years later—Interior, New York

0:23:18   Thatcher dictates a letter to Kane about his fortune.

0:23:48   Thatcher receives a letter from Kane ("I think it would be fun to run a newspaper").

Montage: Thatcher reads the *Inquirer,* New York

0:24:13   Thatcher reads the *Inquirer*'s coverage of traction trust scandals; on train, at home, outside, at office, at breakfast (seven shots).

The *New York Inquirer*—Newsroom

0:24:44   Thatcher holds an *Inquirer* with the headline "Galleons of Spain off Jersey Coast; he and Kane argue about the *Inquirer* and its irresponsible policies; Bernstein and Leland are introduced; Thatcher points out that Kane is the chief critic of the Public Transit Company—as well as one of its major stockholders; Thatcher reminds Kane that the *Inquirer* is losing $1 million a year; Kane says, "I'll have to close this place in . . . sixty years" (two shots).

Thatcher's Memoirs

0:27:15   Close-up of memoir page ("In the winter of 1929 . . .").

Thatcher's Office—Interior, New York

0:27:23   Bernstein reads from financial agreement; Kane signs over control of his empire to Thatcher's bank; Kane discusses what his life might have been.

Thatcher Library—Interior, Philadelphia

0:29:44 Thompson stops reading Thatcher's memoirs; departs the Thatcher Library (two shots).

Bernstein's Office—Interior, New York
(Thompson's interviews with Bernstein)

0:30:16 Bernstein and Thompson talk about Rosebud; Bernstein remembers a girl on the ferry, describes Thatcher, Kane, and Leland; the flashback begins.

The *New York Inquirer*—Exterior Street

0:33:00 Kane and Leland arrive at the *Inquirer;* Bernstein arrives with Kane's belongings.

The *New York Inquirer*—Newsroom

0:33:33 Kane and Leland enter the *Inquirer* newsroom; meet editor Herbert Carter (two shots).
0:34:40 Bernstein crashes through doorway with boxes and furniture.
0:34:45 Kane announces he will live in Carter's office.

The *New York Inquirer*—Kane's Office

0:35:38 Kane and Carter argue about the content of the *Inquirer;* "if the headline is big enough, it makes the news big enough" (eleven shots).

The *New York Inquirer*—Exterior of Kane's Office

0:37:14 Carter leaves the building; refuses to buy a copy of the *Inquirer.*
0:37:24 Exterior of *Inquirer* building.

0:37:29   Exterior of *Inquirer* window; Kane writes against the glass while Leland looks out.

The *New York Inquirer*—Interior of Kane's Office

0:37:39   Kane continues to write; Leland and Bernstein talk about their first edition; Kane completes his "Declaration of Principles"; Kane tells Solly to remake the front page—again; Leland asks to keep the declaration (three shots).

The *New York Inquirer*—Loading Dock

0:39:43   Close-up of the "Declaration of Principles" on the front of the *Inquirer;* shot pulls back to show bundles of *Inquirer*s.

0:39:57   Kane, Leland, and Bernstein look out of the front window of the *Inquirer;* watch newsboys carrying away bundles of their first edition (shown in reflection).

The *New York Chronicle*—Front Window

0:40:05   Kane, Leland, and Bernstein discuss the success of the *Chronicle;* Bernstein points at the photo of the *Chronicle* staff (two shots).

The *New York Inquirer*—Newsroom

0:40:31   Six years later: The *Chronicle* photo shown above dissolves to a photo session of the same men, now in the newsroom of the *Inquirer;* Kane announces that the *Inquirer*'s circulation is the greatest in New York.

0:40:56   Party for the *Inquirer* staff: Kane announces he will take a vacation; Kane and Bernstein talk about statues and promises; Kane whistles; the band and dancing girls arrive; Kane asks Leland if the U.S. is going to declare war on Spain (thirteen shots).

0:42:30   "Charlie Kane" song; Kane dances (twenty-one shots).

0:43:50   Leland and Bernstein discuss the *Inquirer*'s policies, with Kane visible in reflection; Leland points out that the reporters might change Kane (fourteen shots).

0:45:09   Kane poses with the dancing girls; song ends.

The *New York Inquirer*—Outer Newsroom Office

0:45:12   Bernstein enters the outer office with cable from Kane.

The *New York Inquirer*—Interior Office

0:45:24   Bernstein tells Leland about a cable from Kane stating that the publisher wants to buy the world's biggest diamond; they discuss why Leland didn't go to Europe; Bernstein realizes that Kane is "collecting someone who's collecting diamonds" (two shots).

The *New York Inquirer*—Newsroom and Exterior Window

0:46:18   Bernstein reads the inscription on a "Welcome Home" trophy for Kane; Kane returns, gives the society editor an announcement, exits with trophy (two shots).

0:47:16   Copy boy calls the staff to the window; society editor reads announcement that Kane is engaged to Emily Monroe Norton; Leland and Bernstein look out window; Kane sits down in carriage with Emily, drives away (six shots).

The *New York Inquirer*—Exterior Window and *Inquirer* Sign

0:47:49   Leland and Bernstein wave from window.

0:47:51   *Inquirer* staff waves from windows; the flashback ends.

Bernstein's Office—Interior

0:47:55 Bernstein tells Thompson that Emily was "no Rosebud"; wonders if Rosebud was something Kane lost; recommends that Thompson see Leland; Thompson tells Bernstein that Leland is in the hospital; Bernstein says old age is "the only disease . . . you don't look forward to being cured of."

Huntington Memorial Hospital—Exterior, 180th Street, New York

0:49:24 Thompson looks up at the exterior of the hospital.

Huntington Memorial Hospital—Terrace (Thompson's interview with Leland)

0:49:35 Leland talks about Kane—their friendship, Kane's "private sort of greatness," his lack of convictions; asks Thompson for a cigar; says he doesn't believe the *Inquirer;* describes Kane's relationship with Emily; the flashback begins.

Kane Residence—Breakfast Room, New York

0:51:53 The breakfast table montage; six scenes depicting the peak and decline of Kane's marriage to Emily Norton (twenty-seven shots); the flashback ends.

Huntington Memorial Hospital—Terrace

0:54:08 Leland discusses Kane and love; Leland recalls Kane's description of Susan Alexander; the flashback begins.

City Street—New York

0:55:08   Susan Alexander exits a drugstore, meets Kane as he is splashed with mud by a passing wagon; Susan invites Kane to her room to clean up.

Boardinghouse—Susan's Boardinghouse Room, New York

0:56:32   Susan suffers from a toothache; Kane entertains Susan (six shots).

0:57:30   Kane makes hand shadows; Kane describes the search for his youth; Kane and Susan talk about their careers, mothers, singing; Kane asks to hear Susan sing (fourteen shots).

Boardinghouse—Parlor

0:59:59   Susan sings for Kane as the shot dissolves.

Susan's New Apartment—Living Room

1:00:20   Susan continues to sing the same aria from the previous scene, but now in her new home; Kane applauds.

Tenement Alley, New York

1:00:40   Applause transitions to a small "Kane for Governor" gathering; Leland speaks from the backseat of a convertible.

Madison Square Garden—Campaign Rally, New York

1:00:56   Kane delivers a campaign speech to huge audience; promises to fight "Boss" Jim Gettys' political machine; reaction shots of Leland, Bernstein, Emily, Kane's son (fifteen shots).

1:03:04   Gettys observes the rally conclude from the balcony.

1:03:13   Kane is congratulated by officials.

Madison Square Garden—Exterior Street

1:03:29   Kane exits the auditorium with officials; greets his son and Emily; poses for photographs; Emily sends their son home with chauffeur; asks Kane to make a call with her (thirteen shots).

Susan's Apartment Building—Exterior Doorway, 185 W. 74th Street, New York

1:04:39   Kane and Emily arrive at Susan's building; they enter.

Susan's Apartment Building—Staircase and Hallway

1:04:58   Kane and Emily walk up to Susan's apartment; Gettys appears; Kane threatens Gettys (two shots).

Susan's Apartment—Interior

1:05:51   Emily reads a note about Kane and Susan; Gettys threatens to blackmail Kane; Kane refuses to drop out of the election (eight shots).

Susan's Apartment Building—Hallway and Staircase

1:09:34   Kane screams that he will send Gettys to Sing Sing Prison (four shots).

Susan's Apartment Building—Exterior Doorway

1:09:44   Gettys closes the door; asks Emily if she has a car; both walk away.

The *New York Chronicle* Front Page

1:10:04   A freeze frame of the door to Susan's apartment building becomes the front page of the *Chronicle;* headline reads, CANDIDATE KANE CAUGHT IN LOVE NEST WITH "SINGER."

Saloon—Exterior, New York

1:10:13   Leland refuses a *Chronicle* offered by a newsboy; enters saloon.

The *New York Inquirer*—Pressroom

1:10:28   Bernstein chooses the front-page headline for its election edition: FRAUD AT POLLS.

The *New York Inquirer*/Kane Campaign Headquarters—Exterior

1:10:47   Leland steps past a discarded *Inquirer;* throws away his cigar while street sweeper watches.

The *New York Inquirer*—Newsroom

1:11:08   Bernstein says good night to the campaign staff and Kane, then exits. Leland enters; Kane and Leland argue about Kane's motives for wanting to serve the people; Leland talks about the workingman and organized labor and their effect on Kane; Leland asks for a transfer to Chicago; Kane toasts "love on my terms" (three shots).

Headline

1:15:28   KANE MARRIES SINGER.

Town Hall—Exterior, Trenton, New Jersey

1:15:31   Kane and Susan exit Town Hall after marriage; Kane announces that Susan is going to be an opera star; says it won't be necessary to build an opera house.

Headline

1:16:07   KANE BUILDS OPERA HOUSE.

Chicago Opera House—Stage

1:16:12   Backstage panic; Susan rehearses just before performance; Matiste instructs while the stage is prepared; the performance begins (three shots).

Chicago Opera House—Rafters

1:17:10   The camera moves up through the rafters and ropes; a stagehand looks at his colleague and pinches his nose (three shots: live shot transitions to miniature, back to live shot).

The *Chicago Inquirer*—City Room

1:17:34   Bernstein checks on preparations for the newspaper's opera coverage; Kane enters and goes to Leland's office (two shots).

The *Chicago Inquirer*—Leland's Office

1:19:15   Bernstein sees Leland drunk and unconscious at his typewriter; Bernstein reads part of the negative review; Kane asks for a typewriter to finish the review as Leland started it (twelve shots).

Close-up—Page in a Typewriter

1:20:58 Typed letters: "weak."

The *Chicago Inquirer*—Leland's Office

1:21:01 Leland awakens; Bernstein lights his cigar, tells Leland that Kane is finishing his review just as Leland started it (two shots).

The *Chicago Inquirer*—City Room

1:22:13 Kane types the review; Kane fires Leland; Leland walks out; the flashback ends (two shots).

Huntington Memorial Hospital—Terrace

1:23:00 Leland continues his recollection (inset shot of Kane in the right frame); Leland says that Kane "was always trying to prove something"; Leland admits that he refused to respond to Kane's letter; talks about Kane's reasons for building Xanadu; asks Thompson to send him cigars; Leland is escorted away by nurses.

El Rancho Nightclub—Exterior Roof, Atlantic City, New Jersey

1:25:16 The shot travels over the roof and through the skylight.

El Rancho Nightclub—Interior (Thompson's second interview with Susan Alexander)

1:25:33 Susan talks about Kane, her singing, Kane's motivations; the flashback begins.

Kane Residence—Music Room, New York

1:26:41   Susan rehearses while Matiste instructs and Kane watches; Susan sings a note off-key; Matiste says she cannot be taught; Kane insists that the lessons continue.

Chicago Opera House—Stage

1:29:09   Susan rehearses at the last second as the opera begins; the curtain rises; Susan's view of the opera hall and audience; Kane watches; Leland looks bored; Matiste instructs from the prompter's box; Bernstein dozes; Leland shreds his program; Kane reacts to someone saying "perfectly dreadful"; the performance ends with scattered applause; Bernstein and cronies applaud loudly; Susan bows and struggles with bouquets; Kane sits motionless until the applause dies, then he applauds (thirty-six shots).

The *Chicago Inquirer* Drama Page—Close-Up

1:32:40   Leland's "Stage Views" column (two shots).

Hotel Suite—Interior, Chicago

1:32:46   Susan screams at Kane about Leland's review; Kane winces; messenger arrives with an envelope; Kane opens the envelope and finds Leland's $25,000 severance check in pieces and Kane's original "Declaration of Principles"; Kane calls the document "an antique" and tears it up; Susan declares she will refuse to sing; Kane insists she will continue (twenty-six shots).

Montage—Susan's Opera Career

1:34:44   Montage: Kane newspaper coverage of Susan's performances; opera audiences; Matiste prompts, Susan sings; Kane reactions; a lightbulb dims (twenty shots plus newspaper overlays).

Susan's Bedroom—Kane Residence, New York

1:35:27   Susan in bed, breathing weakly; bottle, spoon, and glass in foreground; Kane and a servant break in; Kane orders the servant to call a doctor.

1:36:18   Susan in bed after treatment; Dr. Corey tells Kane that Susan will recover; Kane asks to stay.

1:36:59   Kane watches Susan; Susan awakens and explains that she attempted suicide because of the ridicule of her singing; Kane agrees to let her stop performing (five shots).

Xanadu—Exterior, Night

1:38:20   Long shot of Xanadu under construction.

1:38:24   Close-up shot of Xanadu under construction.

Xanadu—The Great Hall

1:38:29   Susan works on a puzzle; Kane comments about the *Inquirer* "bulldog" edition going to press; Susan complains about being lonely and asks to go to New York; Kane refuses; Susan returns to her puzzle.

1:40:20   Montage: Susan works on puzzles (six shots).

1:40:40   Another day years later: Kane walks down stairs; asks Susan about her puzzles; Kane orders Susan and guests to go on a picnic (nine shots).

Kane Limousine—Driving to Picnic

1:41:38   Susan tells Kane he never gives her anything she cares about.

Florida Beach Road

1:41:46   Caravan of cars traveling to the picnic.

Kane's Everglades Picnic—Exterior

1:41:53   Blues performer sings "It Can't Be Love" lyrics from "In a Mizz"; dancers, barbecue; Raymond supervises.

Kane's Tent—Interior

1:42:25   Kane and Susan argue; Susan says, "You just tried to buy me into giving you something" (nine shots).

Picnic—Exterior

1:43:02   Guests gather around musicians, singing and clapping.

Kane's Tent—Interior

1:43:10   Kane and Susan continue to argue; Susan realizes that Kane doesn't love her, but he will give her anything if she loves him; Kane slaps Susan; a woman screams outside; Susan says, "Don't tell me you're sorry"; Kane says, "I'm not sorry" (ten shots).

Xanadu—Walkway Above the Great Hall

1:43:49   Raymond the butler tells Kane that Susan wants to see him, and she is packing to leave.

Xanadu—Susan's Room

1:44:11   Susan says good-bye; Kane begs her to say; she weakens until he says, "You can't do this to me"; Susan exits; the flashback ends (eleven shots).

El Rancho Nightclub—Interior

1:46:17   Susan talks about losing her money; Thompson describes his trip to Xanadu; Susan suggests that he talk to Raymond; Thompson says he feels sorry for Kane; Susan replies, "Don't you think I do?"

El Rancho Nightclub—Exterior

1:47:06   The roof at dawn.

Xanadu—Front Gate, Florida Gulf Coast

1:47:10   Main gate with *K* at top.

Xanadu—Great Hall Stairway
(Thompson's interview with Raymond the butler)

1:47:13   Raymond asks Thompson for $1,000 for the story of Rosebud; talks about Kane's behavior; the flashback begins (two shots).

Xanadu—Patio

1:48:05   A cockatoo screeching; Raymond watches Susan depart.

Xanadu—Entrance to Corridor

1:48:14   Raymond looks at Kane standing in the doorway of Susan's bedroom.

Xanadu—Susan's Bedroom

1:48:18   Kane stands in the doorway; returns to room; closes suitcase; throws suitcases; destroys bedroom; sees and picks up the snow globe; walks to the door, stands in the doorway, says, "Rosebud" (seven shots).

Xanadu—Susan's Room and the Corridor Outside

1:50:30   Raymond looks in at Kane in doorway; Raymond, staff, and guests watch Kane as he leaves Susan's bedroom with the snow globe (two shots).

Xanadu—Corridor with Mirrors

1:51:06   Kane walks past mirrors; infinite reflections; the flashback ends.

Xanadu—Great Hall Stairway

1:51:27   Raymond says he heard Kane say "Rosebud" when he died; Thompson says his story isn't worth $1,000; walks down the stairs.

Xanadu—Great Hall

1:52:09   Reporters take pictures of Kane's treasures (three shots).
1:52:37   Thompson and Raymond talk about the value of Kane's collection; reporters comment about treasures and junk; reporters ask Thompson about Rosebud; Thompson describes Kane as a man "who got everything he wanted and then lost it"; calls Rosebud a piece in a jigsaw puzzle, "a missing piece" (four shots).
1:54:48   The camera moves over a sea of crates and boxes toward the early mementos from Kane's life; a workman picks up a sled (two shots).

Xanadu—Incinerator Room

1:55:47   Raymond directs the burning of Kane's junk; a workman throws the sled on the fire.

Xanadu—Incinerator

1:56:01   Close-up of Rosebud lettering on the burning sled; the letters disappear in the flames.

Xanadu—Exterior

1:56:25   Xanadu chimney and smoke.
1:56:43   Chain-link fence
1:56:48   "No Trespassing" sign.
1:56:59   Main gate with *K* at top and Xanadu in background with chimney smoke.
1:57::04 "The End."
1:57:11   Fade to black.

Credits

1:57:13   Introduction text for the credits.
1:57:22   Credits with vignettes of the principal actors
          (Joseph Cotten, Dorothy Comingore, Agnes Moorehead, Ruth Warrick, Ray Collins, Erskine Sanford, Everett Sloane, William Alland, Paul Stewart, George Coulouris).
1:58:25   Credit list of the other actors.
1:58:42   Production team credits.
1:59:18   RKO logo.
1:59:21   Fade to black.
1:59:23   Disc ends.

THE BUDGET

These budget figures from RKO's financial report dated March 8, 1941, compare the original budget estimates for *Citizen Kane* with the actual costs absorbed by the studio. Although other expenses were associated with the film during its original release—such as preparing prints of the film for distribution to theaters—this tabulation represents the budget for the actual production of the motion picture.

Today, with film costs routinely topping $50 million, and often much more, it seems hard to appreciate RKO's fussiness in 1940 over a budget that totaled little more than $600,000 in direct expenses. Even requests for additional expenses as small as $10 were itemized by the Mercury staff and approved by RKO management.

RKO may have been concerned about Welles' spending habits, but the single largest category in the budget of *Citizen Kane* was "Indirect Costs," the 20 percent studio surcharge for overhead and administration that was added to the cost of every production. All charges, including those that did not require studio facilities, such as salaries—or such incidentals as the $2,400 payment to Everett Sloane for shaving his head—added an additional 20 percent to the cost of making the film.

Even with indirect costs included, Welles' spending on *Citizen Kane* exceeded his budget target by only 12 percent.

Category	Budget	Actual
Supervision	$81,493.00	$ 83,015.27
Screenplay	34,317.00	34,195.24
Directors	——	458.33
Cast	68,048.00	87,633.68
Extras	13,557.00	16,943.53
Production Staff	16,376.00	18,183.20
Camera Staff	24,270.00	26,684.58
Sound Recording	6,752.00	9,400.74
Film & Laboratory	18,117.00	20,988.94
Set Design & Artwork	12,000.00	15,350.13
Set Construction	58,775.00	59,206.23
Set Maintenance	4,000.00	3,981.17
Set Standby Labor	12,500.00	14,653.71
Set Striking	6,500.00	6,541.43
Properties & Drapery	21,913.00	29,355.18
Lighting	19,895.00	24,171.60
Wardrobe	15,766.00	17,241.64
Makeup	15,586.00	13,675.10
Transportation	14,782.00	11,189.98
Location	1,759.00	1,845.77
Special Effects	2,698.00	5,493.79
Editing	9,560.00	12,132.33
Musical Score	22,464.00	35,435.86
Scoring: Sound & Laboratory	1,788.00	3,582.43
Songs	5,000.00	362.00
Rerecording	7,288.00	16,761.37
Process	24,465.00	38,048.74
Inserts	4,780.00	7,905.84
Main & End Titles	750.00	970.40
Checkup & Master Prints	1,000.00	1,902.88
Tests	20,000.00	16,425.18
Stills	2,463.00	2,854.26
Special Taxes	13,000.00	14,405.28
Insurance	9,000.00	7,952.31
Royalties & Code Certificate	7,005.00	——

Category	Budget	Actual
Miscellaneous	25,500.00	24,811.07
Labor Adjustments	——	2,274.19
Total Direct Costs	**$603,167.00**	**$686,033.38**
Indirect Costs (20%)	**$120,633.00**	**$137,206.67**
Total Picture Cost	**$723,800.00**	**$823,240.05**

RKO SOUNDSTAGES

RKO (Culver City) Stages

The RKO soundstages on Washington Boulevard in Culver City, now part of the Culver Studios, are identified with the same numbers today as in 1940. Here are the soundstages used for *Citizen Kane:*

Thatcher montage 3
Opera scenes
Xanadu, interior corridor

Thatcher's office, 1929 7
Bernstein's office
New York Inquirer exterior street
New York Inquirer building exterior
New York Chronicle office window
Kane and Emily's breakfast room
Madison Square Garden, interior
Xanadu furnace room

Mary Kane's Boarding House 8

Saloon exterior 9

New York Inquirer newsroom 11
Kane's *Inquirer* office
Susan's second apartment and hallway
Madison Square Garden, exterior
New York City street and Susan's boardinghouse
Kane and Susan's picnic tent
Susan's bedroom, Xanadu
Kane's *Inquirer* office window, exterior

Senate investigation room.. 12

Thatcher's office, 1898 14
Thatcher montage—train, breakfast, office

Paramount Stages

In 1967, the main RKO lot at Melrose Avenue and Gower Street in Hollywood—then part of the Desilu Productions organization owned by Lucille Ball—was purchased by Gulf & Western, at the time the parent company of Paramount Pictures. The two production facilities were merged under the Paramount banner, and the RKO soundstages were renumbered.

If you visit Paramount Pictures today and want to see the soundstages where *Citizen Kane* was filmed, here is how the old RKO stage numbers used in this book match up to the new ones:

	RKO	Paramount
Rerecording	2A	24A
El Rancho nightclub	2B	24
City room, *Chicago Inquirer*		
Leland's office, *Chicago Inquirer*		
Chicago hotel room		
Susan's bedroom (suicide attempt)		
Thatcher Library	3	25
Susan's first apartment	4	26

	RKO	Paramount
Xanadu terrace		
Welles' makeup and wardrobe tests	7	29
Car interior (Kane and Susan)		
Hospital roof (Leland interview)	10	32
Florida picnic		
Great Hall of Xanadu		
Kane's bedroom		

RKO Projection Room 4, where Rawlston ordered Thompson to learn about Rosebud, is now an office on the Paramount lot.

RESOURCES ABOUT ORSON WELLES AND *CITIZEN KANE*

There is no shortage of material in print and online for those who want to explore the life of Orson Welles and the creation of *Citizen Kane*. With apologies to those not mentioned, here are several recommended resources.

Archives

Several archives contain extensive collections of material about *Citizen Kane* and the career of Orson Welles:

The principal collection of Orson Welles' papers is housed in the Lilly Library at Indiana University, Bloomington. This collection includes some twenty thousand items regarding Welles' work in entertainment and politics, including correspondence, memos, script drafts, and photographs. Featured prominently in the collection is extensive material about Welles' early career and *Citizen Kane;* especially interesting is the correspondence from lawyer L. Arnold Weissberger, publicist Herb Drake, and Welles regarding the controversy with the Hearst organization over the attempts to suppress the film—some of which is featured in this book (indiana.edu/~liblilly/guides/welles/orsonwelles.html).

The Special Collections Library at the University of Michigan, Ann Arbor, holds the personal papers of Richard Wilson, assistant producer of *Citizen Kane* and a longtime Welles associate. Among the jewels found within the sixty-three linear feet of the Richard Wilson–Orson Welles Papers, 1930–2000, are two folders titled "Late Draft," which include the final-draft eighty-seven-page shooting script for *Citizen Kane* (quod.lib.umich.edu/s/sclead/browse.html, under "Film, Theatre, & Television").

The UCLA Library Special Collections in Los Angeles contains some production files for *Citizen Kane* from the RKO studio archives, including draft scripts of *American* and *Citizen Kane,* daily shooting reports, set drawings, notes, memos, musical scores, and budget information. UCLA Library Special Collections also holds the personal papers of John Houseman (for details on the collections, use the search feature at library.ucla.edu/).

The Margaret Herrick Library of the Academy of Motion Picture Arts and Sciences maintains a large collection of photographs from *Citizen Kane,* as well as files of notes and clippings about the film. The Herrick Library, located in Beverly Hills, California, also has collections of *Variety* (in print) and *The Hollywood Reporter* (microfilm), including the key years of 1939–1942 that cover Orson Welles' early career in Hollywood and the controversy surrounding the release of *Citizen Kane* (www.oscars.org/library).

The library system at the University of Southern California (USC) in Los Angeles holds two particularly interesting resources. The first is the personal collection of Joseph Cotten, which includes six scrapbooks of material and photos—among them publicity stills that show the deleted scenes from *Citizen Kane* that were set in the brothel (usc.edu/libraries/finding_aids/records/finding_aid.php?fa=2115). The second resource, the USC Digital Library, offers online access to one of the most useful documents on *Citizen Kane:* the master's thesis written by Donald Rea, *A Critical-Historical Account of the Planning, Production, and Release of* Citizen Kane. Written at the twenty-fifth anniversary of the release of the film in 1966, Rea's thesis is a thoroughly researched, fact-filled document that also includes interviews with many who participated in the film's creation (digitallibrary.usc.edu; search on "Donald W. Rea").

Books About Orson Welles

Perhaps more is written about Orson Welles than any other director. While every year new volumes appear that focus on specific aspects of Welles' life and work, five books have endured as being particularly illuminating:

This Is Orson Welles, the collected interviews with Welles by director Peter Bogdanovich, offers candid insight into the highlights of Welles' life and films, as gathered by Bogdanovich in an entertaining series of interviews conducted around the world. *Citizen Welles* by Frank Brady was the first and perhaps the most comprehensive biography of Welles' entire life. *Orson Welles: The Road to Xanadu* by Simon Callow provides an extremely detailed, often amusingly subjective view of Welles' life from birth through the release of *Citizen Kane;* (Callow's second volume, *Hello Americans,* is just as enlightening while exploring the darker moments of Welles' early career between the release of *Citizen Kane* through the production of *Macbeth* in 1948.) Barbara Leaming's biography, *Orson Welles,* is a particularly intimate portrait; at Welles' suggestion, Leaming featured details of her own encounters and conversations with Welles that occurred during her research and writing of the book.

Books, Articles, and Unpublished Material About *Citizen Kane* and RKO

The most detailed academic study about *Citizen Kane* is *The Making of* Citizen Kane by Robert Carringer. In addition to Carringer's thorough scholarly perspective about the creation of *Citizen Kane,* the book contains background about Gregg Toland's work that preceded his collaboration with Welles and a chapter about *The Magnificent Ambersons.* The book also includes an exhaustive analysis of the draft scripts, the best published collection of preproduction drawings, and the most extensive bibliography of *Citizen Kane*–related material available.

While one could spend months exploring articles about *Citizen Kane,* two of Carringer's are particularly instructive: his two articles for *Critical Inquiry.* The initial article offers a superb analysis of the first seven script drafts of *Citizen Kane* (*Critical Inquiry* 5, no. 2 [Winter 1978]), and the second explores the creative relationship between Welles and Gregg Toland (*Critical Inquiry* 8, no. 4 [Summer 1982]). The articles are available on the *Critical Inquiry* Web site (criticalinquiry .uchicago.edu; search on "Robert Carringer").

Two books by Ronald Gottesman provide comprehensive collections of articles, reviews, and new material that analyze and appraise *Citizen Kane:* his 1971 book, *Focus on* Citizen Kane, and his much expanded 1996 work, *Perspectives on* Citizen Kane. Among the many highlights in Gottesman's 1996 volume are reviews, critical essays, and Robert Carringer's study of the script drafts.

Another compilation of material, ***Orson Welles' Citizen Kane: A Casebook*** by James Naremore, features many essays, interviews, and excerpts of other works.

Two unpublished research projects are excellent resources: the previously mentioned ***A Critical-Historical Account of the Planning, Production, and Release of* Citizen Kane** by Donald Rea (digitallibrary.usc.edu; search on "Donald W. Rea"); and Richard Jewell's Ph.D. thesis, ***A History of RKO Radio Pictures, Incorporated, 1928–1942***. Much of Jewell's material and other research is contained in his published books, ***The RKO Story*** and ***RKO Radio Pictures: A Titan Is Born***.

For views on *Citizen Kane* from the perspective of two principals associated with the production, see Joseph Cotten's autobiography, ***Vanity Will Get You Somewhere,*** which includes material, although not always accurate, about the actor's work on *Citizen Kane* and his friendship with Orson Welles; and ***Mank: The Wit, World, and Life of Herman Mankiewicz*** by Richard Meryman, which features a wealth of details about Mankiewicz's work on the *Citizen Kane* script.

Orson Welles and Pre–*Citizen Kane* Films

The Hearts of Age (Welles' short film made at the Todd School when he was nineteen) and *Too Much Johnson* (his abortive film project to accompany his stage production of William Gillette's comedy) are in the public domain and available for free online; the full eight-minute *The Hearts of Age,* as well as the uncut footage of *Too Much Johnson,* can be viewed on YouTube (search by their titles).

An edited version of the *Too Much Johnson* footage, based on notes by Welles from the Mercury Theatre files, can be viewed or downloaded from the National Film Preservation Foundation at www.filmpreservation.org. Also on the foundation's site is an excerpt of film from the family of Myron Falk (an investor in the Mercury Theatre) that shows Welles on location directing *Too Much Johnson*—the first footage of Welles directing a film.

Welles' 1937 Screen Test—Available Online

A clip from Welles' hammy screen test shot by Warner Bros. in 1937 is available on many Web sites and on YouTube; search on "Welles 1937 screen test."

Special Effects

In the 1970s, Linwood Dunn was a popular speaker at college film programs, and examples of his special effects presented at these lectures are available on YouTube (some come and go depending on copyright enforcement) and other Web sites. For instance, Critical Commons, a public media archive, features clips of Dunn's work that showcase the use of effects in the predigital world. Included are demonstrations of how optical effects were made for *Bringing Up Baby* and other films from the 1940s, as well as copies of some of Dunn's notes (at www .criticalcommons.org, search on "dunn" only). Shots from *Citizen Kane* are included on the site, but only as examples of scenes that required special effects.

Web Sites

The list of Web sites devoted to Orson Welles and *Citizen Kane* is nearly endless; here are several starting points that will lead a discriminating Welles enthusiast in the right direction. First, the entry on *Citizen Kane* in the *AFI Catalog of Feature Films* is especially comprehensive. (Go to afi.com, choose "catalog," and then "Citizen Kane"; be sure to select the "Movie Detail" view and not the "Summary" view.)

Wellesnet.com, which bills itself as "the leading online source of information about the life, career, and work of Orson Welles," is indeed a reliable focal point for online study. The site also includes a long list of other Web sites and links to Welles-related news. Also useful is orsonwelles.org, which includes interesting summaries of Welles' career in a variety of formats (flipcard, timeslide, etc.).

The Wikipedia entry on *Citizen Kane* is comprehensive and especially handy for its rollover links to other sources. Wikipedia also maintains lengthy lists of Welles' credits in radio, film, and theater.

Note: As mentioned elsewhere in this book, information found online about classic films can be unreliable because much of it circulates without attribution and then recirculates endlessly as if true. Given the large amount of subjective material and analysis of *Citizen Kane* on the Internet, and Welles' colorful storytelling and deliberately liberal interpretation of his life and work, this problem is especially acute when seeking information about this film. If you extend your searches beyond the Web sites previously listed here, use discretion before assuming that information about *Citizen Kane* found online is correct.

Video

Thousands of clips of Welles—including many discussions of *Citizen Kane*—are available online. On YouTube, clips abound of filmmakers talking about *Citizen Kane*, including a series of videos posted by the American Film Institute showing actors and directors such as Martin Scorsese, Steven Spielberg, and others discussing the impact of the film on their own careers. Also on YouTube are many clips of fine opera singers brilliantly performing the pieces that Susan Alexander vainly attempted: Rossini's "Una voce poco fa" from *The Barber of Seville* and the arias from the Bernard Herrmann–composed opera, "*Salammbô.*"

A documentary that provides an objective look at the making of the film is *The Complete Citizen Kane,* an Arena production produced in the United Kingdom. Originally developed for the fiftieth anniversary of the film and now available sporadically online, the documentary takes a journey through the events in Welles' life leading up to his arrival in Hollywood as well as the making of the film. The beginning of *The Complete Citizen Kane* is especially intriguing; it features the opening scene of *Heart of Darkness* as Welles might have produced it, using re-creations of models based on RKO's original drawings, Bernard Herrmann's music from *Citizen Kane,* and Welles' own narration from the radio broadcast of Joseph Conrad's story. Also scattered throughout *The Complete Citizen Kane* is William Alland's narration, spoken in the style he used in 1941 for *News on the March.*

Some other videos and docudramas that supposedly chronicle the story of *Citizen Kane* are nothing more than opinions and speculation—including the idea that Kane and Hearst were somehow predestined by fate to clash. These are of little use, and have received the critical drubbing they deserve.

NOTES

In addition to references for the sources used in this book, this section includes the time in *Citizen Kane* of every scene mentioned in the text. The times are based on the 2011 Blu-ray of *Citizen Kane;* for the conventional DVD of the film, subtract approximately three seconds from each notation.

For the three archives cited most often in these notes, I used these abbreviations:

Bancroft   William Randolph Hearst Papers, Bancroft Library, University of California, Berkeley.

Lilly   Orson Welles Collections, Mercury Productions Files, Lilly Library, Indiana University, Bloomington.

UCLA   RKO Radio Pictures Studio Records (Collection PASC 3), UCLA Library Special Collections, Charles E. Young Research Library, UCLA, Los Angeles.

PART ONE

Chapter One: Asking for the Impossible

3 "There but for the grace of God goes God"   *New York Times,* October 11, 1985
4 "Were Welles' 23 years"   *Time,* May 9, 1938
5 "The word 'genius'"   Orson Welles Interview, BBC

5 "arrived in Kenosha" — Maurice Bernstein letter to Herb Drake, November 29, 1939, Lilly

5 While attending camp as a ten-year-old — Brady

5 "In some ways" — Leaming

6 "I don't know what possessed me" — *Orson Welles Sketchbook*

6 "I saw this brilliant creature" — *Complete Citizen Kane*

6 in July 1934 — Orson Welles theater credits, Wikipedia

6 The production was so enthusiastically received — *New York Times,* January 17, 1937

7 "Declaration of Principles" — Welles and Houseman, *New York Times,* August 29, 1937

7 "The Mercury Theatre which John" — *New York Times,* November 12, 1937

7 "What amazed and awed me" — Houseman

7 "effortless magnificence" — Brady

7 frantic performance schedule — *Orson Welles Story,* BBC

8 Welles was chosen — Brady

8 "Marvelous Boy" — *Time,* May 9, 1938

8 "This is Orson Welles, ladies and gentlemen" — *War of the Worlds, Mercury Theatre on the Air* broadcast (the transcript of the broadcast, and the broadcast itself, are available widely online)

9 "masterful in his astonishment" — *War of the Worlds, American Experience*

9 "Don't believe everything you hear on the radio" — 0:10:57

9 "At the moment" — *War of the Worlds, American Experience*

10 Warner Bros. offered him three scripts — Brady

10 quirky piece of film — Orson Welles screen test, Warner Bros., 1937

10 Welles declined the position — Brady

10 From its creation in 1928 — Jewell/*RKO Story*

11 Among the notables — Jewell in Gottesman, *Perspectives on* Citizen Kane

11 "such a brilliant talent" — Brady

12 "a bundle of laundry" — Ruth Warrick interview with the author

12 "like meeting God" — Meryman

12 "exactly the way he would have been" — *Orson Welles and the Gate Theatre*

12 "the Christ Child" — Many references in Drake correspondence, Lilly

12 "There but for the grace of God" — *New York Times,* October 11, 1985

12 "We used to say" — Meryman

13 "Genius unchecked" — Whipple

13 "The honeymoon is over" — Brady

13 "When you don't really want to go" — *Monitor*

14 "In my case I didn't want money" — Ibid.

Chapter Two: The Beard and the Contract

15 "A genius is a crackpot on a tightrope" *Variety*

15 "each picture shall be under" Welles' contract with RKO dated July 22, 1939, Lilly

15 "control of such cutting" Ibid.

15 *"from time to time"* Ibid.

16 "being a janitor" Bogdanovich audio interview

16 "revolutions and counter-revolutions" *Monitor*

16 Welles' agreements with RKO Contracts dated July 22, 1939, Lilly, also referenced in Rea and Carringer

19 "It was both the beard" Fowler

19 "If George Schaefer had" *Hollywood Reporter,* September 26, 1939

19 Ward Bond *Orson Welles Story*

19 "King Vidor said" Leaming

20 "I would have hated" Ibid.

20 "We stared at each other" Brady

21 the maximum amount Welles Carringer

22 Welles had already gained Videos of *The Hearts of Age* and *Too Much Johnson*

23 "Going into the Maxine Elliott" Brady

24 lush Brentwood estate Leaming, among many references

24 hired researcher Miriam Geiger *Complete Citizen Kane*

25 "I screened *Stagecoach* every night" Bogdanovich audio interview

25 "Welles started work" Drake letter to Leonard Lyons, *New York Post,* September 26, 1939, Lilly

25 "I had my first night" Welles letter to Drake, October 18, 1939, Lilly

25 Welles imported from New York Mercury casting records, Lilly

26 impact of losing overseas ticket sales George Schaefer telegram to Welles, September 15, 1939, Lilly

26 "Every cent will be counted twice" Welles telegram to Schaefer, undated, September 1939, Lilly

27 "We shall have many arguments" John Houseman telegram to Welles, November 9, 1939, Lilly

27 *The Smiler with a Knife* was going to be produced Drake letter to Bernstein, December 14, 1939, Lilly

28 "We came to a parting" Houseman in *Action* magazine

28 "Orson does not think of his income" Arnold Weissberger letter to Richard Baer, December 18, 1939, Lilly

28	$800 a week	Ibid.
29	RKO commissioned Audience Research Institute	Schaefer memo to

Harry Edington, June 5, 1940,
referenced in Jewell in Gottesman, *Perspectives on* Citizen Kane

29	The top choice among viewers	Ibid.
29	survey results were presented to Schaefer	Ibid.
29	"The only way"	Ibid.
30	"Will you accept"	Meryman
31	"was a scandal"	Houseman
31	"throw-away genius"	Hecht
31	he was fired again	Meryman
31	"Like a boulder"	Meryman
31	"I can just see them"	Houseman
32	After recovering in the hospital	Meryman
32	He also toyed	Ibid.
32	The discussions began at Mankiewicz's modest house on Roxbury Drive	Ibid.
32	"Nobody was more miserable"	Bogdanovich audio interview
32	"The actual writing"	Ibid.
32	In the small bedroom	Meryman
32	"He was fun"	Ibid.
33	"I had been nursing an old notion"	Bogdanovich
33	"We discussed an unusual technique"	Meryman
33	Geraldine Fitzgerald remembered	Ibid.
33	"We started searching"	Bogdanovich
34	"an absurd venture"	Houseman

Chapter Three: The Script

35	"I don't know—I'm making it up as I go along"	Meryman
35	"Mankiewicz went to the desert"	Bogdanovich
36	"The only reason Mankiewicz was here"	Lindstrom
36	Alexander handled less traditional chores	Meryman
36	The work started in late morning	Ibid.
36	"Houseman sort of ended up riding herd"	Ibid.
36	"Towards evening around 6 o'clock"	*Complete Citizen Kane*
36	Mankiewicz tried to make light of the alcohol-free policy	Handwritten

note on the front page of an undated early draft of *Citizen Kane*,
Profiles in History; note that Mankiewicz and colleagues used both
"Manky" (used here) and Mankie" to spell his nickname

37	Mankiewicz used a snow globe	Meryman
37	"My dear Mrs. Alexander, I don't know"	Ibid.

38	Mankiewicz's script for *American*	First draft script of *American,* dated April 16, 1940, UCLA
46	*"A Sea of Upturned Faces"*	Bogdanovich audio interview
46	*"Citizen Kane* is the final title"	Collier Young memo to RKO department heads, June 11, 1940, Lilly
48	"It's still 50–60 pages longer"	RKO memo from J. R. McDonough to Schaefer, June 18, 1940 (quoted in Carringer)
48	"Herman would rather talk for three days"	Meryman
48	"It never occurs to him"	Ibid.
48	Welles and Mankiewicz often worked	Ibid.
49	"We went to Mank's garden"	Ibid.
49	"I always wanted Kane to have"	Meryman
49	"I did the breakfast table scene"	Bogdanovich/Welles
49	Mankiewicz also claimed some script victories	Meryman
49	"I wanted the man to seem"	Bogdanovich
50	"I'd call that *the* most valuable thing"	Ibid.
50	"If I were in hell and they gave me a day off"	Ibid.
50	"There is one important detail"	Letter from Joseph Breen to RKO executive J. J. Nolan, July 15, 1940, Lilly
51	$200 worth of glass bead curtains	Daily production reports, RKO production files, UCLA
51	"It will be necessary that you"	Breen to Nolan, July 15, 1940, Lilly
51	poked Bernstein in the crotch	0:45:36

Chapter Four: The Consequences of His Actions

53	I would say I wrote about"	*Lundberg v. Welles et. al.*
53	even though evidence in his own files	Leaming
53	nor did she talk	Bogdanovich and references in media coverage
54	"is in the biggest fever yet"	Drake memo to Welles, August 26, 1940, Lilly
54	"My own secretary"	Welles/*The Times* (London)
54	Houseman backpedaled considerably	*Action*
55	Mankiewicz had waived his right	Mankiewicz agreement with Mercury Productions, undated letter, Lilly
55	"enormous"	Bogdanovich audio interview
55	"Without Mank it would have been"	Meryman
55	"There is a quality in the film"	Ibid.

55 "Mankiewicz is claiming" — Weissberger letter to Baer, September 9, 1940, Lilly

55 "I feel it my modest duty to tell you" — Meryman

55 bickered for weeks — Several letters exchanged in spring 1940 by Welles and Hadley Cantril at Princeton University, Lilly

56 "It would be unwise" — Weissberger letter to Welles, October 1, 1940, Lilly

56 "Mankiewicz has conceded" — Baer letter to Weissberger, January 3, 1941, Lilly

56 if Welles wrote original material — Meryman

56 "I would say I wrote about 98 percent" — Ibid.

57 "One marvels at the debt" — Meryman

57 "The big contribution of Mankiewicz" — Bogdanovich audio interview

58 Ninety-two pages of the script — Untitled ninety-two-page excerpt script draft, Lilly

59 "Third Revised Final" — The final-draft script, the most commonly seen version, is available in Welles Papers and other archives that maintain *Kane* files, including the Lilly Library, UCLA Library Special Collections, the Academy of Motion Picture Arts and Sciences, and the Museum of Modern Art; it is also distributed widely online

60 "adept at handling" — Carringer/*Critical Inquiry 5*

60 "at last out of trial and error" — Ibid.

62 Susan is seen breathing — 1:35:27

63 interviews by Thompson with

Bernstein, — 0:30:16

Leland, — 0:49:34

Susan, — 0:14:48 and 1:25:33

and Raymond — 1:47:13

argument between Kane and Thatcher — 0:24:44

63 Bernstein's delicate recounting of his youth — 0:30:45

63 after the Madison Square Garden speech — 1:04:10

63 "What do you do on a newspaper in the middle of the night?" — 0:52:51

64 "I first encountered Mr. Kane in 1871 . . ." — 0:18:45

65 "damned man" — Bogdanovich, reprinted in Naremore

65 "In his hatred of Hearst" — Meryman

65 "My *Citizen Kane* would have" — Ibid.

65 "I don't say that Mank didn't see Kane" — Ibid.

66 "Mr. Kane was a man who got everything he wanted, and then lost it" — 1:54:09

66 Kane enters a hall of mirrors — 1:51:07

67 Jed Leland's angry outburst after Kane's election defeat   1:11:53

67 "You talk about the people as though you own them"   1:12:40

67 "A toast, Jedediah, to love on my terms"   1:15:16

68 the "basically vague" characterization   Crowther

68 "It fails to provide a clear picture"   Ibid.

Chapter Five: RKO Production #281

69 "During the shooting of *Citizen Kane*"   Cobos

69 He met with George Schaefer   Brady

70 "Orson had no doubt"   William Alland interview with the author

70 "It's the greatest railroad train"   Johnston

71 "I am dying to work there"   Cobos

71 "I happened to be in *Citizen Kane*"   *Action*

72 "Orson told me, 'Emily must be a lady'"   Ruth Warrick interview with the author

72 "frightened, whining, pathetic"   Callow

72 in his search for a "kind of cheapness"   Bogdanovich audio interview

73 "George was known as"   *Rosebud in the Snow*

73 "He phoned me in New York"   Meryman

73 "I'd missed him in my life"   Ibid.

73 Welles casually emptied his pipe   Houseman

73 Welles gave him acting   Alland interview with the author

74 "Perhaps you'll recognize"   Ibid.

74 character actor Edgar Barrier   RKO production files

75 "I never forgot him"   Bogdanovich

75 "He looked to me like a leading man"   Ibid.

75 "Mr. Thompson, you will be required to leave this room"   0:18:13

75 "We will need Hitler"   Baer memo to Robert Palmer, July 18, 1940, Lilly

76 Wilson remembered being in   Richard Wilson interview with the author

76 Welles said he was also   Bogdanovich audio interview

76 When Rawlston asks his reporters what they think of the Kane newsreel   0:12:40

76 Baer . . . played "Hillman"   1:03:30

76 Wilson played a reporter   1:54:09

76 in her only film credit   1:53:21

77 O'Connell is the skinny reporter   1:52:19 and 1:52:56

77 Ladd is the reporter   1:53:08

77 Leland's gentle, thoughtful personality   Bogdanovich audio interview

78 a tribute to Whitford Kane   Carringer

78 While the actor missed his opportunity   Brady

79 "I could never have made"   Bogdanovich audio interview

79 "they didn't have terrible movie habits"   Ibid.
79 waivers were obtained   Several memos about waivers, January 1940, Lilly

Chapter Six: A Great Deal of Doing

81 "These unconventional set-ups impose"   Toland/*Popular Photography*
82 "Toland carries himself"   Blanchard
83 "Toland was the best"   Bogdanovich
83 "The two," said Kahle   Kahle
83 Goldwyn loaned out Toland   Carringer
83 Goldwyn also required RKO   Ibid.
83 "I thought you could"   *Monitor*, BBC
83 Recent developments in both lighting and film   Carringer
84 soft visual tones   Ibid.
84 "From the moment"   Toland/*American Cinematographer*
84 "Welles had a full realization"   Toland/*Popular Photography*
84 "Welles was insistent"   Ibid.
85 "Its keynote"   Toland/*American Cinematographer*
85 "Welles instinctively grasped a point"   Ibid.
85 "Instead, we tried"   Ibid.
85 Bernstein points to a group photo of the newspaper's reporters   0:40:18
85 "These unconventional set-ups"   Ibid.
86 "Depth of field nearly always is sacrificed"   Toland/*Popular Photography*
86 "In life you see everything"   *Rosebud in the Snow*
86 "It took a great deal of doing"   Toland/*Popular Photography*
87 To achieve the "human eye" quality   Rea
87 "During recent years, a great deal"   Toland/*American Cinematographer*
87 "In the course of my"   Ibid.
88 such as the lawn at RKO in Culver City   0:12:07
88 "The classic example"   Ferguson
88 "But a movie night-club"   Ibid.
89 "An even better example"   Ibid.
89 "A severe restriction"   Ferguson
91 "It's disastrous to let"   Bogdanovich audio interview
91 "I don't know why"   Ibid.
91 when Jed Leland and Bernstein are unpacking statues   0:45:18
91 "one must always be on the lookout"   Toland/*American Cinematographer*
92 Sound engineer Bailey Fesler   Rea
92 RKO accountants would question   Multiple memos with questions about budget
                                              items, August 1940–January 1941, Lilly
93 Ferguson suggested a simple solution   Bogdanovich audio interview
93 was the full-cast filming of the projection room sequence   0:12:29

93 Thompson's first visit to interview Susan Alexander   0:14:48
93 her suicide attempt   1:35:27
93 El Rancho nightclub   0:14:22 and 1:25:16
94 on the 40 Acres back lot as they departed from their marriage   0:09:02 and 1:15:37
94 pivotal argument between Kane and Susan   1:42:24
94 Kane speaking from a flag-draped platform   0:09:48
94 being interviewed on a boat deck about the prospects for war   0:10:52
94 Susan's singing lesson   1:26:38
94 Susan confronting Kane in their Chicago apartment   1:32:41
94 Kane shaking hands with Neville Chamberlain   0:08:37
94 Kane standing with Hitler   0:08:42
94 longtime extra Gino Corrado   0:14:52
94 "My whole idea of having only new faces"   Bogdanovich audio interview

Chapter Seven: No Visitors, Please

96 There's a lot of stuff here"   *Orson Welles Story*
96 The breakfast table sequence   0:51:52
96 the sequence was filmed   Rea
96 As the breakfast room   Ibid.
97 "last 60 years"   *New York Times,* July 28, 1940
97 "robber baron industrialist"   *Hollywood Reporter,* July 29, 1940
97 "Orson functioned best"   Wilson interview with the author
97 "I have never observed a director"   Alland interview with the author
97 Welles loved actors   Popper interview
97 "There was no one quite like him"   *Action*
98 "did everything he could"   Warrick interview with the author
98 "There was one terrible moment"   Bogdanovich audio interview
98 "I left for the day"   Ibid.
98 Gettys threatens to destroy Kane's political career   1:04:58
99 "I had no idea what to do"   Bogdanovich audio interview
99 Welles may have tried to work out his conundrum   Third Revised Final
                                        shooting script from Welles' files,
                                        dated July 16, 1940,
                                        Profiles in History
99 "I think it's like lion taming"   Ibid.
99 "I somehow assumed that movie lighting"   Ibid.
99 "He was quietly fixing it"   Ibid.
100 "Orson would rehearse"   Rea
100 "'There's a lot of stuff here'"   *Orson Welles Story*
101 "Orson would set up"   Alland interview with the author
101 "After the take"   Ibid.

101	"My job was not"	Ibid.
101	"Schaefer came with all the bankers"	Bogdanovich audio interview
101	"It drove the brass"	Alland interview with the author
102	"Ford's greeting to him was the first hint"	Bogdanovich audio interview
102	filming scenes of Susan's opera debut	RKO production files, UCLA
102	"has worked this crew harder"	Drake letter to Weissberger, September 12, 1940, Lilly
102	"shot more film than anyone"	Callow
102	"One day he shot"	*Action*
102	Stewart's first day	1:47:13
103	"My first line in"	Callow
103	"I was utterly exhausted"	Alland interview with the author
103	"'That girl isn't an actress'"	Warrick interview with the author
103	"Orson left me completely alone"	Sharp
103	"Working for Orson"	Popper interview
103	"Working with Orson"	Robert Wise interview with the author
104	Cotten faced an inviolate deadline	Callow
104	postelection argument between Kane and Leland	1:11:53
104	Leland unconscious	1:19:14
104	Kane's first night at the *Inquirer*	0:35:39
105	drunk, confronts Kane in the newsroom	1:11:53
105	"The thing you don't do when faced"	Cotten
105	Cotten was so tired that he did a tongue trip	Ibid.
105	"'dramatic crimmitism'"	1:14:35
105	"I remember that the eight o'clock whistle blew"	Cotten
105	"After Orson called an end to the shooting"	Ibid.
105	"I'll never forget actors from other pictures"	Ibid.
105	Kane, Leland, and Bernstein at the *Chicago Inquirer*	1:19:14
106	Kane, Leland, and Bernstein on their first night	0:35:39
106	Leland entering a saloon to get drunk	1:10:18
106	Kane's return to the *Inquirer* after his trip to Europe	0:46:24
106	Leland and Bernstein reacting to Kane's campaign speech	1:02:00
106	"The greatest gift"	Bogdanovich
106	"Orson and Gregg respected each other"	Alland interview with the author
106	Kane's parents tell young Charles he is leaving home	0:20:53
107	Kane and Jed Leland arrive at the *Inquirer* for the first time	0:33:04
107	the lit window in Kane's bedroom	0:0:17
107	Susan looking hatefully at Kane	1:43:47
107	dissolves to a stained-glass window	1:43:47
107	"the background dissolves from one scene to the next"	Toland/*American Cinematographer*
108	"The dissolve is begun by dimming"	Toland/*Popular Photography*
108	Bernstein is talking with Thompson about Leland	0:32:30

108 all of the lighting in the nightclub slowly dims   1:26:32
108 "We actually dimmed"   Bogdanovich
108 the tune in the nightclub quietly changes   1:26:34
108 Leland, as an old man, reminisces   0:49:34
108 As Leland says "toothache"   0:55:04
109 encouraged by the publisher to sing   0:59:57
109 The scene dissolves to Kane still listening to Susan   1:00:19
109 The sound of Kane clapping for Susan continues into the next scene   1:00:39
109 "With one purpose only," roars Kane in the next scene   1:00:57
109 Kane and his wife, Emily, are blackmailed   1:04:25
109 A newsboy offers a copy of the *Chronicle* to Jed Leland   1:10:13
109 Bernstein is forced to choose between two potential headlines   1:10:29
110 a copy of the actual newspaper a few hours later   1:10:48
110 confront Kane in their postelection argument   1:11:53
110 KANE MARRIES SINGER   1:15:29
110 KANE BUILDS OPERA HOUSE   1:16:08
110 Susan frantically preparing   1:16:14
110 the action continues in the newsroom of the *Chicago Inquirer*   1:17:38
110 Kane discovers Leland, passed out   1:19:14
110 Kane finishes the negative review . . . and then fires his former friend   1:22:13
110 Leland as an old man, as he concludes his recollections   1:23:05
110 pops of photographers' flash powder help bridge   1:03:22
110 "Extra, read all about it!"   1:10:04
111 the front room where Susan sings at the piano   0:59:58
111 the breakfast room where the marriage of Kane and Emily deteriorates   0:51:52
111 Raymond the butler directs workmen while they burn Kane's mementos   1:55:47
111 when Thatcher is dictating a letter to Kane   0:23:18
111 "His camera-wise designing of the settings"   Toland/*American Cinematographer*
112 Great Hall of Xanadu   1:38:54
112 Silvera had professional experience   Carringer
112 Susan's second apartment, where she sings for Kane   1:00:19
113 The bedroom in the background   Set-continuity images from *Citizen Kane,* Profiles in History
113 in the tent at the Everglades picnic where Kane slaps Susan   1:42:25
113 the broad and intricate *Inquirer* newsroom   0:33:32
113 In the *Chicago Inquirer* newsroom   1:17:45
114 the reading room at the Thatcher Library   0:17:55
114 Great Hall of Xanadu, with its colossal staircase and walk-in fireplace   1:38:34
114 only a model   1:38:19
114 Kane's room   00:02:13
114 Susan's room and the doorways outside   1:44:11 and 1:46:03
114 the terrace (with its screeching cockatoo)   1:48:05

114 the walkway above the main staircase · · · · · · · · · · · · · 1:43:49
114 the hall of mirrors · 1:51:08
114 the furnace room where Rosebud burns · · · · · · · · · · · · · 1:55:47
114 three types of fences · 00:00:35
114 a seemingly endless Xanadu corridor · · · · · · · · · · · · · · 1:46:11
114 Raymond the butler looks down the hallway · · · · · · · · · · 1:48:13
115 the Great Hall does indeed include real wall details · · · · · · 1:38:34
115 Some expenses for decorating the Great Hall were minimized · · 1:43:45;
Set-continuity images
from *Citizen Kane*,
Profiles in History

115 Toland lit the set so hard shadows would fall on the walls and
      sculptures . . . by hanging rolls of black velvet · · · · · · · · Carringer
115 impenetrable voids · · · · · · · · · · · · · · · · · · · shown at 1:38:34
115 Later, when Xanadu is shown in daylight · · · · · · · · · · · · 1:52:10
115 especially the Venus seen from the back · · · · · · · · · · · · · 1:52:45
116 when Kane is walking across the set while Susan plays
      with her jigsaw puzzles · 1:38:34
116 *not* including furnishings · 1:39:50
116 Later, for Xanadu during the argument about Kane's demand for a picnic · · 1:40:15
116 "You always said you wanted to live in a palace" · · · · · · · · 1:39:19
116 "We can make a foreground piece" · · · · · · · · · · · · · · · Ferguson
116 viewers can see the ill-fated snow globe · · · · · · · · · · · · · 0:57:00
117 a photographer snaps a photo · · · · · · · · · · · · · · · · · · · 1:03:44
117 Amid the luxury of the Kane-acquired apartment · · · · · · · · 1:00:39
117 in her room at Xanadu · 1:44:12
117 for no particular reason carrying a large covered basket · · · · 1:53:04
117 It is the same basket that was one of Kane's original belongings · · 0:33:21 and 0:34:41
117 That doll later shows up, ready for burning, in a box of castoffs · · 1:55:41
117 one of last items knocked to the floor · · · · · · · · · · · · · · 1:41:51
118 the set is crammed with packing crates · · · · · · · · · · · · · 1:54:55
118 the ornate metal bed frame · 1:55:24
118 that Kane brought with him · · · · · · · · · · · 0:33:21 and 0:34:41
118 tattered bundle of decaying newspapers · · · · · · · · · · · · · 1:55:28
118 When Kane and Susan Alexander are married · · · · 0:09:07 and 1:15:37
118 In the bedroom of the psychologically scarred Susan · · · · · · 1:44:06
118 Fabricated newspapers . . . appear throughout *Citizen Kane*
        the *Inquirer* that Kane reads and the *Chronicle* that Emily reads · · 0:53:51
        CANDIDATE KANE CAUGHT IN LOVE NEST WITH "SINGER" · · 0:10:16 and 1:10:10
        five front pages . . . that feature Susan's opera "triumphs" · · 1:34:44
        DETROIT HAS "SELL OUT" FOR SUSAN ALEXANDER · · · · · · 1:16:22
        thousands of copies of Kane's first edition of the *Inquirer* · · 0:39:42
119 the *Chronicle* that Kane sees involving a "Mrs. Silverstone" · · 0:35:48

119 the montage of newspapers that show the coverage of Kane's death   0:05:13

120 W. R. HEARST'S DEATH MOURNED BY NATION   *Los Angeles Examiner,* August 15, 1951

120 WILLIAM RANDOLPH HEARST DIES AT 88   *New York Times,* August 15, 1951

120 he was already thinking ahead to his next projects   Notes and memos about potential film projects, September 1940, Lilly

120 a biopic on the life of Christ   Correspondence between Welles and U.S. Christian leadership, August and September 1940, Lilly

121 "Script exciting and powerful"   Herrmann telegram to Welles, July 23, 1940, Lilly

121 "We could see from the rushes"   Wise interview with the author

121 "we have just about completed half of the picture"   Baer letter to Weissberger, September 6, 1940, Lilly

122 "I couldn't leave for New York today"   Nolan memo to Welles, September 6, 1940, Lilly

122 "as of September 30"   Drake letter to Welles, October 4, 1940, Lilly

122 "There is a slowly rising buzz of anticipation"   Weissberger letter to Welles, November 26, 1940, Lilly

Chapter Eight: Giggling Like Schoolboys

123 Each time, he threw himself into the action"   Alland, interview with the author

123 shots of Kane's campaign speech and the aftermath   1:00:57

123 During Susan Alexander's operatic debut as described by Leland   1:16:22

124 RKO's background material on *Citizen Kane* reported   RKO press releases, UCLA

124 Susan's devastating debut as she described it to Thompson   1:29:09

125 Kane interrupts Susan's singing lesson   1:27:36

125 "Instead of following the usual practice of cutting from a close-up "   Toland/*Popular Photography*

125 the scene in which Kane signs over control of his empire   0:27:25

126 postelection argument between Kane and Leland   1:11:53

126 when the *Inquirer* staff members prepare to present a trophy to Kane   0:46:18

127 "It is too much like a play"   Drake letter to Welles, August 26, 1940, Lilly

127	an $875 expense	Budget overage request, UCLA
127	One of the elevated sets is visible	(Trailer) 0:01:11
128	"giggling like schoolboys"	Warrick interview with the author
128	postelection argument	1:11:53
128	Kane's destruction of Susan Alexander's room	1:48:27
128	"I must admit"	Toland/*American Cinematographer*
128	"It's impossible to say"	Bogdanovich audio interview
128	To film Susan Alexander's attempted suicide	1:35:25
129	Mary Kane signing away the guardianship of her son	0:19:21
129	"It was . . . a complex mixture of art and mechanics"	Toland/*Theatre Arts Magazine*
130	The final shot used in the film is not perfect	00:19:24
130	Welles said he had not seen any of the films from that period	Bogdanovich
131	The party table for the reporters was lit with long sets of small lights	0:40:46
131	when Kane and Susan Alexander chat in her boardinghouse room	0:56:33
131	when Jed Leland and Bernstein talk about Kane at the party	0:44:12
131	young Kane in the snow about to be taken away by Thatcher	0:21:20
131	Susan as she performs the closing scene of her operatic debut	1:30:33
131	Kane is in his office describing his "Declaration of Principles"	0:37:29
131	"I'm the one that gets the razzberries!"	1:34:20
131	As Kane approaches Susan, his shadow overwhelms her	1:34:33
131	film's closing scenes, most of the shots of reporters . . . contrasts of light and dark	1:52:10
131	As Thompson takes a jigsaw puzzle from one of his colleagues	1:53:50
131	An inventive use of lighting makes an intentional on-screen appearance	0:41:50
132	When Kane whistles to summon the band	0:41:44
132	they blaze directly into the camera	0:43:36
132	photography required for Kane's campaign speech	1:00:57
132	lengthy sessions needed to shoot Susan's opera debut	1:29:09
132	Welles filmed Raymond the butler and Thompson on the staircase	1:47:30
133	"We knew . . . that a successful"	Alland interview with the author
133	Welles tripped while rehearsing	Daily production report, UCLA
133	It was a painful injury	Popper interview
134	Welles directed Joseph Cotten's first scenes	0:49:34
134	confrontation between Kane and Leland	1:11:53
134	For Kane's destruction of Susan Alexander's bedroom at Xanadu	1:48:27
134	Ferguson's crew used real perfume	Rea
134	"Each time, he threw himself into the action"	Alland interview with the author
135	"I was bleeding like a pig"	Bogdanovich
135	"He literally went berserk"	Alland interview with the author
135	Raymond the butler delivered the film's final line	1:55:47
135	"Each time, all of us were there"	Wilson interview with the author
136	when retakes of the cellar scenes were filmed	Daily production report, UCLA

136	whom Welles called "the best makeup man in the world"	Welles ad in *Daily Variety*, May 8, 1941
136	"Maurice is an alchemist"	RKO press release, UCLA
136	"No one held my hand"	*Hollywood the Golden Years: The RKO Story*
136	"I had a little corner"	Ibid.
137	"Orson saw me playing with noses and ears"	Ibid.
137	"When *Citizen Kane* came out in script form"	Gambill
137	"our wizard of the rubber"	RKO press release, UCLA
137	"When I was satisfied with the appearance"	Gambill
137	Welles immobilized in coatings of hydrocolloid	Ibid.
137	Welles did not wear a padded costume	Ibid.
137	Such a massive padding project	Press release, RKO production files
138	Sloane's balding head was no simulation	RKO daily production report, October 8, 1940, UCLA
138	The inconvenience of having his head shaved	Ibid.
138	Seiderman worked with Charles Wright	Gambill
138	"multidirectional makeup"	Ibid.
138	individual pores	Ibid.
138	As editor Robert Wise recalled, he first met Welles	Wise interview with the author
139	"I never looked as young as that"	*Monitor*
139	"that terrible round moon face"	Bogdanovich audio interview
139	"Note how Orson either never smiles on camera"	Vidal
139	"My whole face was yanked up with pieces of fish skin"	*Monitor*
139	"Norman Mailer wrote once"	Bogdanovich/*This Is Orson Welles*
139	Seiderman created three different noses	Gambill
139	Complex applications of old-age makeup required up to four hours	Many RKO daily production reports, UCLA
139	a job accomplished with sponged-on vodka	Rea
139	Welles was sometimes in his makeup chair as early as three A.M.	Ibid.
140	Seiderman often slept on a cot	Gambill
140	"Orson and I never had a chance"	Ibid.
140	Leland's eyeshade was Cotten's own contribution	Cotten
140	"Flurp"	Cotten
140	"drove you mad with pain"	Bogdanovich
140	Seiderman's skills could not reduce the time required	Several RKO daily production reports, UCLA
141	"We agree that to give credit to Seiderman"	Sid Rogell memo to J. R. McDonough, November 23, 1940, UCLA
141	when Baer ordered the makeup credits	Baer memo to Doug Travers, January 8, 1941, Lilly

141	five days later Baer ordered	Baer memo to James Wilkinson, January 13, 1941, Lilly
141	"After *Citizen Kane* was exhibited"	Gambill
142	fashion trends of more than seventy years	RKO press release
142	even when she wore a tightly tailored evening dress	1:07:51
142	meeting Kane for the first time when she was still quite slender	0:55:12
142	Susan had to be shown standing as she confronts Kane	1:44:11
142	While playing with jigsaw puzzles	1:38:05 and 1:40:50
142	the outfit he wore to pose for the massive banner	1:00:57
142	for his confrontation with Matiste during Susan's unsuccessful singing lesson	1:26:58
143	the overarching *K* on the front gate at Xanadu	00:01:08, 1:47:10, and 1:56:59
143	the ice-block *K* as a centerpiece at the newsroom party	0:40:52
143	the row of *K*s (forward and backward) on the ornate Moroccan-style hanging lamp	1:43:11
143	Kane's velvet robe in his apartment after Susan's opera debut	1:33:16
143	the gold pin he wears on his cravat	0:08:52
143	the even larger tiepin that Kane-the-candidate displays	1:01:48
143	a *K* monogram on the front of Kane's shirt at the picnic tent	1:42:29
143	on Kane's watch chain when he destroys Susan's room	1:50:19
143	exquisitely embroidered collar and cuffs of the shirt	0:24:46
143	going to the studio at two in the morning	Popper interview
143	"It is not possible"	*Lundberg v Welles et al.*
143	"If a shot didn't work"	Popper interview
144	Matiste coaches and sings	1:28:38
144	two-sentence speech . . . "evil domination of 'Boss' Jim Gettys"	1:00:39
144	Welles also shortened Kane's speech	1:00:56
145	Thatcher confronting Kane, now twenty-seven	0:24:46
145	a river of new budget requests began to flow	Many RKO daily overage reports, September and October 1940, UCLA
146	a single shot of his sled covered in snow	0:22:54
146	a completely white screen in the next scene	0:23:07
146	"And a Happy New Year," as he dictates a letter	0:23:18
146	"I think it would be fun to run a newspaper"	0:23:48
146	seven brief scenes, each showing Thatcher reading an *Inquirer* headline	
	Thatcher sits on a train and whispers the banner headline	0:24:13
	TRACTION TRUST BLEEDS PUBLIC WHITE	0:24:24
	TRACTION TRUST SMASHED BY INQUIRER	0:24:26
	LANDLORDS REFUSE TO CLEAR SLUMS	0:24:29
	INQUIRER WINS SLUM FIGHT	0:24:33
	WALL STREET BACKS COPPER SWINDLE	0:24:38
	Thatcher yells, "Copper Robbers Indicted!"	0:24:42
147	final and most preposterous headline, "Galleons of Spain off Jersey Coast!"	0:24:44

147 "I'll have to close this place in . . . sixty years"   0:27:10
147 "In the winter of 1929 . . ."   0:27:16
148 provided some of the film's few observations by Kane   0:29:42
148 each of the eight editions of the *Inquirer* that riled Thatcher   0:24:13
149 "This is an added set, not figured in the original budget"   Several RKO overage
                                                    reports, September and October 1940, UCLA
149 For Leland's brief back-alley speech, Perry Ferguson loaded the set   1:00:39
149 For Thatcher's Depression-era office, Ferguson created a spartan chamber 0:27:25
149 he shot the "Merry Christmas" scene   0:23:07
149 "Welles sent everyone home"   Wise interview with the author
149 But Richard Wilson remembered   Carringer/*Critical Inquiry* 5
149 In the first week of October   Several RKO daily production reports,
                                                              October 1940, UCLA
150 Welles may have been writing whenever he could   Third Revised Final
                                                        shooting script from Welles' files,
                                                                 dated July 16, 1940,
                                                                 Profiles in History
150 George Coulouris and Everett Sloane were held   RKO overage reports,
                                                        October 15 and 17, 1940, UCLA
150 Welles filmed the single-shot, two-minute, twenty-one-second scene   0:27:25
150 Toland shot the reporters rummaging through the vast sea of crates   1:52:10
150 Welles directed himself and Dorothy Comingore in the Great Hall   1:38:34
150 After filming the demolition of Susan's bedroom and cutting himself   1:47:27
150 The last shot of the regular production schedule   1:51:08
151 Production #281 as eighteen days behind schedule   RKO production reports,
                                                               October 1940, UCLA
151 The original budget for direct costs   RKO budget report, UCLA

Chapter Nine: Cryptic Notes and Bigger Hams

152 "Mark [Robson] and I would be"   Wise, interview with the author
152 brief clip of Sonny Bupp as Kane's son   1:03:54
152 Susan and Kane driving in a limousine to the Florida picnic   1:41:38
152 retakes of Susan and Kane
        in the picnic tent   1:42:24
        their Chicago apartment   1:32:42
        and Susan's now repaired Xanadu bedroom   1:44:23
        additional shots of the reporters in the Great Hall   1:52:09
        set up the shots of Kane's death   0:2:19
152 protest speaker, played by Art Yeoman   0:07:35
152 Kane with the foreign generals   0:08:40
153 six close-up shots of puzzle construction   1:40:18

153	Kane and Thatcher argue about the paper's credibility	0:24:46
153	while the staff waves at Kane and Emily	0:47:49
153	Stewart appeared in the outdoor scenes of the Everglades picnic	1:42:04
153	bursting the snow globe when Kane dies and drops it	0:02:38
153	Wild filmed Kane's death	0:02:19
153	Cully filmed William Alland—again showing his left side	0:49:24
153	"Mr. Welles has completed with the shooting"	Baer memo to Darrel Silvera, January 6, 1941, Lilly
154	Dunn was a popular guest	Linwood Dunn presentation, attended by the author
154	Susan's suicide attempt	1:35:25
155	the *Inquirer* staff looks out the windows	0:47:35
155	when Kane and Jed Leland arrive at the *Inquirer*	0:33:04
155	The caravan of cars traveling alongside the sand	1:41:47
155	the brief background scenes of birds in flight	1:42:12
156	smoke from Kane's burning mementos pours from the chimney	1:56:25
156	The rain-swept roof of Susan Alexander's nightclub	0:14:23
156	a simpler version of the effect is repeated without the storm	1:25:15
156	when Susan and Thompson complete their discussion	1:46:59
156	Raymond the butler looks down a long corridor and sees Kane in the distance	1:48:13
156	When reporter Thompson visits the Thatcher Library	0:17:27
156	George Coulouris actually posed for the statue	Brady
156	the camera rises through the rafters of the Chicago Opera House	1:17:01
157	Even the impact of Rosebud burning was enhanced	1:56:01
157	the scene opens with a startling shot of a screeching cockatoo	1:48:05
157	Welles admitted thirty years later	Bogdanovich audio interview
157	when the camera moves through Xanadu and the vast trove	1:54:55
158	the trailer begins with a shot of the door to RKO Stage 10	(Trailer) 0:00:04
158	dancers from the *Inquirer* party to run onto a set	(Trailer) 0:00:42
158	The clip of Ruth Warrick shows the actress leaning against a set	(Trailer) 0:01:11
158	model of Xanadu can be seen when Paul Stewart is introduced	(Trailer) 0:01:51
158	Everett Sloane is shown . . . on RKO's massive Stage 10	(Trailer) 0:01:34
159	two actors had to lie down in a bathroom stall	Alland interview with the author
159	crystal wind chimes in the shot of the snow globe	0:02:30
159	the booming salvo of Kane's campaign speech	1:00:56
159	"Sound became for us became an integral part"	Alland interview with the author
159	"The motion picture business as a whole"	*The Complete Citizen Kane*
159	Attentive listening reveals a melding of on-screen action	
	early-twentieth-century street noises	0:55:15
	train whistles	0:22:54

echo-filled conversations between Kane and Susan   1:38:34

a woman's scream when Kane slaps Susan   1:43:34

the moan of a solitary steamship whistle   0:49:34

Kane whispering, "Rosebud"   0:02:31

159 the fading gasp achieved by blending two separate sound tracks   Carringer

160 the auditory power of Kane's speech   1:00:56

"Orson adopted the manner of speaking"   *Action*

160 "You're a bigger ham than I am"   Ibid.

160 "In my enthusiasm"   Ibid.

160 the "clunk" of the carriage   1:22:12

160 As "Boss" Jim Gettys leaves Susan's apartment building   1:09:20

160 "I'm going to send you to Sing Sing!"   1:09:40

161 "Orson would describe what he wanted"   Wise interview with the author

161 Watching a final film, Welles said   Bogdanovich audio interview

162 he did not recall ever seeing footage   Wise interview with the author

162 The only existing outtakes are included in the closing credits   1:57:20

162 the same idea is conveyed in the scene that remains   0:39:30

162 one of Susan's puzzles in a state of completion   1:38:29 compared with 1:39:05

162 when Kane departs Madison Square Garden   1:03:30, 1:03:57, and 1:04:01

162 When Kane returns to the *Inquirer* newsroom after his vacation   0:46:24

163 Welles could see his own bracelet on his left wrist   1:36:01

163 "I had a girlfriend who made me wear it"   Bogdanovich audio interview

163 Raymond the butler tells Thompson he was present at Kane's death   1:51:37

163 the breakfast table montage, which . . . captures the decline   0:51:52

163–64 To assemble the newsreel, the production acquired stock footage   0:03:11

striking workers   0:07:36

mass demonstrations   0:07:40

animals being shipped   0:04:27

General Film Library provided a snippet of U.S. Cavalry   0:08:10

Kane's meetings with world leaders such as Adolf Hitler   0:08:42

British prime minister Neville Chamberlain   0:08:37

anonymous foreign military officers   0:08:40

campaigning on a whistle-stop train tour with Theodore Roosevelt   0:08:15

and 0:08:33

mob protest . . . during which Kane is burned in effigy   0:08:19

"Kane for Governor" torchlight parade   0:10:02

Scenes of Kane in a wheelchair as an old man   0:12:02

an excerpt from Richard Wagner's overture from *Tannhäuser*   0:09:19

the bouncy theme music for *News on the March* itself   0:03:12

the romantic sweep of violins that is heard   0:03:23

Kane responds to charges that he is a Communist   0:07:49

text about Kane as "the greatest newspaper tycoon"   0:05:33

in the scene of "1941's biggest, strangest funeral"   0:04:51

164	"Mark and I would be in our cutting room"	Wise interview with the author
165	*News on the March* was perhaps too realistic	Bogdanovich audio interview
165	he told his friend Henry Jaglom	Henry Jaglom interview with the author
165	"Here is [a] chance for you to do something witty"	Welles telegram to Bernard Herrmann, July 18, 1940, Lilly
165	"This not only gave me ample time"	Herrmann
165	"The problem was to create"	Ibid.
166	"a girl with a modest voice . . . would be completely hopeless"	Herrmann Q&A
166	she sings for Kane in the scene that transitions	1:00:19
166	for her hapless performance during the singing lesson	1:26:38
166	"In this way, I had a sense"	Herrmann
167	The first, a theme for Kane	0:00:34
167	A haunting eleven-note them to identify Rosebud	0:01:35
167	"Both themes came to me rather automatically"	Herrmann Q&A
167	"The permutations of this theme are complex"	Ibid.
167	"The Rosebud theme is heard again and again"	Herrmann
167	when young Kane is shown playing on his sled	0:18:59
168	As Kane leaves Susan's room in Xanadu after destroying it	1:50:22
168	the Rosebud theme is playing softly and continues into Susan's room	0:56:18
168	For the breakfast table sequence	0:51:54
168	"The popular music of this period"	0:51:52
168	the music stops abruptly with the "plunk" of a harp and violins	0:19:04
168	When Thompson departs the Thatcher Library	0:30:12
168	"I would do the same thing again"	0:30:12
168	When Susan is playing with her puzzles	1:40:18
168	The lighthearted song is performed during the party	0:42:42
168	as Leland enters the *Inquirer* building to confront Kane	1:10:57
169	When Thompson first visits Susan Alexander at the El Rancho nightclub	0:14:57
169	On his second visit, a solo piano plays the same tune	1:25:32
169	Later, as Susan recovers from her suicide attempt	1:37:04
169	"Most composers would go right through the roof"	Wise interview with the author
169	Herrmann . . . "understood the type"	*Music of the Movies*
170	while Thompson reads the line in Thatcher's memoirs	0:27:16
170	the full orchestra is played in the final minutes of the film	1:54:43
170	"The ending of *Citizen Kane* gave me a wonderful opportunity"	Herrmann
170	"Bernie's particular talent"	*Music of the Movies*
171	"I had heard of the many handicaps"	Herrmann
171	Independent of Herrmann, a key musical segment	Research by Ron Gottesman and Buddy Collette
171	"I kind of based the whole scene around that song"	Bogdanovich

PART TWO

Chapter Ten: Conflict

175 "What I saw appalled me"   Hopper
176 "the script of Orson Welles' first movie"   *Newsweek*
177 Lederer said he read the script   Meryman
177 "[Mankiewicz] asked me if I thought Marion"   *This Is Orson Welles*
177 "exactly . . . what we were trying"   RKO correspondence, UCLA
178 "When I heard that the film"   Parsons
178 "I was refusing"   Richard Berlin letter to Joseph Willicombe,
                                                  January 2, 1941, Bancroft
179 Brad Sears, the general manager   Ibid.
179 "The Orson Welles interests"   *Hollywood Reporter,* December 30, 1940
180 "Orson Welles' first motion picture"   *Friday,* January 17, 1941
180 "There was only one script"   Ibid.
180 " 'Wait until the woman finds out' "   Ibid.
181 "I wish you could have seen my little home"   Hopper letter to Welles,
                                                   January 9, 1940, Lilly
181 "a dread secret"   Drake letter to W. Schneider,
                                                  January 15, 1941, Lilly
182 "Dearest Hedda, . . . I owe you"   Welles telegram to Hopper,
                                                   January 3, 1941, Lilly
182 "James Francis Crow, a reviewer for *Look*"   Drake letter to W. Schneider,
                                                  January 15, 1941, Lilly
182 "She was . . . violently angry"   Ibid.
182 "What I saw appalled me"   Hopper
182 "Hedda has for some time been"   Meryman
183 "If Mr. Welles makes"   Louella Parsons column, nationally syndicated,
                                                    October 13, 1939
183 "Orson Welles wins"   Ibid., December 31, 1939
183 "I can hardly wait"   Ibid., July 29, 1940
183 Welles appeared in Parsons' column   Drake memo to Welles,
                                                    October 4, 1940, Lilly
184 "the devoted slave of Mr. Hearst"   Douglas Fairbanks, Jr., interview with the author
184 "As the story was reported to me"   Parsons
184 "Across the cerulean Hollywood sky"   Hopper
184 "Mr. Hearst called me and asked that"   Parsons
184 "*Friday Magazine* this week carries a vicious lie"   Welles letter to Parsons
184 "A good deal of nonsense"   Ibid.
184 "several audible gasps"   Rea
185 "She was purple"   Warrick interview with the author

185	"one of the classic double crosses"	Parsons
185	"one of the most beautiful lawsuits"	RKO production files
185	Within days, Parsons called	Drake notes, Mercury Files, Lilly
185	"total press blackout"	Parsons letter to Willicombe, Bancroft
185	"called everybody but St. Peter"	Drake letter to Schneider, January 15, 1941, Lilly
185	the entire organization was alerted	*Variety*, January 10, 1941
186	"Chief requests that you omit"	Willicombe night letter to Berlin, January 8, 1941, Bancroft
186	"As a result of the fury"	Ibid.
186	Parsons called every member	Drake letter to Schneider, January 15, 1941, Lilly
186	she promised Nelson Rockefeller	Ibid.
186	"if you boys want private lives"	Ibid.
187	"Mr. Hearst might like to know"	Parsons letter to Willicombe, January 14, 1941, Bancroft
187	"Had long talk with George"	Nelson Rockefeller telegram to Parsons, January 14, 1941, Bancroft
187	"You can't blame a fellow for trying"	Wilkerson "Tradeviews" column, *Hollywood Reporter*, January 14, 1941
	"It was not a good effort"	Ibid.
	"This comment is not written"	Ibid.
	"So far they have never uncovered"	Ibid.
188	"I do not see how Orson can lose"	Drake letter to Weissberger, January 10, 1941, Lilly
188	"We have been asked by Mr. Schaefer to say nothing"	Drake letter to Schneider, January 15, 1941, Lilly
189	"I am going slowly mad because my hands are tied"	Ibid.

Chapter Eleven: Negotiating and Placating

190	"This is not a tempest in a tea pot"	Weissberger letter to Welles, January 20, 1941, Lilly
190	"We have not used Hearst's name"	Weissberger letter to Welles, January 13, 1941, Lilly
191	"I don't believe in lawsuits"	Parsons
191	"making a direct request"	Anonymous by request, interview with the author
192	"Dear Louella—this is a note"	Willicombe letter to Parsons, February 1, 1941, Bancroft

192 "Schaefer is not phased" Weissberger letter to Drake, January 14, 1941, Lilly

192 "in the slightest way" Ibid.

192 "Had Mr. Hearst and similar financial barons" *New York Times,* January 11, 1941

192 "It is essential" Weissberger letter to Drake, January 14, 1941, Lilly

192 "There is no serious consideration" *Variety,* January 13, 1941

192 "No one on or off this lot" McDonough memo to RKO department heads, January 17, 1941, UCLA

193 Late in January *New York Times,* February 2, 1941

193 "I asked Schaefer whether there were" Weissberger letter to Welles, January 17, 1941, Lilly

193 "If they fail to release the picture" Ibid.

194 "The more I regard the situation" Weissberger letter to Welles, January 20, 1941, Lilly

194 "This is not a tempest in a tea pot" Ibid.

194 RKO announced a mammoth advertising campaign RKO press announcement, reported widely in trade press, January 22, 1941

195 "the owners of RKO have an interest" *Variety,* March 19, 1941

195 *Variety* reported that he was neutral Ibid.

195 "How can you tell what a board" Weissberger letter to Welles, January 20, 1941, Lilly

196 "As you can see, I'm just as ill-tempered" Welles letter to Dan Gillmor, January 1941, UCLA

196 "*Citizen Kane* is the portrait" *Friday,* February 14, 1941

"*Friday* ran a series of stills" Ibid.

"Worst of all" Ibid.

"Retractions are notoriously valueless" Ibid.

196 "Louie asked me to speak to you about this picture" Crowther

197 "Such an extraordinary suggestion" Ibid.

197 "The request comes from Louie" Ibid.

197 "The idea of the screening" Wise interview with the author

197 "Orson talked to them first" Ibid.

197 "The next day I got a list" Ibid.

198 The resulting compromise Carringer

198 Paul Stewart recorded two replacement lines Ibid.

198 "acted kind of funny sometimes" 1:47:36

198 "The second time we screened it" Wise interview with the author

198 "We *didn't* expect that the film" Bogdanovich audio interview

198 Parsons told Willicombe Parsons letter to Willicombe, January 29, 1941, Bancroft

198 "If they are sincere" Ibid.

199 Hearst papers lifted their ban *Variety,* January 22, 1941

199 "I did the listening and he did the talking" — Berlin letter to Willicombe, January 27, 1941, Bancroft

"Then . . . he admitted" — Ibid.
"I told him that I had not discussed" — Ibid.
"Mr. Wheelock informed me" — Ibid.
200 John Houseman "had spoken to Welles" — Ibid.
200 "There was nothing said" — Ibid.
200 "I couldn't blame her" — Bogdanovich audio interview
200 Hopper practically endorsed — Hopper column, nationally syndicated, March 6, 1941
200 "I think she's a louse" — Parsons letter to Joseph Willicombe, March 19, 1941, Bancroft

201 "I got a rosary" — Bogdanovich audio interview
201 RKO probably could not have destroyed — Welles contract with RKO, Lilly
202 "The threat of action on your part" — Weissberger letter to Welles, January 31, 1941, Lilly
202 "Never in my experience" — Schaefer letter to Welles, February 15, 1941, referenced in Brady and Gottesman
203 "I loved Citizen Kane" — Brady
203 "half-crazy in his declining years" — Weissberger letter to Welles, January 22, 1941, Lilly
203 "This is not the story of any man" — Schaefer letter to Welles, March 11, 1941, Lilly
203 "Cannot express my disapproval of revised title" — Welles telegram to Schaefer, inaccurate written date (probably March 14, 1941), Lilly
203 "Citizen Kane is an examination of" — Welles telegram to Schaefer, undated [March 1941], Lilly

204 "unleash their guns" — Variety, March 5, 1941
204 "Few movies have ever come from Hollywood" — Life, March 17, 1941
205 "The situation is also said" — New York Times, January 11, 1941
205 "The judgment of its executives" — Ibid., January 19, 1941
205 "didn't carry private fights between two gentlemen" — Brady
205 "A few obsequious" — O'Hara
205 "Will Hollywood stand up" — Sage
206 "according to a spokesman for the studio" — New York Times, February 28, 1941
207 "I managed to say very little" — Welles letter to Schaefer, March 6, 1941, Mercury Files, Lilly

"no real reasons" — Ibid.
"I have to sit up until" — Ibid.
"Don't tell me to get a good night's rest" — Ibid.
"been trying to get you on the telephone" — Schaefer telegram to Welles, March 7, 1941, Lilly
208 "I believe that the public" — Welles press statement, March 11, 1941

208	"Under my contract"	Ibid.
208	"I have been advised"	Ibid.
208	"There is nothing to warrant"	Ibid.
209	"Under ordinary circumstances"	*Variety,* April 16, 1941
209	Mortimer blasted Hollywood	Ibid.
209	Welles' draft status	Medical records and reports in Mercury Files, Lilly
209	"Don't go back to your hotel"	BBC interview with Welles, 1982
210	"Our friend, Welles, is a pretty bad boy"	Berlin letter and report to Willicombe, January 21, 1941, Bancroft
	"preliminary, and rather hasty"	Ibid.
	"acted as a front"	Ibid.
	other supposedly notorious activities	Ibid.
	"We have the complete assurance"	Ibid.
211	With initial input	Brady
212	helping to *increase* their ratings	Callow
212	list of articles criticizing his work	Undated summary by Welles of Hearst headlines through May 7, 1941, Lilly
212	"I have stood silently by"	Welles public statement, Mercury files, Lilly
213	"Optimism of a few weeks ago"	*Variety,* March 5, 1941
213	His friends printed	Shown in a photograph in Bogdanovich/ *This Is Orson Welles*
214	Although Welles was denied his own print	Brady
214	"to most of the several hundred"	*Time,* March 17, 1941

Chapter Twelve: Mr. Hearst

215	Historical information about George Hearst, Phoebe Hearst, William Randolph Hearst, and Millicent Hearst gathered from many general online biographical sources	
216	In one of several	Weissberger letter to Welles, June 5, 1940, Lilly
216	Hearst, like Kane, was expelled from Harvard	Carringer
216	In retaliation against a proposed boycott	Ibid.
216	two other characters	Brady
218	"You can crush a man"	Fairbanks interview with the author
220	"completely unconcerned"	Rea
221	Mankiewicz's idea to write Susan	Carringer
221	"no one wanted to hurt Marion"	Trosper interview
221	"We were terribly unfair to Marion"	*Monitor*
221	"I always felt Hearst had the right"	Bogdanovich

221 "Hearst built more than one castle"   Davies
221 However, a much more intimate subject   Gottesman
224 The Casa Del Prado, with its twin towers   0:04:40
224 Photos of the Hearst estate were indeed referenced   Carringer
225 As an attempted peace gesture   RKO production files, UCLA
225 film columnist John Chapman   Nasaw
225 "When the film ended and the lights came up"   Ibid.
225 "He looked away thoughtfully and replied"   Tebbel
225 "but my sister Rose did"   Davies
226 "Marion once told me"   Bacon
226 "We have [*Citizen Kane*] here"   Swanberg
226 The inventory of the estate's contents   Interview by the author with
                                multiple members of the archival staff at Hearst Castle
226 "the old man would be thrilled by it"   Bogdanovich audio interview
226 "I found myself alone with Hearst"   Ibid.
227 "I wished to make a motion picture"   Gottesman
227 "For a time I considered making him"   Ibid.
227 "As in the case of a great deal of fiction"   Welles testimony, *Lundberg v. Welles et. al.*
228 "William Randolph Hearst is conducting a series"   Brady
228 "Do you think . . . Willie Hearst"   *PM*
228 "I told Welles that I would be interested"   Meryman
228 "If we keep it in . . . we'll never have any trouble"   Ibid.
229 "But how is he different from Ford"   0:13:13
229 "I'll have to close this place in . . . sixty years"   0:27:11
229 response to a cable from Wheeler   0:25:15
229 "it is the only purely Hearstian"   Davies
230 "This happens to be the gist"   Notes on Mankiewicz's copy
                                of the Third Revised Final script, UCLA,
230 "Who else?"   Ibid.
230 "I'm always glad to be back, young man"   0:11:13
230 "He was right. . . . He was dead right"   Bogdanovich
231 "Mr. Welles says the film"   *New York Times*, January 19, 1941
231 "It is my opinion that Mr. Hearst"   Meryman
231 "Many years back"   Parsons, *Modern Screen*
232 the few stars   Barbas

Chapter Thirteen: Release

233 Seeing [*Citizen Kane*], it's as if you never really saw a movie before"   Ager
233 "Show it in tents"   Welles undated memo to Schaefer, RKO production files
234 included news briefs   *Los Angeles Times,* mini-articles and photographs
                                in the "Screen" section, May 2, 3, 4, 5, 6, 7, and 8, 1941

234 "I'm usually criticized" | Welles statement to reporters at Los Angeles premiere, May 8, 1941
234 "incur the wrath" | *Variety*, May 7, 1941
234 "one of the largest representative gatherings" | *Los Angeles Times*, May 9, 1941
234 "Now that the wraps are off" | Crowther, *New York Times*, May 2, 1941
234 *Citizen Kane* has found" | *Time*, March 17, 1941
234 "After you've seen Orson Welles' first film" | Boehnel
235 "*Citizen Kane* will be around, will be remembered" | Mishkin
235 "Before *Citizen Kane* . . . it's as if the motion picture" | Ager
235 "Tonight I was present" | Lesser
235 "*Citizen Kane* is a film possessing" | *Variety*, April 16, 1941
236 "There's been so much written" | Hopper column, *Los Angeles Times*, May 4, 1941
236 "The Kid" | Ibid., May 10, 1941
236 "They were making bets out here" | Schaefer letter to C. B. McDonald, April 14, 1941, Lilly
238 "It's Terrific!" | RKO marketing materials, Margaret Herrick Library
239 The Fox West Coast theater chain | *New York Times*, September 7, 1941
242 even younger Ben Affleck | Welles was twenty-six years and nine months old when he won his Oscar; Affleck was twenty-five years and seven months old; Damon was twenty-seven years and five months old
242 "Congratulations and best wishes" | Meryman
242 "Dear Mankie" | Ibid.
242 "I am very happy" | Callow
243 The voting rules | Academy of Motion Picture Arts and Sciences rules for awards voting
243 Welles figured strongly in the nominations | *Variety*
243 Just as likely an explanation | *Variety*, July 18, 1939
244 loss of more than $150,000 | Budget reports, RKO production files
245 "Showmanship in Place of Genius" | RKO 1942 publicity material, Herrick Library

Chapter Fourteen: Triumph

246 "With the changes" | *Sight & Sound*
247 "We're not that hard up for a buck" | *Variety*, August 29, 1951
247 "Some Called Him a Hero" | RKO 1956 publicity material, Herrick Library
247 740 RKO films were sold to C&C Super Corporation | Carringer

Chapter Fifteen: Walking on the Edge of a Cliff

249 "I had luck as no one had" | Cobos
250 "Orson said to me" | Jaglom interview with the author

250 "This is sickening" — Elliot Silverstein press conference statement, January 30, 1989, covered widely in media

251 "Our attorneys" — Statement by Roger Mayer, February 14, 1989, covered widely in media

251 "a victory from the grave" — *Time,* February 27, 1989

251 "This is one of the outstanding" — RKO memo from Reg Armour to Rogell, April 16, 1941, RKO production files

252 Kodak ceased production — Kodak online background paper

252 "The three prints had different strengths and weaknesses" — Multiple source coverage of the release of the 2011 Blu-ray

253 A Rosebud sled . . . purchased by Steven Spielberg — Broad media coverage, June 1982 (1:55:39)

253 But what of the Rosebud — Broad media coverage, December 1996 (0:21:25)

254 Mankiewicz's family sold

254 In 2012, the Oscar sold again — Broad media coverage of both sales, February 2012

254 Welles' own Oscar — Broad media coverage, December 2011

254 The cup given to Kane — Broad media coverage, June 2012 (0:46:20 and 1:53:00)

254 The gray three-piece suit — Broad media coverage, December 2013 (1:43:56 and 1:48:18)

254 a single article of clothing — Broad media coverage, October 2014

254 The dress that Ruth Warrick wore — Broad media coverage, December 2013 (0:47:35)

254 The mink coat that Kane wore — Broad media coverage, May 2014 (1:17:40)

254 the RKO camera crane — Broad media coverage, December 2011

254 His second-draft script — Broad media coverage, February and March 2014

255 In April — Broad media coverage, April 2014

255 "a sexy steno" — Profiles in History action results, September 2015

255 "I tossed out the idea" — Wendy Eidson comments covered extensively in most media, March 2012

255 "a great opportunity to draw" — Steve Hearst comments reported in most national media, January 19 and 20, 2012; January 2015

256 "*Citizen Kane* is a classic American film" — Ibid.

256 "The character Orson Welles depicted" — Ibid.

256 "was a beacon in a way" — AFI video

257 "I don't regret that" — *Monitor*

257 "I think it was the first time" — *Rosebud in the Snow*

258 "has inspired more vocations to the cinema" — Ibid.

258 "I simply think of it" — Ibid.

258 "*Citizen Kane* means everything to me." — AFI video

258 "I had the confidence of ignorance" — *Monitor*

BIBLIOGRAPHY

Archives and Collections

Orson Welles Collections (memos, letters, telegrams, contracts, newspaper clippings), Lilly Library, Indiana University, Bloomington.

Citizen Kane files (notes, reviews, souvenir programs, clippings, photographs; publicity material from the 1956 re-release of *Citizen Kane*), Margaret Herrick Library, Academy of Motion Picture Arts and Sciences, Beverly Hills, California.

Joseph Cotten Collection, USC Libraries, Cinematic Arts Library, University of Southern California, Los Angeles

Profiles in History, Calabasas, California. Orson Welles auction lots (scripts, photographs, and negatives) for Hollywood Auction 74, September 28–October 1, 2015

Richard Wilson–Orson Welles Papers, 1930–2000, Special Collections Library, University of Michigan, Ann Arbor.

RKO Radio Pictures Studio Records (Collection PASC 3), UCLA Library Special Collections, Charles E. Young Research Library, UCLA, Los Angeles.

William Randolph Hearst Papers, Bancroft Library, University of California, Berkeley.

Interviews

William Alland, interview with the author, April 1990.

Douglas Fairbanks, Jr., phone interview with the author, February 1989.

Ralph Hernandez, Sr., Earl Hays Press, phone interview with the author, January 2015.

Hearst Castle, interviews by the author with several of the archival staff, April 1990

Henry Jaglom, phone interview with the author, February 1991.

Frank Mankiewicz, phone interview with Dallas Adams, August 2011.

Kathryn Trosper Popper, several interviews with Joseph Popper, 2004.

Ruth Warrick, interview with the author, August 1991.

Richard Wilson, interviews with the author, March and April 1990.

Robert Wise, interviews with the author, March 1990.

Scripts

Text of *American;* drafts, shooting scripts, partial scripts, and cutting continuity of *Citizen Kane,* dated April through July 1940—UCLA Library Special Collections, UCLA, Los Angeles.

Third Revised Final script, dated July 16, 1940—Orson Welles Collections, Lilly Library, Indiana University, Bloomington.

Third Revised Final script, dated July 16, 1940, photocopy of Herman Mankiewicz's personal copy, with notes added by lawyers from the Hearst organization—UCLA Library Special Collections, UCLA, Los Angeles.

Untitled script marked "Late Draft"—Richard Wilson Papers, Special Collections Library, University of Michigan, Ann Arbor.

Untitled script marked "Correction Script"—Film Study Center, Museum of Modern Art, New York City, New York.

Musical Scores

Compositions and orchestrations for *Citizen Kane* by Bernard Herrmann—UCLA Library Special Collections, UCLA Library, Los Angeles.

Books, Articles, and Documents

Action (Directors Guild of America magazine). "Raising Kane," May–June 1969.

Ager, Cecelia. Review of *Citizen Kane. PM,* May 2, 1941.

Atkinson, Brooks. Review of *Julius Caesar. New York Times,* November 12, 1937.

Barbas, Samantha. *The First Lady of Hollywood: A Biography of Louella Parsons.* Berkeley: University of California Press, 2006.

Blanchard, Walter. "Aces of the Camera XIII: Gregg Toland." *American Cinematographer,* January 1942.

Boehnel, William. Review of *Citizen Kane. New York World-Telegram,* May 2, 1941.

Bogdanovich, Peter. "The Kane Mutiny." *Esquire,* October 1972.

———, and Orson Welles. *This Is Orson Welles.* Edited by Jonathan Rosenbaum. New York: HarperCollins, 1992.

Brady, Frank. *Citizen Welles: A Biography of Orson Welles.* New York: Scribner, 1989.

Callow, Simon. *Orson Welles: The Road to Xanadu.* New York: Penguin Books, 1996.

Carringer, Robert. *The Making of* Citizen Kane. Berkeley: University of California Press, 1985.

———. "The Scripts of *Citizen Kane." Critical Inquiry* 5, no. 2 (Winter 1978).

———. "Orson Welles and Gregg Toland: Their Collaboration on *Citizen Kane*." *Critical Inquiry* 8, no. 4 (Summer 1982).

Cobos, Juan, Miguel Rubio, and J. A. Pruneda. "A Trip to Don Quixoteland: Conversations with Orson Welles." *Cahiers du Cinéma in English*, number 5, 1966

Cotten, Joseph. *Vanity Will Get You Somewhere*. San Francisco: Mercury House, 1987.

Crowther, Bosley. *Hollywood Rajah: The Life and Times of Louis B. Mayer*. New York: Holt, 1960.

———. Review of *Citizen Kane*. *New York Times*, May 2, 1941.

———. "The Ambiguous *Citizen Kane*." *New York Times*, May 4, 1941.

Daily Variety. Various articles, 1938–1941.

Davies, Marion. *The Times We Had: Life with William Randolph Hearst*. Foreword by Orson Welles. Indianapolis: Bobbs-Merrill, 1975.

Ferguson, Perry. "More Realism from 'Rationed' Sets?" *American Cinematographer*, September 1942.

Fowler, Roy Alexander. *Orson Welles*. London: Pendulum Publications, 1946.

Friday. "Orson Delivers," January 17, 1941.

Gambill, Norman. "Making Up Kane." *Film Comment*, November–December 1978.

Gottesman, Ronald, ed. *Focus on* Citizen Kane. Englewood Cliffs, NJ: Prentice-Hall, 1971.

———. *Perspectives on* Citizen Kane. New York: G. K. Hall, 1996.

Griffith, Richard. " 'Kane' Rouses Manhattan Ovation; Dissenter Speaks." *Los Angeles Times*, May 12, 1941.

Hecht, Ben. *A Child of the Century*. New York: Simon & Schuster, 1954.

Hollywood Reporter. Various articles, 1938–1941. (See also "Wilkerson.")

———. Review of *Citizen Kane*, March 12, 1941.

Hopper, Hedda. Various columns. *Los Angeles Times*, 1939–1941.

———, and James Brough. *The Whole Truth and Nothing But*. Garden City, NY: Doubleday, 1963.

Houseman, John. *Run-Through: A Memoir*. New York: Simon & Schuster, 1972.

Jewell, Richard B., and Vernon Harbin. *The RKO Story*. New York: Arlington House, 1982.

Johnston, Alva, and Fred Smith. "How to Raise a Child: The Education of Orson Welles, Who Didn't Need it." *Saturday Evening Post*, February 3, 1940.

Kahle, Alexander. "Welles and the Cameraman." *International Photographer*, January 1941.

Leaming, Barbara. *Orson Welles: A Biography*. New York: Viking Penguin, 1985.

Lesser, Genee Kobacker. "*Citizen Kane* Hailed as a Triumph of Cinema." *Columbus* (Ohio) *Citizen*, April 6, 1941.

Life. "Movie of the Week: *Citizen Kane*," March 17, 1941.

———. "Orson Welles: Once a Child Prodigy, He Has Never Quite Grown Up," May 26, 1941.

Lindstrom, Natasha. "*Citizen Kane* Penned on Quiet Victorville Ranch." *Victorville Daily Press*, December 19, 2011.

Lundberg v. Welles et al. United States District Court, S.D. New York. August 18, 1950.

McGilligan, Patrick. *Young Orson*. New York: HarperCollins, 2015.

Meryman, Richard. *Mank: The Wit, World, and Life of Herman Mankiewicz.* New York: William Morrow, 1978.

Mishkin, Leo. Review of *Citizen Kane. New York Morning Telegraph,* May 2, 1941.

Naremore, James. *Orson Welles'* Citizen Kane: *A Casebook.* New York: Oxford University Press, 2004.

Nasaw, David. *The Chief: The Life of William Randolph Hearst.* Boston: Houghton Mifflin, 2001.

Newsweek. "Hearst vs. Orson Welles," January 20, 1941.

New Yorker. "Citizen Kane," May 10, 1941.

New York Times. "Hearst Objects to Welles Film," January 11, 1941.

O'Hara, John. Preview of *Citizen Kane. Newsweek,* March 17, 1941.

Parsons, Louella. *Tell It to Louella.* New York: Putnam, 1961.

———. Various columns. *Los Angeles Examiner,* 1939–1941.

Program prepared by RKO for premieres of *Citizen Kane.* UCLA Library Special Collections, UCLA, Los Angeles.

Program prepared for Los Angeles premiere of *Citizen Kane,* El Capitan Theatre. Margaret Herrick Library, Academy of Motion Picture Arts and Sciences, Beverly Hills, California.

Sage, Michael. Feature on *Citizen Kane* and the Hearst controversy. *New Republic,* February 24, 1941.

Sharp, Kathleen. "Destroyed by HUAC: The Dorothy Comingore Story." *Los Angeles Review of Books,* September 13, 2013.

Smith, Steven C. *A Heart at Fire's Center: The Life and Music of Bernard Herrmann.* Berkeley: University of California Press, 1991.

Swanberg, W. A. *Citizen Hearst: A Biography of William Randolph Hearst.* New York: Scribner, 1961.

Tebbel, John William. *The Life and Good Times of William Randolph Hearst.* New York: Dutton, 1952.

Thomas, François. "Musical Keys to *Citizen Kane.*" Originally published in Jean-Pierre Berthomé and François Thomas, *Citizen Kane* (Paris: Flammarion, 1992). Reprinted in Gottesman, *Perspectives on* Citizen Kane.

Time. "Marvelous Boy," May 9, 1938.

———. "Citizen Welles Raises Kane," January 27, 1941.

———. "Kane Case," March 17, 1941.

Toland, Gregg. "I Broke the Rules in '*Citizen Kane.*'" *Popular Photography,* June 1941.

Toland, Gregg. "The Motion Picture Cameraman." *Theatre Arts Magazine, September 1941*

———. "Realism for *Citizen Kane.*" *American Cinematographer,* February 1941.

"Top 10 Best Films." *Sight & Sound* 2, no. 8 (December 1992). Truffaut, François. "*Citizen Kane.*" *L'Express,* November 26, 1959.

Trosper (Popper), Kathryn. Notes from meeting with Orson Welles, Herman Mankiewicz, and John Houseman, May 23, 1940.

Variety. "Orson Welles Signed by RKO," July 18, 1939.

————. Review of *Citizen Kane,* April 16, 1941.

Variety (weekly):

"RKO, Despite Hearst's Ire, Announces Huge National Campaign for 'Kane,'" January 22, 1941.

"Welles East to Talk 'Citizen Kane' Future," January 29, 1941.

"Welles, as 25% Owner of 'Kane,' Would 'Force' RKO to Release Pic," February 5, 1941.

"Decide Future of Welles' Pic by This Week," February 12, 1941.

"Hearst Opens Blast on RKO-Schaefer; 'Citizen Kane' Release Still Indef," February 19, 1941.

"'Citizen Kane' Release Date Not Yet Set," February 26, 1941.

"Luce's Time-Life Steamup by Welles to Force 'Citizen Kane' Release; $800,000 Prod. Now May Be Stalled," March 5, 1941.

"Welles Suing RKO on 'Citizen Kane' in Effort to Force Pic's Release," March 12, 1941.

"Welles' Threat to Raise 'Kane' Puts Him in Spot Between Odlum-Schaefer," March 19, 1941.

"N.Y. Legiter to House 'Citizen Kane' Day-and-Date with RKO Palace, B'way," April 9, 1941.

"Hearst Papers' Anti-'Citizen Kane' Gripe Takes It Out on Welles-CBS," April 16, 1941.

"Add: Hearst vs. Welles ('Citizen Kane'); More Newspaper Attacks," April 23, 1941.

"RKO's Watchful Waiting on Hearst Papers' Further Reaction to 'Kane,'" May 7, 1941.

Voting rules. Academy of Motion Picture Arts and Sciences, 1941 and 1998.

Welles, Orson. "*Citizen Kane* Is Not About Louella Parsons' Boss." *Friday,* February 14, 1941.

Welles, Orson. "The Creation of *Citizen Kane,*" Welles letter to *The Times* (London), November 17, 1971.

Wilkerson, W. R. "Tradeviews" column. *Hollywood Reporter,* January 14, 1939.

Video

American Film Institute. Videos of Martin Scorsese, Steven Spielberg, and Sydney Pollack discussing the impact of *Citizen Kane* on their careers, AFI video channel, YouTube

Citizen Kane (Blu-ray). Warner Bros., 2011.

Citizen Kane Special Edition (DVD). Warner Bros., 2001.

Citizen Kane (laser disc). Criterion Collection, Janus Films, and Voyager Company, 1987.

Citizen Kane (VHS videotape), RKO Collection. Turner Home Entertainment, 1988.

Citizen Kane (Beta videotape). VidAmerica edition, 1987.

Citizen Kane (VHS videotape). VidAmerica edition, 1982.

The Complete Citizen Kane. Arena, 1991.

The Hearts of Age. Public domain, 1934.

Hollywood the Golden Years: The RKO Story. BBC, 1987

Monitor. BBC interview with Orson Welles, 1960.

Music for the Movies: Bernard Herrmann. Alternate Current International/Les Films d'Ici, Channel Four Films, La Sept Cinéma, 1992.

Orson Welles and the Gate Theatre. TG4 Ireland, November 17, 2011.

Orson Welles interview. BBC, 1982.

Orson Welles Story. BBC Arena production, 1982.

Orson Welles Sketchbook. BBC, 1955.

Orson Welles Directs *Too Much Johnson* (excerpt of film from the family of Myron Falk). National Film Preservation Foundation, 1938.

Reflections on Citizen Kane. Turner Home Entertainment, 1991.

Screen test of Orson Welles. Warner Bros., 1937.

Too Much Johnson, raw footage. Public domain, 1938.

Too Much Johnson, "reimagined" edited version. National Film Preservation Foundation, 1938.

War of the Worlds. American Experience, PBS, 2013.

Audio and Sound Track Recordings

Bogdanovich, Peter. Audio interviews with Orson Welles, selections publicly available at https://archive.org/details/InterviewsWithOrsonWelles.

Citizen Kane—Film Music by Bernard Herrmann. Bernard Herrmann Conducts the London Philharmonic Orchestra and National Philharmonic Orchestra. Decca, 1990.

Citizen Kane sound track. *Bernard Herrmann Anthology,* vol. 2, *Tony Bremner and the Australian Philharmonic Orchestra.* Preamble/Fifth Continent Music, 1991.

Citizen Kane sound track. Joel McNeeley and the Royal Scottish National Orchestra. Varese Sarabande, 1991.

Classic Film Scores of Bernard Herrmann. Charles Gerhardt and the National Philharmonic Orchestra. RCA, 1991.

Rosebud in the Snow. BBC Radio Production, May 1991.

Public Presentations

Linwood Dunn, speech and special effects presentation. Grossmont College, El Cajon, California, 1975. Attended by the author.

Bernard Herrmann, speech and question and answer session, George Eastman House, Rochester, New York, 1973. Retrieved from http://www.wellesnet.com.

Unpublished Research

Jewell, Richard B. *A History of RKO Radio Pictures, Incorporated, 1928–1942*. Ph.D. thesis, University of Southern California, Los Angeles, 1978.

Rea, Donald W. *A Critical-Historical Account of the Planning, Production, and Release of* Citizen Kane. Master's thesis, University of Southern California, Los Angeles, 1966.

Web Sites

AFI Catalog of Feature Films. Listing for *Citizen Kane,* afi.com/members/catalog /DetailView.aspx?s=&Movie=27624.

Citizen Kane. Wikipedia.

Federal Theatre Project. "American Memory." Library of Congress, memory.loc.gov /ammem/fedtp/fthome.html.

Mercury Theatre of the Air page, www.radioarchives.com/The_Mercury_Theatre_on _the_Air_p/ra580.htm.

National Film Preservation Foundation. Excerpt from *Voodoo Macbeth,* www .filmpreservation.org/preserved-films/screening-room/voodoo-macbeth.

———. *Too Much Johnson,* www.filmpreservation.org/preserved-films/screening-room /too-much-johnson-work-print.

———. Orson Welles Directs (home movie from the Falk Collection), www .filmpreservation.org/preserved-films/screening-room/falk-home-movie.

"Orson Welles Theatre Credits." Wikipedia.

Wellesnet, the Orson Welles web resource. www.wellesnet.com.

LIST OF ILLUSTRATIONS

1. Orson Welles at *War of the Worlds* press conference. Corbis Images
2. *The Hearts of Age.* Frame still extracted from the public domain video on YouTube
3. *Too Much Johnson.* Frame still from the public domain video on the Web site for the National Film Preservation Foundation
4. Set design for *Julius Caesar.* Federal Theatre Project Archives, Library of Congress
5. Set design for *Voodoo Macbeth.* Federal Theatre Project Archives, Library of Congress
6. George Schaefer on the dock. Provided by Michael Reynolds
7. RKO annual report: Online excerpt
8. Herman Mankiewicz. Margaret Herrick Library, Academy of Motion Picture Arts and Sciences
9. Clip from *The New York Times.* Online excerpt
10. Writing sessions with Orson Welles, Herman Mankiewicz, and John Houseman. *Victorville Daily Press*
11. On the set. Bill's Collectibles
12. Makeup. MovieStillsDB.com
13. Portrait of Perry Ferguson. Provided by Jeff Ferguson and the Estate of Perry Ferguson
14. Ruth Warrick on the soundstage. Frame still from the trailer for *Citizen Kane*
15–18. Example of scene dissolve. Frame stills from *Citizen Kane*

19–20. Examples of deep focus and deep sets. Frame stills from *Citizen Kane*

21. Bernard Herrmann in rehearsal. Getty Images

22. Singers on the set for "Georgie's Place." Frame still from the trailer for *Citizen Kane*

23. Hedda Hopper and Louella Parsons at the Mocambo. © 1948 King Features Syndicate, Inc. World Rights Reserved

24. William Randolph Hearst portrait. Library of Congress

25. Marion Davies in formal gown. Library of Congress

26–27. Photos of Hearst Castle. Photographs by Victoria Garagliano/©. Hearst Castle®/CA State Parks

28. Great Hall at Xanadu: frame still from *Citizen Kane*

29. Premiere of *Citizen Kane*. Margaret Herrick Library, Academy of Motion Picture Arts and Sciences

30. RKO advertisement: Excerpt from *Daily Variety*

31. "Big Screen Attraction" ad. Excerpt from *Los Angeles Examiner*

32. Xanadu statues in storage. Photo by the author

33. Orson Welles at the AFI Life Achievement Award presentation. American Film Institute © 1975

INDEX

40 Acres back lot, 90, 94, 135

A Sea of Upturned Faces (proposed title), 46

Academy Awards, 240–42, 243–44

advertising campaign, 194, 237, 238

Ager, Cecelia (critic, *PM*), 233, 235

Alland, William (played Jerry Thompson; newsreel narrator; assistant director), ix, xvi, 73–74, 76, 78, 93, 103, 133, 153, 159

    face not shown on screen, 74

    on Toland-Welles relationship, 106

    on Welles acting, 123, 134

    on Welles directing style, 70, 97

    Welles' eyes and ears on set, 100–101

Alexander, Rita (secretary), 35, 36, 37, 77

Alexander, Susan (Kane's second wife played by Dorothy Comingore), xx, xxi, 39, 43, 44, 45, 47, 52, 58, 62, 63, 64, 90, 93, 98–99, 72, 77, 107, 108, 109, 110, 111, 112–13, 114, 115, 116, 117, 118, 127, 128–29, 131, 142, 143, 144, 150, 152, 155, 157, 162, 164, 166, 168, 169, 171, 198, 218, 221, 238

American (first draft of *Citizen Kane*), 36, 38–46, 50, 59, 66, 198

Anderson, Bertha (librarian played by Georgia Backus; not named in film), 75

Atkinson, Brooks (drama critic for *The New York Times*), 7

Backus, Georgia (as Bertha Anderson), 75

Baer, hard (associate producer; played Hillman, reporter in projection room), 28, 55–56, 75, 76, 121 141, 143, 153

    described rewriting, 143

    in continuity error, 76, 162

    recalled origins of *Citizen Kane*, 33

    saw Welles dissatisfaction with drafts, 38

Balboa Park, San Diego (as Xanadu), 223

Barrier, Edgar 74, 75, 93

Bazin, André (film writer), 246

behind-the-scenes footage, 158

Benton (character in *American*), 41–42

Berlin, Richard (Hearst executive), 178, 186

    declined *Citizen Kane* ad, 178–79

    investigations of Welles, 210–11

    lunch meeting with Schaefer, 199–200

    plotted with studio heads, 179

Berns, Mel (RKO makeup head), 141

Bernstein (Kane's general manager played by Everett Sloane), 40, 41, 43, 50, 63, 71, 72, 85, 91, 105, 106, 108, 109–10, 125, 131, 148, 160, 162, 216, 238

Bernstein, Dr. Maurice (Welles' guardian and surrogate father), 5, 27, 77

"Big Screen Attraction" (cover name for *Citizen Kane* in Hearst newspapers), 240

Blake, Elmore Draper "Ed" (writer of prop newspapers), 118–119, 148

Bogdanovich, Peter, ix, 129, 130, 163, 177, 201, 230

    analyzed scripts, 53–54

Bonanova, Fortunio (played Signor Matiste), 75, 79, 94, 144

breakfast table montage, 58, 96, 111 119, 163, 168, 217, 219

Breen, Joseph (director, Production Code Administration), 50, 51, 200–01

budget, 88, 85, 92–93, 95, 149–151, 301

Bupp, Sonny (played Kane Jr.), 75, 152

Cahiers du Cinéma, 246, 248

Carringer, Robert (scholar), ix, 58, 60, 84, 129, 146

Carter, Herbert (editor of the Inquirer played by Erskine Sanford), 41, 75

Carvalho, Solomon (possible model for Bernstein), 216

CBS Radio, 73, 159, 200

"Charlie Kane" song, 132, 168

Chicago Inquirer, 57, 104–105, 110, 113, 134, 160, 222, 254,
    set design, 113–114

Churchill, Douglas (writer), 182, 205, 231

Citizen Kane, film—see specific topics throughout the index, such as "budget" or "deep focus"

Collins, Ray (played "Boss" Jim Gettys), 25, 72, 77, 78, 79, 99

colorization, 202, 250–51

Comingore, Dorothy (played Susan Alexander), 72, 78, 79, 94, 108, 137, 152, 241
    encouraged to hate Welles, 103
    pregnant during filming, 142

continuity errors, 110, 162

Corrado, Gino (extra), 94

Correction Script (probable final script), 61–63, 65, 143–44, 145

Cosmopolitan, 178–79

costumes, 142–143

Cotten, Joseph (played Leland, projection room reporter), 49, 71, 78, 79, 93, 105–06, 131, 132, 134, 137, 139, 144, 227, 241
    in Too Much Johnson, 22
    pressures of production schedule, 104–5
    used Welles' makeup, 140

Coulouris, George (Thatcher in Citizen Kane), 25, 73, 78–79, 93, 137, 149, 150, 156, 240–41

Craig, Charles Foster (original name for lead character in American), 38, 59, 78

creative control, Welles, 15–21

Crowther, Bosley (film critic), 68, 234

"Crusader" (gift sled to young Kane), 146

Cully, Russell (cameraman), 153, 154

cuts after screening by studio chiefs, 198

Davies, Marion (actress, mistress of William Randolph Hearst), 30, 112, 177, 220, 221
    alcoholism, 218, 225
    as film actress, 220–21
    as palace hostess, 221
    supported Hearst financially, 220
    worked on jigsaw puzzles, 221

deep focus, 84, 86–87, 110, 124–26, 128

delays in filming, 132, 150–51
    caused by Welles' inexperience, 98–99

deleted scenes, 161–62

depth of field, 111

"Destiny" (musical theme), 170

dissolves for transitions, 107–08, 114

dissolves, 109, 153, 154

Donahue, Eddie (assistant director), 102

Drake, Herbert (publicist for Mercury Theatre), 5, 12, 25, 27, 54, 122, 126–27, 137, 181, 182, 188, 189
    described Parsons' antics, 185
    memos about Schaefer, 102, 192
    on "no comment" policy, 188–89
    reported on Mankiewicz's anger, 54

Dunn, Linwood (special effects), 154

Earl Hays Press (prop newspapers) 118–119

editing, 160

Edwards, Hilton (Gate Theatre), 6

El Rancho nightclub (setting), 47, 93–94, 108, 127, 156, 169,

extras and bit parts, 75, 174

fades, 154

FBI, file on Welles, 212

Federal Theatre Project, 6, 23, 78

Ferguson, Perry (art director), 81, 87–88, 90, 95, 115, 116, 141, 224, 149, 241, 242
    as cost-cutting designer, 82, 88
    created deep sets 110–111
    featured on 2003 postage stamp, 116
    suggested shooting "tests," 93
    transformed Welles' ideas into plans, 89
    views about set design vs. reality, 88–89

Fesler, Bailey (sound), 92, 159

film negative destroyed, 251

film withdrawn from circulation, 244

fire on set, 135–136

Flanagan, Hallie (director of the Federal Theatre Project), 23

Flynn, Errol, 19, 21

Ford, John (director, Welles' idol), 19, 25, 35, 82, 101, 241, 242, 244

Forward, Jean (sang for Comingore), 166

Fowler, Roy (Welles' first biographer), 19

Fox West Coast Theater Chain, 239–240

France, study of film as art, 246–47

Friday magazine, 179–180, 196

Garvin, Edward (cameraman), 83

Gate Theatre, Dublin, 6, 12

Geiger, Miriam (RKO researcher), 24

George Eastman House, 22, 275

"Georgie's Place" (brothel in deleted scenes), 50, 64, 158

Gettys, "Boss" Jim W (corrupt politician played by Ray Collins), xx, 63, 72, 77, 98–99, 109, 133, 144, 216, 238,

Gillingwater, Claude (staff artist), 89

Gillmor, Dan (editor of *Friday*), 180, 196

Gottesman, Ronald (scholar), ix

Grant, Cary, 52, 71, 126, 154, 164, 203, 241

Greenspoon, R. (optometrist), 140

Griffith, D.W., 20, 203

Griffith, Richard (writer), 68

Gunga Din, 52, 87,164

Hays, Will, 185, 253

Hearst Castle (San Simeon), 219, 223–24

Hearst compared to Kane, 215–20, 218–24

Hearst Corporation, today, 255

Hearst San Simeon State Historical Monument, 219

Hearst, George (William's father), 216

Hearst (organization), 101, 195

    attacks against RKO and *Citizen Kane*, 175–78, 186–87, 190–91, 208–09, 234

    attempted frame-up of Welles, 209

    bans RKO and *Citizen Kane*, 186

    cooperated with Congress, 211

    first mention of *Citizen Kane*, 240

    lifted ban on RKO; not *Citizen Kane*, 199

    media coverage, 191–92, 204, 233

    rallied anti-Welles views, 212

    red-baiting of Welles, 176, 209–211

    reviewed Welles' draft status, 209

Hearst, Phoebe (William's mother), 229

Hearst, Steve (great-grandson of William Sr., manager of family interests), 255–56

Hearst, William Randolph Jr. , 220, 225

Hearst, William Randolph Sr., 30, 49, 101, 175, 176, 178, 180, 182, 191, 196, 198, 205, 213, 215–220, 224, 226, 230, 231, 232, 233, 235

    allowed action against *Citizen Kane*, 192

    collected antiquities, 217, 218

    constructed San Simeon, 218–219

    criticized President McKinley, 217

    death in 1951, 120, 219

    declining credibility, 218

    directed attack, 185–186

    financial crisis, 217, 220

    life with Marion Davies, 191, 220–21

    marriage to Millicent, 220

    mentioned in *Citizen Kane,* 228–29

    question if he saw *Citizen Kane*, 224

    response about lack of war in Cuba, 229

    supported war against Spain, 217

Heart of Darkness (proposed film by Welles) 21, 24–25, 26, 52, 69, 71,183, 314

Hearts of Age, The (first Welles film), 22, 23

Hecht, Ben (writer), 30, 31, 228

Herrmann, Bernard (composer), 93, 121, 147, 165–170, 171, 241, 242

    composed elements of opera, 165–166

    composed two main musical themes: "Destiny" and "Rosebud," 167

    composing methods, 166–167

    conflicts with Welles, 170

    hinted at Rosebud in music, 167–168

Hill, Roger (Welles' close friend), 5

Hillman (played by Richard Baer), 162

Hoge, Ralph (grip), 83, 100

Hollywood Reporter, The, 18, 29–30, 97, 141, 179, 181, 187, 204, 206, 236

Hoover, J. Edgar, 212

Hopper, Hedda (columnist), 176, 178, 181, 185, 200, 231–32

    alerted Hearst, 75, 182, 230, 231

    as supporter of Welles, 175, 181

    attended Los Angeles premiere, 234

    hosts radio series about Welles, 200

    opinions about *Citizen Kane*, 175, 182

    power struggle with Parsons, 175–76, 182

    writes about premiere, 236

Houseman, John (producer, editor), 27, 31, 38, 46, 57, 69, 78, 200

    concerns about Kane's character, 68

    conflicts with Welles, 6, 7, 8, 210

    edited drafts, 35, 36, 47, 48

Houseman, John (*continued*)
  views on Mankiewicz, 31
  views about script authorship, 53, 54
  wrote lyrics for *Salammbô*, 166
House Un-American Activities Committee, 210, 211
How Green Was My Valley, 241, 242, 244
Huettner, John (stand-in for Welles, reporter in Xanadu), 100
Hughes, Howard (possible subject for Welles' film), 34, 152, 227

"In a Mizz" (song) 108, 169, 171
inspiration to filmmakers, 257–58
It's All True, 242, 245
"It's Terrific!" (ad slogan), 238, 247

Jaglom, Henry, 165, 249, 250, 258
John (waiter played by Gus Schilling), 75
John Citizen, USA (temporary name for Welles' project), 38, 46
Journey into Fear, 71, 141, 244–45
Julius Caesar, 11, 23, 71, 73, 120

"K" (visual symbol in Kane's life), 143
Kael, Pauline, 53
Kane compared to Hearst, 215–19, 218–24
Kane Jr. (Sonny Bupp), 106, 129, 146
Kane, age 8 (Buddy Swan), 152
Kane, Charles Foster (principal character played by Orson Welles in *Citizen Kane*), xix, xxi, 38–47, 49, 60, 62, 63, 64, 67, 78, 85, 90, 94, 96, 97, 99, 104–05, 106, 107, 109, 110, 111, 113, 114, 115, 116, 117, 125, 126, 128, 131, 132, 133, 139, 143, 144, 148, 150, 152, 153, 155, 157, 162, 164, 167, 168, 170, 171, 198, 212, 215, 216, 218, 219, 230–32, 238
  character as "damned man," 65
  gaps in knowledge about his life, 145
  Welles explored "truths," 66–67
Kane, Jim (Charles' father played by Harry Shannon), 44, 75, 78, 106, 129
Kane, Mary (Charles' mother played by Agnes Moorehead), xix, 39, 72, 129, 215
Kane, Whitford (actor-director), 78
Keene, Ivy (extra) 152–153
Kemper Campbell Ranch, 35
Kent, Molly (script supervisor), 98–99
King Kong, 11, 135, 154

Kitty Foyle, 117, 186
Kodak Super XX film, 83–84
Koerner, Charles (RKO president), 245

Ladd, Alan, background, 77
Larrinaga, Mario (matte artist), 154
Lawler, Oscar (attorney), 182, 184–85
Lederer, Charles (screenwriter, nephew of Marion Davies), 177, 220, 222, 225, 230
Leland, Brad (name for Jed in *American*), 40
Leland, Jed (Kane's best friend and drama critic for the *Inquirer* played by Joseph Cotten), xx , 41, 42, 43, 44, 57, 60, 63, 64, 67, 71, 85, 91, 104–105, 106, 197, 108, 109, 110, 126, 128, 131, 142, 153, 155, 160, 162, 198, 216, 238,
Lent, Eugene (Leland model) 216–17
Lesser, Genee Kobacker (writer), 235
Life, 181, 187, 188, 194, 204, 206, 237
lighting, 84, 130–31
  and dissolves, 107–108
  and shadow, 131
  contrast of light and dark, 131
  "psychological look," 130
  shown deliberately, 132
  under ceilings, 130–31
lists of best films, 240, 248
long takes (master shots), 129–30
Look, 181, 187, 188, 194
Los Angeles Examiner, 120, 183, 186, 233
Lot 891 (prop) and Project 891, 78
Luce, Henry, 204, 208

Macbeth, 23, 141, 256
MacLiammóir, Micheál (The Gate), 6, 12
Magnificent Ambersons, The, 71, 141, 244
makeup, 136–141
  caused delays 139, 140–41
Maltese Falcon, The, 250, 253
"Mangel-Wurzel" (Mankiewicz nickname), 54
Mankiewicz, Herman J. (co-writer of *Citizen Kane*), 30–31, 36, 62, 126–27, 183, 198, 220, 223, 231, 254, 255
  as self-destructive, 30, 31, 36, 55
  conflict over authorship, 53–55, 56
  described Orson Welles, 3, 12
  discussions/arguments with Welles about scripts, 33–35, 46, 47, 48, 49, 68
  gave script to Charles Lederer, 177
  included snow globe in script, 37

learned about Rosebud's origin, 222

mentioned Hearst and Davies in script planning, 228

personal details in script, 37

said Kane not based on Hearst, 227–28

testimony about role in writing, 56

visited Hearst Castle, 223

wanted to include murder, 228

won Academy Award, 241–42, 243

wrote for the Campbell Playhouse, 32

wrote joke shopping list, 36, 255

wrote, edited *American*, 32, 36, 38, 48, 49, 50, 54, 57, 58, 59, 69, 221

Mankiewicz, Sara (Herman's wife), 30, 31, 32, 37, 48, 229

March of Time, 33, 38, 74, 163, 204

Martin, Jerry (character in *American*), 44

Matiste, Signor ("Matisti" in script, "Matiste" in credits; played by Fortunio Bonanova), 64, 75, 108, 112, 144, 166

matte paintings, 153, 155–156

Max Factor & Company, 138

Mayer, Louis B. (MGM production chief), 18, 31, 185, 187, 194–95, 202

plan to buy and burn *Citizen Kane*, 197

McClellan, William (gaffer), 83, 130

McDonough, J.R. (RKO), 48, 141, 177, 192

media coverage of Hearst actions, 205

Mercury productions, 12, 55, 73, 165, 245

Meryman, Richard (Mankiewicz's biographer), 56, 57

Messenger, Lillie (story editor), 11

Metty, Russell (cinematographer), 93, 158

Mishkin, Leo (critic), 235

Mitchell, A. Laurence (lawyer), 184, 185

Moorehead, Agnes, 72–73, 78, 130

described Welles directing style 97–98

models, 89, 153, 155–57

"Mrs. Silverstone" (subject of discussion in Kane's office), 47, 119

Munsey, Frank (executive), 184, 222

Murphy, Charles F. (political boss), 216

Museum of Modern Art, 61, 247

music for newsreel, 164

music, 165–171

National Board of Review, 240

National Film Registry, 248

National Screen Service (trailer), 158

Native Son, 202, 210, 212

natural movement on set, 125

New Republic, 205

New York Film Critics Circle, 241

New York Times, The, 30, 97, 120, 192, 205, 213, 227, 240

New Yorker, The, 30, 212

News on the March, 74, 90, 93, 97, 120, 164, 204, 218, 223

newspapers as props, 118–119

Newsweek, 176, 186, 205, 206

New York Inquirer (fictional newspaper owned by Kane), 4, 41, 47, 50, 62, 63, 64, 67, 85, 91, 96, 104–105, 106, 107, 108, 109–10, 113, 117, 118, 119, 126, 131, 139, 142, 143, 146, 153, 212, 229, 230

set design, 113

Nicholson, Virginia (ex-wife of Welles), 225

nicknames for Welles, 19, 235, 236

Nolan, J.J. (RKO executive), 121–122

North, John Ringling (circus owner), 223

Norton, Emily Monroe (Kane's first wife played by Ruth Warrick), xx, 42, 43, 49, 58, 63, 67, 72, 96, 97, 99, 109, 110, 142, 143

Norton, President James (character in *American*), 217

O'Connell, Arthur, 76–77, 117

O'Hara, John (writer), 205

Odlum, Floyd (financial stakeholder in RKO) 194–95, 198, 202, 245

Oheka Castle, 223

Ohmann, Charles (storyboards), 82, 89

optical printing, 153

outtakes, 162

Palace Theatre (New York premiere), 214, 233, 234, 237, 238

Parker, Jefferson (character in *American*), 39

Parlo, Dita (actress), 28

Parsons, Louella (Hearst columnist), 54, 176, 178, 183, 196, 232, 255

"audible gasps" at screening, 231

defended Welles, 175, 181, 183

described Hopper as "a louse," 200

described possible destruction of *Citizen Kane*, 198

informed *Variety* about suppression tactics, 186

loses credibility, 231–32

Parsons, Louella (*continued*)
  power struggle with Hopper, 175, 182
  reaction to viewing *Citizen Kane*, 184–85, 218, 230, 231
  recalled Hearst prevented lawsuit, 191
  suppression of *Citizen Kane*: threatens RKO board, demands support from studio chiefs, 175, 185, 186, 192, 196
  threatened Nelson Rockefeller, 185, 186
Pathé News, 163
Peck, Orrin (friend of Hearst), 222
Perkins, Frances (secretary of labor), 141
Phair, George (film columnist), 18
Philadelphia Story, The, 71, 104
Phipps, Thomas (writer), 31
physical demands on cast/crew, 102–03
Pierson, Frank (Screen Writers Guild), 56
Pizzitola, Louis (author) , 222
Point Mugu, California, 155
Pollack, Sydney, 257–58
Pollard, Richard (film critic), 182
Popper, Kathryn (Trosper), see Trosper
Popper, Martin (lawyer), 47
post-production, 152–172
premiere, 234
press event during filming, 96–97
press screening, 202, 233
preview attempt in Salt Lake City, 193
Price, Ned (ran Blu-ray technical team), 252
Production Code Administration (PCA), 50–51, 185
production planning, 70–71
props, 109, 118
  used for passage of years, 118
  used for visual bridges, 117
Profiles in History (auction house), 255
public preview, 193
publicity, 238
Pulitzer, Joseph, 184, 216, 222

Radio City Music Hall, 194, 197
Rawlston (head of newsreel company played by Philip Van Zandt), xix, 59, 74, 75, 76, 93, 94, 127
  mentions Hearst, 228–29
Raymond (Kane's butler played by Paul Stewart), xxi, 44, 45, 46, 63, 64, 73, 74, 111, 114, 115, 135, 157, 163,
Rea, Donald (researcher), 129
realism, 111, 112
Redbook, 181, 187
rehearsals, 93

release delayed, 194, 201–02
release, 238–39
Remington, Frederic (artist, Hearst correspondent in Cuba), 215, 229
re-released in 1956, 247
restoration for Blu-ray, 252–53
retakes, 152
reviews, 234–36
RKO (Radio-Keith-Orpheum studios), x, 3, 4, 15, 22, 51, 52, 88, 89–90, 92, 93, 95, 97, 141, 164, 186, 188, 227, 245, 301
  alerted to Hearst attacks, 178
  background, 10
  declined to re-release of *Citizen Kane* after Hearst death in 1951, 247
  options for *Citizen Kane*, 201, 202
  potential impact of WW2 on studio earnings, 26
  risk from Welles' contract, 21
  sells films to C&C Super Corp., 247
RKO "40 Acres" back lot, 90, 94, 135
RKO "ranch" in Encino, 90
RKO Production #281 (administrative name for *Citizen Kane*), 69, 75, 82, 87, 92, 96, 97, 112, 116, 121, 123, 132, 136, 151, 171, 172, 259,
Robson, Mark (asst. editor), 161, 197, 198
Rockefeller family, 194–95
Rockefeller, Nelson,
  mentioned in early script draft, 229
  sent telegram hinting that CK could be shelved, 187
  threatened by Parsons, 186
Rogell, Sid (RKO executive), 141, 251
Rogers, Charles Foster (original name for lead character in *American*), 38, 59, 79
Rogers, Edward P. (corrupt politician in *American*), 43, 77–78
Rogers, Hugo (New York politician), 78
Roosevelt, Franklin, 141
Roosevelt, Theodore, 75, 164
Rosebud (central plot device in *Citizen Kane*), xx–xxi, 38, 39, 40, 43, 45, 46, 50, 57, 59, 66, 73, 74, 76, 77, 93, 94, 103, 114, 116, 117, 118, 132, 135, 146, 150, 157, 159, 163, 167, 168, 170, 221, 222, 226, 228, 253, 276, 277
  auction of sled used in film, 253–54
  balsa sled sold to Spielberg, 253
  Hearst name for Davies' genitalia, 221
  origins of name, 221–22
Rosebud theme, 170
Rossini, Gioachino, 108, 166

Rubin, Benny (Smathers; scene deleted), 162
Ruby, Herman (lyrics), 168
rumors about Hearst, 176
Rushmore, Howard (writer), 211

Sage, Michael (writer), 205–06
Salammbô (opera by Herrmann), 131, 166
Samuel Goldwyn Productions, 93
San Diego Zoo (bird sanctuary), 223
San Luis Obispo Film Festival, 255
San Simeon (location of Hearst estate), 30
Sanford, Erskine (played Carter), 25, 74–75, 76, 78
Sarnoff, David, 10
Saturday Evening Post, The, 194
Schaefer, George J. (president, RKO), 11, 19, 21, 28, 29, 48, 92, 101, 188, 189, 192, 193–95, 201, 203–04, 215, 242, 244, 251
    approved script, 69
    arranged screenings 202, 203, 214
    attacked in *Hollywood Reporter*, 18, 29–30, 187–88
    buys thank-you ads for Welles, 240
    conflict with other executives, 16, 29
    contract with Welles, 11, 13, 14
    created name for the film, 46
    described possible war impact, 26
    extended Welles' deadline, 28
    forced to resign, 245
    held screening for studio CEOs, 197
    lunch meeting with Berlin, 199–200
    met with Nicholas Schenck about destroying *Citizen Kane,* 196–197
    pressured by Parsons, 185
    refused to commit to release, 202
    reported enthusiasm, 202–03
    risk of Welles' creative control, 15, 22, 80
    sent Hearst a print of *Citizen Kane*, 224
    vindicated with accolades, 236–37
Schenck, Nicholas, (Loew's CEO), 187, 196
Schilling, Gus (played John the waiter), 25, 75, 76, 94
Scorsese, Martin (director), 256, 258,
Screen Writers Guild, 55, 56
screened at Hearst Castle, 255
Scripps-Howard newspaper chain, 8
seamless photography, 85, 106, 109, 110
Sears, Bradwell (Warner Bros), 179
secrecy on set, 102
Seiderman, Maurice (makeup artist), 96, 102, 136–141, 223, 241

aged characters, 136, 137, 138
created pads, casts, for Welles, 137
created pores for Welles, 138
created noses for Welles, 139
created wigs with Charles Wright, 138
improvised makeup for Cotten, 140
prepared Welles as a young man, 139
Selznick International Pictures, 11
Selznick, David O. (producer), 10, 90, 135, 185, 203
Sepulveda Basin Recreation Area, 90
sets, 51, 81, 88–90, 94, 110–18
    built on platforms, 127–128
    depth, 110–11,
    illusion of width, 113
shadow, used for emphasis, 131
Shannon, Harry (played Jim Kane), 75
Shipman, Bert (camera operator), 83
shooting schedule, 97
Sight & Sound (film magazine), 246, 247
Silvera, Darrell, 112, 153, 241
Skouras, Spyros (20th Century-Fox), 179
Sloane, Everett (played Bernstein), 25, 71–72, 77, 78, 137, 150, 158, 241
    shaved head, 138, 301
Smathers (deleted character), 162
Smiler with a Knife, The, 33, 69, 71, 183
smooth transitions, 107
snow globe (prop), xix, 37, 38, 45, 59, 66, 116–17, 135, 150, 153, 159, 168, 254
Snow White and the Seven Dwarfs, 224
Solly (printer played by Al Eben), 162
sound, 159–60
Spanish-American War, 163, 230, 231
special effects, 109, 153–57
Spielberg, Steven (director), 253, 258
spies on set, 102
Spitz, Leo (RKO studio chief), 11
Stagecoach, 25, 35
staging, off-camera planning, 129
stand-ins for Welles, 100
statues for set design, 115
statues used for visual bridges, 117–118
Sterbini, Cesare (librettist), 166
Stevens, Ashton (model for Leland), 77, 226
Stevenson, Edward (costumes), 142, 143
Stewart, James G., (sound), 159, 169
Stewart, Paul (Raymond the butler), 73, 74, 78, 102, 111, 135, 152, 153, 158, 170, 198
storyboards, 82, 89
Swan, Buddy (Kane, age 8), 75, 149, 219

Tannhäuser, 164

Tebbel, John (Hearst biographer), 225

Technicolor, 84, 130

tests, filming, 93

Thaïs, 166

Thatcher Jr. (character in *American*), 40, 45

Thatcher Library, 74, 112, 114

Thatcher, Walter (Kane's banker and
    guardian played by George Coulouris)
    xix, 40, 47, 57, 59, 60, 63, 64, 74, 106,
    114, 125, 129, 139, 143, 145, 146, 148,
    153, 158, 170, 217, 230, 238,

theatrical trailer, 158

Third Revised Final script, 59, 60, 61, 62,
    63, 145, 150

Thompson, Jerry (reporter seeking the secret
    of Rosebud played by William Alland),
    xix, xx, xxi, 39, 45, 46, 47, 49, 50, 59,
    63, 64, 66, 73, 74, 76, 93, 108, 127,
    163, 169, 170, 198,

Time, 4–5, 186, 204, 206, 214, 251

Times We Had, The (Davies' book), 225

Todd School, 22

Toland, Gregg (cinematographer), 82–84,
    86, 87, 94, 126, 142, 81, 82, 83, 84, 92,
    94, 115, 116, 125, 128, 130, 131, 150,
    152, 246
  as mentor to Welles, 98–100
  avoided direct cuts, 85
  cost-cutting, 123
  created continuity, 107
  created realism, 85, 125
  created seamless quality, 85, 106
  creative breakthroughs, 124–125
  deep focus, 86, 110, 125, 126
  unconventional methods needed for
      Welles, 81, 84, 128
  developed visual plan, 83
  edited in camera, 154, 161
  lighting for Xanadu, 115, 131
  lighting for dissolves, 108
  lighting, 131, 132, 138
  long takes, 129–30
  low-angle filming, 91, 127–128, 158
  open spaces for depth at Xanadu, 115
  planned transitions, 85, 107
  praise for Ferguson 111–112
  requested fine grain prints, 251
  shared screen credit with Welles,
      128
  shot directly into lights, 124, 132
  shot footage logged as "tests," 93
  simplified the visuals, 125–126

  simulated deep focus in camera,
      128–129
  supported Welles' goal of maintaining a
      theatrical style, 125
  use of extras to imply hundreds, 123–24
  used coated lenses, 86
  used wide-angle lenses, 87

Too Much Johnson (unproduced film shot by
    Welles), 22, 23, 71, 74 ⟵ *The Trial*, 25

Touch of Evil, 71, 93, 141, 256

transitions, 106, 107

Travers, Douglas (montage effects), 154

Trenton Town Hall (setting), 90, 94, 118

Trosper, Kathryn (Welles' assistant; played
    reporter at Xanadu), ix, 254
  arrived at 2 am for script work, 143
  as reporter at Xanadu, 76
  described Welles' injury, and drunk at
      hospital, 133–134
  described Welles' writing and editing, 37,
      47, 60, 68, 143, 221
  took notes about Kane's character, 68
  on working with Welles, 97, 103
  reported Welles-Mankiewicz meeting,
      47

Welles' reactions to early drafts, 37–38

true incidents about Hearst in film, 229

Truffaut, François (director), 246, 258

Turner Classic Movies, 158–159

Turner Entertainment, plan to colorize
    Citizen Kane, 250–51

Turner, Ted, 250

"Una voce poco fa" (aria) 166, 169,

United Press, 205

U.S. postage stamp, "American Filmmaking
    Behind the Scenes" series. 116

Van Schmus, W.G. (managing director of
    Radio City Music Hall), 185

Van Zandt, Philip (played Rawlston)), 74,
    75, 76, 84, 94

Variety, 18, 141, 181, 186, 189, 195, 203,
    204, 206, 209, 213, 235, 243

Verde Guest Ranch (aka Kemper Campbell
    Ranch), 35

Victorville, CA (writing location), 35–38,
    57, 58, 69, 77,

Vidor, King, 19, 234

visual bridges, 117–18

visual plan, 81, 82, 83, 106

Wagner, Richard, 164

Walker, Vernon (special effects), 154

War of the Worlds, The, 8, 10, 13, 73, 239

Warner Bros. studio, 18, 77, 179, 252

Warner Bros. Technical Operations, 252

Warner, Harry (CEO, Warner Bros.), 179

Warner, Jack (Warner Bros.), 18, 185

Warrick, Ruth (played Emily Monroe
    Norton), ix, xvi, 12, 72, 78, 79, 93, 96,
    127, 128, 158
  on Welles directing, 98
  pregnant during filming, 142
  tested to play Susan Alexander, 72

Watts, Richard (theater writer), 13

Weissberger, L. Arnold (Welles' lawyer and
    financial counselor), 122, 188,
  explored legal methods to release, 193–94
  insisted that no one say that Hearst was
    connected to Kane, 227
  negotiated fate of *Citizen Kane*, 188–192,
    193, 194, 195, 201, 202
  on Mankiewicz screen credit, 55, 56
  on Welles spending, 28

Welles, Beatrice (Orson's mother), 5

Welles, Christopher (daughter), 225

Welles, (George) Orson, (played Charles
    Foster Kane; producer, director,
    co-writer), *see also individual listings
    about the production throughout the
    index,* ix, 4, 5, 6, 7, 9, 10, 11–12, 13, 19,
    20, 24, 25, 26–27, 31–32, 50, 51, 52, 57,
    64, 66, 71, 72, 74, 76, 79–80, 83, 93,
    94, 95, 96, 99, 104–05, 124–25, 131,
    134,136, 137, 140, 141, 142–43, 149,
    150, 163–64, 171, 182, 188, 216, 239,
    241, 244, 249, 256
  acknowledged Mankiewicz's role, 53, 55
  acting while directing, 100–01
  announced lawsuit, 202, 207, 208
  as Hollywood outsider, 242
  attacked in media, 54, 187–88
  banned in Hearst publications, 186
  beard, 19, 27
  began training as filmmaker, 24
  career damaged by Hearst, 215, 232
  charmed Hopper and Parsons, 181, 230
  complaints about McDonough, 177
  concerns about his nose, 139
  confidence to make *Citizen Kane*, 258
  conflict at RKO post-*Citizen Kane*, 244
  conflict with *Friday*, 179–180, 184, 196
  considered sole screen credit, 56
  contract details, 15–16, 20, 21
  contract protected *Citizen Kane* from
    colorization, 251
  courted by Hollywood, 10
  created two-part visual plan 83–85
  creative control, 14, 15–16, 17–18
  credited Mankiewicz for Bernstein, 50
  credited Schaefer for *Citizen Kane*, 234
  death, 71, 256
  deliberately rude to Comingore, 103
  demands as actor-producer-writer, 79–80
  denied Kane was Hearst, 226–27
  described actors' inexperience in film, 79
  described favorite scene, 50
  described his role in writing, 53, 56
  described in divine terms, 12
  described makeup for young Kane, 139
  described Mankiewicz's view of Kane, 65
  described origin of Rosebud, 57, 222
  described origins of *Citizen Kane*, 32–33
  discussed in *Cahiers du Cinéma*, 246
  discussed project at RKO meeting, 38
  discussions with Mankiewicz, 30, 32, 37,
    47, 48–49, 33–34, 228
  draft status, 209
  dropped rosary with Joseph Breen, 201
  drunk after injury, 133–134
  early days in Hollywood, 24–25
  economy of dialogue, 60–61
  edited drafts, 53, 54, 57–58
  editing instincts, 60
  envisioned *Inquirer* party in brothel, 50
  experimented with film gear, 25
  financial problems, 13, 24, 28
  formed creative team 70–71, 81
  gift for collaboration, 70
  goal of theatrical style for film, 125
  honored by film industry, 249
  hosted private screenings, 203, 213
  inexperience caused delays, 22, 23, 98–99
  injuries and illness, 132, 134, 135,
    149–50
  interests in stagecraft, 23
  invited Hearst to see *Citizen Kane*, 226
  involvement with Hopper, 181–82, 200
  Kane as "damned man," 65–66
  kept closed set, 101
  lack of Hollywood experience, 4
  mentored by Toland, 84, 98–99, 128
  nominated for awards, 241, 243
  on being "out of step," 249
  on Hearst and Kane, 227, 229, 230
  on others hating him, 12, 20
  performs story for Schaefer, 69

philosophy of directing, 99
physical presence as actor, 11
pictured on the cover of *Time*, 8
plan for "all new faces," 94
prepared *Heart of Darkness*, 24, 25
proposed biopic on Christ, 120–121
proposed *The Smiler with a Knife*, 27
radio background, goals for sound, 159
radio star, 8–9
received awards, 240–43, 249
reduced budget, improved plot, 59
refined master shots, 63
reshaped views about Hearst, 226–27
responded to Hearst attacks, 212, 227
responded to Parsons about *Friday*, 184
rewrites scenes, 62, 63–64, 66–67, 143
rewrites with cast and crew, 143–144
screen test in 1937, 10
screened film for Henry Luce, 204
screened film for studio CEOs, 197
script credit fights, 55–56
shot "tests," 93
shot extensive footage, 102–03
stabbed Joseph Holland, 133
strengths as writer and editor, 23, 60
support from other directors, 16
testified about Kane origins, 227
"under budget and on schedule," 151
unimpressed by early drafts, 37–38
used depth of field for innovative
    placement of performers, 125
viewed *Stagecoach*, 25
views about early good luck, 256–57
views about Mankiewicz, 32
views about Susan-Marion parallels, 221
weight problems, 12
wins Academy Award, 241–42, 243
work as a producer, 69–70
work with Herrmann, 121, 165–166, 170
work, conflict with Houseman, 6–8, 28,
worked with Herrmann on music, 166
worked with Toland, 83, 106, 111–112
wrote late in production, 65, 144–48,
youth and early years in acting, 5–10
Wells, Richard (Orson's father), 5
Wells, H.G. (author, *The War of the
    Worlds*), 8

Wheeler (unseen character), 215, 229
Wheelock, Ward (ad executive), 199–200
wide-angle lenses, 87
Wild, Harry (cinematographer), 152, 153
Wilder, Thornton (playwright), 49
Wilkerson, W.R. (*Hollywood Reporter*), 18, 179
    apologized for criticism, 235–36
    criticized Schaefer and Welles, 19, 29–30,
    187–88
Williams, Guinn "Big Boy," 19
Willicombe, Joseph (personal assistant to
    Hearst), 178, 186, 198, 199, 200,
    210–11
    reported on Hearst's knowledge of actions
    against *Citizen Kane*, 192
Wilson, Richard (assistant producer; reporter
    in projection room and at Xanadu), ix,
    xvi, 61, 76, 135
    recalled last-minute filming, 149
    on Welles working in chaos, 97
Wise, Robert (editor-director), ix, xvi, 121,
    138, 161, 198, 241
    edited breakfast table montage, 58, 163
    edited in New York, 197
    on Herrmann's flexibility, 169
    on working with Welles, 103, 161
    recalled last-minute shooting, 149
    witnessed Welles' speech, 197
    worked on newsreel 152, 163–165
    worked on newsreel, 163–165
Woollcott, Alexander, 7, 31, 55, 183, 231
Wright, Charles (wigs), 138

Xanadu (Kane's Florida hilltop estate), x,
    38–39, 44, 46, 50, 59, 76, 77, 90, 91,
    112, 114–15, 117, 131, 143, 152, 157,
    164, 167, 170, 198, 219, 223, 224
    boxes and crates for set design, 115
    corridor, special effects, 114
    illusion of size, 116
    set depth created with open spaces, 115
    simulated corridor, 114

Yeoman, Art (Union Square speaker), 152
Youngman, Gordon (attorney), 201, 203